NORTH ATLANTIC
SEAWAY
Volume 2

NORTH ATLANTIC SEAWAY

Volume 2

An illustrated history
of the passenger services linking the old world with the new
in four volumes

by

N. R. P. BONSOR

with illustrations by
J. H. ISHERWOOD
Extra Master

BROOKSIDE PUBLICATIONS
JERSEY   CHANNEL ISLANDS

ISBN   0 905824 01 6

First published by T. Stephenson & Sons Ltd 1955, and with Supplement 1960.

Enlarged and completely revised edition published by Brookside Publications, Jersey, Channel Islands 1978.

© N. R. P. Bonsor 1978.

Drawings © J. H. Isherwood 1978.

Photoset in 11 on 12 Times Roman and printed by The Garden City Press Ltd. Letchworth, Herts.
for Brookside Publications, Brookside, Petit Port, St Brelade, Jersey, Channel Islands.

UK, British Commonwealth and European Distributors: Patrick Stephens Ltd, Bar Hill, Cambridge, CB3 8EL.

CONTENTS

477

*New chapter
§Major alterations and additions

SUMMARY

Volume I   Contents
Introduction
Introduction to Second Edition
Acknowledgements
Explanatory Notes
Chapters 1 - 55

Volume II   Chapters 56 - 99

Volume III   Chapters 100 - 173

Volume IV   Chapters 174 - 258
Appendices A - I
Index of Lines
Index of Ships
Addenda and Corrigenda

LIST OF ILLUSTRATIONS

EXPLANATORY NOTES

(Shortened Version of Abbreviations used in Fleet Lists)

EXAMPLES

1862[1] CHINA[2]
    2,638.[3] 99,42 x 12,31.[4] (326.2 x 40.4).[5] C[6]—1[7]—2.[8] I[10]—S[11]—GO2[12]—
    12.[13] Robert Napier, Glasgow.[14]

(1945)[1] FALSTRIA[2] (M/S)
    6,993.[3] 131,79 [138,07] x 19,23.[4] (432.4 [453.0] x 63.1).[5] O[7]—4[8]—C.[9]
    S[11]—2SC.DA[12]—15.[13]

1.   DATE
    Year of maiden voyage on North Atlantic.
    (Dates in brackets indicate that the ship had been in previous employment - not necessarily for the same owners or under the same name).

2.   NAME OF SHIP
    Where (c) (chartered) follows the name, this should not necessarily be used in the literal sense. In some cases ships so noted were 'managed', 'loaded on the berth', etc.
    (M/S) after the name denotes motorship.

3.   GROSS TONNAGE

4.   DIMENSIONS
    Length between perpendiculars (BP) in metres and hundredths of metres x beam. Length overall (OA) where shown is in square brackets.

5. DIMENSIONS
Length between perpendiculars (BP) in feet and tenths of feet x beam. Length overall (OA) where shown is in square brackets.

6. TYPE OF BOW
C — Clipper
S — Straight
This information is normally omitted after about 1900.

7. NUMBER OF FUNNELS

8. NUMBER OF MASTS

9. CRUISER STERN
When the number of funnels and masts is followed by 'C', this indicates that the ship had a cruiser stern.

10. CONSTRUCTION
W — Wood
I — Iron
S — Steel
Where this information is omitted - usually after about 1900 - the ship was built of steel.

11. PROPULSION
P — Paddle
S — Single screw
2S — Twin-screw
3S — Triple-screw
4S — Quadruple-screw

12. ENGINES
B — Beam
C — Compound
D — Diagonal
DE — Diesel Electric
G — Geared
H — Horizontal
HT — Horizontal trunk
I — Inverted

O — Oscillating
Q — Quadruple-expansion
SL — Side lever
ST — Steam turbines (direct acting)
ST(SR) — Steam turbines (single-reduction)
ST(DR) — Steam turbines (double-reduction)
T — Triple-expansion
TE — Turbo-electric
T & ST — Combination of triple-expansion reciprocating engines and steam turbines
2SC.DA — Two stroke double-acting engines (motorships)
4SC.SA — Four stroke single-acting engines (motorships)
   The number immediately following I, C, T or Q indicates the number of cylinders.

13. SERVICE SPEED (in knots)

14. BUILDER

SHIP'S ACTIVITIES
1977 (5/1) — 1977 (5 January)
MV — Maiden voyage
FV — First voyage (ie on that particular route or for that particular company)
LV — Last voyage
RV — Round voyage
   The number in brackets following the loss of a ship indicates the number of fatal casualties.

HOUSEFLAGS
Houseflags have been divided into five different shapes, as follows:
(1) Flag — rectangular
(2) Burgee — as (1) except for a 'swallow-tail' at fly
(3) Pennant — triangular
(4) Long pennant — as (3) but longer
(5) Swallow-tailed pennant — as (3) but with a 'swallow-tail' at fly.
Note: Unless otherwise stated, the houseflags described at the end of the fleet lists are 'flags'.

Where, in the fleet lists, the reader is referred to another company the number that follows is the chapter number of that company.

(More detailed notes are in Volume I).

NOTE
The original Isherwood drawings of the funnels of certain CGT ships were finished in the company's red and black colours, while others remained white and black. The former circumstance explains why some of the CGT funnels in Chapter 71 appear all black. Unfortunately, there was no apparent way of avoiding a similar occurrence in the case of some of the Cunard ships in Chapter 13, Volume I.

Chapter 56

1857

NORTH ATLANTIC STEAM NAVIGATION COMPANY

(British)

The NORTH ATLANTIC STEAM NAVIGATION COMPANY can be said to have started in 1857 where the Liverpool, Newfoundland & Halifax Steam Navigation Company (Chapter 54) left off in 1856. Like its predecessor, it was managed by the Liverpool firm of Weir, Cochrane & Co, but a new feature was the 'forwarding of telegraphic despatches for the continent of America via the submarine telegraph from Newfoundland.'[1] This was made possible by the activities of the General Screw Company's steamer PROPONTIS, which in 1856 had laid the first cable from Newfoundland to Nova Scotia (Chapter 42).

The service was opened by the 1,387 ton iron screw CIRCASSIAN, which sailed from Liverpool on 7 March 1857 with cargo and 200 passengers for St John's (Newfoundland), Halifax and Portland, but put back a week later after experiencing a succession of terrific gales. The voyage was resumed on 19 March. It is interesting to note that the CIRCASSIAN 'had a house on deck forming a promenade of 230 feet (70 metres). The sleeping berths have been placed in the 'midships', thus avoiding the motion and noise of the propeller usually so much complained of by passengers.'[2] She appears to have been some years before her time as the White Star OCEANIC, completed in 1871, is usually credited with having introduced amidships passenger accommodation on the North Atlantic. The OCEANIC was a product of Harland & Wolff of Belfast, successors to Robert Hickson & Co, builders of the CIRCASSIAN. In all probability, however, the CIRCASSIAN's dining saloon, unlike that of the OCEANIC, was situated aft, as was that of the Cunard CHINA, built in 1862, but the latter also had some of her cabin accommodation amidships.

The 1,409 ton KHERSONESE, which had been responsible for the predecessor company's only transatlantic sailing in 1856, followed in April. She had the misfortune to fracture her propeller shaft in mid Atlantic on the homeward run, but thanks to her sails managed to complete the crossing from St John's to Liverpool in 12 days.

After her second round voyage, the KHERSONESE was taken up as an Indian Mutiny transport, and the 1,152 ton GENERAL WILLIAMS was chartered to replace her. A month later the CIRCASSIAN, after

1856 KHERSONESE 1,409 tons
Built by Robert Hickson & Co of Belfast,
predecessors of Harland & Wolff.

completing three round voyages, also became a transport and was replaced by the 1,007 ton ANTELOPE, which made two round voyages for the Company, the second ending at Liverpool on 23 December 1857. By that time, however, a severe slump had set in and the Company was forced to suspend operations.

The ANTELOPE had an interesting and varied career. Built in 1846 as an auxiliary iron screw steamer, she was a contemporary of the SARAH SANDS (Chapter 19) and a product of the same firm. A few years later she is said to have made a record passage of 27 days to Rio de Janeiro 'under sail', from where she proceeded to California via Cape Horn. Upon return to Liverpool in 1853 she was sold to Miller & Thompson, who sent her to John Laird to be lengthened and re-engined. [3] She was despatched to Australia in March 1853 at approximately the same time as the famous clipper ship MARCO POLO, which reached Melbourne in 75 days whereas she herself took 163, having twice had repairs and adjustments made to her engines. After her North Atlantic Steam Navigation Company service, she was bought by J.O.Lever and made a voyage to Karachi as an Indian Mutiny transport, later being sold by Lever to the Atlantic Royal Mail Steam Navigation Company (Galway Line), but did not sail for them. She was sold again in 1864 to become the CORAL QUEEN and survived until 1890.

[1]   *The Times* 5/3/1857
[2]   *Mitchell's Maritime Register* 21/2/1857
[3]   *Illustrated London News* 5/3/1853

1. 1857 CIRCASSIAN
   1,387. 77,72 x 11,92. (255.0 x 39.1). C—1—3. I—S—GB2—9. (Cabin; intermediate; III). Robert Hickson & Co, Belfast (engines Randolph, Elder & Co, Glasgow. 1856 (18/7) launched. 1857 (7/3) MV Liverpool—St John's, NF—Halifax—Portland; put back to Liverpool 14/3. 1857 (19/3) voyage resumed. 1857 (11/7) LV ditto (3RV). 1857 (Sep) Indian Mutiny transport. 1858 (26/10) FV for Galway (c), Galway—New York. 1860 (5/3) LV ditto (8RV). 1862 (May) captured by USS SOMERSET when blockade running; seized; transferred to US flag. 1865 (19/8) FV New York—Southampton—Bremen (Ruger Bros, agents). 1865 (20/10) stranded at Arichat, Cape Breton Island. 1865 (Nov) refloated; steamed to New York (arr 20/11). 1866 (18/7) FV for Continental (c), New York—Antwerp. 1866 (12/10) LV ditto (2 RV). 1867 (2/8) FV for Ruger Bros (c), New York—Bremen (dep 5/10)—Falmouth—New York (1 RV). 1868 (25/4) FV for Ruger's Atlantic Line (c), New York—Bremen. 1868 (25/7) LV ditto (2 RV). 1874 engines removed. 1876 wrecked at Bridgehampton, Long Island (O).

2. (1857) KHERSONESE

　　1,409. 75,00 x 11,86. (246.1 x 38.9). C—1—3. I—S—GB2—9. (I; inter-
mediate; III). Robert Hickson & Co, Belfast (engines Randolph, Elder &
Co, Glasgow). 1855 (4/10) launched. 1856 (Apr) sailed Liverpool—Black
Sea; repatriated British troops from Crimea. 1856 (23/8) FV Liverpool—
St John's, NF—Halifax—Portland—St John's—Liverpool, (arr 16/10)
for Liverpool, Newfoundland & Halifax SN Co (1 RV). 1857 acquired by
North Atlantic SN Co. 1857 (4/4) FV Liverpool—St John's, NF—Halifax
—Portland. 1857 (Jun) LV ditto (2 RV). 1857 (29/8) sailed Portsmouth—
Madras as Indian Mutiny transport. 1863 (25/1) FV London—New York
for George Duncan & Co (1 RV). 1865 (approx) engines removed. 1889
KHERSONESE (Dutch). 1891 (21-2/7) destroyed by fire at Montevideo.

2a. (1857) GENERAL WILLIAMS (c)

　　1,152. 68,27 x 10,06. (224.0 x 33.0). C—1—3. I—S—?—9. A. Leslie & Co,
Hebburn-on-Tyne. 1856 (20/8) launched. 1857 (17/8) FV for North
Atlantic SN Co (c), Liverpool—St John's, NF—Halifax—Portland (in
place of KHERSONESE (1 RV). 1858 GENERAL WILLIAMS (Greek &
Oriental (Br)). 1859 (3/4) foundered on voyage London—Piraeus.

2b. (1857) ANTELOPE (c)

　　1,007. 72,19 x 7,98. (236.9 x 26.2). C—2—3. I—S—I(2)—9. (I & II—120).
Hodgson & Son, Liverpool (engines George Forrester & Co, Liverpool).
1846 (/) launched for H McTear & Co, Liverpool, as auxiliary
steamer. 1853 bought by Miller & Thompson, Liverpool; lengthened by
John Laird, Birkenhead, from 57,90 metres (190.0 feet); new engines. 1857
(8/9) FV for North Atlantic SN Co (c), Liverpool—St John's, NF—
Halifax—Portland (in place of CIRCASSIAN). 1857 (Nov) LV ditto
(2 RV) 1858 (10/3) bought by J.O. Lever; sailed Gravesend—Karachi as
Indian Mutiny transport. 1859 (8/2) ANTELOPE (Atlantic RMSN Co
(Galway Line)) but did not run for them. 1864 CORAL QUEEN (British).
1866 new engines by M. Samuelson & Co, Hull. 1890 (Feb) sunk in
collision in North Sea.

Total 8 RV.

FUNNEL: Black.

Chapter 57

1857

EUROPEAN & AMERICAN STEAM SHIPPING COMPANY

(British)

The General Screw Steam Shipping Company (Chapter 42) made no serious attempt to resume operations on the North Atlantic after the Crimean War but, instead, laid up most of the ships and advertised them for sale. In fact·, first rumours of a sale had been heard as long previously as February 1854, some months before the short-lived pre-war North Atlantic service started. It was stated in February 1856 that eight of the ships had been sold to a French Company to run between France, Ceylon and India and between France and Brazil, but the announcement was premature and it was not until February 1857 that disposal of the ships to the British-owned EUROPEAN & AMERICAN STEAM SHIPPING COMPANY was formally completed. The purchase price of £320,000 was paid in shares, and the new company was under the sole management of T.R.Croskey, American Consul at Southampton, who was to receive no remuneration until the shareholders got six per cent.[1]

This new service was, by and large, merely a repetition of the pre-war aspirations of the General Screw Company as four iron screw steamers - the QUEEN OF THE SOUTH, INDIANA, ARGO and JASON, in that order, sailed between Bremen , Southampton and New York at fortnightly intervals starting on 25 April 1857. As previously, sailings were interspersed between those of the wooden paddle steamers of the American-owned Ocean Steam Navigation Company on the New York - Southampton - Bremen route and the New York & Havre Steam Navigation Company on the New York - Southampton - Havre route. First, second and third class passengers were carried.

Of the other four steamers - the GOLDEN FLEECE, HYDASPES, CALCUTTA and LADY JOCELYN - the first-named sailed from Hamburg on 20 April 1857 via Southampton in a joint service with the PETROPOLIS and TEUTONIA of the Hamburg-Brasilianische Linie. Before a fourth sailing could take place the steamers were chartered by the East India Company to carry troops to the Indian Mutiny, which was fortunate as the three completed voyages had resulted in a loss of £11,602.

All told, 11 round voyages were completed between Bremen, Southampton and New York, and in fairness it must be stated that although the westbound voyages averaged 17½ days from Southampton and most of

491

the eastbound took at least 14 or 15, the service was carried out with pretty good regularity. There was a loss of £899 on the New York line.

At a general meeting held on 3 February 1858 the hope was expressed that the service would be resumed later in the year 'with a fair prospect of larger receipts and a more economical scale of expenditure.' It was never resumed however, and in 1859-60 the ARGO, JASON, BRAZIL (ex- LADY JOCELYN) and GOLDEN FLEECE made some voyages for the Galway Line between Galway and New York, the first-named being wrecked on her first homeward voyage. In the autumn of 1859 THE MILFORD HAVEN (ex-QUEEN OF THE SOUTH), PORTUGAL (ex-CALCUTTA) and BRAZIL had been running under the Portuguese flag betweeen England, Portugal and Brazil, but this service was also a failure and soon afterwards the East India & London Shipping Company acquired all the surviving ships and placed them in service between London, Madras and Calcutta via the Cape of Good Hope - a similar route, apart from the absence of intermediate calls, to that for which most of them had been built.

The failure of the European & American Steam Shipping Company can be attributed to the slump that followed the short boom after the Crimean War, but high operating costs combined with the inadequate power of the ships' engines were contributory causes. Moreover, the service was not in operation long enough to give it a reasonable chance of success.

[1] *New York Daily Tribune* 27/1/1857

1. (1857) QUEEN OF THE SOUTH
      2,221. 74,06 x 11,98. (243.6 x 39.3). C—1—3. I—S—D2—9. C.J. Mare & Co, London (engines Maudslay, Sons & Field, London). 1851 (29/10) launched for General Screw (1,850 tons). 1852 (20/6) MV Plymouth—Cape Town—Calcutta (3 RV). 1854 (4/4) FV Southampton—Cape Town—Australia. 1854 (28/10) scheduled to sail Bremen—Southampton—New York, but voyage cancelled. 1854 (Oct) Crimean War transport. 1857 QUEEN OF THE SOUTH (European & American). 1857 (25/4) FV Bremen—Southampton—New York. 1857 (22/6) LV ditto (2 RV). 1857 (29/8) sailed Portsmouth—Madras as Indian Mutiny transport. 1859 THE MILFORD HAVEN (Anglo-Luso-Brazilian). 1861 QUEEN OF THE SOUTH (East India & London). 1872 MALTA (British) (sailing ship). 1885 (24/11) wrecked near Sandy Hook USA.

2. (1857) INDIANA
      2,365. 74,06 x 11,98. (243.6 x 39.3). C—1—3. I—S—D2—9. C.J. Mare & Co, London (engines Maudslay, Sons & Field, London). 1852 (/) launched for General Screw (1,850 tons). 1852 (15/9) MV Plymouth—Cape Town—Calcutta (3 RV). 1854 (15/7) FV Havre—Southampton—

New York. 1854 (3/10) LV ditto (2 RV). 1854 (Nov) Crimean War transport. 1857 INDIANA (European & American). 1857 (9/5) FV Bremen—Southampton—New York. 1857 (31/8) LV ditto (3 RV). 1861 INDIANA ʏ(East India & London). 1870 FERDINAND DE LESSEPS (British). 1873 GREAT QUEENSLAND (British). 1876 (Aug) went missing.

3. (1857) ARGO

2,315. 74,06 x 11.98. (243.6 x 39.3). C—1—3. I—S—D2—9. C.J. Mare & Co, London (engines Maudslay, Sons & Field, London). 1852 (23/12) launched for General Screw (1,815 tons). 1853 (8/5) MV Southampton—Cape of Good Hope—Australia—Cape Horn—Southampton (first steamer to encircle the Globe). 1854 (15/2) FV Plymouth—Cape Town—Calcutta. 1854 (4/10) resumed Southampton—Australia. 1855 (12/4) sailed from Southampton as Crimean War transport. 1857 ARGO (European & American). 1857 (23/5) FV Bremen—Southampton—New York. 1857 (12/9) LV ditto (3 RV). 1857 (15/12) sailed Portsmouth—Calcutta as Indian Mutiny transport. 1859 (28/5) FV for Galway (c), Galway—New York. 1859 (28/6) wrecked at Trepassey Bay, NF, on homeward voyage (0).

4. (1857) JASON

2,667. 77,41 x 11,89. (254.0 x 39.0). C—1—3. I—S—D2—9. C.J. Mare & Co, London (engines Watt & Co, London). 1853 (6/8) launched for General Screw. 1854 (May) MV to Constantinople as Crimean War transport. 1857 JASON (European & American). 1857 (8/6) FV Bremen—Southampton—New York. 1857 (28/9) LV ditto (3 RV). 1858 (12/1) sailed London—Calcutta as Indian Mutiny transport. 1859 (20/8) FV for Galway (c), Galway—New York. 1859 (15/10) LV ditto (2 RV). 1861 JASON (East India & London). 1862 (27/12) wrecked north of Madras.

Total 11 RV.

LONDON & CANADA STEAMSHIP LINE

(British)

The pioneer steamship service between London, Quebec and Montreal was established in 1857, and according to contemporary advertisements was undertaken by the 'Royal Mail steamers of the Grand Trunk Railway of Canada'. [1] This is a surprising statement as there is no evidence that the Grand Trunk owned any ocean-going steamers at the time, and according to other sources the new service was known as the LONDON & CANADA STEAMSHIP LINE. Moreover, announcements were made simultaneously that the North Atlantic Steam Navigation Company (Chapter 56) was running 'in direct communication with the Grand Trunk Railway of Canada, giving through bills of lading and through tickets to all the principal Canadian towns.' There is every reason to suppose that similar facilities, and nothing more, were offered by the railway in connection with the London & Canada Steamship Line.

The steamers undertaking the service - the 903 ton UNITED SERVICE and the 853 ton ELIZABETH JANE - were stated to have superior accommodation for chief cabin, second class and third class passengers, fares to Quebec or Montreal being £18, £12 and £8, respectively, including 'dietary of the first quality.'

The iron screw UNITED SERVICE sailed from London on 27 July 1857 and reached Quebec on 27 August with general cargo and 73 passengers, [2] the protracted nature of her voyage being partly due to the fact that she put in at Sydney, Cape Breton Island, for coal. [3] She sailed again on 23 September and four days later 'while disconnecting the screw a sea struck the propeller and washed it away.' The UNITED SERVICE anchored in the Downs, between Dover and Ramsgate, on 9 October, after making a homeward passage of 16 days under sail alone. [4]

The ELIZABETH JANE left Gravesend, London, on 13 August for Quebec and Montreal, and on the 15th was in collision with a Spanish brig. She put in at Plymouth for repairs [5] and so far as is known the voyage was never completed.

The UNITED SERVICE only undertook the one round voyage for the Company and there were no further steamship sailings between the Thames and the St Lawrence for several years. It is interesting to note that the London agency of the Company was shared between Alfred Hill and

Temperleys, Carter & Darke, the latter firm becoming in due course agents for the British Colonial Steamship Company, which started operations on the same route in 1864. (Chapter 72).

[1]   *The Times* 23/7/1857 (advt).
[2]   *Quebec Mercury* 27/8/1857.
[3]   *Quebec Mercury* 29/8/1857.
[4]   *Quebec Mercury* 31/10/1857.
[5]   *Quebec Mercury* 3/9/1857.

1. (1857) UNITED SERVICE
903. 65,52 x 9,54. (215.0 x 31.3). C—1—3. I—S—I(2)—9. (I; II; III). J.Laing, Sunderland.1857 (/   ) launched for W. Gray & G. Swainston. 1857 (27/7) FV London—Sydney, CBI (for coal)—Quebec (arr 27/8; dep 23/9). 1857 (27/9) lost propeller and completed voyage to London under sail. 1858 UNITED SERVICE (Bombay owner). 1870 ditto (Hong Kong owner). 1871 ditto (Singapore owner). 1875 lengthened to 80,28 metres (263.4 feet); 1,459 tons; masts reduced to two; compound engines; renamed CHEANG HOCK KIAN (?KIANG) (Singapore owner). 1903 (approx) CHEANG HOCK KIAM (Dutch). 1915 owner and flag deleted from *Lloyd's Register*. 1923 ship deleted from *Lloyd's Register*.

ELIZABETH JANE
853. 64,45 x 9,32 (211.5 x 30.6). C—1—3. I—S—I(2)—9. (I; II; III). J. & G. Thomson, Glasgow. 1856 (11/12) launched. 1857 (13/8) left London for Quebec and Montreal. 1857 (15/8) collided with Spanish brig; put in at Plymouth for repairs; voyage believed never to have been completed. 1859 sold to French Government.

GALWAY LINE

(British)

1858. Atlantic Steam Navigation Company
1859. Atlantic Royal Mail Steam Navigation Company

Geographically, Galway is ideally situated as a jumping-off place for a steamship service to North America, lying half-way down the Atlantic coast of Ireland, about 120 miles due west of Dublin. Railway communication between Dublin and Galway was established in 1851 by the Midland & Great Western Railway,which a year previously had subscribed much of the capital for an unsuccessful attempt to start a steamship line between Galway and New York (Chapter 26).One of the arguments put forward in favour of Galway was that it is about 300 miles nearer to New York than is Liverpool, then the principal British transatlantic port, representing a saving of over 24 hours steaming time.

A·Government commission had reported in 1852 that Foynes and Tarbert, on the River Shannon, would be less expensive than Galway to equip with the necessary harbour works, but an Admiralty report in 1859 stated that 'Galway Bay is to a great extent a harbour already formed by nature. Its approach from the ocean is well-defined, it is easy of access and free from outlying dangers. It has a width of 20 miles between outer headlands which shelter the bay, while the magnificent natural breakwater of the Aran Islands arrests the force of the swell of the Atlantic, leaving on either side a navigable channel or sound of some four miles in width, well-defined by day and admirably lighted by night'.[1]

A Manchester businessman, John Orr Lever, and a group of associates had already anticipated the findings of this report and in the previous year had established the ATLANTIC STEAM NAVIGATION COMPANY[2] with a view to starting a steamship service between Galway, Halifax and New York. From the earliest days the Company was best-known as the GALWAY LINE.

The 2,516 ton wooden paddle steamer HANSA, built in America in 1848 as the UNITED STATES, and having subsequently had a varied career as a German Warship, a North Atlantic liner and a Crimean War transport, was bought by J. O. Lever, re-named INDIAN EMPIRE, inspected at Southampton on 29 May 1858 by a large number of guests and despatched to Galway. She struck a rock entering Galway harbour but sustained only slight damage and was able to open the service on 19 June, carrying 11 passengers and a small letter mail. Further trouble was in store, however, as she fractured a piston in mid-Atlantic and the remainder of the passage was made on one cylinder. She reached Halifax after a voyage of 12 days instead of the eight optimistically forecast by Mr. Lever, and then proceeded to New York.

The Company's second voyage was advertised for 27 July by the AMERICAN EMPIRE, stated to be of 3,000 tons burden [3] but likely to have had a gross tonnage only half that figure. She was not completed in time but Mr. Lever had already chartered the 2,028 ton PRINCE ALBERT [4] which had been built for the short-lived Belgian transatlantic line of 1855-7 and whose only activity hitherto had been a trooping voyage to India, completed in record times of 53 days outwards and 54 days homewards. Leaving Galway on 27 June, as scheduled, the PRINCE ALBERT arrived at Halifax with 172 passengers in 10 days and at New York in 12. It was at this time that the AMERICAN EMPIRE was scheduled to take a later sailing for the Company, as was a steamer named BRITISH EMPIRE, but neither actually did so. It looks as if it may originally have been intended to give most, if not all, the Galway Line fleet names ending with 'EMPIRE'.

It was proposed to run a service to Boston as well as New York, and the 603 ton iron screw PROPELLER was bought by J. O. Lever from the North of Europe Steam Navigation Company and sailed from Galway on 21 August 1858 for St John's, Newfoundland, and Boston, where she arrived on 3 September. She left again on the 14th and reached Galway in a sinking condition on the 30th. She was one of several ships sold by J. O. Lever to the Atlantic Royal Mail Steam Navigation Company on 8 February 1859 (the ANTELOPE, PACIFIC and PRINCE ALBERT were others), but she was not employed again on the North Atlantic. The ANTELOPE did not run thereon for the Company at all, perhaps because experience had shown that she was too small.

On her return from New York the INDIAN EMPIRE ran on the rocks at Galway when in charge of a pilot. She was sent to Southampton for repairs and J. O. Lever bought the 1,469 ton iron paddle steamer PACIFIC to undertake the fourth voyage on 24 August, New York being reached in 13 days. The PRINCE ALBERT and INDIAN EMPIRE followed at approximately fortnightly intervals, the latter carrying over 400 passengers. Homewards, she was involved in a slight collision after leaving New York and put in at Halifax for temporary repairs. But this was only the beginning of her troubles as a succession of south-easterly gales caused her to run out of coal when still 300 miles from Galway. For 10 days she lay to under canvas in hopes of a fair wind and then, in desperation, the captain decided

1858 PACIFIC 1,469 tons
Made four voyages for Galway Line.
In 1866 converted to screw.

to burn the masts, bulwarks and part of the cargo of cotton to provide fuel. By this means the ship reached port after a voyage of 34 days from New York. She was not employed again.

The PACIFIC started her second voyage on 12 October 1858. Among her 337 passengers was Lord Bury, who was travelling to St John's to discuss with the Newfoundland Government the advisability of granting the Company a mail contract. Agreement was soon reached, and in February 1859 the Company was provisionally informed that it would receive a subsidy of £3,000 a round voyage for a fortnightly service from Galway to St John's, thence alternately to New York and Boston. The contract was formally confirmed in April 1859 and was due to come into operation in June 1860. A fine of £5 an hour was to be levied in the event of the late arrival of the mails and double that sum for each hour of lateness in excess of 24. It was also stipulated that during the months of April to October inclusive letters must be delivered at New York in 11 days 2 hours from Galway, an additional time allowance being made in the case of Boston and for voyages undertaken between November and March inclusive; the summer allowance from New York to Galway was 10 days.

Meanwhile, the Company's name was changed to ATLANTIC ROYAL MAIL STEAM NAVIGATION COMPANY, and plans were completed for the construction of four iron paddle steamers of about 3,000 tons. One of the Company's objects was to carry messages from Galway to St John's for despatch thence by telegraph to all parts of North America or *vice versa* as, although an Atlantic cable was in operation for a few days in August 1858, it was not until 1866 that permanent telegraphic communication was established between the two continents.

The PRINCE ALBERT made an excellent eastbound voyage in December 1858, taking 5 days 16½ hours from St John's to the Aran Islands lights. [5] On her following homeward voyage she was delayed by ice floes off Cape Race and must have been more seriously damaged than was realised as on 11 April 1859, two days after the start of her next voyage from Galway, she was compelled to put back there and did not sail again until 10 December. In January 1859 the 1,387 ton iron screw CIRCASSIAN had met with a minor mishap while paying a brief visit to Cork, and this was followed by the loss of her propeller during her ensuing transatlantic voyage - her second for the Company - so that she arrived at New York in tow, no fewer than 31 days after leaving Galway.

The Company undertook 24 sailings between the departure of the PACIFIC in October 1858 and that of the first of the new steamers in July 1860, eight by the CIRCASSIAN, six by the PRINCE ALBERT and two by the PACIFIC, which was sold in 1861, converted to screw about five years later and wrecked on Whalsey Island, Shetlands, on 7 February 1871. No fewer than six steamers were chartered for the eight remaining sailings -

the ADELAIDE, ARGO, JASON, BRAZIL, GOLDEN FLEECE and PARANA, the first three being required as temporary replacements for the PRINCE ALBERT. All except the PARANA were screw-propelled. The ARGO was wrecked in Trepassey Bay, Newfoundland, on her first homeward voyage owing to incorrect information given by a fisherman. She became a total loss, but her passengers and crew were rescued and taken to St John's.

During the summer of 1859, Mr Lever made an offer to the directors of the Great Ship Company to charter the GREAT EASTERN for a voyage to America and back. He stipulated that the ship would have to show at a speed trial that she was capable of 14 knots, and would have to be fitted with accommodation for 2,000 passengers. The price suggested was £20,000, but the offer was declined.[6]

It had been stated in November 1858, some months before the Company was awarded the mail subsidy, that orders had been given to Palmers of Tyneside for three large iron paddle steamers intended to have a speed of 20 miles an hour (sic) in smooth water.[7] In fact, two contracts went to Palmers and two to Martin Samuelson & Co of Hull. The Tyneside ships were the CONNAUGHT and LEINSTER, the former being scheduled to sail on 26 June 1860; the Hull pair were the ULSTER and MUNSTER. As laid down, accommodation was provided for 197 first class and 360 steerage passengers, but the steerage capacity was subsequently increased.

1860 CONNAUGHT 2,959 tons
Sister ship of iron paddle steamers
COLUMBIA, HIBERNIA and ANGLIA.

The maiden voyage of the CONNAUGHT was postponed to 10 July 1860. Meanwhile, a great deal had been going on behind the scenes and the Company was receiving a lot of unfavourable publicity. In reply to a critical article in *The Times* the secretary denied that his company was *in extremis*, but admitted that arrangements were being made to dispose of the Newfoundland mail contract. [8] It transpired that the Allan Line were to take it over, and an advertisement stated that their NORTH BRITON, due to leave Liverpool on 11 July, would call at Galway *en route* to St John's and Quebec. As it turned out, there was a last-minute hitch, and negotations between the two lines fell through.

It had been intended that the CONNAUGHT would leave without the mails, but just as she was casting off a message was received that they were being despatched from London. She eventually sailed for Boston on 11 July 1860 and took eight days instead of the appointed six to reach St John's. The homeward voyage from Boston to Galway took no fewer than 13 days, partly due to fog, which made it impossible for the ship to call at St John's, and partly to a mechanical defect. The second new steamer, the LEINSTER, due to sail early in September, was still in the hands of her builders and her departure was indefinitely postponed.

The CONNAUGHT's second voyage started on 25 September 1860. She left Galway with 462 passengers and all went well until she sprang a leak about 150 miles from Boston. To make matters worse it was found impossible to work the pumps, fire broke out shortly afterwards in the stokehold and very soon the ship was well ablaze. In the nick of time the brig MINNIE SCHIFFER hove in sight and took off everyone on board, but the CONNAUGHT was completely destroyed.

The PRINCE ALBERT was now the only ship in full commission and on 25 January 1861 the Postmaster-General announced that he had agreed to suspend the Company's contract until 26 March, when it was confidently expected that they would start a regular service in accordance with the conditions laid down. The steamer scheduled for this resumed sailing was the HIBERNIA, which was none other than the LEINSTER under a new name. The ULSTER and MUNSTER had been renamed COLUMBIA and ANGLIA, respectively.

The HIBERNIA and COLUMBIA reached Southampton from their builders in time for a party of guests to visit them on 16 March 1861, and on the following day the HIBERNIA set out for Galway in preparation for her maiden voyage. She encountered a severe storm, put into Cork in a sinking condition and instead of continuing to Galway was diverted to Liverpool for major repairs. The COLUMBIA left Southampton a few days later, having meanwhile recorded a mean speed of only 13.9 knots over the measured mile. She sailed from Galway on 9 April for St John's and Boston and should have been followed on 23 April by the final ship of the series, the ANGLIA, which, however, had not left her builder's yard.

It was announced in March 1861 that the 3,670 ton wooden paddle steamer ADRIATIC, formerly of the Collins Line, had been bought by the Company. She sailed from New York on 13 March for Queenstown, Cowes and Havre, taking the Cunard AUSTRALASIAN's passengers and mails to the first-mentioned. After terminating the voyage at Southampton she recorded a mean speed of 15.9 knots at the Stokes Bay measured mile; before leaving Southampton for Galway on 17 April she was docked and fitted with steerage berths for several hundred passengers. She sailed from Galway on 23 April for New York via St John's, which she reached in 5 days

19¾ hours, and she did even better homewards with a time of 5 days 12 hours. She was, in fact, the first of the Company's fleet to cross in less than the standard time of six days laid down in the mail contract.

Repairs to the HIBERNIA took much longer than expected and, consequently, the PARANA was chartered for the next voyage. A few days later the Postmaster-General announced that owing to the Company's failure to fulfil their undertakings he had cancelled the contract. However, the Company decided to despatch two more steamers. The PRINCE ALBERT sailed on 21 May in place of the COLUMBIA, which had been damaged on her recent homeward voyage, and the ADRIATIC left on 5 June, in each case without any mails. It was stated [9] that the ADRIATIC reached St John's in 5 days 2 hours, but other reports give the time as 5 days 12 hours and the writer believes them to be correct. The distance steamed is not known, but assuming that it was about 1,677 nautical miles, the average speed was about 12.70 knots, that is to say, over ¼ knot slower than the fastest westbound passage of the Collins Line ships, whereas had the shorter time been confirmed the average would have been about 13.75 knots.

Sailings were suspended for well over two years while the three surviving new steamers received drastic treatment at the hands of Laird of Birkenhead. One is apt to think of all Galway Line steamers as having one or more white funnels with black tops. It is, therefore, important to point out that an illustration of the HIBERNIA and COLUMBIA under repair at Birkenhead shows each as having two black funnels with a broad white band. [10] As likely as not the funnel colours were changed at or about the same time as the names.

All the ships had been passed as seaworthy by the early summer of 1863, but lay idle until the following August, when the Postmaster-General announced that Her Majesty's Government had decided to revive the Company's contract, and that a fortnightly service to St John's and New York or Boston alternately would start forthwith. An important change was made in the itinerary, Liverpool becoming the terminal in place of Galway where, however, the steamers were due to call outwards and homewards. One of the Company's many difficulties had been the small volume of outward and inward cargo at Galway, and it was hoped that much more would be moving via Liverpool.

First of the reinstated sailings was taken by the HIBERNIA on 14 August 1863 from Liverpool and 18 August from Galway, the ADRIATIC ANGLIA and COLUMBIA following at the appointed intervals. On her second outward voyage the ANGLIA struck the Black Rock in Galway Bay and although she was refloated without any difficulty it was decided that she should return to Liverpool for survey. In order to avoid any further interference with the schedule, the COLUMBIA terminated her next eastbound voyage at Galway. The HIBERNIA did the same a fortnight

1861 HIBERNIA 3,008 tons
Seen under repair after extensive storm
damage. Note unfamiliar funnel markings.

later, sailed again on 19 January 1864 and this, as things turned out, was the Company's last westbound sailing.

There were many reasons for the Galway Line's lack of success, one of the principal b eing over-anxiety to get the service started before suitable ships were ready. The Company also sacrificed strength for speed in the four paddle steamers they built and they were unable to stand up to the severe weather conditions of the North Atlantic, in addition to which their speed was very much less than anticipated. One cannot but feel sympathetic towards Palmer Brothers, builders of two of the ships, who in a letter to *The Times* said *inter alia*:'We prepared a specification with additional strength, based on Lloyd's rules for a nine years classification, but they [the Galway Line] determined to considerably increase and alter the dimensions from those first contemplated, and employed an eminent surveyor of shipping in the port of London to prepare the specifications upon which we tendered and obtained the contract. The vessels were from time to time strengthened and altered at considerable cost, which was paid us, showing that we were not responsible for the specification.' [11]

No fewer than 16 steamers had been employed to carry out a total of 51 completed round voyages. Of these, only the ADRIATIC was an unqualified success, but some credit must be given to the PRINCE ALBERT, which made 13 round voyages - five more than her nearest rival, the CIRCASSIAN.

Looking at the other side of the picture, the Company undoubtedly filled a long-felt want in providing regular steamship accommodation between Ireland and North America, and after a slow start the Irish public did not hesitate to patronise the ships. It is hardly surprising therefore that the Inman and Cunard lines cast envious eyes on what appeared to them to be lucrative traffic with the result that in May and November 1859, respectively, they arranged for their steamers to call at Queenstown (Cobh).

The Galway Line had also shown enterprise in quoting through fares from any of the principal towns in the United Kingdom, the additional charge over and above the ocean fare being only 24s first class and 11s second, irrespective of starting point. In the case of steerage passengers a rail ticket was provided free.

During 1860, the Galway Line carried the surprisingly high total of 4,244 westbound and 1,621 eastbound passengers between Galway and New York and 1,099 westbound and 290 eastbound between Galway and Boston making a grand total of 7,254 compared with 7,558 by the Cunard services to and from the same American ports. It must be pointed out, however, that first and second class passengers only were carried by Cunard whereas the Galway Line carried first, second and steerage. The Galway Line's New York voyages in 1860 averaged 15 days outwards and 13 days homewards.

It cannot be denied that in those days Queenstown was far preferable to

Galway as an Atlantic port. The following outspoken comment was published in 1863: 'A Belfast theological professor once declared that Londonderry was at the back of God-speed. If the dictum had been applied to Galway it would have been more readily accepted. Even a most patriotic company, with a subsidy of £70,000 per annum cannot force that city upon the groove of Irish progress. The subsidy was obtained in order to make Galway a packet station, but the mail packets appear in the bay only as birds of passage, on their way from Liverpool to America. The passengers who go to that port for convenience are subjected to the greatest possible inconvenience, being without any proper accommodation for themselves and their luggage while waiting to embark. Amid noise, hurry, confusion, wet, dirt and all sorts of discomforts they are taken out a mile or two through the breakers in a small steamer, and perhaps they commence their voyage across the Atlantic thoroughly drenched with sea water.' [12]

[1] *The Times* 29/3/1859
[2] *The Times* 1/6/1858
[3] *The Times* 3/7/1858 (advt)
[4] *The Times* 16/7/1858
[5] *The Times* 20/12/1858
[6] *The Times* 17/8/1859
[7] *The Times* 30/11/1858
[8] *The Times* 12/7/1860
[9] *The Times* 24/6/1861
[10] *Illustrated London News* 27/7/1861
[11] *The Times* 25/6/1861
[12] *The Times* 12/11/1863

ANTELOPE
(Did not run for Galway. See text and North Atlantic SN Co - 56).

1. (1858) INDIAN EMPIRE
2,516. 74,54 x 14,63. (244.6 x 48.0). C—1—3. W—P—SL2—10. (I—100; II—50; III—450). Wm H. Webb, New York (engines T.F. Secor Co, New York). 1847 (20/8) launched as UNITED STATES (US). 1858 (18/5) INDIAN EMPIRE (J.O. Lever). 1858 (19/6) FV Galway—New York. 1858 (28/9) LV ditto (2 RV). (See Chapter 22).

AMERICAN EMPIRE (c)
(Did not run for Galway).

2. (1858) PRINCE ALBERT (c)
(1858) PRINCE ALBERT
2,028. 87,17 x 11,58. (286.0 x 38.0). C—1—3. I—S—I(2)—10. Société

NAS–3 **
505

Cockerill, Antwerp. Laid down as DUC DE BRABANT (Société Belge des Bateaux à Vapeur Transatlantiques); renamed PRINCE ALBERT. 1857 (15/10) MV London—India as Indian Mutiny transport. 1858 (27/7) FV for Galway (c), Galway—New York. 1858 (20/10) PRINCE ALBERT (J.O. Lever). 1859 (8/2) ditto (Atlantic RMSN Co (Galway Line)). 1861 (21/5) LV galway—New York (13 RV). 1861 PRINCE ALBERT (Jose Yglesias, London). 1862 ISLA DE CUBA (A. Lopez y Cia). 1877 (1/4) wrecked near Havana.

3. (1858) PROPELLER

603. 57,05 x 8,84. (187.2 x 29.0). C—1—2. I—S—I(2)—9. T.D. Marshall, South Shields (engines Humphrys & Pearson, Hull). 1855 (/) launched for W.S. Andrews. 1858 (16/7) PROPELLER (J.O. Lever). 1858 (21/8) FV Galway—Boston (1 RV). 1859 (8/2) PROPELLER (Atlantic RMSN Co (Galway Line)), but did not run for them. 1861 ROLAND (German). 1899 (approx) scrapped.

4. (1858) PACIFIC

1,469. 77,50 x 9,93. (254.3 x 32.6). C—2—2. I—P—O2—10. Scott Russell & Co, London. 1854 (23/9) launched for Sydney & Melbourne SP Co. 1858 (16/8) PACIFIC (J.O. Lever). 1858 (24/8) FV Galway—New York. 1859 (8/2) PACIFIC (Atlantic RMSN Co (Galway Line)). 1859 (6/3) LV Galway—New York (4 RV). 1861 sold. 1865 PACIFIC (Henry Lafone). 1866 converted to screw. 1866 PACIFIC (United States & United Kingdom). 1871 (7/2) wrecked on Whalsey Island, Shetlands.

4a. (1858) CIRCASSIAN (c)

1,387. 77,72 x 11,92. (255.0 x 39.1). C—1—3. I—S—GB2—9. Robert Hickson & Co, Belfast (engines Randolph, Elder & Co, Glasgow). 1856 (18/7) launched for North Atlantic SN Co. 1858 (26/10) FV for Galway (c), Galway—New York. 1860 (5/3) LV ditto (8 RV). (See North Atlantic SN Co - 56).

4b. (1859) ADELAIDE (c)

1,653. 79,39 x 11,18. (260.5 x 36.7). C—2(abreast)—4. I—S—?—9. (I—80; III—120). Scott Russell & Co, London. 1852 (12/11) launched for Australian RMSN Co. 1859 (30/4) FV for Galway (c), Galway—New York. 1859 (30/6) LV ditto (2 RV). (See Stock Line - 67)-

4c. (1859) ARGO (c)

2,315. 74,06 x 11,98. (243.6 x 39.3). C—1—3. I—S—D2—9. C.J. Mare & Co, London (engines Maudslay, Sons & Field, London). 1852 (23/12) launched for General Screw. 1859 (28/5) FV for Galway (c), Galway—New York. 1859 (28/6) wrecked at Trepassey Bay, NF, on homeward voyage (0). (See European & American - 57).

4d. (1857) JASON (c)

2,667. 77,41 x 11,89. (254 x 39.0). C—1—3. I—S—D2—9. C.J. Mare &
Co, London (engines Watt & Co, London). 1853 (6/8) launched for
General Screw. 1859 (20/8) FV for Galway (c), Galway—New York. 1859
(15/10) LV ditto (2 RV). (See European & American - 57).

4e. (1859) BRAZIL (c)

1,824. 77,41 x 11,89. (254.0 x 39). C—1—3. I—S—D2—9. C.J.MARE &
Co, London (engines Maudslay, Sons & Field, London). 1852 (/)
launched for General Screw as LADY JOCELYN. 1859 BRAZIL (Anglo-
Luzo-Brazilian). 1860 (28/4) FV for Galway (c), Galway—New York
(1 RV). 1861 LADY JOCELYN (East India & London). 1868 ditto (Shaw,
Savill & Albion); engines removed. Later used as meat hulk in West India
Dock, London. 1922 scrapped in Holland.

4f. (1860) GOLDEN FLEECE (c)

2,768. 77,41 x 11,89. (254.0 x 39.0). C—1—3. I—S—D2—9. C.J. Mare &
Co, London (engines Maudslay, Sons & Field, London). 1853 (/)
launched for General Screw. 1860 (23/6) FV for Galway (c), Galway—
New York (1 RV). 1869 (10/9) foundered in Penarth Roads.

4g. (1860) PARANA (c)

2,250. 92,96 x 12,80. (305.0 x 42.0). C—2—3. W—P—SL2—11. Wigram &
Sons, Southampton (engines Caird & Co, Greenock). 1851 (15/7)
launched for RMSP Co. 1860 (27/6) FV for Galway (c), Galway—New
York. 1860 (7/8) 2nd voyage ditto. 1861 (7/5) LV ditto (3 RV). 1868 hulk
at St Thomas. 1876 scrapped.

5. 1860 CONNAUGHT

2,959. 109,72 x 12,19. (360.0 x 40.0). S—2—2. I—P—O3—12. (I—200;
III—600). Palmer Bros & Co, Jarrow-on-Tyne. 1860 (21/4) launched. 1860
(11/7) MV Galway—St John's, NF—Boston. 1860 (25/9) 2nd voyage
Galway—St John's, NF (destination Boston). 1860 destroyed by fire about
150 miles from Boston (0).

6. 1861 COLUMBIA

2,913. 111,24 x 12,19. (365.0 x 40.0). S—2—2. I—P—O2—12. (I—197;
III—360). Martin Samuelson & Co, Hull. Laid down as ULSTER. 1860
(/) launched as COLUMBIA. 1861 (9/4) MV Galway—St John's,
NF—Boston (1 RV). 1861 strengthened by Laird, Birkenhead. 1863 (25/9)
FV Liverpool—Galway (dep 29/9)—St John's, NF—New York. 1863
(20/11) 3rd voyage ditto. 1864 (5/1) LV Galway—St John's, NF—Boston
(total 4 RV). 1864-6 laid up. 1866 sold to Turkish Govt.

7. (1861) ADRIATIC

  4,154. 105,15 x 15,24. (345.0 x 50.0). S—2—2. W—P—O2—13. George &
  James Steers, New York (engines Novelty Iron Works, New York). 1856
  (7/4) launched for Collins. 1861 ADRIATIC (Galway). 1861 (23/4) FV
  Galway—New York. 1861 (Dec) carried British troops to Canada; winter-
  ed at Halifax. 1862 (May) returned to Spithead. 1863 (18/12) LV Galway
  —St John's, NF—New York (5 RV). (See Collins - 25).

8. 1863 HIBERNIA

  3,008. 109,72 x 12,19. (360.0 x 40.0). S—2—2. I—P—O3—12. (I—200;
  III—600). Palmer Bros & Co, Jarrow-on-Tyne. 1860 (1/9) launched as
  LEINSTER; renamed HIBERNIA. 1861 (17/3) sailed Southampton—
  Galway; put into Cork in sinking condition; strengthened by Laird,
  Birkenhead. 1863 (14/8) MV Liverpool—Galway (dep 18/8)—St John's,
  NF—Boston. 1863 (9/10) 2nd voyage ditto. 1863 (4/12) 3rd voyage ditto.
  1864 (10/1) LV Galway—St John's, NF—New York (4 RV); LV of line.
  1864-9 laid up. 1869 sold to Telegraph Construction & Maintenance Co;
  converted to twin-screw; name unchanged. 1877 (22/11) wrecked at
  Maranhão, Brazil.

9. 1863 ANGLIA

  2,913. 111,24 x 12,19. (365.0 x 40.0). S—2—2. I—P—O2—12. (I—200;
  III—600). Martin Samuelson & Co, Hull). laid down as MUNSTER. 1860
  (/) launched as ANGLIA. 1861 strengthened by Laird, Birkenhead.
  1863 (11/9) MV Liverpool—Galway (dep 15/9)—St John's, NF—Boston
  (1 RV). 1863 (6/11) sailed Liverpool—Boston but struck Black Rock in
  Galway Bay; returned to Liverpool for repairs. 1863-6 laid up. 1866 sold to
  Turkish Govt.

Total 53 completed westbound voyages; 51 eastbound.

FUNNEL: (a) White; black top
        (b) Black; broad white band.

FLAG: Blue; red cross with golden harp.

NORDDEUTSCHER LLOYD

(North German Lloyd)

NDL - NGL

(German)

Hermann Heinrich Meier, founder of NORDDEUTSCHER LLOYD, was born in Bremen on 16 October 1809, and on 1 January 1834 became a partner in his father's firm of H. H. Meier & Co, which had been established in 1805. Trading extensively with the USA, the firm also acted as emigration agents for a number of sailing ships running between Bremen and ports in the New World. Nearly 20 years later Meier became a director of the Weser & Hunte Dampfschiffahrtsgesellschaft (Weser& Hunte Steamship Company), which was operating three small vessels between Bremen, Oldenburg and Bremerhaven. In the same year he founded the Schleppschiffahrtsgesellschaft auf der Unterweser (Lower Weser Towing Company) and joined the board of the Dampfschleppschiffahrtsgesellschaft auf der Oberweser (Upper Weser Steam Towing Company). In addition, he became an important member of the Allgemeine Assekuranzanstalt für die Oberweser (Upper Weser Insurance Company).[1]

It was already, in 1854, Meyer's intention to amalgamate these four companies into one concern of sufficient size to include also an ocean steamship line based on Bremen. But money was scarce and no progress was made until the early part of 1856, when Meier met a young Berlin banker and merchant, Eduard Crüsemann, who, he discovered, was planning to establish a shipping and trading firm under the style Bremer Handelscompagnie. They realised at once that they had basically similar aims and decided to pool their ideas.

The outcome was that on 26 November 1856 the four above-mentioned firms agreed to amalgamate. It was decided that the new concern would be known as NORDDEUTSCHER LLOYD and that the share capital would be 4,000,000 talers (£600,000), of which more than half was subscribed by the beginning of February 1857. The Company received its first charter in the Bremen Senate on 18 February, and two days later was well and truly established, with Meier as chairman of the board of directors and Crüsemann as general manager. There seems no doubt that the choice of name was prompted by that of the Lloyd Austriaco, founded at Trieste in 1833 and sometimes referred to as the South German Lloyd.

The principal objects of the new Bremen concern were not only to continue and develop the shipping interests of the component companies on the River Weser and its tributaries as well as the existing insurance activities, but also to inaugurate a steamship service across the North Sea betwen Germany and England and, more particularly, a transatlantic steamship service between Bremen and New York. In Germany the name Norddeutscher Lloyd is frequently abbreviated to NDL or Lloyd; in England and America it is often referred to as the North German Lloyd, NGL or NDL.

Orders were placed on Tyneside with Palmer Brothers for the 500 ton iron screw ADLER, MÖWE, SCHWAN and SCHWALBE and with Humphrys & Pearson of Hull for the FALKE and CONDOR, enabling a passenger and cargo service to be inaugurated betwen Bremen and London in October 1857.

The Hamburg American Line had started steamship operations between Hamburg and New York in 1856. Their fourth unit, the SAXONIA, was launched by Caird & Co of Greenock on 21 August 1857, and it was stated that the keel of a similar but slightly larger vessel would be laid down immediately for NDL on the same slipway.[2] The resulting ship,the 2,674 ton BREMEN, was launched only a little over five months later and sailed on 19 June 1858 to inaugurate her owner's service from Bremen (or to be exact, Bremerhaven) to New York, where she arrived on 4 July with 22 cabin passengers, 93 steerage and 150 tons of cargo. She sailed again on the 17th, reaching her home port on the 30th after a remarkably fast passage of 12 days 5 hours. For many months, NDL advertisements claimed that the 'BREMEN has made the quickest passage on record.' [3] It is evident that the Company was anxious to attract business from the United Kingdom, as it was announced that passengers would be conveyed from London to New York in connection with their twice-weekly service of steamers from London to Bremen at through fares of £24 first class, £14.10.0 second and £9.5.0 third.

1858 BREMEN 2,674 tons
NDL's pioneer North Atlantic unit.
Sister ship: NEW YORK.

1858 HUDSON 2,166 tons
A contemporary of the BREMEN. After a
serious fire became National Line
LOUISIANA. Sister ship: WESER

A sister ship, the NEW YORK, followed in August and the HUDSON in September, the latter differing from the first two in that she was a product of Palmers and had two funnels instead of one. The HUDSON was badly damaged by fire at her berth at Bremerhaven just before starting her second voyage. This was the end of her NDL career, but she was subsequently towed to the Tyne, rebuilt and in due course returned to the North Atlantic under new ownership. The fourth ship, the WESER, also by Palmers, was badly damaged by heavy seas in mid-Atlantic during her maiden voyage in December 1858 and had to put back to Cork for repairs. She did not sail again until 6 March 1859, and after only three round voyages was sold to France to become a naval transport.

22 March 1859 was a red-letter day for the port of Southampton as the NEW YORK sailed with over 450 passengers for New York, 44 of them having embarked there. The homeward-bound BREMEN also called at the end of the same month and from then onwards the NDL ships made a regular call, outwards and homewards.

It was announced at the second annual general meeting of NDL held on 18 April 1859 that in all probability the New York line would shortly be augmented by the 1,902 ton wooden paddle steamer ERICSSON, laid down in 1852 as a caloric ship but subsequently fitted with orthodox steam machinery. This ship has already cropped up in two earlier chapters and will do so again in at least two more. There was an unexpected hitch in the arrangements, which was probably just as well as it is unlikely that the ERICSSON would have enhanced the Company's prestige.

The Company suffered a further misfortune when the BREMEN was out of commission for about six months in 1860 with a fractured propeller shaft, leaving the NEW YORK to carry on the North Atlantic service alone.

London agents for NDL were Phillips, Graves & Phillips, [4] of 11 Rood Lane, E.C. Until 1861 their Southampton representatives were Croskey & Co, who had acted in a similar capacity for the Ocean, New York & Havre and Vanderbilt lines, as well as for the Hamburg American Line (Hapag)

1861 HANSA 2,992 tons
A successor to NDL's North Atlantic pioneers.

and the European & American Steam Shipping Company, but were then replaced by Keller Wallis & Postlethwaite, predecessors of the well-known firm of Keller, Bryant & Co, of London and Southampton.

In 1861, also, a limited measure of agreement was reached between NDL and Hapag, the former adopting the latter's description 'First class, upper saloon' and 'First class, lower saloon' instead of the more usual first and second class.

More significantly, some months before the completion of their 2,992 ton HANSA in 1861, NDL announced that as soon as a fourth steamer was commissioned they and Hapag would run a joint weekly service to New York during eight months of the year and a fortnightly one during the remainder. The newcomer, the 2,752 ton AMERICA, started her maiden voyage from Bremen on 25 May 1863, subsequent sailings alternating between the ships of the two lines. As it was clear by this time that the Company was likely to expand much further, the lease of some extensive dock property was acquired at Hoboken, on the New Jersey bank of the Hudson River. Six years later, in 1869, NDL bought it outright.

The outbreak of the Prusso-Danish War of 1864 resulted in the BREMEN, HANSA and AMERICA being transferred to the Russian flag in order to protect them from the Danish corsairs, but the New York arrivals column of the *New York Herald* still showed the NEW YORK under the Bremen flag. Whether or not this was correct is not clear. At any rate, the Russian-flag arrangement was only in effect for two or three round voyages by each of the steamers concerned.

The 2,800 ton HERMANN, DEUTSCHLAND, UNION and WESER (II) were commissioned during 1865/7 and enabled a weekly NDL service to be introduced. They were similar in most respects to their predecessors and all had clipper bows, but they had two masts instead of three. During 1865 the average duration of NDL passages from Southampton to New York was 11 days 19 hours, and in the opposite direction 11 days 6 hours. The HANSA had been responsible for the fastest eastbound passage of 10 days 9½ hours in June 1863 and a month later she also completed a record westbound passage of 10 days 11 hours. The number of transatlantic passengers carried by the Company rose in 1867 to 33,427, compared with 28,501 in 1866, 15,116 in 1864 and 7,029 in 1859. The tonnage of cargo carried also rose steeply.

It was decided at an extraordinary general meeting on 22 January 1867 to order two steamers from Caird & Co, for a new service between Bremen and Baltimore, a special issue of Litera B shares to the value of £105,000 being made to finance the ships, half being subscribed by the Baltimore & Ohio Railroad. The first of the newcomers, the 2,321 ton BALTIMORE, was laid down on 27 February 1867 and was launched only five months and four days later. However she did not sail from Bremen for Baltimore until 1

March 1868 and it transpires that she was laid up in the Gareloch, River Clyde, between August and November 1867 owing to the non-arrival of her propeller shaft from Germany. In this connection, it is of interest to note that following a succession of fractured shafts in the earlier steamers, the AMERICA of 1863 was fitted with a cast-steel shaft manufactured by the Krupp Works in Essen. It would seem that the BALTIMORE, and perhaps some or all of the intervening ships, had been similarly treated.

The BALTIMORE had accommodation for 84 first class and 600 steerage passengers, and was followed by the BERLIN. Advertisements stated that 'the North German Lloyd will despatch their full-powered, first class, Clyde-built steamships from Southampton to Baltimore',and despite the railroad interest the line was invariably referred to as the Norddeutscher Lloyd or North German Lloyd in advertisements, newspaper articles and, for that matter, in the NDL annual reports. The new service met with instant success, and the slightly larger OHIO and LEIPZIG were placed in service in March and May 1869 respectively. The Litera B capital was doubled in order to provide for these additions.

The 3,000 ton RHEIN and MAIN were completed for the New York service in 1868, followed by the DONAU in 1869. The RHEIN was actually the second of that name as the NDL annual report for 1868 revealed that following the loss of several Royal Mail Steam Packet Company ships during a hurricane in the West Indies, a steamer under construction by Caird & Co for NDL was taken over by the RMSP and renamed NEVA. The report added that NDL had placed a new order with Caird for a steamer to be ready by January 1869. As the steamer subsequently commissioned as the RHEIN first sailed from Bremen on 3 October 1868 it must be assumed that the name had been transferred to the earlier of two ships already under construction for the Company.

Until 1870 seven or preferably eight steamers were required to maintain a weekly service to New York. From the autumn of 1868 onwards the available number was ten, so it was decided to despatch the NEW YORK in November 1868 on an experimental voyage from Bremen and Southampton to Havana and New Orleans, while in the following spring, when the total of ships was 11, there were extra sailings once a fortnight from Bremen to New York via Havre. Southampton remained the port of call of the principal New York service.

The New Orleans voyage having proved successful, the new 2,600 ton FRANKFURT and HANNOVER entered service between Bremen, Havre and New Orleans in the autumn of 1869, one or two additional sailings being made by the BREMEN and NEW YORK. This service was only intended to operate during the autumn, winter and early spring, and in consequence first the HANNOVER and then the FRANKFURT were detailed to New York during the early summer of 1870. By this time four more steamers were in an advanced stage of construction - the 2,555 ton KÖLN for the New Orleans service and the remainder for a new venture to Central America due to start in the autumn.

The outbreak of the Franco-Prussian War in July 1870 played havoc with the Company's transatlantic services, which for a time were suspended altogether. To avoid the risk of capture by the French Navy four of the ships were laid up at Southampton, six at New York and the remainder at Bremen or Baltimore. On 1 October 1870 it was considered safe, however, for the HANSA to sail from Bremen for New York via the north of Scotland, the RHEIN, DEUTSCHLAND, DONAU, HERMANN and MAIN following at weekly intervals, while the AMERICA sailed home from New York on 8 October by the same route, succeeded by the UNION, HANNOVER and HANSA. On 28 November the UNION, bound from Bremen to New York with 300 passengers, had the misfortune to strand near Rattray Head, Aberdeenshire. Her passengers and crew were saved, but she became a total loss.

The Southampton call of the New York steamers was resumed in February 1871, as it was in the case of Baltimore and New Orleans, to the latter of which the KÖLN sailed on her maiden voyage at the beginning of April. The start of the Central American service had been delayed by the war, the first sailing being taken by the 2,550 ton KÖNIG WILHELM 1 in March 1871, followed at monthly intervals by the KRONPRINZ FRIEDRICH WILHELM and GRAF BISMARCK. To begin with, the ships proceeded from Bremen to Southampton, thence direct to Colon (Panama), Savanilla, Puerto Cabello and La Guayra.

Fourth unit of the New Orleans fleet, the 3,025 ton STRASSBURG was completed in the summer of 1872 and was the first of the NDL transatlantic ships to have a straight stem. Her maiden voyage took place to New York. She was followed by the 3,200 ton MOSEL for the New York service, the BRAUNSCHWEIG and NÜRNBERG for Baltimore and the FELDMARSCHALL MOLTKE and MINISTER ROON for Central America. All had compound engines. The two Baltimore ships were products of R.Steele & Co, near neighbours of Caird at Greenock, who were responsible for the others.

There was a short-lived boom on the North Atlantic at the conclusion of the war, and during 1871 NDL carried 50,759 passengers on the New York route. The next two years were even more successful and in May 1872 the 2,717 ton NEMESIS, which had already made a few voyages for Cunard and Inman, started the first of four NDL voyages at a time when the Company was awaiting the completion of several new ships. Unfortunately, the charter was not financially profitable. From March to October 1873 and again from March to September 1874 the fortnightly extra service between Bremen and New York became a weekly one - until May 1874 via

Southampton and subsequently via Havre. Accommodation on the weekly Bremen-Southampton-New York mail steamers was still described as first class, upper saloon; first class, lower saloon; and steerage, but from 1871 onwards the extra steamers were advertised as carrying cabin and steerage passengers only. This was by no means the first time that the description cabin had been used on the North Atlantic, but it was a new development for the descriptions first class and cabin to be used simultaneously to indicate varying standards of luxury. NDL was anticipating by nearly half a century a custom that came into general use after World War 1.

Although the STRASSBURG and MOSEL were the first newly-built NDL steamers to appear with compound engines, the AMERICA's machinery had been compounded in 1871, followed by the HERMANN and DEUTSCHLAND in 1872 and many other steamers from 1875 onwards.

The Central American service was far from being a success and was withdrawn in 1874. The KÖNIG WILHELM 1 had already been transferred to the North Atlantic and was wrecked during the concluding stages of her third homeward voyage thereon in November 1873. The MINISTER ROON made three North Atlantic voyages in 1874 and the FELDMARSCHALL MOLTKE was scheduled for one later in the year but this was subsequently cancelled; within a few months both were sold to the P&O. In addition the pioneer BREMEN and NEW YORK were sold in 1874 to a Liverpool owner, who subsequently ran them as sailing ships.

By the middle of 1874 a severe slump had set in on the North Atlantic. Passengers on the New York service, which had carried 52,428 in 1873, dropped to 35,305 in 1874, 31,050 in 1875, 27,505 in 1876 and 23,015 in 1877. It cannot be denied that the Company had been over-ambitious, and within eight years had commissioned no fewer than 26 new ships averaging nearly 3,000 tons each. Between 1872 and 1875 inclusive the additions totalled 16, of which the 3,120 ton NECKAR and the 3,265 ton ODER were completed in 1874 for the New York service and the GENERAL WERDER for the West Indies. These were the last three ships to be built for the Company by Caird. In addition, the 3,100 ton HOHENZOLLERN, HOHENSTAUFEN, SALIER and HABSBURG were built by Earle's Shipbuilding Company of Hull for a new service between Bremen, Brazil and the River Plate, which was opened by the HOHENZOLLERN in March 1876.

At the height of the slump in 1875 as many as 19 ships were laid up. The outlook was black but the Company succeeded in weathering the storm despite two serious disasters during the year. On 6 December the DEUTSCHLAND was wrecked off the Kentish Knock in the Thames estuary with the loss of 157 lives,and only five days later a bomb explosion on the MOSEL in Bremerhaven resulted in the death of 128 people, injuries to many more and serious damage to the ship.

1874 ODER 3,265 tons
Bremen—Southampton—New York service.
Sister ships: MOSEL, NECKAR.

When NDL reached its majority in February 1878 its founder, H.H.Meier,was still president of the board of directors. Herr J.G.Lohmann had just taken over the management of the Company after two predecessors had died in quick succession. He was a man of vast energy and was determined to put the Company back on its feet. The time was not opportune to build new ships and to begin with he had to be content with continuing the policy of fitting the earlier units with compound engines, this work being, by degrees, undertaken in Germany instead of Great Britain. There were still some surplus ships and in 1878 services were started from Genoa to Rio de Janeiro and from Genoa to Montevideo and Buenos Aires. They only remained in operation for about three years, by which time separate services were in operation from Bremen, via Antwerp, to the same destinations.

At first, the Baltimore line had been affected much less by the depression than the New York one. The number of passengers to and from Baltimore in 1873 was 11,114, in 1874 9,874 and in 1875 7,617. By 1877 however, the number had fallen to 3,226 westbound and 922 eastbound. It was decided, therefore, to wind up the Litera B shares, and as from 1 January 1879 the six ships of the Baltimore service were transferred to the account of the main shareholders. It is clear that the Company would have liked to abandon the service altogether but they wisely adopted the attitude that if they did so someone else would almost certainly step in. It remains to add that the first and second class passenger accommodation of the BALTIMORE, BERLIN, OHIO and LEIPZIG had been considerably reduced in 1876-7 in order to increase the amount of space available for cargo.

Although NDL had kept pace with the rival Hapag, they had fallen behind the principal British lines in the size and speed of their ships. Herr Lohmann decided to make drastic changes in the Company's building policy and ordered an 'express' steamer which would be comparable with

517

the best non-German ships. It was originally intended to build the ship in Germany, but none of the German shipyards had sufficient experience to turn out a ship of the high standard required and the order eventually went to John Elder & Co of Glasgow, builders of the Guion Line's record-breaker ARIZONA. The new ship was the 4,510 ton iron single-screw ELBE, which had accommodation for 120 first class, 130 second and 1,000 steerage passengers and sailed on 26 June 1881 from Bremen to New York via Southampton. On her second westbound voyage, in August, she proceeded from Southampton to Sandy Hook in 8 days 12 hours 50 minutes, which was a record for the English Channel route, and in the reverse direction completed an even faster passage of 8 days 9 hours 10 minutes.

1882 WERRA 4,817 tons
Second of nine express steamers built
in Scotland.

The ELBE is stated to have made a profit equal to about one-fifth of her total cost during the five round voyages she undertook in 1881. Not surprisingly, orders were placed for two slightly larger and faster ships, the WERRA and FULDA, followed in 1884 by the EIDER and EMS. All these ships were lighted throughout by electricity, the ELBE being converted thereto in 1883. It was now possible to run a weekly express service as well as a weekly extra service. The newcomers arrived on the scene at an opportune time as the number of passengers carried between Bremen and New York increased from 27,269 in 1879 to 60,424 in 1880, 86,636 in 1881, 100,764 in 1884 and 108,174 in 1885.

Ill-luck continued to dog the MOSEL, victim of the bomb explosion, and in 1882 she was wrecked near the Lizard. Two years previously, the 2,513 ton HANSA (11), built at Southampton in 1879 and the first purely cargo North Atlantic steamer to be owned by the Company, was wrecked on Terschelling Island, off the Dutch coast. The HANSA (1) had been sold earlier in the same year.

The New Orleans service had never been a great success for either passengers or freight, the maximum number of passengers carried in any one year being well under 5,000. Monthly sailings took place during September, October and November of each year with, as a rule, one or two more in the spring. From 1882 onwards the service was extended to serve both New Orleans and Galveston, with calls at Havre and Havana, but this did not produce any improvement and the service was withdrawn in 1886. Instead, two new routes were opened in that year - from Bremen to the Far East and from Bremen to Australia, in each case via the Suez Canal, an annual subsidy of £222,000 having been awarded the Company by the German Government. In preparation for these activities, the ODER, NECKAR, HOHENZOLLERN and GENERAL WERDER were refitted at Bremen, and shortly afterwards the newly-built 4,500 ton PREUSSEN, BAYERN and SACHSEN were commissioned. They and the 1,800 ton feeder steamers STETTIN, LÜBECK and DANZIG were notable as the first oceangoing ships of the Company's fleet to be laid down in Germany. The first three spent practically all their lives in the Far Eastern trade.

The 4,970 ton ALLER, TRAVE and SAALE were completed for the express service in 1886. Like their five predecessors they had two buff funnels (compared with the black funnels of earlier units) and four masts, but they were built of steel instead of iron. The ALLER was the first North Atlantic express liner to be fitted with triple-expansion engines, which gave her a speed of nearly 18 knots. The 5,099 ton LAHN, which followed in 1887, had a trial speed of 19½ knots and for a time was the third fastest ship on the North Atlantic.

An interesting new series of 13 knot steamers was turned out from 1889 onwards, and was one of the last building orders placed by the Company outside Germany. First to appear were the 4,530 ton DRESDEN, and MÜNCHEN, followed by the 5,000 ton KARLSRUHE, STUTTGART, GERA, WEIMAR, OLDENBURG and DARMSTADT. They started a new policy of interchangeability between the Company's different services - that is to say, New York, Baltimore, South America, Far East and Australia. All ran extensively on the North Atlantic - to New York or to Baltimore and sometimes to both.

The German shipbuilding yards made great progress during the 1880s, and towards the end of the decade NDL felt that the time was ripe to entrust Vulcan of Stettin with orders for two express steamers as well as a slightly less pretentious ship, the 4,773 ton KAISER WILHELM 11, which was the first to appear. At that time she was the longest ship in the fleet but her speed did not exceed 16 knots. The 6,900 ton SPREE and HAVEL started their maiden voyages from Bremen to New York inNovember 1890 and February 1891, had a trial speed of 20 knots and differed in appearance from their predecessors in that they had three masts instead of four. They failed to create quite the sensation expected as they were slightly smaller and slower, and less imposing in appearance than the four twin-screw ships recently commissioned by the rival Hapag. NDL undeniably had made a great mistake in fitting them with single screws.

The Company had been running a bi-weekly service from Bremen to New

1901 HOHENZOLLERN 6,661 tons
Built 1889 as KAISER WILHELM II and
renamed in 1901.

York, usually via Southampton, since the early 1880s. This required eight steamers, and as by August 1891 no fewer than 12 express steamers were available the service was increased to tri-weekly, with departures from Bremen on Saturdays, Tuesdays and Wednesdays and from Southampton one day later. It was soon found that results did not justify the increase and the third service remained in operation for only a few weeks. While it lasted, however, it was the most outstanding long-distance service ever provided by any steamship company on any route.

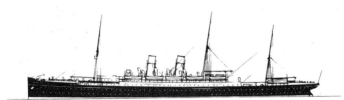

1891 HAVEL 6,875 tons
German-built single screw express steamer.
Sister ship: SPREE.

The problem was how to find employment for the surplus ships, and was partially solved by the stranding of the EIDER on the Isle of Wight in dense fog on 31 January 1892. She was refloated, but was too badly damaged to be worth repairing and was scrapped. Unfortunately, also, the ELBE was sunk in collision in the North Sea on 30 January 1895 with the appalling loss of 332 lives. Meanwhile, it had been decided to start a new service between New York and Italy, as emigration from Italy to the USA was booming and comparatively small steamers were still being employed by the Italian, French and British lines already in the trade. The first sailing was taken by the FULDA, which left New York on 21 October 1891 for Genoa, the WERRA followed about a month later and in the autumn and winter of 1892-3 they were augmented by the EMS, KAISER WILHELM 11 and KRONPRINZ FRIEDRICH WILHELM. The last-named had been fitted with quadruple-expansion engines in 1887, but at the time was running to South America and consequently does not qualify as the first steamer on the North Atlantic with that advanced type of machinery.

NDL announced in 1893 that owing to the withdrawal of their Brindisi-Port Said feeder service the 1,800 ton STETTIN and DANZIG would be transferred to the New York - Genoa route, but this never came about - probably because, on reflection, it was decided that they were too small to withstand the rigours of the North Atlantic. Instead, the DANZIG inaugurated a weekly feeder service between Genoa, Naples and Palermo. It should be added that in the autumn of 1893 Hapag decided to participate in the New York - Mediterranean trade and it was soon agreed with NDL that sailings should be on a joint basis. After a twelve-month trial of running all the year round - in summer by some of the smaller steamers - Hapag subsequently arranged temporarily for their express steamers to represent them in the Mediterranean during autumn and winter only.

The North Atlantic Steamship Lines' Association was started in Hamburg in 1892 by Hapag, NDL, Holland America and Red Star. Revised steerage fares were fixed and each line was guaranteed a percentage share of the steerage trade according to its total tonnage employed, with provision for adjustments from time to time.

It was in 1892 that NDL published details of passengers landed at New York by each of the North Atlantic lines during the 11 years between 1881 and 1891 inclusive. The total was 817,169 cabin (that is to say, first and second combined) and 4,075,000 steerage, making a grand total of 4,892,169. Of these, 815,749 (or 16.7 per cent) were carried by NDL; 609,216 (or 12.4 per cent) by Hapag; 407,203 (8.3 per cent) by White Star; 369,284 (7.6 per cent) by Inman; and 347.823 (7.1 per cent) by Cunard.

For many years after the foundation of NDL there had been no serious rivalry with Hapag. On the contrary, there had been a normal semi-friendly relationship up to the time of the near-disaster which befell Hapag soon after the acquisition of the Adler Line. But there was a drastic change when Albert Ballin joined Hapag, which quickly regained the important position it had formerly occupied. There was intense rivalry between the two lines from 1889, when the first of the twin-screw Hapag express steamers was commissioned, until August 1914, and again after World War 1 until 1930. Publication of these statistics in 1892 was undoubtedly aimed at telling the world that NDL was supreme in the passenger field and caused quite a sensation, as few outside Germany had realised the magnitude of the NDL success.

The arrival of a Hapag steamer at New York in September 1892 with a number of cases of cholera resulted for a time in the virtual cessation of westbound steerage business to USA ports. So drastic were the steps taken to prevent further outbreaks that by mid November the NDL ships were again operating normally. Instead of it being a slack time of year, the backlog of business caused the DRESDEN to arrive at New York on 29 November 1892 with 1,632 steerage passengers and the STUTTGART on 15 December with no fewer than 2,263 steerage, which was probably the highest number of civilian passengers carried to date on a North Atlantic steamer.

The autumn of 1892 was a turning point as regards accommodation on NDL ships as there were further occasions when the DRESDEN and her consorts carried steerage passengers exclusively. Moreover, it seems that this group of ships seldom if ever again carried first class on the North Atlantic. For examples,the *New York Herald,* in reporting the arrival of the WEIMAR on 9 March 1893, stated that she was carrying 423 second cabin and nine steerage passengers, and that the DARMSTADT landed 744 steerage passengers at New York on 5 April 1893, 117 second class and 670 steerage being carried to Baltimore, her final destination.

Another event of 1892 was the commissioning of the 5,140 ton H.H.MEIER, which had been bought on the stocks for the South American trade and was the first twin-screw unit of the fleet. In fact, her maiden voyage, on which she carried 46 first class and 259 second class passengers, took place to New York, and apart from five round voyages to South America she ran exclusively on the North Atlantic for upwards of eight years. On her second voyage she carried 354 second class and 24 steerage, and it seems that she catered exclusively for second and steerage on all subsequent North Atlantic occasions.

It was announced at the 36th annual general meeting of the Company in April 1893 that in order to strengthen the cargo traffic it had been decided to establish with chartered tonnage a new line to be known as the 'Roland Line of the Norddeutscher Lloyd' between Bremen and New York. The first sailing was taken by the 3,172 ton British-flag GULF OF MEXICO, which sailed from Bremen on 13 April 1893 and reached New York on 30 April with cargo and 296 steerage passengers, the fare paid being appreciably lower than on the other steamers. The 2,436 ton LAUGHTON followed on 26 April and, between them, the pair undertook five round voyages. Meanwhile, the Company had bought on the stocks in England a 3,603 ton single-screw steamer, which was named ROLAND and sailed from Bremen on 13 September. She had accommodation for 28 second class and 800 steerage passengers, but on her maiden voyage and most subsequent occasions carried steerage exclusively, as did her two succesors. They were the 4,760 ton twin-screw WITTEKIND and WILLEHAD, built by Blohm & Voss of Hamburg. They joined the Roland Line in April and May 1894, respectively, by which time the ROLAND had made at least one voyage to South America. Before long she made several more.

At the beginning of 1893 the Company still owned no fewer than 21 of the 31 transatlantic steamers they had commissioned between 1862 and 1875. The HERMANN and GENERAL WERDER were taken in part payment for the H.H.MEIER in 1893, seven more were sold in 1894, two in 1895, four in 1896, two in 1897, two in 1898 and finally the HOHENZOLLERN in 1899. The SALIER was wrecked with heavy loss of life on the north coast of Spain in 1896. By the middle of 1893 these old-timers had been completely ousted from the Far East service and by mid-1895 from the Australian service. Final voyages of four of the last five survivors were to South America.

1894 WITTEKIND 4,755 tons
Built for Roland Line of NDL.

In replacement, NDL commissioned the 3,800 ton PFALZ and MARK in 1893-4 for the South American trade, the 6,288 ton PRINZREGENT LUITPOLD in 1894 for Australia and a sister ship, the PRINZ HEINRICH, in 1895 for the Far East. In 1895, also, the 3,900 ton CREFELD, BONN, AACHEN and HALLE started running to South America, as did the 3,200 ton twin-screw COBLENZ, MAINZ, and TRIER in 1897-8. The PRINZREGENT LUITPOLD was responsible for ten round voyages to New York and on some of them carried first, second and third class passengers, but on at least two second was the top class. The CREFELD and sisters made many voyages to New York or Baltimore and usually carried steerage passengers only, although on a few occasions they carried second class as well. The MAINZ and COBLENZ each made three round voyages on the North Atlantic, all but one to Baltimore; the TRIER made two voyages to New York.

A further replacement programme was obviously necessary and orders were placed in German yards for four twin-screw ships of over 10,500 tons propelled by quadruple-expansion engines. The newcomers, the KÖNIGIN LUISE, FRIEDRICH DER GROSSE, BARBAROSSA and BREMEN (11), inaugurated an extra service from Bremen and Southampton to New York in spring and summer and made an autumn or winter voyage to Australia.

The commissioning of these steamers was overshadowed a few months later by the ship of the decade, the KAISER WILHELM DER GROSSE. Built by Vulcan of Stettin on the unusual arrangement that she could be handed back to them if her maiden outward and homeward voyages were completed at less than a specified speed, she was a twin-screw ship of 14,349 tons, was propelled by two sets of triple-expansion engines and had a striking appearance with four funnels, arranged in pairs, and two pole masts. She left Bremen on 19 September 1897, Southampton a day later and steamed from the Needles to Sandy Hook Lightship at an average speed of 21.39 knots, which was faster than any previous maiden voyage. On her third homeward voyage in November 1897 she averaged 22.27 knots between Sandy Hook and the Needles, and thereby acquired the distinction of being the fastest as well as the largest liner in the world. In March 1898 she proceeded from the Needles to Sandy Hook in 5 days 20 hours at an average speed of 22.29 knots and thereby gained the 'double'. But much more important than an occasional burst of speed is the performance of a ship over a period, and in this connection the 'KWDG' put up a very satisfactory mean speed of 21.94 knots during six successive round voyages in 1899.

One of the reasons behind the decision to build this ship was the Company's determination to carry a higher proportion of British and American passengers. Not only did they succeed but in 1897, when the

1897 KAISER WILHELM DER GROSSE 14,349 tons
First of the NDL record-breakers, which did so
much to popularise German ships.

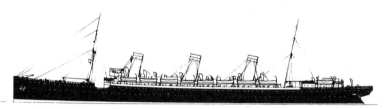

1898 KAISER FRIEDRICH 12,480 tons
Built as a consort of KAISER WILHELM DER
GROSSE but failed as a high-speed ship.

'KWDG' only made four voyages, the Company landed 11,583 first and second class and 24,562 steerage passengers at New York, whereas in 1898, when she made ten voyages, the numbers were 17,895 and 53,223 respectively. The combined total of 71,118 represented nearly 24 per cent of all North Atlantic passengers landed at New York and, almost for the first time, the Company's first and second class totals exceeded those of Cunard.

A second would-be record-breaker was ordered from Schichau of Danzig on similar conditions of acceptance or refusal. This was the 12,480 ton KAISER FRIEDRICH, which was propelled by two sets of five-cylinder quadruple-expansion engines and differed in many respects from her rival, including her three funnels. However, this ship proved a great disappointment and the fastest of her eight round voyages was made at an average speed of no more than 20 knots. The Company persevered for more than a year before returning her to the builders; she subsequently made a few voyages under charter to Hapag, although many years passed before a buyer could be found.

Reverting to 1897, the 5,350 ton ELLEN RICKMERS was chartered from the Rickmers Line for service between Bremen and Baltimore. The MARIA RICKMERS and ELISABETH RICKMERS followed in 1898, all three having accommodation for 18-19 second class and 600 steerage passengers. They were bought by NDL in 1900, the first two renamed

BORKUM and HELGOLAND respectively, making a few more North Atlantic voyages.

During the summer of 1897 the line between Bremen and British ports was sold to the Argo Steamship Company together with seven steamers, most of which bore names similar to those of the vessels which opened the service in 1857.

After the outbreak of the Spanish-American War in 1898 the HAVEL was sold to the Spanish Government. The FULDA helped to repatriate Spanish troops after the war, and at the conclusion of these duties proceeded to Birkenhead to be sold to the Canadian Steamship Company (Chapter 149). On 2 February 1899 she was badly damaged in a mishap in dry dock and broken up. The sale of the WERRA, and probably of the EMS, to the same concern fell through owing to their inability to pay.

During the spring of 1899 NDL was running a weekly express service between Bremen, Southampton and New York with the KAISER WILHELM DER GROSSE, KAISER FRIEDRICH, LAHN and TRAVE; a weekly twin-screw service between the same ports with the BARBAROSSA, BREMEN, FRIEDRICH DER GROSSE, KÖNIGIN LUISE and PRINZREGENT LUITPOLD; the ROLAND, WILLEHAD, H.H.MEIER, MÜNCHEN, DRESDEN, BONN and CREFELD were responsible for the Bremen - Baltimore service; the KAISER WILHELM 11, EMS, SAALE and ALLER took care of the New York - Naples - Genoa service.

Owing the the success of the KÖNIGIN LUISE class, the 10,643 ton KÖNIG ALBERT and the 10,881 ton PRINZESS IRENE were completed for the Far East service in 1899-1900. The latter's maiden voyage was to New York, and in later years both undertook many voyages between New York and the Mediterranean. A slightly larger ship, the 13,182 ton GROSSER KURFÜRST, was employed on the North Atlantic apart from some seasonal voyages to Australia.

In October 1899 Far East sailings were increased from monthly to fortnightly. Hapag had already started a mainly cargo service of their own to that destination and arranged to share the mail contract with NDL. It should be added that in the summer of 1900 NDL played an important part in transporting troops and munitions to the Boxer War in China.

Sailings between Bremen and Galveston, discontinued in 1886 and resumed on an occasional basis in 1898, became fairly regular in 1899, at first with the three steamers chartered from the Rickmers Line.

The HAVEL's sister ship, the SPREE, had suffered from fractured propeller shafts in 1892 and again in 1897. By that time the single-screw express steamer was fast becoming obsolete, and the opportunity was taken to lengthen her by 19,81 metres (65 feet), fit her with twin-screws and make drastic alterations to her passenger accommodation. She reappeared in

527

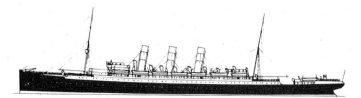

1900 KAISERIN MARIA THERESIA 7,840 tons
Built 1891 as SPREE. Lengthened in 1899,
converted from single to twin-screw and renamed.

March 1900 as the 7,840 ton three-funnelled KAISERIN MARIA
THERESIA. The time was opportune as the KAISER FRIEDRICH had
been returned to her builders some months previously, but unfortunately
the conversion was by no means a success and in their annual report for
1902 the Company admitted that she could no longer compete with the
other units. Apart from acting as a reserve ship she was employed largely on
cruising until 1904, when the Company took the opportunity of selling her
to Russia. She became the auxiliary cruiser URAL and was sunk on 27 May
1905 at the Battle of Tsushima. The LAHN, also, was sold to Russia at
about the same time.

Three further series of ships, all twin-screw, now call for mention,
namely, the 7,400 ton KOLN (11), HANNOVER (11) and FRANKFURT
(11) of 1899-1900; the 10,000 ton RHEIN (11), MAIN (11) and NECKAR
(11) of 1899-1901; and the 7,500 ton CASSEL, BRESLAU, CHEMNITZ
and BRANDENBURG of 1901-2. The 10,000 tonners ran extensively to
New York and started by carrying first, second and steerage passengers, but
soon catered for second and steerage only, as did all the others from the
start. All made many Baltimore voyages.

Arrangements had been made from June 1896 onwards for some of the
steamers to call at Cherbourg instead of Southampton. Before long, certain
steamers called at both ports and by 1900, the year of the Paris Exhibition,
the dual call became a regular feature of the express service. During the same
year the extra steamers of the BARBAROSSA class, instead of calling at
Southampton every week, began to call there one week and at Cherbourg
the next. Several of the 'KWDG's early homeward voyages had been made
via Plymouth instead of Southampton. This practice was then discontinued
until September 1901, when Plymouth became a regular eastbound port of
call for the express steamers, but not for the others.

A disastrous fire broke out in the Company's docks at Hoboken on 30
June 1900. The 'KWDG' was towed to safety, but the BREMEN, MAIN
and SAALE were not so fortunate and the last-named was so severely
damaged that she was sold. The BREMEN, like the MAIN, required an

extensive refit and the opportunity was taken to lengthen her by 7,62 metres (25 feet). Altogether, over 150 lives were lost, many because the ships' portholes were too small to provide a means of escape.

The 16,703 ton DEUTSCHLAND was commissioned by Hapag in 1900 and succeeded in wresting the 'Blue Riband' from the 'KWDG'. Other events of the year were the experiments carried out with the Marconi system of wireless telegraphy between the 'KWDG' and a German lightship, and the purchase of the four-masted barque ALBERT RICKMERS, which was converted into a cadet school ship and renamed HERZOGIN SOPHIE CHARLOTTE. She sailed in April 1900 with 40 cadets for Philadelphia and thence to Japan, returning via San Francisco. A second cadet ship, the HERZOGIN CECILIE, was added in 1902. Also of interest was the lengthening of the WITTEKIND from 116,85 metres (383.4 feet) to 135,93 metres (446.0 feet) in order to increase her cargo capacity. The work was undertaken in Britain owing to the rush of orders in the German shipyards, and for some unexplained reason was not recorded in *Lloyd's Register*. It was intended also to lengthen the WILLEHAD, but this never took place.

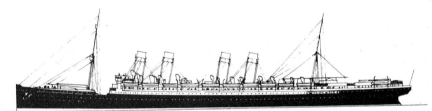

1901 KRONPRINZ WILHELM 14,908 tons
An improved KAISER WILHELM DER
GROSSE and a rival of Hapag DEUTSCHLAND.

The spectacular success of the 'KWDG' led to the building of a consort, the 14,908 ton KRONPRINZ WILHELM, which was completed during the summer of 1901 and was similar in most respects except that her propelling machinery consisted of two sets of six-cylinder quadruple-expansion engines. An important safety device was the provision of mechanically-operated watertight doors. It was claimed in June 1902 that the KRONPRINZ WILHELM had made an eastbound crossing at 23.53 knots compared with the DEUTSCHLAND's best effort of 23.51 knots, but two months later a joint statement was issued by NDL and Hapag that the captain's calculations were incorrect and that the DEUTSCHLAND still held the record. A month later the 'KRONPRINZ' did win the westbound record with a 23.09 knot trip, and was certainly a more consistent performer.

529

When the International Mercantile Marine Company was formed in 1902, NDL at first remained aloof, but was later drawn into the discussions. It was eventually arranged that the IMM Company would guarantee payment by both NDL and Hapag of a dividend of six per cent in return for a share of any dividend exceeding that figure. NDL benefitted handsomely as in 1903-11 inclusive their nett dividend averaged only four per cent and, consequently, they received about 4½ million marks from the combine. In association with IMM and Hapag, NDL obtained a substantial interest in the Holland America Line.

The KRONPRINZ WILHELM had been laid down while Hapag's DEUTSCHLAND was still building. A successor, the 19,361 ton KAISER WILHELM 11, was designed as a result of experience gained from three outstanding ships. The most important new features related to her propelling machinery, which consisted of four separate sets of quadruple-expansion engines, two to each propeller shaft, and each in a separate watertight compartment. Her tonnage was exceeded only by that of the White Star CELTIC and CEDRIC. Her maiden voyage started on 14 April 1903, and in the following year she completed a westbound crossing at just over 23 knots. However, she never quite succeeded in gaining either the westbound or the eastbound record.

1908 DERFFLINGER 9,060 tons
Built for Far East trade but employed extensively
on North Atlantic after World War I.

Despite these important additions to the express service, NDL was by no means neglecting its other routes and, starting in 1902, commissioned the 7,000 ton SCHLESWIG for the South American service in addition to the 8,000 ton ZIETEN, ROON, SEYDLITZ, GNEISENAU and SCHARNHORST, which were designed principally for the Far East and Australian trades. The 9,000 ton PRINZ EITEL FRIEDRICH was in a class by herself and was completed in 1904 to run to the Far East. The 9,000 ton BÜLOW, YORCK, GOEBEN, KLEIST, LÜTZOW and DERFFLINGER completed the 'Feldherrn' ('Field Marshal') class and were normally detailed to the Far East or Australia. But all these ships except the SCHLESWIG, PRINZ EITEL FRIEDRICH and GOEBEN ran for NDL on the North Atlantic, the GNEISENAU being responsible for as many as 10 round voyages.

With the completion of the ZIETEN and ROON, the KÖNIG ALBERT and PRINZESS IRENE joined the HOHENZOLLERN (11) (ex-KAISER-WILHELM 11) on the New York - Mediterranean line, from which the ALLER had already been withdrawn, as were the TRAVE and LAHN soon afterwards. The Company was well aware that these ships were out of date and no longer an attraction to American travellers. The KÖNIGIN LUISE joined the Mediterranean service in 1904 and superseded the HOHENZOLLERN (11), which was detailed to a new Marseilles - Naples - Alexandria line in partnership with the SCHLESWIG.

Owing to differences betwen NDL and Hapag the latter withdrew from the Far East mail service in 1903. The Hapag KIAUTSCHOU, one of two 11,000 ton steamers built specially for the trade, was sold to NDL soon afterwards, being renamed PRINCESS ALICE (not PRINZESS ALICE). She was, in fact, an almost exact replica of the PRINZESS IRENE. Although subsequently employed largely to the Far East, she made 16 round voyages on the North Atlantic between 1904 and 1910.

Final unit of the NDL express fleet was the 19,400 ton

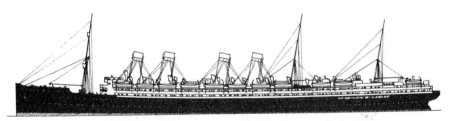

1907 KRONPRINZESSIN CECILIE 19,400 tons
Last of the German four-funnelled express
steamers.

KRONPRINZESSIN CECILIE, which started her maiden voyage from Bremen to Southampton, Cherbourg and New York in August 1907. Like her predecessors, she was propelled by reciprocating engines, after careful consideration had been given to the possibility of substituting turbines. She averaged 21.81 knots outwards and 22.65 homewards but, outside Germany, no great interest was taken in her subsequent achievements as public attention was focussed on the newly-completed LUSITANIA and MAURETANIA, which regained the 'Blue Riband' for Britain. It is worth noting, however, that in July 1908 she proceeded from Cherbourg to Sandy Hook in 5 days 15 hours 23 minutes at an average speed of 23.21 knots, and in the following month from Sandy Hook to Eddystone in 5 days 11 hours

12 minutes at an average of 23.4 knots. Her westbound crossing was apparently the fastest ever made in that direction by a German pre-World War 1 steamer, but soon afterwards the KAISER WILHELM 11 crossed from Sandy Hook to Eddystone in 5 days 9 hours 55 minutes at an average of 23.71 knots,which is believed to have been the fastest voyage, eastbound or westbound, ever achieved by one of these steamers. The completion of the KRONPRINZESSIN CECILIE enabled the Company to maintain a weekly expres service from Bremen, Southampton and Cherbourg to New York. Long-distance wireless telegraphy kept the ships in constant touch with England or the North American coast.An innovation on the KRONPRINZESSIN CECILIE was an *à la carte* restaurant for first class passengers, who were seated at small tables. Similar arrangements were soon introduced on the other three express steamers.

NDL had already placed orders for three large ships of medium speed, and had in mind plans for even larger tonnage to meet the British competition. Before anything could be done a severe slump set in and 1908 turned out to be one of the blackest years in the Company's history, with receipts plunging by nearly £900,000. No fewer than 47 departures to North America were cancelled. Trading conditions improved considerably in 1909, and by 1910 payment of a dividend was resumed.

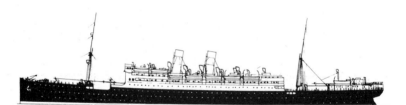

1908 PRINZ FRIEDRICH WILHELM 17,082
Bremen—New York intermediate service

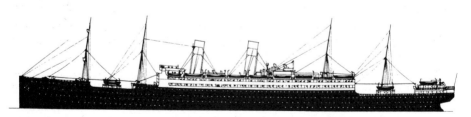

1909 GEORGE WASHINGTON 25,570 tons
NDL's reply to Hapag's AMERIKA and
KAISERIN AUGUSTE VICTORIA.

First of the new steamers was the 17,082 ton PRINZ FRIEDRICH WILHELM (laid down as the WASHINGTON), which was detailed to the extra service between Bremen, Southampton and New York. Her sister ship, the BERLIN (11), was placed in service between New York and the Mediterranean. Third newcomer was the 25,570 ton GEORGE WASHINGTON which, although having a speed no greater than 19 knots, was the largest German-built steamer and was exceeded in size only by the new Cunarders. She had accommodation for 520 first class, 377 second, 614 third and over 1,000 fourth class passengers. When completed in June 1909 she joined the PRINZ FRIEDRICH WILHELM on the extra service.

After a preliminary sailing by the Hapag PRINZ OSKAR on 19 March 1909 to Halifax and St John, New Brunswick, the WILLEHAD inaugurated a new summer service from Hamburg and Bremen to Quebec and Montreal, jointly with Hapag, Holland America and Red Star. The NDL report for 1909 stated that results came up to expectations, and in consequence the frequency of sailings was increased. In 1911, the WITTEKIND made two round voyages in addition to those of her sister ship. Sailings were increased still further in 1912. NDL ships employed being the ZIETEN, WILLEHAD, KÖLN and FRANKFURT, while in 1913-4 the WITTEKIND and HANNOVER replaced the ZIETEN and KÖLN.

It was arranged in March 1910 for the Bremen - Galveston steamers to call at Philadelphia, where some additional sailings from Bremen terminated. Steamers proceeding to or via Philadelphia during the year included the FRANKFURT, BRESLAU, HANNOVER, MAIN, KÖLN and BRANDENBURG.

The Company declared a dividend of three per cent in 1910, increased to five per cent in 1911, seven in 1912 and eight in 1913. This satisfactory state of affairs made it possible to consider further improvements to the fleet, and a ship of 34,000 tons was laid down, extreme comfort combined with medium speed being the keynote. She was launched on 17 December 1913 as the COLUMBUS, but never saw service under the NDL flag as completion did not take place until after the outbreak of World War 1, and at the end of the war she was taken over by Britain. The 15,000 ton ZEPPELIN and the 19,000 ton MÜNCHEN (11) were also under construction when war broke out.

The year 1913 produced results just as satisfactory as its three predecessors. An important step was the commissioning of the 8,200 ton SIERRA VENTANA, SIERRA CORDOBA, SIERRA NEVADA and SIERRA SALVADA for the Bremen . Montevideo - Buenos Aires service. A further development at the end of the year was the departure of the HANNOVER on a new service to Boston and New Orleans, the KÖLN and FRANKFURT following at intervals of three weeks.

The Company carried no fewer than 175,000 westbound and 64,000 eastbound passengers on the Bremen - New York services during 1913, the combined total of 239,000 being over 25,000 more than the rival Hapag total, and not far short of the White Star and Cunard totals from Southampton and Liverpool to New York put together. NDL did not, of course, by any means depend on the Bremen - New York trade. Their other activities included services from New York to the Mediterranean (fortnightly), Bremen to Baltimore (weekly), to Philadelphia and Galveston (fortnightly), Quebec and Montreal (monthly in summer), Brazil (fortnightly), River Plate (fortnightly), Cuba (monthly), China and Japan (fortnightly), Australia via Suez (fortnightly), Australia via the Cape (fortnightly), in addition to various local services in the North Sea, Mediterranean and the Orient. The total number of passengers carried by the Company in 1913 amounted to the staggering total of 662,385. The grand total for all routes since operations were started in 1857 was 10,408,113; the equivalent total of cargo carried was 4,178,133 tons. The NDL fleet consisted of 131 ocean-going steamers of over 800,000 tons gross, ten more totalling 100,000 tons being under construction. Tonnage of the fleet was exceeded only by that of the Hamburg American Line.

As from March 1914 the KAISER WILHELM DER GROSSE was refitted to carry third and fourth class passengers only and she consequently omitted the calls at Southampton and Cherbourg.

The Company's annual report for 1913 included the interesting statement that NDL and Hapag had reached agreement to share equally for a period of 15 years the results of their activities to and from North America. Unfortunately, the outbreak of World War I not long afterwards was responsible for the arrangement being allowed to lapse.

It was also reported that a four-year agreement had been reached with the Prussian Government for regular calls to be made at the German port of Emden. Steamers of the Australian and River Plate services put in there as early as October 1913, but it was not until the spring of 1914 that a vessel destined to New York followed suit. Another news item was that the arrangement preventing NDL from running cargo lines to East Asia had been cancelled, with the result that a new fortnightly cargo service was introduced in December 1913. What the report did not indicate was that, in the autumn of 1914, Hapag was intending to resume the passenger and mail service to the Far East, which it had withdrawn in 1903.

At the outbreak of World War 1 in August 1914 the KRONPRINZESSIN CECILIE was homeward bound with a large consignment of specie. She hastily retraced her tracks and was interned in Boston. Her consort, the KRONPRINZ WILHELM, escaped from New York and for eight months acted as a commerce raider before taking shelter at Philadelphia. Ships interned at New York were the GEORGE

WASHINGTON, KAISER WILHELM 11, GROSSER KURFÜRST, BARBAROSSA, FRIEDRICH DER GROSSE and PRINZESS IRENE; the RHEIN and NECKAR were interned at Baltimore; the KÖLN and WITTEKIND at Boston; the WILLEHAD at New London, Connecticut; and the BRESLAU at New Orleans. All were seized and entered United States service in April 1917.

Among the ships safely in port at Bremerhaven were the KAISER WILHELM DER GROSSE, BERLIN, BREMEN, CASSEL, CHEMNITZ, FRANKFURT, HANNOVER and KÖNIGIN LUISE, and only the first two saw active service. The KAISER WILHELM DER GROSSE was fitted out as an armed cruiser and was sunk by HMS HIGHFLYER at Rio de Oro, West Africa, on 27 August 1914. Of much greater value to the German cause was the BERLIN, which was fitted as a minelayer and was responsible for sinking the British battleship AUDACIOUS. Many other NDL ships were held in a variety of ports throughout the world.

In 1915 NDL played a prominent part in the formation of the Deutsche Ozean Reederei, which intended to run a regular freight service by submarine between Germany and the USA. The submarine DEUTSCHLAND did make two round voyages in 1916, but the BREMEN was lost on her first outward voyage. Owing to the severance of diplomatic relations between the USA and Germany and the subsequent entry of the former into the war in 1917, the service was not continued.

After the Armistice, the Company were deprived of every worthwhile ocean-going steamer, the largest left in their possession being the 800 ton GRÜSSGOTT. In consequence they entered into arrangements with the United States Mail Steamship Company, which started a passenger and cargo service between New York and Bremen in August 1920 with ships chartered from the United States Shipping Board. NDL were appointed their general agents for Central Europe and placed at their disposal their docks and quays at Bremerhaven. NDL reserved the right to run their own or chartered steamers up to a total of 200,000 tons. The United States Mail Company soon got into financial difficulties, and in September 1921 their services were taken over by the United States Lines, leaving NDL a free hand to carry on by themselves.

In September 1920 NDL despatched the first of their newly-built ocean-going cargo steamers, the 2,350 ton VEGESACK, to Brazil and the River Plate, a sister ship, the BREMERHAVEN, following in due course. Owing to a gradual relaxation of the rules prohibiting the resale to Germany of ex-German ships, the 7,942 ton SEYDLITZ came back into the Company's possession towards the end of 1921. She left Bremen for South America on 11 December 1921 and soon after completion of this, the first NDL post-war ocean passenger sailing, was responsible for restarting the New York passenger service. She sailed from Bremen on 11 February 1922 and arrived at New York on 25 February with 75 cabin and 65 third class passengers. Two further units of the pre-war fleet, the 7,305 ton HANNOVER (11) and the 8,901 ton YORCK followed at fortnightly intervals. On 20 February 1922 NDL were readmitted to the North Atlantic Passenger Conference.

Meanwhile, several ships were under construction for other routes, of which the 8,753 ton SIERRA NEVADA, although intended for the South American trade, made two round voyages to New York, while the 11,452 ton SIERRA VENTANA, also intended for the South Atlantic, made no fewer than 21 round voyages to New York between 1923 and 1932.

The first of the new ships actually designed for the New York service, the 13,325 ton MÜNCHEN (111), was commissioned during the summer of 1923. At about the same time the Company reacquired three more of their pre-war fleet - the 10,881 ton BREMEN (111) (formerly the PRINZESS IRENE), the 9,060 ton DERFFLINGER and the 8,818 ton LÜTZOW. The STUTTGART (II), a sister ship of the MÜNCHEN, sailed on her maiden voyage to New York in January 1924.

In 1923 there were 49 passenger sailings from Bremen to New York. In two of these cases passengers disembarked at Boston on account of congestion at Ellis Island, New York, where third class passengers were normally landed, and in two more Portland and Philadelphia were the ports of disembarkation. During the year the cargo steamers EISENACH and PORTA, which had accommodation for 12 passengers, made nine round voyages between Bremen, Philadelphia and Baltimore. In subsequent years there were one or two continuations to Philadelphia and Baltimore by New York passenger steamers, as well as some calls at Halifax or Boston.

As already mentioned, completion of the 34,000 ton COLUMBUS, a product of F. Schichau of Danzig, did not take place until after the outbreak of the war. Under the Treaty of Versailles, Danzig became a Free State, and there was consequently no way of compelling NDL to surrender the ship. But although technically they were entitled to keep her it was out of the question for them to place her in one of their own services so soon after the war. Eventually, she was handed over to Britain, becoming the White Star HOMERIC, and in return NDL were allowed to retain some of their older and smaller ships, which were still lying in the neutral ports where they had taken refuge in 1914 - the SEYDLITZ, YORCK, GÖTTLINGEN, GOTHA, HOLSTEIN and WESTFALEN.

A sister ship of the COLUMBUS had been laid down at Danzig in 1914, and owing to the length of time she had been under construction she stuck halfway when an attempt was made to launch her on 17 June 1922. She reached the water safely on 12 August. Here again there were no means of insisting on the surrender of the ship, but by this time the Allies did not particularly want her and, on the other hand, NDL felt fully competent to take her over for their own use. Laid down as the HINDENBURG, she was actually named COLUMBUS (11), had a tonnage of 32,354, twin-screws propelled by eight-cylinder triple-expansion engines gave her a service speed of 19 knots and she had accommodation for 478 first class, 644 second and 602 third class passengers. Her maiden voyage started on 22 April 1924 from Bremen direct to New York, returning via Plymouth and Cherbourg, but subsequent westbound voyages were made via Southampton and, very soon, via Cherbourg also. She was by far the largest ship NDL had ever commissioned.

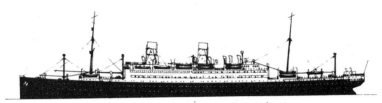

1925 BERLIN 15,286 tons
Bremen—Southampton—New York service.

The 15,286 ton BERLIN (111) was delivered by Bremer Vulkan in September 1925 for the New York service, several other ships having been completed during the previous year or two for the Far East and South American trades. She was one of the last North Atlantic liners to be fitted with reciprocating engines.

In December 1925 the NDL Board gave its approval to the acquisition of the Hamburg - Bremen Afrika Linie, the Dampfschiff Reederei Horn and the Roland Linie, which had no connection with the NDL service of similar name started in 1893 but had, nevertheless, been founded by NDL and to all intents and purposes had been an NDL subsidiary during its entire existence. NDL bought a controlling interest in several other lines.

It was announced in January 1927 that in and after the following May some eastbound NDL calls would be made at Galway. The results were so satisfactory that before long Hamburg American, Cunard and White Star steamers followed suit. The MÜNCHEN was responsible for making the first westbound NDL call at Galway on 5 May 1928.

The remarkable recovery staged by NDL is evident from the fact that during 1926 they carried 46,000 westbound and 23,000 eastbound passengers on the Bremen - New York route. Their total of 69,000 was under 10,000 less than those of either the Cunard or White Star lines on their

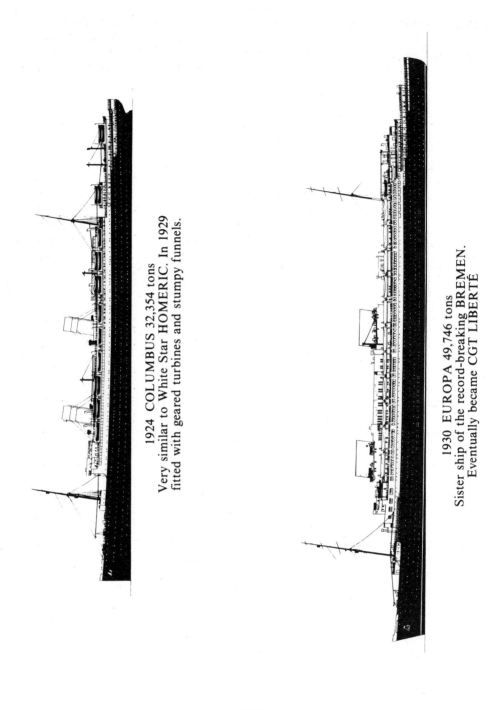

1924 COLUMBUS 32,354 tons
Very similar to White Star HOMERIC. In 1929
fitted with geared turbines and stumpy funnels.

1930 EUROPA 49,746 tons
Sister ship of the record-breaking BREMEN.
Eventually became CGT LIBERTÉ

Southampton - Cherbourg - New York services, and beat by a comfortable margin the New York totals of the Compagnie Générale Transatlantique, Hamburg American, Red Star and Holland America. It is not surprising, therefore, that this satisfactory showing, combined with the success of the COLUMBUS, should have brought to mind the exploits of the KAISER WILHELM DER GROSSE in 1897 and made NDL decide to build two ships capable of regaining the speed record from the Cunarder MAURETANIA. The 50,000 ton BREMEN and EUROPA were accordingly ordered in December 1926 from AG Weser of Bremen and Blohm & Voss of Hamburg, respectively, their keel plates being laid some six months later.

The 14,588 ton DRESDEN (11), surrendered to Britain in 1919 as the ZEPPELIN and subsequently becoming the Orient Line ORMUZ, started her first voyage for the Company on 5 August 1927 from Bremen to Southampton, Cherbourg and New York. This was one of the few occasions when she called at Southampton, most subsequent voyages until the summer of 1928 being via Cherbourg and Cobh, after which Boulogne was substituted as the French port of call.

It was decided in 1928 to reintroduce a passenger and cargo service between Bremen, Quebec and Montreal, last undertaken in 1914. After one or two sailings by cargo steamers, the 9,573 ton CREFELD (11) left Bremen in June 1928, and was joined in July by a sister ship, the 9,265 ton KÖLN (111), both having accommodation for 40 cabin and 500 third class passengers. The same two steamers undertook nine round voyages in 1929, when they landed 198 cabin and 1,562 third class passengers in Canada. The CREFELD made one further sailing in 1930, after which she undertook two voyages to Halifax and Galveston, her place on the St Lawrence run being taken by the 9,415 ton twin-screw TRIER (11). Owing to the then-prevailing slump the service was withdrawn in the autumn of 1930 and was not reinstated.

The express steamers EUROPA and BREMEN were launched on consecutive days during the summer of 1928, but the EUROPA was seriously damaged by fire while fitting out and the BREMEN was completed many months before her. In appearance she differed considerably from any predecessor with two squat streamlined funnels, two masts and a raked stem. Her propelling machinery consisted of single-reduction geared turbines driving quadruple screws. Two unusual features were the bulbous stem and the forward, instead of aft, overlapping of her plating, which is stated to have increased her speed by about half a knot.

Great interest was shown in the Bremen's maiden voyage in July 1929, and she did all that was expected of her by steaming from Cherbourg to Ambrose in 4 days 17 hours 42 minutes at an average speed of 27.83 knots. Homewards, she did even better with a time of 4 days 14 hours 30 minutes from Ambrose to Eddystone at an average of 27.9 knots. Thus, after 20 years, she regained the 'Blue Riband' for Germany.

There were a number of differences between the two ships, the BREMEN having a tonnage of 51,656 and a length of 273,91 metres (898.7 feet) compared with the EUROPA's 49,746 tons and 271,32 metres (890.2 feet). The BREMEN's funnels were pear shaped instead of oval and were three metres (ten feet) less in height than her consort's. At a later date those of both ships were lengthened by $4\frac{1}{2}$ metres (15 feet) in order to keep the decks free of smuts. The EUROPA started her maiden voyage in March 1930, and during the same year succeeded in capturing the westbound record by a passage of 27.91 knots. Three years later, however, the BREMEN left the issue in no doubt by steaming from Ambrose to Cherbourg in 4 days 16 hours 15 minutes at an average speed of 28.51 knots. Her success was short-lived as within a few weeks the Italian liner REX made an appreciably faster passage from Gibraltar to Ambrose, and since then the NORMANDIE, QUEEN MARY and UNITED STATES have all left her far behind.

An interesting feature of the BREMEN and EUROPA were the catapults, which enabled a seaplane with a consignment of mails to leave the ships hundreds of miles out to sea. At the New York end delivery of mail was expedited sometimes by as much as 24 hours. Letters for European destinations often arrived two days before the ships.

At the time of the EUROPA's completion, the NDL fleet consisted of 149 ships totalling 860,000 tons - roughly the same size as it was in 1914. A tremendous achievement!

The COLUMBUS had a breakdown of her starboard engine on 2 August 1927 during a westbound voyage. She returned light from New York to Bremen and was temporarily fitted with an engine from one of the Company's cargo steamers so that her next westbound voyage, in October, took nine days instead of the customary eight. She was withdrawn from service in July 1929, and when she put in a reappearance in the following December had been re-engined with single-reduction geared turbines, which increased her speed to 23 knots. In addition, she was given two broad squat funnels to make her appearance blend with that of the BREMEN and EUROPA. The earlier BREMEN was renamed KARLSRUHE (II) in 1928 and was scrapped in 1932. The MÜNCHEN was badly damaged by fire at New York in 1930, patched up at Brooklyn, sailed for Bremen in ballast, was extensively rebuilt and reappeared in 1931 as the GENERAL VON STEUBEN.

The BREMEN and EUROPA carried first, second, tourist third cabin and third class passengers from the start. The COLUMBUS originally catered for first, second and third class, but tourist third cabin was added in March 1928 and consisted of the less luxurious second class cabins and the best of the third. It was officially renamed tourist class in 1931. By 1932 the

BERLIN, GENERAL VON STEUBEN and STUTTGART all carried cabin, tourist and third classes, while in April of that year the COLUMBUS discontinued carrying second. Second class was rapidly dying out on the North Atlantic and, in fact, the BREMEN and EUROPA were the only ships of any line still carrying it - except those running to and from the Mediterranean. Early in 1934, the BREMEN and EUROPA became first, tourist and third class carriers. Moreover, the description first class was also dying out, and the two NDL giants had already become 'cabin' ships when the Cunard - White Star QUEEN MARY entered service in this capacity in 1936.

Intense and often harmful rivalry had existed between NDL and Hapag for several decades. There had often been rumours of the pending fusion of the two concerns, and mention has already been made of an important agreement provisionally reached shortly before the outbreak of World War 1. Even so, a good deal of surprise was caused in 1930 by the announcement that an alliance, known as the Hapag-Lloyd Union, had been entered into whereby all services were to be jointly operated, and all costs, profits and losses pooled. Neither company lost its separate identity. Four years later it was announced that the 'Union' was to be dissolved, but in fact it was merely loosened and modified. Alterations principally affected the passenger and cargo services to North America and the mainly-cargo services to the Pacific coasts of America, to Cuba and Mexico and to the Far East. These were still jointly operated, but only the net proceeds were pooled. Among services to be operated independently by NDL was the Far Eastern passenger service, and an 18,000 ton liner under construction by Hapag for this trade was transferred to NDL.

In June 1932 the capital of NDL was reduced from 148,500,000 marks to 49,500,000. There was a further reduction in March 1936 to 11,530,000 marks, but simultaneously new stock valued at 34,360,000 marks was issued in satisfaction of bank debts amounting to $2\frac{1}{2}$ times that amount, thereby making the new capital of the Company 45,890,000 marks. It was stated that losses were largely due to the devaluation of sterling and the dollar, but an important reason was the boycotting of German ships by Jews in retaliation for their ill-treatment in Germany. At this time the Company's fleet consisted of 86 ocean-going ships of 614,000 gross tons.

The EUROPA was lying in her home port when World War 11 started in September 1939. At a later date the BREMEN managed to get back to Germany after an adventurous voyage via Murmansk, but the COLUMBUS was not so lucky and was intercepted by the British destroyer HYPERION when attempting to return from Mexico in December 1939. She was promptly scuttled. The BREMEN did not survive the war as she was set on fire on 18 March 1941 by a mentally-unbalanced seaman and later broken up. The EUROPA, although often a target for British and

American bombers, was not seriously damaged. After the war she made one or two voyages as a United States transport and later became the French Line's LIBERTÉ.

It was announced in January 1942 that a new company, DEUTSCHE-AMERIKA LINIE HAMBURG-BREMEN GmbH, had been registered in Germany with a capital of 40 million marks to carry on the North Atlantic services of NDL and Hapag. NDL contributions to the joint fleet were the EUROPA and BERLIN, while Hapag were able to set aside six ships, five of which, like the BERLIN, did not survive the war. At its conclusion the EUROPA and the Hapag MILWAUKEE were handed over to the Allies. The Deutsche-Amerika Linie was disbanded. For a second time within 30 years, Norddeutscher Lloyd lost almost its entire fleet, only survivors being one 1,230 ton motor ship and one small cargo steamer.

It was disclosed at the annual general meeting of the Society of Naval Architects and Marine Engineers on 14 November 1946 that Germany had been planning to build a super liner of over 80,000 tons if she won the war. She would have been named VIKTORIA, for the victory that never came, would have had a length of 304,73 metres (1,000 feet) between perpendiculars, have been driven by five propellers powered by huge steam turbines giving her a speed in excess of 34 knots, and operated by NDL. The plans were filed away when the tide turned against Germany. [5]

A relaxation of restrictions on German shipping made it possible for NDL to despatch the 8,000 ton chartered cargo steamer HERMOD from Emden to Baltimore in ballast in March 1950. Having loaded 2,500 tons of grain there, she reached New York five days later, on 29 March, and was the first German-flag vessel to visit the port since September 1939. It was soon arranged for NDL and Hapag to run a joint service between Bremen and Hamburg and New York, calls being made at Antwerp and Rotterdam on the homeward voyages. To begin with, chartered tonnage was used, but by 1952 both lines had taken delivery of their own ships, most of which had accommodation for 10-12 passengers. Later still, joint services were started to Cuba, Mexican Gulf ports, Central America, the west coast of South America, the Far East and Australia.

From 1951 onwards many Swedish American sailings from Gothenburg to New York were made via Bremerhaven. At the beginning of 1954 the Swedish American liner GRIPSHOLM, an 18,600 ton ship built in 1925, was sold to the BREMEN - AMERIKA LINIE, in which both Swedish American and NDL held a substantial interest. She sailed from Bremen on 1 February 1954 under NDL management and without change of name, calling at Gothenburg on the following day and, proceeding via Halifax, reached New York on the 13th. The agreed purchase price was paid by NDL in instalments. The newcomer was renamed BERLIN (1V) on 7 January 1955, and from then onwards wore the black hull which had long been standard for the North Atlantic fleet of NDL, but her registration in the name of the Bremen - Amerika Linie continued until 1959. NDL and Swedish American ran a joint service from Bremen to New York until 1962.

1959 BREMEN 32.336 tons
Completed 1939 as French PASTEUR. In 1957
sold to NDL, rebuilt and renamed.

It was not to be expected that NDL would long be content to run a one-ship passenger service to New York, and in September 1957 the 30,000 ton French liner PASTEUR , completed immediately before the outbreak of World War 11, was bought for £2¼ million. She was renamed BREMEN (V), sailed from Brest for Bremerhaven on 26 September and was extensively rebuilt by Bremer Vulkan at a cost of nearly £6 million. New turbines, boilers and generators were installed, Denny-Brown stabilisers were added and accommodation for passengers and crew was remodelled. She started her first transatlantic voyage under the German flag on 9 July 1959 from Bremen to New York via Southampton and Cherbourg. Accommodation was provided for 216 first class and 906 tourist passengers.

The 26,677 ton KUNGSHOLM (111) was commissioned by Swedish American in 1966, making the 22,071 KUNGSHOLM (11) surplus to their requirements. She was, therefore, transferred to Norddeutscher Lloyd, who renamed her EUROPA (11), and she sailed from Bremen for New York on 9 January 1966. The BERLIN, by this time over 40 years old, made a few more trips but before the end of the year proceeded to Italy to be scrapped. Thus, the BREMEN (V) and EUROPA (11) undertook a Bremen - Southampton - Cherbourg - New York service similar in many respects to that provided by their pre-war namesakes.

The long-expected amalgamation of Hapag and NDL was announced in April 1970 and took place on 1 September 1970 under the title HAPAG - LLOYD AKTIENGESELLSCHAFT. It is surprising that outside Germany, at any rate, the fusion attracted very little attention - perhaps because it was recognised as one of those things that had to happen sooner or later. There was no outward change in the appearance of the BREMEN and EUROPA as they still wore their plain buff funnels and, like the entire

NDL and Hapag fleets, continued to fly the NDL houseflag, but all other ships had Hapag-type black-white-red tops to their buff funnels. Subsequent activities of the combine are dealt with in Chapter 258.

[1]   GEORG BESSELL: *Norddeutscher Lloyd* 1857-1957
[2]   *North British Daily Mail* 21/8/1857
[3]   *The Times* 11/9/1858
[4]   *The Times* 10/8/1858
[5]   *New York Herald-Tribune* 15/11/1946

1. 1858 BREMEN (I)
     2,674. 97,53 x 11,88. (320.0 x 39.0). C—1—3. I—S—I(2)—10. (I—160; II—110; III—400). Caird & Co, Greenock. 1858 (1/2) launched. 1858 (19/6) MV Bremen—New York. 1860 fractured propeller shaft; out of service for 6 months. 1873 (5/11) LV Bremen—Southampton—New York. 1874 BREMEN (Edward Bates, Liverpool); engines removed. 1882 (16/10) wrecked on South Farralone Islands, Calif.

2. 1858 NEW YORK
     2,674. 97,53 x 11,88. (320.0 x 39.0). C—1—3. I—S—I(2)—10. I—60; II—110; III—400). Caird & Co, Greenock. 1858 (31/3) launched. 1858 (14/8) MV Bremen—New York. 1873 (20/12) LV Bremen—Southampton —New York. 1874 NEW YORK (Edward Bates, Liverpool); engines removed. 1891 (20/4) wrecked near Staten Island, NY.

3. 1858 HUDSON
     2,266. 93,57 x 12,43. (307.0 x 40.8). C—2—3. I—S—I(2)—10. (I—70; II—100; III—450). Palmer Bros & Co, Jarrow-on-Tyne. 1858 (12/6) launched. 1858 (11/9) MV Bremen—New York (1 RV). 1858 (2/11) damaged by fire in dock at Bremerhaven; towed to Newcastle; rebuilt; LOUISIANA (National - 69); (qv).

4. 1858 WESER (I)
     2,266. 93,57 x 12,43. (307.0 x 40.8). C—2—3. I—S—I(2)—10. (I—70; II—100; III—450). Palmer Bros & Co, Jarrow-on-Tyne. 1858 (21/10) launched. 1858 (4/12) MV Bremen—New York; damaged by heavy seas and had to put back to Cork for repairs. 1859 (6/3) sailed Cork—New York (arr 18/3). 1859 (1/7) LV Bremen—Southampton—New York (3 RV). 1859 WESER (French naval transport). 1861 (16/1) wrecked 60 miles from Poulo Condor, Cochin China.

5. 1861 HANSA (I)
     2,992. 100,05 x 12,80. (328.2 x 42.0). C—1—3. I—S—I(2)—11. (I—75;

II—105; III—480). Caird & Co, Greenock. 1861 (23/8) launched. 1861 (24/11) MV Bremen—Southampton—New York. 1878 (12/11) LV Bremen—New York. 1879 HANSA (British). 1881 compound engines. 1881 (May) FV London—Boston for Adamson & Ronaldson (c), 1882 (Mar) LV ditto (6 RV). 1883 LUDWIG (White Cross). 1883 (2/7) sailed Antwerp—Montreal; went missing (70-80).

6. 1863 AMERICA
2,752. 96,92 x 12,19. (318.0 x 40.0). C—1—3. I—S—I(2)—11. (I—76; II—107; III—480). Caird & Co, Greenock. 1862 (Nov) launched. 1863 (25/5) MV Bremen—Southampton—New York. 1871 engines compounded by Day, Summers & Co, Southampton. 1894 (27/1) LV Bremen—New York—Baltimore. 1894 ORAZIO (Italian). 1895 scrapped at Spezia.

7. 1865 HERMANN
2,873. 96,92 x 12,19. (318.0 x 40.0). C—1—2. I—S—I(2)—11. (I—80; II—120; III—500). Caird & Co, Greenock. Laid down as EUROPA (NDL). 1865 (Jun) launched as HERMANN. 1865 (17/12) MV Bremen—Southampton—New York. 1872 engines compounded by Day, Summers & Co, Southampton. 1892 (22/12) LV Bremen—New York. 1893 sold to Sir W.G. Armstrong, Mitchell & Co in part exchange for H. H. MEIER. 1896 scrapped.

8. 1866 DEUTSCHLAND
2,800. 99,05 x 12,19. (325.0 x 40.0). C—1—2. I—S—I(2)—11. (I—60; II—120; III—700). Caird & Co, Greenock. 1866 (29/5) launched. 1866 (14/10) MV Bremen—Southampton—New York. 1872 engines compounded. 1875 (6/12) wrecked off Kentish Knock, R Thames estuary(157).

9. 1867 UNION
2,800. 99,05 x 12,19. (325.0 x 40.0). C—1—2. I—S—I(2)—11. (I—60;II—120; III—700). Caird & Co, Greenock. 1866 (27/10) launched. 1867 (13/1) MV Bremen—Southampton—New York. 1870 (28/11) wrecked on Rattray Head, Aberdeenshire(0).

10. 1867 WESER (II)
2,870. 99,05 x 12,19. (325.0 x 40.0). C—1—2. I—S—I(2)—11. (I—60; II—120; III—700). Caird & Co, Greenock. 1867 (19/3) launched. 1867 (1/6) MV Bremen—Southampton—New York. 1881 compound engines by builders. 1895 (13/6) LV Bremen—New York—Baltimore. 1895 (3/8) FV Bremen—S America (2 RV). 1896 scrapped.

11. 1868 BALTIMORE
2,321. 86,86 x 11,88. (285.0 x 39.0). C—1—2. I—S—I(2)—10.(I—84;

III—600). Caird & Co, Greenock. 1867 (27/2) keel laid. 1867 (3/8) launched. 1868 (1/3) MV Bremen—Southampton—Baltimore. 1872 (22-23/5) collision off Hastings with ss LORENZO SEMPRUN (Spanish); beached; towed to Southampton for repairs. 1881 engines compounded by AG Weser, Bremen. 1883 (10/10) LV Bremen—Baltimore; subsequently to S America. 1893 (30/12) LV Bremen—S America. 1894 scrapped.

12. 1868. BERLIN (I)
2,333. 86,86 x 11,88.(285.0 x 39.0). C—1—2. I—S—I(2)—10. (I—84; III—600). Caird & Co, Greenock. 1867 (1/10) launched. 1868 (Apr) MV Bremen—Southampton—Baltimore. 1882 engines compounded by AG Weser, Bremen. 1894 (3/3) LV Bremen—S America. 1894 M. BRUZZO (Italian). 1895 scrapped in Italy.

13. 1868. RHEIN (I)
2,901. 101,19 x 12,19. (332.0 x 40.0). C—1—2. I—S—I(2)—13. (I—70; II—100; III—600). Caird & Co, Greenock. 1868 (Aug) launched. 1868 (3/10) MV Bremen—Southampton—New York. 1878 engines compounded by builders. 1889 (16/10) LV Bremen—New York—Baltimore. 1890 (18/9) LV Bremen—Baltimore. 1891 RHEIN (British). 1893 scrapped.

14. 1868 MAIN (I)
3,087. 101,19 x 12,19. (332.0 x 40.0). C—1—2. I—S—I(2)—13. (I—70; II—100; III—600). Caird & Co, Greenock. 1868 (22/8) launched. 1868 (28/11) MV Bremen—Southampton—New York. 1878 engines compounded by builders. 1890 (6/3) LV Bremen—New York. 1890 (10/7) LV Bremen—Baltimore. 1891 MAIN (Br). 1892 (23/3) destroyed by fire at Fayal, Azores.

15. 1869 DONAU
2,896. 101,19 x 12,19. (332.0 x 40.0). C—1—2. I—S—I(2)—13. (I—60; III—700). Caird & Co, Greenock. 1868 (17/10) launched. 1869 (16/1) MV Bremen—Southampton—New York. 1877 engines compounded by builders. 1887 (16/1) LV Bremen—New York. 1889 (25/9) LV Bremen—Baltimore. 1889 (21/10) DONAU (German). 1895 (16/3) destroyed by fire on N Atlantic; abandoned.

16. 1869 OHIO
2,394. 88,46 x 11,88. (290.2 x 39.0). C—1—2. I—S—I(2)—10. (I—84; III—600). Caird & Co, Greenock. 1868 (18/12) launched. 1869 (Mar) MV Bremen—Southampton—Baltimore. 1871 (6/9) FV Bremen—Southampton—New York (11 RV-last in 1883). 1880-1 engines compounded by AG Vulcan, Stettin. 1883 (3/10) LV Bremen—Baltimore. 1884 (24/3)

FV Bremen—S America. 1893 (25/11) LV ditto. 1894 sold to Sir W.G. Armstrong, Mitchell & Co in part payment for PFALZ and MARK; AMAZZONE (Argentine Govt). 1897 RIO SANTA CRUZ (ditto). 1903 hulked.

17. 1869 LEIPZIG

2,388. 88,46 x 11,88. (290.2 x 39.0). C—1—2. I—S—I(2)—10. (I—84; III—600). Caird & Co, Greenock. 1869 (13/2) launched. 1869 (May) MV Bremen—Southampton—Baltimore. 1872 (13/1) FV Bremen—Southampton—New York (5 RV). 1883 engines compounded by Henniges, Bremen. 1886 (12/5) LV Bremen—Baltimore. 1894 (19/5) LV Bremen—S America. 1894 sold to Hamburg owners. 1898 scrapped at Hamburg.

18. (1870) HANNOVER (I)

2,571. 91,43 x 11,88. (300.0 x 39.0). C—1—2. I—S—I(2)—10. (I—60; III—700). Caird & Co, Greenock. 1869 (28/7) launched for NDL New Orleans service. 1870 (19/5) FV Bremen—New York. 1870 (6/7) 2nd voyage ditto; laid up at New York. 1870 (27/10) sailed New York —Bremen. 1871-4 mainly New Orleans service but 4 RV to New York; 4 RV to West Indies. 1880 (15/7) LV Bremen—New York. 1880-1 engines compounded by AG Vulcan, Stettin. 1881 (12/10) LV Bremen—Baltimore; subsequently to S America. 1894 (27/1) LV ditto. 1894 scrapped in Italy.

19. (1870) FRANKFURT (I)

2,582. 91,43 x 11,88. (300.0 x 39.0). C—1—2. I—S—I(2)—10. (I—60; III—600). Caird & Co, Greenock. 1869 (18/6) launched for NDL New Orleans service. 1870 (30/6) FV Bremen—Havre—New York. Laid up at New York during Franco-Prussian War. 1871-4 mainly New Orleans service but 6 RV to New York. 1880 engines compounded by builders. 1882 (8/3) LV Bremen—Baltimore; subsequently to S America. 1893 (30/9) LV ditto. 1894 sold to Sir W.G.Armstrong, Mitchell & Co in part payment for PFALZ and MARK: FRANKFURT (British). 1895 sold to Italy. 1897 scrapped in Italy.

20. (1871) KÖLN (I)

2,555. 91,43 x 11,88. (300.0 x 39.0). C—1—2. I—S—I(2)—10. (I—60; III—700). Caird & Co, Greenock. 1870 (11/8) launched for NDL New Orleans service. 1871 (Apr) MV Bremen—Southampton—New Orleans. 1871 (8/6) FV Bremen—New York. 1877 (12/9) LV ditto (13 RV). 1880 (29/9) FV Bremen—Baltimore. 1884 compound engines. 1887 (2/4) LV Bremen—Baltimore. 1895 (23/3) LV Bremen—S America. 1895 scrapped in Germany.

20a (1872) NEMESIS (c)

2,717. 107,46 x 12,65. (352.6 x 41.5). C—1—3. I—S—C2——11. Tod & McGregor, Glasgow (engines Rankin & Blackmore, Greenock). 1872 (2/5) FV for NDL (c), Bremen—Southampton—New York. 1872 (18/9) LV ditto (4 RV). (See Cunard - 13).

21. 1872 STRASSBURG

3,025. 106,67 x 11,89. (350.0 x 39.0). S—1—2. I—S—C2—10. (I—60; II—120; III—900). Caird & Co, Greenock. 1872 (24/5) launched for NDL New Orleans service. 1872 (3/9) MV Bremen—Southampton—New York. 1872 (16/10) FV Bremen—Havre—New Orleans. 1881 (16/2) FV Bremen—Baltimore. 1883 (19/9) LV ditto. 1883-96 mainly to S America. 1893 (2/8) LV Bremen—New York (12 RV). 1896 (25/1) LV Bremen—S America. 1896 sold. 1897 scrapped at Genoa.

22. 1873 MOSEL

3,200. 106,37 x 12,28. (349.0 x 40.3). S—1—2. I—S—C2—13. (I—90; II—126; III—680). Caird & Co, Greenock. 1872 (20/8) launched. 1873 (4/1) MV Bremen—Southampton—New York. 1875 (11/12) bomb explosion when in dock at Bremen (128). 1881 new compound engines by John Elder & Co, Glasgow. 1882 (2/7) LV Bremen—Southampton—New York. 1882 (9/8) wrecked near Lizard, Cornwall.

23. (1873) KRONPRINZ FRIEDRICH WILHELM

2,387. 95,18 x 11,91. (312.3 x 39.1). C—1—2. I—S—I(2)—10. (I—105; II—50; III—400). Caird & Co, Greenock. 1870 (13/9) launched for NDL West Indies service. 1871 (7/4) MV Bremen—Southampton—Panama. 1873 (14/5) FV Bremen—Southampton—New York. 1875 engines compounded. 1876 mainly to S America. 1884 (10/8) LV Bremen—New York (9 RV). 1887 quadruple-expansion engines by Denny, Dumbarton. 1893 (23/3) FV Genoa—Naples—New York. 1895 (8/5) LV Naples—New York (16 RV). 1895 (7/7) FV Bremen—S America. 1897 (10/4) LV ditto. 1897 scrapped in Italy.

24. (1873) GRAF BISMARCK

2,406. 96,46 x 11,91. (316.5 x 39.1). C—1—2. I—S—I(2)—10. (I—105; II—50; III—400). Caird & Co, Greenock. 1870 (9/11) launched for NDL West Indies service. 1871 (7/5) MV Bremen—Southampton—Panama. 1873 (11/6) FV Bremen—Southampton—New York—Bremen; laid up. 1874 (9/6) Bremen—Havre—New York (4 RV). 1875-6 laid up. 1877 mainly to S America but 3 RV to New York. 1879 compound engines by AG Weser, Bremen. 1890 (3/4) LV Bremen—New York. 1896 (10/11) LV Bremen—S America. 1898 scrapped.

25. (1873) KÖNIG WILHELM I
2,550. 95,09 x 11,91. (312.0 x 39.1). C—1—2. I—S—I(2)—10. (I—105; II—50; III—400). Caird & Co, Greenock. 1870 (6/7) launched for NDL West Indies service. 1871 (7/3) MV Bremen—Southampton—Panama. 1873 (25/6) FV Bremen—Southampton—New York. 1873 (Aug) FV Bremen—Southampton—Baltimore. 1873 (15/10) LV Bremen—Southampton—New York. 1873 (26/11) wrecked at Nieuwediep, Holland, during 3rd N Atlantic voyage (0). 1874 (Mar), refloated but sank again. 1951 wreck removed by Dutch Navy.

26. 1873 BRAUNSCHWEIG
3,079. 107,07 x 11,91. (351.3 x 39.1). S—1—2. I—S—C2—12. (I—34; II—33; III—600). R. Steele & Co, Greenock. 1873 (1/4) launched. 1873 (9/9) MV Bremen—Southampton—Baltimore. 1880 (16/10) FV Bremen—New York (4 RV). 1887 (13/1) FV Bremen—Suez Canal—Far East. 1891 (8/7) FV Bremen—Suez Canal—Australia. 1894 (13/1) resumed Bremen—New York. 1896 (14/1) LV ditto (11 RV). 1896 (15/4) FV Naples—New York. 1896 (30/5) LV ditto (2 RV). 1896 scrapped.

FELDMARSCHALL MOLTKE
3,060. 106,67 x 12,01. (350.0 x 39.4). S—1—2. I—S—C2—12. (I—144; II—68; III—500). Caird & Co, Greenock. 1873 (18/4) launched for W Indies service. 1874 (31/10) scheduled Bremen—Southampton—New York but did not sail; 4 RV to W Indies; 1 RV to New Orleans. 1875 ASSAM (P&O) 1896 KAIJO MARU (NYK). 1899 scrapped.

27. 1874 NÜRNBERG
3,116. 106,98 x 11,91. (351.0 x 39.1). S—1—2. I—S—C2—12. (I—34; II—33; III—600). R. Steele & Co, Greenock. 1873 (9/9) launched. 1874 (17/2) MV Bremen—Southampton—Baltimore. 1880 (11/9) FV Bremen—Southampton—New York (9 RV). 1886 (15/12) FV Bremen—Suez Canal—Far East. 1887 (13/7) FV Bremen—Suez Canal—Australia. 1891 (11/6) LV ditto (8 RV). 1892 (21/1) LV Bremen—Baltimore. 1895 sold. 1896 scrapped at Vegesack.

28. (1874) MINISTER ROON
3,068. 106,67 x 12,01. (350.0 x 39.4). S—1—2. I—S—C2—12. (I—144; II—68; III—502). Caird & Co, Greenock. 1873 (16/6) launched for W Indies service. 1873 (7/10) MV Bremen—Southampton—Panama. 1874 (25/3) FV Bremen—Southampton—New York (1 RV). 1874 (Jun) FV Bremen—Southampton—Baltimore (1 RV). 1874 (11/8) FV Bremen—Havre—New York. 1874 (29/9) LV ditto (2 RV). 1875 SIAM (P&O). 1897 YORIHIME MARU (NYK). 1901 scrapped.

29. 1874 NECKAR (I)

3,120. 106,67 x 12,19. (350.0 x 40.0). S—1—2. I—S—C2—13. (I—144; II—68; III—502). Caird & Co, Greenock. 1873 (10/11) launched. 1874 (18/4) MV Bremen—Southampton—New York. 1886 (3/1) LV ditto. 1886 rebuilt at Bremerhaven; (I—50; II—21; III—574). 1886 (28/7) FV Bremen—Suez Canal—Far East. 1894 (14/2) FV Naples—New York. 1895 (23/3) LV ditto (9 RV). 1895 (15/6) FV Bremen—New York. 1895 (Aug) LV ditto (2 RV). 1896 scrapped in Italy.

30. (1874) HOHENZOLLERN (I)

3,092. 107,59 x 11,91. (353.0 x 39.1). S—1—2. I—S—C2—12. (I—142; III—800). Earle's Shipbuilding Co, Hull. 1873 (24/5) launched. 1873 (7/12) MV Bremen—Southampton—Panama. 1874 (12/5) FV Bremen—Havre—New York. 1875 (6/2) LV Bremen—Southampton—New York (6 RV). 1876 (1/3) FV Bremen—S America (FV of service). 1878 (5/5) FV Bremen—Southampton—New York.1886 (11/8) FV Bremen—Suez Canal—Australia. 1890 triple-expansion engines by AG Vulcan, Stettin; (I—44; II—18; III—558). 1894 (1/8) LV dito. 1895 (9/12) LV Bremen—New York (7 RV). 1899 sold to Hong Kong; converted to barge; scrapped.

31. 1874 ODER

3,265. 106,67 x 12,28. (350.0 x 40.3). S—1—2. I—S—C2—13. (I—90; II—126; III—650). Caird & Co, Greenock. 1873 (Dec) launched. 1874 (23/5) MV Bremen—Southampton—New York. 1885 (26/4) LV ditto. 1886 (30/6) FV Bremen—Suez Canal—Far East (FV of service). 1887 (30/5) wrecked on Socotra Island, Indian Ocean.

32. 1874 HOHENSTAUFEN

3,098. 107,59 x 11,91. (353.0 x 39.1). S—1—2. I—S—C2—12- (I—142; III—800). Earle's Shipbuilding Co, Hull. 1873 (24/9) launched. 1874 (1/9) MV Bremen—Havre—New York. 1874 (20/12) LV Bremen—Southampton—New York (3 RV). 1880 (4/4) FV Bremen—Christiania—New York (2 RV). 1885 (29/4) LV Bremen—New York. 1886 (14/4) FV Bremen—Baltimore (1 RV). 1887 (26/1) FV Bremen—Suez Canal—Australia. 1890 triple-expansion engines by AG Vulcan, Stettin; (I—44; II—18; III—558). 1895 (8/5) LV ditto. 1895 (10/10) FV Bremen—S America. 1897 (11/2) LV ditto. 1897 scrapped at London.

33. 1874 GENERAL WERDER

3,020. 105,79 x 11,94. (347.1 x 39.2). S—1—2. I—S—C2—12. (I—144; II—68; III—502). Caird & Co, Greenock. 1874 (4/3) launched. 1874 (16/9) MV Bremen—Southampton—Baltimore—Bremen; laid up. 1887 (7/7)

FV Bremen—Southampton—New York. 1886 (11/9) LV Bremen—New York (40 RV). 1886 (3/11) scheduled to sail Bremen—Far East, but no trace of this or further NDL voyages. 1893 sold to Armstrong Mitchell in part payment for H.H.MEIER; became MIDNIGHT SUN (British cruise liner); triple-expansion engines. 1899 PRINCESS OF WALES (Boer War hospital ship). 1901 MIDNIGHT SUN. 1912 scrapped on R Tyne.

34. 1875 SALIER

3,083. 107,59 x 11,91. (353.0 x 39.1). S—1—2. I—S—C2—12. (I—142; III—800). Earle's Shipbuilding Co, Hull. 1874 (15/6) launched. 1875 (14/7) trials. 1875 (8/9) MV Bremen—Southampton—New York. 1876 (5/2) LV ditto (4 RV). 1876 (1/4) FV Bremen—S America. 1880 (2/5) FV Bremen—New York. 1886 (10/4) LV ditto (30 RV). 1886 (14/7) FV Bremen—Suez Canal—Australia (FV of service). 1890-1 triple expansion engines by AG Vulcan, Stettin; (I—63; II—30; III—641). 1894 (9/5) LV ditto. 1894 (1/12) resumed Bremen—New York. 1895 (20/8) LV ditto (6 RV). 1895 (10/12) resumed Bremen—S America. 1896 (7/12) wrecked on north coast of Spain (279).

35. 1876 HABSBURG

3,094. 107,59 x 11,91). 353.0 x 39.1). S—1—2. I—S—C2—12. (I—142; III—800). Earle's Shipbuilding Co, Hull. 1875 (9/1) launched. 1876 (11/3) MV Bremen—Southampton—New York (1 RV). 1876 (May) FV Bremen—S America. 1880 (21/4) resumed Bremen—Southampton—New York. 1886 (28/3) LV ditto (30 RV). 1887 (23/2) FV Bremen—Suez Canal—Australia. 1891 triple-expansion engines by AG Vulcan, Stettin; (I—63, II—30; III—641). 1894 (24/10) LV ditto. 1895 (28/4) resumed Bremen—New York (2 RV). 1895 (10/11) resumed Bremen S America. 1896 (10/3) LV ditto. 1898 sold to Italy; when bound thereto stranded near Cadiz. 1899 refloated; scrapped.

36. 1879 HANSA (II) §

2,513. 101,31 x 10,85. (332.4 x 35.6). S—1—2. I—S—C2—11. Oswald, Mordaunt & Co, Southampton. Laid down as NETLEY (British). 1879 (/) launched as HANSA (NDL); first NDL ocean freighter. 1879 (25/11) MV Bremen—New York. 1880 (4/1) wrecked on Terschelling Island, Holland (0).

37. 1881 ELBE

4,510. 126,94 x 13,71. (416.5 x 45.0). S—2—4. I—S—C3—15. (I—120; II—130; III—1,000). John Elder & Co, Glasgow. 1881 (2/4) launched. 1881 (26/6) MV Bremen—Southampton—New York. 1895 (29/1) sailed Bremen—New York. 1895 (30/1) sunk in North Sea in collision with ss CRAITHIE (British) (332).

38. **1882 WERRA**

4,817. 132,00 x 13,98. (433.1 x 45.9). S—2—4. I—S—C3—16. (I—125; II—130; III—1,000). John Elder & Co, Glasgow. 1882 (4/7) launched. 1882 (12/10) MV Bremen—Southampton—New York. 1891 (9/11) LV ditto. 1892 (4/1) FV Genoa—New York. 1898 (10/11) LV ditto. 1898(Dec)-1899(Summer) chartered to Cia Trasatlántica to repatriate Spanish troops. 1899 (24/9) sailed Bremen—Southampton—New York—Naples—Genoa. 1901 (28/8) LV Genoa—Naples—New York. 1901 (Sep) scrapped at Genoa.

39. **1883 FULDA**

4,816. 130,99 x 13,98. (429.8 x 45.9). S—2—4. I—S—C3—16. (I—120; II—130; III—1,000). John Elder & Co, Glasgow. 1882 (15/11) launched. 1883 (14/3) MV Bremen—Southampton—New York. 1886 (14/3) rescued passengers and crew of Cunard OREGON. 1891 (7/10) LV Bremen—Southampton—New York. 1891 (24/10) FV New York—Genoa (dep 11/11)—New York. 1898 (27/10) LV Genoa—Naples—New York. 1898 chartered to Cia Trasatlántica to repatriate Spanish troops. 1899 (2/2) serious damage in dry dock at Birkenhead after provisional sale to Canadian SS Co; deal abandoned; scrapped.

40. **1884 EIDER**

4,722. 130,99 x 14,32. (429.8 x 47.0). S—2—4. I—S—C3—16. (I—120; II—130; III—1,000). John Elder & Co, Glasgow. 1883 (15/12) launched. 1884 (19/3) MV Bremen—Southampton—New York. 1892 (9/1) LV ditto. 1892 (31/1) stranded on Atherfield Ledge, Isle of Wight; refloated; scrapped.

41. **1884 EMS**

4,730. 130,99 x 14,32. (429.8 x 47.0). S—2—4. I—S—C3—16. (I—125; II—130; III—1,000). John Elder & Co, Glasgow. 1884 (27/2) launched. 1884 (4/6) MV Bremen—Southampton—New York. 1896 masts reduced to two. 1896 (14/3) LV ditto. 1896 (16/4) FV Genoa—Naples—New York. 1900 (25/10) LV ditto. 1901 LAKE SIMCOE (Elder Dempster). 1901 (20/8) FV Liverpool—Quebec—Montreal. 1903 (4/3) LV Liverpool—St John, NB. 1903 (18/8) FV for Can Pac (c) Liverpool—Quebec—Montreal (1 RV). 1905 scrapped at Genoa.

42. **1886 ALLER**

4,966. 133,53 x 14,56. (438.1 x 47.8). S—2—4. S—2—4. S—S—T3—17. (I—150; II—90; III—1,000). Fairfield Co Ltd, Glasgow. 1886 (18/2) launched. 1886 (24/4) MV Bremen—Southampton—New York. 1897 masts reduced to two. 1897 (18/9) LV ditto. 1897 (21/10) FV

Genoa—Naples—New York. 1902 (6/11) LV ditto. 1902 sold. 1904 scrapped.

43. 1886 TRAVE
   4,969. 133,50 x 14,66. (438.0 x 48.1). S—2—4. S—S—T3—17. (I—150; II—90; III—1,000). Fairfield Co Ltd, Glasgow. 1886 (18/2) launched. 1886 (5/6) MV Bremen—Southampton—New York. 1896-7 refitted; masts reduced to two. 1901 (29/1) LV ditto. 1901 (20/3) FV Genoa—Naples—New York. 1903 (23/4) LV ditto. 1903-6 laid up. 1906 (11/3) resumed Bremen—New York. 1907 (26/10) LV ditto (9 RV). 1908 sold. 1909 scrapped.

44. 1886 SAALE
   4,967. 133,98 x 14,66. (439.6 x 48.1). S—2—4- S—S—T3—17. (I—150; II—90; III—1,000). Fairfield Co Ltd, Glasgow. 1886 (21/4) launched. 1886 (18/8) MV Bremen—Southampton—New York. 1896-7 refitted; masts reduced to two. 1900 (30/6) severely damaged in New York dock fire (109); sold; J.L.LUCKENBACH (US cargo steamer); one funnel; new triple-expansion engines. 1921 PRINCESS (US). 1923 MADISON (US). 1924 scrapped in Italy.

45. 1888 LAHN
   5,099. 136,66 x 14,93. (448.4 x 49.0). S—2—4. S—S—T5—18. (I—224; II—106; III—700). Fairfield Co Ltd, Glasgow. 1887 (7/9) launched. 1888 (1/2) MV Bremen—Southampton—New York. 1896 masts reduced to two. 1901 (1/10) LV ditto. 1901 (13/11) FV Genoa—Naples—New York. 1904 (4/2) LV ditto. 1904 RUSS (Russian Navy). 1927 scrapped.

46. 1889 DRESDEN (I)
   4,527. 119,01 x 14,23. (390.5 x 46.7). S—1—2. S—S—T3—13. (I—38;II—20; III—1,759). Fairfield Co Ltd, Glasgow. 1888 (1/12) launched. 1889 (10/4) MV Bremen—Baltimore. 1889 (29/5) FV Bremen—Suez Canal—Far East (1 RV). 1889 (30/12) FV Bremen—S America. 1890 (9/7) FV Bremen—Suez Canal—Australia (1 RV). 1892 (18/5) FV Bremen—New York. 1902 (15/5) LV Bremen—Baltimore. 1902 (15/11) LV Bremen—S America (5 RV). 1903 (12/5) LV Bremen—New York—Baltimore (19 RV on N Atlantic). 1903 HELIUS (Houston). 1904 ditto (Union Castle); laid up. 1906 TIRIMUJGHIAN (Turkish Govt). 1914 sunk by Russians in Black Sea.

47. (1889) MÜNCHEN (I)
   4,536. 119,01 x 14,23. (390.5 x 46.7). S—1—2. S—S—T3—13. (I—38; II—20; III—1,763). Fairfield Co Ltd, Glasgow. 1889 (23/1) launched. 1889 (11/3) MV Bremen—Montevideo—Buenos Aires. 1889 (5/6) FV

Bremen—Baltimore. 1890 (25/9) FV Bremen—New York—Baltimore. 1892 (10/11) LV Bremen—S America (6 RV). 1900 (24/3) LV Bremen—New York—Baltimore (19 RV on N Atlantic). 1900 (23/5) FV Bremen—Suez Canal—Australia (1 RV). 1902 (3/2) stranded on Yap Caroline Islands; refloated; GREGORY MORCH (Northern SS Co (Russian)). 1906 (27/10) FV Odessa—Piraeus—New York. 1907 (18/1) LV ditto (2 RV). 1910 scrapped.

48. 1889 KAISER WILHELM II (I)
    (1901) HOHENZOLLERN (II)
    4,773. 137,03 x 15,54. (449.6 x 51.0). S—2—4. S—S—T3—16. (I—120; II—80; III—1,000). AG Vulcan, Stettin. 1889 (23/4) launched. 1889 (27/8) MV Bremen—Southampton—New York (1 RV). 1889 (2/10) FV Bremen—Suez Canal—Australia. 1892 (17/2) LV ditto (6 RV). 1892 tonnage 6,661. 1892 (22/10) LV Bremen—Southampton—New York (10½ RV). 1892 (30/11) FV Genoa—Naples—New York. 1893 (5/6) sank at berth in Genoa. refloated. 1893 (8/7) resumed Bremen—Southampton—New York. 1893 (8/11) resumed Genoa—Naples—New York. 1900 (18/12) LV New York—Naples—Genoa; renamed HOHEN-ZOLLERN. 1901 (9/1) FV Genoa—Naples—New York. 1906 (21/5) LV Naples—New York—Naples; subsequently ran within Mediterranean. 1908 (10/5) stranded at Alghero, Sardinia; refloated; scrapped in Italy.

49. (1890) KARLSRUHE (I)
    5,057. 126,49 x 14,63. (415.0 x 48.0). S—1—2. S—S—T3—13. (I—44; II—36; III—1,955). Fairfield Co Ltd, Glasgow. 1889 (31/8) launched. 1889 (10/11) MV Bremen—Montevideo—Buenos Aires. 1890 (13/2) FV Bremen—New York—Baltimore. 1892 (28/9) FV Bremen—Suez Canal—Australia. 1894 (31/1) FV Bremen—Suez Canal—Far East (7 RV). 1902 (8/2) LV Bremen—New York—Baltimore. 1902 (18/12) LV Bremen—Baltimore (37 RV on N Atlantic). 1906 (16/5) LV Bremen—Australia (19 RV). 1906 (22/9) LV Bremen—S America (3 RV). 1908 scrapped.

50. (1890) STUTTGART (I)
    5.048. 126,49 x 14,63. (415.0 x 48.0). S—1—2. S—S—T3—13. (I—44; II—36; III—1,955). Fairfield Co Ltd, Glasgow. 1889 (26/10) launched. 1890 (10/1) MV Bremen—Montevideo—Buenos Aires. 1890 (28/8) FV Bremen—Baltimore. 1891 (11/1) FV Bremen—New York. 1896 (1/7) FV Bremen—Suez Canal—Australia. 1899 (3/12) LV Bremen—New York (35 RV on N Atlantic). 1900 (16/5) FV Bremen—Suez Canal—Far East. 1903 (7/4) LV ditto (8 RV). 1904 (13/7) LV Bremen—Australia (9 RV). 1907 (12/1) resumed Bremen—S America. 1907 (14/12) LV ditto. 1908

scrapped.

51. 1890 SPREE
(1900) KAISERIN MARIA THERESIA
6,963. 141,11 x 15,78. (463.0 x 51.8). S—2—3. S—S—T5—18. (I—244; II—122; III—460). AG Vulcan, Stettin. 1890 (17/5) launched. 1890 (11/10) MV Bremen—Southampton—New York. 1892 (26/11) fractured propeller shaft; towed to Queenstown by LAKE HURON (Beaver); repaired at Milford Haven. 1897 (2/7) fractured propeller shaft. 1897 (5/7) sighted by ATL MAINE and towed to Queenstown. 1897 (16/11) LV Bremen—Southampton—New York. 1899 lengthened to 160,31 metres (526.0 feet); 7,840 tons; twin-screw (T8); S—3—2; renamed KAISERIN MARIA THERESIA: (I—405; II—114; III—387). 1900 (13/3) FV Bremen—Southampton—New York. 1903 (26/9) LV ditto (29 RV as 'KMT', of which 7 RV Mediterranean—New York. 1904 URAL (Russian auxiliary cruiser). 1905 (27/5) sunk at Battle of Tsushima.

52. 1891 HAVEL
6,875. 141,11 x 15,81. (463.0 x 51.9). S—2—3. S—S—T5—18. (I—244; II—122; III—460). AG Vulcan, Stettin. 1890 (30/8) launched. 1891 (5/2) MV Bremen—Southampton—New York. 1898. (19/4) LV ditto. 1898 METEORO (Spanish armed cruiser). 1899 ALFONSO XII (Cia Trasatlántica). 1916 (30/10) FV Bilbao—Coruña—Vigo—Havana—New York. 1918 (7/2) LV New York—Coruña—Bilbao (9 RV). 1926 scrapped in Italy.

53. 1891 GERA
5,005. 126,49 x 14,63. (415.0 x 48.0). S—1—2. S—S—T3—13. (I—49; II—38; III—1,901). Fairfield Co Ltd, Glasgow. 1890 (8/11) launched. 1891 (2/4) MV Bremen—Baltimore. 1891 (24/6) FV Bremen—S America. 1892 (28/7) FV Bremen—New York—Baltimore. 1893 (19/7) FV Bremen—Suez Canal—Far East. 1893 (22/11) FV Bremen—Suez Canal—Australia. 1903 (25/3) FV Genoa—Naples—New York (3 RV). 1903 (10/12) FV Hamburg—Far East (5 RV). 1905 (1/4) LV Bremen—Baltimore. 1906 (8/8) LV Bremen—Australia (18 RV). 1906 (15/12) resumed Bremen—S America. 1907 (12/4) LV Bremen—New York (22 RV on N Atlantic). 1907 (7/9) LV Bremen—S America. 1908 VALPARAISO (Lloyd del Pacifico (Italian)). 1917 (14/10) torpedoed and sunk by German submarine off Libya.

54. 1891 WEIMAR
4,996. 126,49 x 14,63. (415.0 x 48.0). S—1—2. S—S—T3—13. (I—49; II—38; III—1,907). Fairfield Co Ltd, Glasgow. 1891 (9/2) launched. 1891 (21/5) MV Bremen—Baltimore. 1891 (17/12) FV Bremen—New

York—Baltimore. 1897 (2/6) FV Bremen—Suez Canal—Australia. 1900 (7/2) FV Bremen—Suez Canal—Far East (2 RV). 1903 (25/2) FV Naples—New York. 1905 (23/9) FV Bremen—S America. 1906 (11/5) LV Naples—New York (8 RV). 1906 (13/6) LV Bremen—Australia (9 RV). 1907 (11/5) LV Bremen—Baltimore (57 RV on N Atlantic). 1908 SANTIAGO (Lloyd del Pacifico (Italian)). 1909 ARMONIA (Chilean). 1917 ditto (Canadian). 1918 (15/3) torpedoed and sunk by German submarine near Porquerolles Island, Mediterranean France.

55. (1891) OLDENBURG

5,006.126,49 x 14,63. (415.0 x 48.0). S—1—2. S—S—T3—13. (I—49; II—38; III—1,901). Fairfield Co Ltd, Glasgow. 1890 (13/12) launched. 1891 (11/2) MV Bremen—Montevideo—Buenos Aires. 1891 (11/6) FV Bremen—Baltimore. 1892 (18/2) FV Bremen—New York. 1892 (22/6) FV Bremen—Suez Canal—Far East. 1892 (26/10) FV Bremen—Suez Canal—Australia. 1904 (3/3) LV Bremen—Far East (8 RV). 1905 (19/1) LV Bremen—Baltimore. 1906 (18/4) LV Bremen—Australia (18 RV). 1906 (25/8) resumed Bremen—S America. 1910 (10/4) LV Bremen—New York (24 RV on N Atlantic). 1910 (15/10) LV Bremen—S America. 1911 AK-DENIZ (Turkish). 1923 scrapped.

56. (1891) DARMSTADT

5,012. 126,49 x 14,63. (415.0 x 48.0). S—1—2. S—S—T3—13. (I—49; II—38; III—1,904). Fairfield Co Ltd, Glasgow. 1890 (27/9) launched. 1891 (10/3) MV Bremen—Montevideo—Buenos Aires. 1892 (8/3) FV Bremen—New York. 1892 (11/10) FV Bremen—Suez Canal—Far East. 1895. (10/4) FV Bremen—Suez Canal—Australia. 1905 (27/4) LV Bremen—Far East (6 RV). 1905 (4/11) resumed Bremen—S America. 1906 (21/3) LV Bremen—Australia (16 RV). 1907 (24/5) LV Bremen—Baltimore. 1910 (28/2) LV Bremen—New York (27 RV on N Atlantic). 1910 (12/11) LV Bremen—S America. 1911 KARA DENIZ (Turkish). 1914 seized at Bombay; laid up. 1923 scrapped.

57. 1892 H.H.MEIER

5,140. 128,31 x 14,63. (421.0 x 48.0). S—1—3. S—2S—T6—13. (I—75; II—300; III—1,000). Sir W.G. Armstrong, Mitchell & Co, Walker-on-Tyne (engines Hawthorn, Leslie & Co, Newcastle). 1891 (19/10) launched as LUCANIA (MacIver). 1892 H.H.MEIER (NDL). 1892 (27/12) MV Bremen—Southampton—New York. 1893 (20/7) FV Bremen—New York—Baltimore. 1894 (23/3) FV Bremen—S America. 1895 (26/7) LV ditto (5 RV). 1901 (21/9) LV Bremen—New York. 1901 MANUEL CALVO (Cia Trasatlántica); 5,617 tons; (I—84; II—32; III—1,100). 1902 (21/3) FV Genoa—Barcelona—Cadiz—New York—Havana—Vera

Cruz. 1919 (29/3) damaged by mine off Turkish coast when repatriating 400 foreigners (151 lost). 1931 (May) LV Barcelona—Cadiz—New York—Havana. 1936 laid up at Port Mahon, Minorca. 1939 (Oct) sailed for Cadiz; rebuilt as cargo steamer. 1950 laid up at Santander. 1952 DRAGO (Spanish). 1959 (Dec) scrapped in Spain.

57a. (1893) GULF OF MEXICO (c)

3,172. 100,58 x 12,89. (330.0 x 42.3). S—1—2. S—S—T3—11. (III—300). Raylton Dixon & Co, Middlesbrough (engines Blair & Co, Stockton). 1883 (24/4) launched for Greenock SS Co. 1893 (13/4) FV for NDL (c), Bremen—New York. 1893 (30/5) LV ditto (2 RV). 1898 VIENNA (Austro-Americana). 1900 VEGA (J.White, Genoa). 1904 YAHIKO MARU (Jap). 1920 (2/5) wrecked in Tsugaru Strait, Japan.

57b. (1893) LAUGHTON (c)

2,436. 91,55 x 12,28. (300.4 x 40.3). S—1—2. I—S—C2—10. (III—450). Raylton Dixon & Co, Middlesbrough (engines T.Richardson & Sons, Hartlepool). 1882 (14/8) launched as NOORD BRABAND (Stoomvaart Maatschappij Rotterdam). 1891 LAUGHTON (Commercial). 1893 (26/4) FV for NDL (c), Bremen—New York. 1893 (27/9) LV ditto (3 RV). 1899 (23/1) sailed Newport News—Copenhagen; went missing.

58. 1893 ROLAND

3,603. 105,15 x 13,34. (345.0 x 43.8). S—1—2. S—S—T3—12. (II—28; III—800). Sir W.G.Armstrong, Mitchell & Co, Walker-on-Tyne (engines Wallsend Slipway Co). Bought on stocks. 1893 (1/5) launched. 1893 (13/9) MV Bremen—New York 1893 (9/12) FV Bremen—S America. 1896 (27/8) FV Bremen—Baltimore. 1906 (15/2) LV Bremen—Baltimore (30 RV on N Atlantic). 1909 (7/8) LV Bremen—S America (16 Rv). 1910 (11/11) LV Bremen—Havana (3 RV). 1911 BAHRIAHMER (Turkish). 1914 (7/11) sunk by Russian Navy off Eregli, Black Sea.

59. 1894 WITTEKIND

4,755. 116,85 x 14,02. (383.4 x 46.0). S—1—2. S—2S—T6—13. (II—174; III—1,366). Blohm & Voss, Hamburg. 1894 (3/2) launched. 1894 (14/4) MV Bremen—New York. 1895 (8/8) LV ditto (11 RV). 1895 (21/9) FV Bremen—S America. 1900 lengthened by Wigham Richardson, Wallsend-on-Tyne, to 135,93 metres (446.0 feet); tonnage 5,640. 1906 (24/2) FV Bremen—Baltimore. 1911 (6/4) FV Bremen—Philadelphia—Galveston. 1911 (16/6) FV Hamburg—Quebec—Montreal. 1912 (14/9) LV Bremen—S America (33 RV). 1914 (2/4) LV Bremen—Philadelphia—Galveston. 1914 (25/6) LV Hamburg—Quebec—Montreal (4 RV). 1914 (24/7) sailed Hamburg—Quebec—Montreal, but diverted to Boston and took refuge there. 1917 (Apr) seized by USA; IROQUOIS (US Govt). 1919 FREE-

DOM (ditto). 1924 scrapped.

60. 1894 WILLEHAD
4,761. 116,85 x 14,02. (383.4 x 46.0). S—1—2. S—2S—T6—13. (II—105; III—1,196). Blohm & Voss, Hamburg. 1894 (21/3) launched. 1894 (24/5) MV Bremen—New York. 1894 (10/11) FV Bremen—S America. 1896 (4/12) FV Bremen—New York—Baltimore. 1903 (23/5) LV Bremen—S America (12 RV). 1904 (3/5) FV Stettin—Helsingborg—Gothenburg—Christiansand—New York (3 RV). 1909 (16/4) FV Hamburg—Quebec—Montreal. 1912 (4/1) FV Bremen—Philadelphia. 1912 (31/12) LV Bremen—Philadelphia—Baltimore. 1914 (10/7) LV Hamburg—Quebec—Montreal (24 RV). 1914 (Aug) took refuge at New London, Connecticut. 1917 (Apr) seized by USA; WYANDOTTE (US Govt). 1924 scrapped at Baltimore.

61. (1895) CREFELD (I)
3,829. 108,35 x 13,31. (355.5 x 43.7). S—1—2. S—S—T3—13. (II—32; III—1,013). AG Vulcan, Stettin. 1895 (23/3) launched. 1895 (11/5) MV Bremen—Rio de Janeiro—Santos. 1895 (12/9) FV Bremen—New York. 1896 (10/9) FV Bremen—Baltimore. 1902 (13/3) LV Bremen—New York (19 RV on N Atlantic). 1902 (19/4) FV Bremen—Galveston (1 RV). Subsequently to S America. 1914 (Oct) took refuge at Tenerife. 1918 handed to Spain; ESPANA No. 4. 1925 TEIDE (Cia Trasatlántica). 1932 (10/6) wrecked at Barta, Spanish Guinea.

62. (1895) BONN
3,969. 108,23 x 13,28. (355.1 x 43.6). S—1—2. S—S—T3—13. (II—20; III—1,043). Germaniawerft, Kiel (engines Germania, Berlin). 1895 (25/1) launched. 1895 (7/9) MV Bremen—Montevideo—Buenos Aires. 1895 (21/12) FV Bremen—New York. 1897 (18/2) FV Bremen—Baltimore. 1901 (9/2) LV ditto (13 RV on N Atlantic). Subsequently to S America. 1913 GREGOR (German). 1920 (Feb) stranded in Black Sea.

63. (1896) AACHEN
3,833. 108,29 x 13,31. (355.3 x 43.7). S—1—2. S—S—T3—13. (II—28; III—1,045). AG Vulcan, Stettin. 1895 launched. 1895 (15/6) MV Bremen—Montevideo—Buenos Aires. 1896 (12/1) FV Bremen—New York. 1896 (9/11) FV Bremen—Baltimore. 1897 (17/6) LV ditto (12 RV on N Atlantic). Subsequently to S America. 1915 (30/7) torpedoed and sunk by British submarine E.1 in Baltic, when German naval auxiliary.

64. (1896) HALLE
3,960. 108,23 x 13,25. (355.1 x 43.5). S—1—2. S—S—T3—13. (II—19; III—1,071). Germaniawerft, Kiel (engines Germania, Berlin). 1895 (3/8)

launched. 1895 (2/11) MV Bremen—Montevideo—Buenos Aires. 1896 (15/2) FV Bremen—New York. 1896 (13/8) FV Bremen—Baltimore. 1899 (28/9) LV ditto (9 RV on N Atlantic). Subsequently to S America. 1913 PAWEL (German). 1915 WOUDRICHEM (Dutch). 1919 LLOYD (US). 1923 ditto (Italian). 1924 IRIS (Italian). 1926 scrapped.

65. 1897 KÖNIGIN LOUISE
10,566. 160,01 x 18,29. (525.0 x 60.0). 2—2. 2S—Q8—15. (I—227; II—235; III—1,564). AG Vulcan, Stettin. 1896 (17/10) launched. 1897 (22/3) MV Bremen—Falmouth (arr 29/3 to repair steering gear; dep 22/4)—New York. 1897 (17/11) FV Bremen—Suez Canal—Australia. 1904 (25/2) FV Genoa—Naples—New York. 1911 (25/5) LV ditto. 1911 (25/10) LV Bremen—Australia (10 RV). 1912 (16/3) resumed Bremen—New York. 1914 (18/4) FV Bremen—Philadelphia—Baltimore. 1914 (25/6) LV ditto (3 RV). 1914 (Aug) laid up at Bremen. 1919 (Apr) surrendered to Britain. 1921 OMAR (Orient). 1924 EDISON (Byron). 1924 (16/10) FV Piraeus—Patras—Naples—New York. 1928 (Aug) EDISON (National Greek). 1932 (29/12) LV New York—Boston—Piraeus. 1935 scrapped at Genoa.

66. (1897) FRIEDRICH DER GROSSE
10,531. 159,40 x 18,29. (523.0 x 60.0). 2—2. 2S—Q8—15. (I—226; II—235; III—1,671). AG Vulcan, Stettin. 1896 (1/8) launched. 1896 (11/11) MV Bremen—Suez Canal—Australia. 1897 (4/4) FV Bremen—Falmouth (to embark passengers ex KÖNIGIN LOUISE)—New York. 1907 (22/3) FV Naples—New York. 1912 (25/7) LV Genoa—Naples—New York (16 RV). 1913 (22/11) LV Bremen—New York. 1914 (21/1) LV Bremen—Australia (14 RV). 1914 (4/6) FV Bremen—Baltimore. 1914 (9/7) LV Bremen—Philadelphia—Baltimore. 1914 (Aug) took refuge at New York. 1917 (Apr) seized by USA; HURON (US Govt). 1922 CITY OF HONOLULU (Los Angeles SS Co). 1922 (12/10) damaged by fire during FV Honolulu—Los Angeles. 1922 (17/10) sunk by gunfire from US transport THOMAS.

67. (1897) PRINZREGENT LUITPOLD
6,288. 138,77 x 15,30. (455.3 x 50.2). 1—2. 2S—T6—14. (I—224; II—101; III—850). F. Schichau, Danzig. 1894 (20/3) launched. 1894 (29/8) MV Bremen—Suez Canal—Australia. 1897 (1/5) FV Bremen—New York. 1900 (22/12) LV ditto (10 RV). 1904 (26/5) FV Hamburg—Suez Canal—Far East. 1910 (11/5) LV Bremen—Australia (22 RV). Subsequently to Far East. 1914 (Aug) sheltered in Italy. 1915 (May) seized by Italy; PIETRO CALVI. 1928 scrapped.

68. (1897) BARBAROSSA
10,769. 160,01 x 18,29. (525.0 x 60.0). 2—2. 2S—Q8—15. (I—230; II—227; III—1,935). Blohm & Voss, Hamburg. 1896 (5/9) launched. 1897 (8/1)

559

MV Bremen—Suez Canal—Australia. 1897 (24/5) FV Bremen—
Southampton—New York. 1906 (16/3) FV Genoa—Naples—New York.
1910 (21/12) LV Bremen—Australia (11 RV). 1912 (4/9) FV Bremen—
New York—Philadelphia—Baltimore—Galveston. 1913 (6/11) LV Genoa
—Naples—New York (18 RV). 1914 (30/4) LV Bremen—Philadelphia—
Baltimore (3 RV). 1914 (18/7) LV Bremen—New York. 1914 (Aug) took
refuge at New York. 1917 (Apr) seized by USA; MERCURY (US Navy).
1919 ditto (USSB). 1920 chartered to Baltic Steamship Corporation but
did not run for them. 1924 scrapped in USA.

69. 1897 BREMEN (II)
10,525. 160,04 x 18,38. (525.1 x 60.3). 2—2. 2S—Q8—15. (I—230; II—250;
III—1,850). F. Schichau, Danzig. 1896 (14/11) launched. 1897 (5/6) MV
Bremen—Southampton—New York. 1897 (20/10) FV Bremen—Suez
Canal—Australia. 1900 (30/6) damaged in New York dock fire; length-
ened by Vulcan, Stettin, to 167,78 metres (550.5 feet); refitted; 11,570 tons.
1901 (12/10) resumed Bremen—Southampton—New York. 1911 (27/9)
LV Bremen—Australia (16 RV). 1914 (20/6) LV Bremen—Southampton
—New York; laid up at Bremen. 1919 (Apr) surrendered to Britain; name
unchanged; ran for P&O. 1921 CONSTANTINOPLE (Byron). 1921
(5/12) FV Constanza—Constantinople—Piraeus—New York. 1923 (4/9)
LV ditto (8 RV). 1924 KING ALEXANDER (Byron). 1924 (24/5) FV
Piraeus—Patras—New York. 1925 (21/4) LV ditto (6 RV). 1929 scrapped
at Venice.

70. 1897 KAISER WILHELM DER GROSSE
14,349. 191,22 x 20,11. (627.4 x 66.0). 4—2. 2S—T8—22. (I—332; II—343;
III—1,074). AG Vulcan, Stettin. 1897 (4/5) launched. 1897 (19/9) MV
Bremen—Southampton—New York—Plymouth—Bremen. 1897 (Nov)
record passage Sandy Hook—Needles. 1898 (Mar) record passage Needles
—Sandy Hook. 1906 (21/11) collided with ORINOCO (RMSP) outside
Cherbourg harbour in fog; slight damage. 1913 (28/10) LV Bremen—
Southampton—Cherbourg—New York. 1914 III and IV only; 13,952 tons.
1914 (18/3) FV Bremen—New York direct. 1914 (21/7) LV New York—
Bremen. 1914 (Aug) armed merchant cruiser. 1914 (27/8) sunk by British
cruiser HIGHFLYER at Rio de Oro, Spanish Sahara.

71. (1897) ELLEN RICKMERS (c)
(1900) BORKUM
5,350. 124,66 x 15,39. (409.0 x 50.5). S—1—2. S—T3—10. (II—18;
III—950). J.L. Thompson & Sons, Sunderland (engines J. Dickinson &
Sons, Sunderland). 1896 (27/2) launched for Rickmers. 1897 (24/9) FV for
NDL (c), Bremen—Baltimore. 1900 (5/1) LV ditto (6 RV). 1900
BORKUM (NDL). 1900 (13/9) FV Bremen—Baltimore—Galveston.

560

1905 (Feb) LV ditto (3 RV). 1905-13 Bremen—S America. 1914 Bremen—
Far East. 1915 seized by Italy; ASTI. 1917 (13/8) torpedoed and sunk by
German submarine 220 miles SW of Scilly Isles.

72. (1898) MARIA RICKMERS (c)
    (1900) HELGOLAND
    4,888. 124,66 x 15,39. (409.0 x 50.5). S—1—2. S—T3—10. (II—18;
    III—950). J.L. Thompson & Sons, Sunderland (engines G. Clark Ltd,
    Sunderland). 1896 (16/1) launched for Rickmers. 1898 (10/2) FV for NDL
    (c), Bremen—Baltimore. 1899 (20/3) LV ditto (8 RV). 1900 HELGO-
    LAND (NDL). 1900 (22/11) FV Bremen—Baltimore (1 RV). 1901-10
    Bremen—S America. 1911-3 Bremen—Cape Town—Australia. 1914
    Bremen—Far East. 1914 seized by Britain; POLYXENA. 1917 (11/6)
    torpedoed and sunk by German submarine 57 mile W of Fastnet.

72a. (1898) ELISABETH RICKMERS (c)
    5,211. 124,96 x 15,39. (410.0 x 50.5). S—1—2. S—Q4—10. (II—19;
    III—975). Wigham, Richardson & Co, Walker-on-Tyne. 1896 (28/3)
    launched for Rickmers. 1898 (24/2) FV for NDL (c), Bremen—Baltimore.
    1899 (27/1) LV ditto (5 RV). 1900 NORDERNEY (NDL). 1900-13
    Bremen—S America. 1914 Bremen—Far East. 1916 (25/7) lost near
    Sassnitz, Baltic.

73. 1898 KAISER FRIEDRICH
    12,480. 177,29 x 19,47. (581.7 x 63.9). 3—2. 2S—Q(10)—20. (I—400;
    II—250; III—700). F. Schichau, Danzig. 1897 (5/10) launched. 1898 (7/6)
    MV Bremen—Southampton—New York. 1899 (6/6) LV ditto (8 RV);
    returned to builders. 1899 (1/10) FV for Hapag (c), Hamburg—
    Southampton—New York. 1900 (11/10) LV ditto (10 RV); laid up. 1912
    BURDIGALA (Cie Sud Atlantique). 1916 (14/11) sunk in Aegean Sea by
    mine laid by German submarine U.73.

74. 1899 HANNOVER (II)
    7,305. 131,02 x 16,46. (429.9 x 54.0). 1—2 2S—Q8—13. (II—120;
    III—1,850). Wigham Richardson & Co, Walker-on-Tyne. 1899 (22/8)
    launched. 1899 (2/12) MV Bremen—Baltimore. 1902 (8/3) FV Bremen—
    New York—Baltimore. 1910 (7/4) FV Bremen—Philadelphia. 1913 (6/4)
    FV Hamburg—Portland, Maine. 1913 (16/5) FV Hamburg—Quebec—
    Montreal (1 RV). 1913 (31/12) FV Bremen—Boston—New Orleans. 1914
    (4/3) LV ditto (2 RV). 1914 (16/5) FV Bremen—Quebec. 1914 (27/6) LV
    ditto (2 RV). 1914 (Aug) laid up at Bremen. 1919 surrendered to Britain;
    name unchanged. 1922 resold to NDL; (cabin; III). 1922 (25/3) FV Bremen
    —New York. 1926 (24/1) LV ditto. 1932 scrapped at Bremen.

75. 1899 RHEIN (II)

10,058. 152,70 x 17,83. (501.0 x 58.5). 1—4. 2S—Q8—14. (I—148; II—116; III—2,500). Blohm & Voss, Hamburg. 1899 (20/9) launched. 1899 (9/12) MV Bremen—New York. 1900 (6/5) FV Bremen—Baltimore. 1901 (11/4) sailed New York—Bremen with I; II; III; subsequently carried II—369; III—217; IV—2,865. 1901 (11/9) FV Bremen—Suez Canal—Australia. 1904 (23/11) LV ditto (4 RV). 1900-11 mainly Bremen—New York &/or Baltimore. 1911 (18/5) FV Bremen—Philadelphia. 1914 (9/4) LV Bremen—New York—Baltimore. 1914 (16/7) LV Bremen—Baltimore (arr 29/7). 1917 (Apr) seized by USA at Baltimore; SUSQUEHANNA (US Govt; 9,959 tons). 1920 (4/8) FV for US Mail (c), New York—Bremen—Danzig; (cabin 500; III—2,500). 1921 (6/4) LV ditto (6 RV). 1922 (4/3) FV for US Lines, New York—Plymouth—Cherbourg—Bremen. 1922 (31/8) LV ditto (5 RV). 1928 (Nov) sold to Japan; scrapped.

76. (1899) KÖLN (II)

7,409. 130,72 x 16,55. (428.9 x 54.3). 1—2. 2S—T6—13. (II—120; III—1,850). J.C. Tecklenborg, Geestemünde. 1899 (24/7) launched. 1899 (20/10) MV Bremen—Galveston. 1899 (21/12) FV Bremen—Baltimore. 1902 (4/1) FV Bremen—New York. Subsequently mostly Bremen—Baltimore or Galveston; occasionally to or via New York. 1910 (7/9) FV Bremen—Philadelphia. 1912 (26/4) FV Hamburg—Quebec—Montreal (2 RV). 1914 (21/1) FV Bremen—Boston—New Orleans. 1914 (29/7) LV Bremen—Boston (arr 11/8). 1917 (Apr) seized by USA at Boston; AMPHION (US Govt). 1923 scrapped.

77. 1900 FRANKFURT (II)

7,431. 131,15 x 16,55. (430.3 x 54.3). 1—2. 2S—T6—13. (II—108; III—1,889). J.C. Tecklenborg, Geestemünde. 1899 (17/12) launched. 1900 (31/3) MV Bremen—Baltimore. 1901 (25/12) FV Bremen—Galveston; subsequently Bremen—Baltimore &/or Galveston. 1908 (19/9) FV Bremen—S America (6 RV). 1910 (10/3) FV Bremen—Philadelphia—Galveston. 1914 (13/2) FV Bremen—Boston—New Orleans. 1914 (7/6) LV ditto. 1914 (Aug) laid up at Bremen. 1919 surrendered to Britain; name unchanged. 1922 SARVISTAN (Hong Kong). 1931 scrapped in Japan.

78. 1900 MAIN (II)

10,200. 152,70 x 17,71. (501.0 x 58.1). 1—4. 2S—Q8—14. (I—148; II—116; III—2,500). Blohm & Voss, Hamburg. 1900 (10/2) launched. 1900 (28/4) MV Bremen—Cherbourg—New York. 1900 (30/6) sank after involvement in New York dock fire. 1900 (27/7) refloated; reconditioned at Newport News; (II—369; III—217; IV—2,865). 1902 (21/8) FV Bremen—New York—Baltimore; subsequently Bremen—New York &/or Baltimore. 1914 (Jun) LV Bremen—Baltimore (arr 1/7; dep 8/7)—

Bremen. 1914-8 laid up at Antwerp. 1919 allocated to Britain; name unchanged. 1921 MAIN (French Govt). 1925 scrapped.

79. 1900 GROSSER KURFÜRST

13,182. 170,86 x 18,99. (560.6 x 62.3). 2—2. 2S—Q8—16. (I—424; II—176; III—1,211). F. Schichau, Danzig. 1899 (2/12) launched. 1900 (5/5) MV Bremen—Southampton—New York. 1900 (7/11) FV Bremen—Suez Canal—Australia. 1912 (17/1) LV ditto (9 RV). 1914 (11/7) LV Bremen—New York (arr 21/7). 1917 (Apr) seized by USA at New York; AEOLUS (US Govt). 1922 CITY OF LOS ANGELES (Los Angeles SS Co). 1924 SR geared turbines. 1937 (Feb) scrapped in Japan.

80. (1900) MAINZ

3,204. 93,35 x 12,80. (306.3 x 42.0). 1—2. 2S—T6—13. (II—20; III—793). J.C. Tecklenborg, Geestemünde. 1897 (15/5) launched. 1897 (May) MV Bremen—Rio de Janeiro—Santos. 1900 (Aug) FV Bremen—Baltimore. 1900 (Sep) LV ditto (2 RV). 1900 (10/11) FV Bremen—New York (1 RV). 1912 LYDIE (Belgian). 1928 (Mar) scrapped in Holland.

81. (1900) COBLENZ

3,169. 93,26 x 12,80. (306.0 x 42.0). 1—2. 2S—T6—13. (II—24; III—700). Blohm & Voss, Hamburg. 1897 (18/3) launched. 1897 (Aug) MV Bremen—Rio de Janeiro—Santos. 1900 (1/9) FV Bremen—Baltimore. 1900 (11/10) LV ditto (2 RV). 1900 (22/11) FV Bremen—Philadelphia—Baltimore (1 RV). 1917 seized at Manila; renamed SACHEM. 1920 CUBA (Pacific Mail). 1923 (8/9) wrecked in Santa Barbara Channel, California.

82. 1900 PRINZESS IRENE
(1923) BREMEN (III)
(1928) KARLSRUHE (II)

10,881. 159,55 x 18,35. (523.5 x 60.2). 2—2. 2S—Q8—15. (I—240; II—162; III—1,954). AG Vulcan, Stettin. 1900 (19/6) launched for Far East service. 1900 (9/9) MV Bremen—Southampton—Cherbourg—New York (1 RV). 1900 (31/10) FV Bremen—Suez Canal—Far East (7 RV). 1903 (30/4) FV Genoa—Naples—New York. 1910 (6/4) stranded on Long Island, NY. 1910 refloated; repaired at Newport News. 1914 (9/7) LV Genoa—Naples—New York (arr 22/7). 1917 (Apr) seized by USA at New York; POCAHONTAS (US Govt). 1921 (26/2) FV for US Mail (c), New York—Naples—Genoa (2 RV); (cabin 350; III—900). 1921 (22/5) 3rd voy New York—Gibraltar, where laid up with machinery defect. 1922 bought by NDL at Gibraltar; towed to Germany where reconditioned; renamed BREMEN. 1923 (7/4) FV Bremen—New York. 1926 (Apr) cabin; tourist third cabin; III. 1927 (28/9) LV Bremen—Cobh—New York. 1928 re-

563

named KARLSRUHE to make way for new express liner. 1928 (29/1) FV Bremen—Cobh—New York. 1931 (16/8) LV Bremen—Boulogne—Galway—Halifax—New York—Havana—Vera Cruz—Tampico. 1932 (Jun) FV Bremen—Halifax—Galveston. 1932 (20/8) LV Bremen—Galveston. 1932 scrapped at Bremerhaven.

83. (1900) TRIER (I)

3,168. 94,05 x 12,83. (308.6 x 42.1). 1—2. 2S—T6—13. (II—20; III—700). G. Seebeck AG, Bremerhaven. 1898 (5/6) launched. 1898 (10/6) MV Bremen—Rio de Janeiro—Santos. 1900 (10/10) FV Bremen—New York. 1901 (1/12) LV ditto (2 RV). 1902 (6/7) wrecked near Langosteira Point, Spain.

84. 1900 WÜRZBURG

4,985. 122,58 x 14,35. (402.2 x 47.1). 1—2. S—T3—12. (II—31; III—1,012). Bremer Vulkan, Vegesack. 1900 (25/9) launched. 1900 (8/12) MV Bremen—Baltimore (1 RV). 1901 (30/1) FV Bremen—Galveston (1 RV). 1901 (2/5) FV Hamburg—Suez Canal—Far East. 1903 (Oct) LV ditto. 1904 (23/4) FV Bremen—S America. 1906 (13/2) FV Bremen—New York. 1907 (12/3) LV ditto (3 RV). Subsequently to S America. 1914 (30/5) LV Bremen—S America. 1916 seized by Portugal in Cape Verde Is; SAO VICENTE (Portuguese). 1921 (21/5) FV Lisbon—Azores—New York (Transportes Maritimos do Estado). 1921 (18/8) LV ditto (2 RV). 1925 LOANDA (Cia Colonial). 1938 scrapped in Italy.

85. 1901 NECKAR (II)

9,835. 152,18 x 17,71. (499.3 x 58.1). 1—4. 2S—Q8—14. (I—148; II—116; III—2,500). J.C. Tecklenborg, Geestemünde. 1900 (8/12) launched. 1901 (4/5) MV Bremen—New York. 1901 (8/10) FV Bremen—Suez Canal—Australia (1 RV). 1902 (12/5) FV Naples—New York. 1902 (19/6) FV Bremen—Baltimore; subsequently Bremen—New York &/or Baltimore or Mediterranean—New York. 1905 (4/11) New York—Mediterranean I; II; III carried; subsequently II—369; III—217; IV—2,865. 1910 (27/5) LV Naples—New York (22 RV). 1912 (16/5) FV Bremen—Philadelphia—Baltimore. 1914 (2/7) LV Bremen—Baltimore (arr 14/7). 1917 (Apr) seized by USA at Baltimore; ANTIGONE (US Govt). 1921 (20/3) FV for US Mail (c), New York—Bremen—Danzig (1 RV); (cabin 200; III—550). 1921 (5/5) FV ditto as POTOMAC (ditto). 1921 (10/8) LV ditto (2½ RV). 1921 (3/9) FV for US Lines, Bremen—New York. 1922 (1/3) LV ditto (4½ RV). 1928 scrapped in Holland.

86. 1901 KRONPRINZ WILHELM

14,908. 194,24 x 20,20. (637.3 x 66.3). 4—2. 2S—Q(12)—22. (I—367; II—340; III—1,054). AG Vulcan, Stettin. 1901 (30/3) launched. 1901

(17/9) MV Bremen—Southampton—Cherbourg—New York. 1902 (Sep) record voyage Cherbourg—Sandy Hook. 1914 (21/7) LV Bremen—Southampton—New York (arr 29/7). 1914 (3-4/8) escaped from New York; acted as commerce raider. 1915 (10/4) interned at Newport News. 1916 (Oct) escorted to Philadelphia. 1917 (Apr) seized by USA at Philadelphia; VON STEUBEN (US Govt). 1919 ditto (USSB). 1923 scrapped.

87. 1901 CASSEL
7,543. 130,72 x 16,55. (428.9 x 54.3). 1—2. 2S—T6—13. (II—140; III—1,938). J.C. Tecklenborg, Geestemünde. 1901 (31/7) launched. 1901 (26/10) MV Bremen—New York. 1902 (26/6) FV Bremen—Baltimore. 1910 (17/11) FV Bremen—Philadelphia—Galveston. 1911 (7/10) FV Bremen—Cape Town—Australia (3 RV). 1913 (8/10) FV Bremen—Boston. 1914 (14/5) FV Bremen—New York—Philadelphia—Galveston. 1914 (Aug) laid up in Germany. 1919 MARECHAL GALLIENI (Messageries Maritimes). 1926 scrapped at La Seyne.

88. 1901 BRESLAU
7,524. 130,84 x 16,55. (429.3 x 54.3). 1—2. 2S—Q8—13. (II—60; III—1,660). Bremer Vulkan, Vegesack. 1901 (14/8) launched. 1901 (23/11) MV Bremen—New York. 1902 (3/4) FV Bremen—Baltimore. 1903 (10/9) FV Bremen—Baltimore—Galveston. 1910 (24/3) FV Bremen—Philadelphia. 1914 (6/5) FV Bremen—Boston—New Orleans. 1914 (8/7) LV Bremen—Emden—Boston—New York (arr 24/7)—New Orleans. 1917 (Apr) seized by USA at New Orleans; BRIDGEPORT (US Navy transport). 1943 LARKSPUR (US hospital ship). 1946 BRIDGEPORT (US Army transport). 1948 scrapped.

89. 1902 CHEMNITZ
7,542. 130,51 x 16,55. (428.2 x 54.3). 1—2. 2S—T6—13. (II—129; III—1,935). J.C. Tecklenborg, Geestemünde. 1901 (27/11) launched. 1902 (21/3) MV Bremen—Baltimore. 1902 (30/11) FV Bremen—New York—Galveston. 1910 (1/12) FV Bremen—Philadelphia—Baltimore. 1914 (11/6) LV Bremen—New York—Philadelphia—Galveston. 1914 (Aug) laid up at Bremen. 1919 surrendered to Britain; name unchanged. 1923 (Nov) scrapped in Holland.

90. 1902 BRANDENBURG
7,532. 130,84 x 16,55. (429.3 x 54.3). 1—2. 2S—Q8—13. (II—60; III—1,660). Bremer Vulkan, Vegesack. 1901 (21/12) launched. 1902 (22/3) MV Bremen—New York. 1902 (1/5) FV Bremen—Baltimore. Subsequently Bremen—New York &/or Baltimore. 1910 (14/7) FV Bremen—Philadelphia. 1914 (23/7) LV Bremen—Philadelphia (arr 5/8)—Trondhjem (Norway), where interned. 1919 surrendered to Britain; name unchanged.

1922 HECUBA (Alfred Holt). 1922 (Jul) run down by MAID OF MILOS (Byron) when anchored at Constantinople. 1925 scrapped.

91. 1903 ZIETEN

8,066. 136,91 x 16,88. (449.2 x 55.4). 1—2. 2S—T6—14. (I—104; II—97; III—1,700). F. Schichau, Danzig. 1902 (12/7) launched. 1903 (25/1) MV Bremen—New York (1 RV). 1903 (24/3) FV Bremen—Suez Canal—Far East (12 RV). 1903 (25/11) FV Bremen—Suez Canal—Australia. 1907 (14/10) resumed Bremen—New York. 1911 (4/3) LV ditto (6 RV). 1912 (23/2) FV Hamburg—Portland (1 RV). 1912 (13/4) FV Hamburg—Quebec—Montreal (1 RV). 1914 (6/5) sailed Bremen—Suez Canal—Australia (15th RV). 1914 (5/8) took refuge at Mozambique. 1916 seized by Portugal; TUNGUE (Portuguese). 1917 (27/11) torpedoed and sunk by German submarine in Mediterranean.

92. (1903) KÖNIG ALBERT

10,643. 152,18 x 18,35. (499.3 x 60.2). 2—2. 2S—Q8—15. (I—227; II—119; III—1,799). AG Vulcan, Stettin. 1899 (24/6) launched. 1899 4/10) MV Hamburg—Suez Canal—Far East (8 RV). 1903 (14/3) Bremen—Cherbourg—New York. 1903 (16/4) FV Genoa—Naples—New York. 1903-14 mainly ditto. 1914 (11/6) LV ditto. 1914 (Aug) took refuge in Italy. 1915 (May) seized by Italy ; FERDINANDO PALASCIANO (hospital ship). 1920 ditto (NGI (c)). 1920 (15/6) FV Genoa—Naples—New York. 1921 (13/4) LV ditto (6 RV). 1922 ITALIA (floating exhibition ship). 1926 scrapped in Italy.

93. 1903 KAISER WILHELM II (II)

19,361. 208,56 x 22,03. (684.3 x 72.3). 4—3. 2S—Q(16)—23. (I—775; II—343; III—770). AG Vulcan, Stettin. 1902 (12/8) launched. 1903 (14/4) MV Bremen—Southampton—Cherbourg—New York. 1904 record voyage Cherbourg—Sandy Hook. 1906 (Sep) record voyage Sandy Hook —Eddystone. 1914 (28/7) LV Bremen—Southampton—Cherbourg—New York (arr 5/8). 1917 (Apr) seized by USA at New York; AGAMEM-NON (US Govt). 1919 ditto (USSB). 1927 MONTICELLO (USSB). 1940 scrapped at Baltimore.

94. (1904) PRINCESS ALICE *(sic)*

10,911. 159,55 x 18,32. (523.5 x 60.1). 2—2. 2S—Q8—15. (I—255; II—115; III—1,666). AG Vulcan, Stettin. Planned as Hapag BORUSSIA; later TEUTONIA. 1900 (14/9) launched as KIAUTSCHOU (Hapag). 1900 (25/12) MV Hamburg—Far East. Subsequently ditto except:- 1902 (2/5) FV Hamburg—Southampton—Cherbourg—New York (1 RV). 1904 PRINCESS ALICE (NDL). 1904 (22/3) FV Bremen—New York. 1904 (30/7) LV ditto (5 RV). 1904 (31/8) FV Bremen—Suez Canal—Far East.

1905-14 mainly ditto. 1905 (9/5) resumed Bremen—Cherbourg—New York. 1910 (14/5) LV Bremen—New York (11 RV). 1914 (25/6) LV Bremen—Far East. 1914 (Aug) sheltered at Cebu, Philippine Is. 1917 (Apr) seized by USA; PRINCESS MATOIKA (US Govt). 1921 (20/1) FV for US Mail (c), New York—Naples—Genoa (10,421 tons; cabin 350; III—500). 1921 (17/5) LV Genoa—Naples—Boston—New York (3 RV). 1921 (14/6) FV New York—Bremen (2 RV). 1921 (15/9) FV ditto (US Lines). 1922 (6/2) LV New York—Queenstown—Bremen—Danzig (4 RV); renamed PRESIDENT ARTHUR. 1922 (27/5) FV New York—Queenstown—Bremen. 1923 (18/10) LV Bremen—Southampton—Cherbourg—New York (11 RV). 1925 PRESIDENT ARTHUR (American Palestine). 1925 (12/3) FV New York—Naples—Haifa (dep 17/4)—Naples—Halifax—New York. 1925 (19/7) LV ditto (3 RV). 1925 CITY OF HONOLULU (Los Angeles SS Co). 1930 (25/5) damaged by fire at Honolulu; returned to Los Angeles; laid up. 1933 scrapped in Japan.

95. (1905) GNEISENAU

8,081. 138,34 x 16,96. (453.9 x 55.7). 1—2. 2S—T6—14. (I—124; II—116; III—1,862). AG Vulcan, Stettin. 1903 (1/4) launched. 1903 (2/9) MV Bremen—Suez Canal—Australia. 1904 (6/7) FV Bremen—Suez Canal—Far East (7 RV). 1905 (18/3) FV Bremen—New York. 1909 (3/4) LV ditto (10 RV). 1914 (29/7) sailed Bremen—Australia (17th RV). 1914 (Aug) seized by Belgium at Antwerp. 1914 (Oct) scuttled to obstruct fairway of R Scheldt. 1917 (May) raised by Germans; docked at Antwerp. 1918 (Nov) seized by Belgium. 1919 (20/6) sold to Italy; rebuilt at Antwerp; CITTÀ DI GENOVA (Italian). 1930 scrapped at Naples.

96. (1906) SEYDLITZ

7,942. 137,18 x 16,91. (450.1 x 55.5). 1—2. 2S—T6—14. (I—101; II—105; III—1,700). F. Schichau, Danzig. 1902 (25/10) launched. 1903 (5/8) MV Bremen—Suez Canal—Far East (6 RV). 1905 (22/2) FV Bremen—Suez Canal—Australia (18 RV). 1906 (31/3) FV Bremen—New York. 1913 (15/3) FV Bremen—S America (1 RV). 1913 (3/10) FV Bremen—Philadelphia (1 RV). 1914 (25/4) LV Bremen—New York (8 RV on N Atlantic). 1914 (3/6) LV Bremen—Australia. 1914 (3/8) dep Sydney; took refuge at Bahia Blanca, Argentina; retained by NDL after Armistice; (cabin; III). 1921 (12/11) resumed Bremen—S America. 1922 (11/2) resumed Bremen—New York (FV of service). 1927 (7/9) LV Bremen—New York. 1928 (May) cabin; tourist third cabin; III. 1930 (Mar) LV Bremen—Halifax—New York (arr 12/4)—Bremen. 1931 (27/6) LV Galveston—Bremen. 1933 scrapped at Bremerhaven.

97. 1906 YORCK

8,901. 141,26 x 17,49. (463.5 x 57.4). 1—2. 2S—Q8—14. (I—108; II—112; III—1,858). F. Schichau, Danzig. 1906 (10/4) launched. 1906 (23/11) MV Bremen—New York. 1907 (12/1) LV ditto (2 RV). 1907 (20/2) FV Bremen —Suez Canal—Australia. 1907 (23/10) FV Bremen—Suez Canal—Far East (16 RV). 1908 (25/11) LV Bremen—Australia (4 RV). 1909 (20/3) resumed Bremen—New York (1 RV). 1914 (10/6) sailed Bremen—Far East. 1914 (Aug) at Tsingtao; served as hospital ship in Graf von Spee's squadron; later interned at Valparaiso; retained by NDL after Armistice; (cabin; III). 1922 (11/3) FV Bremen—New York. 1927 (Apr) cabin; tourist third cabin; III. 1930 (20/9) LV ditto. 1932 (1/6) LV Galveston—Bremen. 1933 scrapped at Elbing.

98. KRONPRINZESSIN CECILIE

19,400. 208,89 x 22,00. (685.4 x 72.2). 4—3. 2S—Q(16)—23. (I—617; II—326; III—798). AG Vulcan, Stettin. 1906 (1/12) launched. 1907 (6/8) MV Bremen—Southampton—Cherbourg—New York. 1914 (14/7) LV ditto. 1914 (28/7) sailed New York—Bremen but returned to Boston. 1917 (Apr) seized by USA; MOUNT VERNON (US transport). 1918 (5/9) torpedoed by German submarine in N Atlantic but reached port (36). 1919 onwards laid up. 1920 MOUNT VERNON (USSB). 1940 scrapped at Baltimore.

99. (1908) BÜLOW

9,028. 140,93 x 17,55. (462.4 x 57.6). 1—2. 2S—Q8—14. (I—108; II—106; III—1,828). J.C. Tecklenborg, Geestemünde. 1906 (21/4) launched. 1906 (26/9) MV Bremen—Suez Canal—Far East (18 RV). 1907 (23/1) FV Bremen—Suez Canal—Australia (3 RV). 1908 (11/1) FV Bremen—New York. 1913 (25/1) LV ditto (5 RV). 1914 (23/7) sailed Bremen—Far East; took refuge in Portugal. 1916 seized by Portugal; TRAS-OS-MONTES. 1922 laid up at Lisbon. 1924 NYASSA (Cia Nacional). 1940 (14/11) arr Lisbon from Mozambique. 1940 (Nov) FV Lisbon—New York (dep 10/12)—Lisbon. 1944 (17/9) LV Lisbon—Philadelphia (13 RV on N Atlantic). 1951 scrapped at Blyth.

100. 1908 LÜTZOW

8,818. 140,90 x 17,55. (462.3 x 57.6). 1—2. 2S—Q8—14. (I—104; II—104; III—1,700). AG Weser, Bremen. 1907 (17/12) launched. 1908 (11/4) MV Bremen—New York. 1908 (20/6) LV ditto (3 RV). 1908 (29/7) FV Bremen —Suez Canal—Far East. 1913 (14/6) resumed Bremen—New York (1 RV). 1914 (8/7) LV Bremen—Far East. 1914 (Aug) at Port Said; forced out and captured by British; HUNTSEND (Br). 1924 resold to NDL; reverted to LÜTZOW; (cabin; III). 1924 (14/6) FV Bremen—Halifax— New York. 1929 (May) cabin; tourist third cabin; III. 1932 (7/4) LV

Bremen—New York. 1933 scrapped in Germany.

101. 1908 DERFFLINGER

9,060. 141,11 x 17,58. (463.0 x 57.7). 1—2. 2S—Q8—14. (I—104; II—104; III—1,919). F. Schichau, Danzig. 1907 (9/11) launched. 1908 (9/5) MV Bremen—New York (1 RV). 1908 (1/7) FV Bremen—Suez Canal—Far East. 1914 (30/4) ditto. 1914 (Aug) at Port Said; forced out and captured by British; HUNTSGREEN (Br). 1923 DERFFLINGER (NDL); (cabin; III). 1923 (20/9) resumed Bremen—New York. 1927 (Feb) cabin; tourist third cabin; III. 1928 (17/3) LV ditto. 1928 (3/5) LV Bremen—Halifax—Galveston. 1932 scrapped at Bremerhaven.

102. 1908 PRINZ FRIEDRICH WILHELM

17,082. 179,85 x 20,81. (590.1 x 68.3). 2—2. 2S—Q8—17. (I—416; II—338; III—1,726). J.C. Tecklenborg, Geestemünde. Laid down as WASHING-TON. 1907 (21/10) launched as PRINZ FRIEDRICH WILHELM. 1908 (6/6) MV Bremen—Southampton—Cherbourg—New York. 1914 (13/6) LV ditto. 1914 (Aug) took refuge at Odda, Norway, during pleasure cruise. 1919 (31/3) surrendered to Britain; chartered by US Navy Dept. 1920 (14/7) FV for Can Pac (c), Liverpool—Quebec as PRINZ FRIEDRICH WILHELM. (See Canadian Pacific - 159).

103. (1908) SCHARNHORST

8,131. 138,22 x 17,00. (453.5 x 55.8). 1—2. 2S—T6—14. (I—114; II—115; III—1,800). J.C. Tecklenborg, Geestemünde. 1904 (14/5) launched. 1904 (31/8) MV Bremen—Suez Canal—Australia. 1905 (25/5) FV Hamburg —Suez Canal—Far East (3 RV). 1908 (5/12) FV Bremen—New York. 1914 (21/2) LV ditto (5 RV). 1914 (8/4) LV Bremen—Australia (19 RV). 1919 seized by France at Cherbourg while in prisoner exchange service. 1921 LA BOURDONNAIS (CGT); (cabin 122; III—500). 1921 (2/4) FV Havre—New York. 1923 (20/1) LV ditto. 1923 (3/3) FV Bordeaux—New York. 1931 (31/1) LV Bordeaux—Vigo—Halifax—New York. 1934 scrapped at Genoa.

104. (1909) ROON

8,022. 138,28 x 17,00. (453.7 x 55.8). 1—2. 2S—T6—14. (I—109; II—102; III—1,700). J.C. Tecklenborg, Geestemünde. 1902 (1/11) launched. 1903 (15/4) MV Bremen—Suez Canal—Far East. 1908 (19/2) FV Bremen—Suez Canal—Australia (10 RV). 1909 (2/3) FV Bremen—New York. 1911 (5/10) LV Hamburg—Far East (14 RV). 1913 (6/7) LV Bremen—New York (9 RV). 1914 (1/7) sailed Bremen—Australia. 1914 took refuge at Tjilatjap, Java. 1919 surrendered to Britain. 1920 CONSTANTINOU-POLIS (Greek). 1925 (May) scrapped in Germany.

105. **1909 BERLIN (II)**

17,324. 179,88 x 21,24. (590.2 x 69.7). 2—2. 2S—Q8—17. (I—266; II—246; III—2,700). AG Weser, Bremen. 1908 (7/11) launched. 1909 (1/5) MV Bremen—Southampton—Cherbourg—New York. 1909 (15/5) FV New York—Naples—Genoa. 1914 (14/5) LV Genoa—Naples—New York. 1914 (4/6) FV New York—Bremen. 1914 (18/7) LV ditto. 1914 (Aug) minelayer. 1914 (26/10) one of BERLIN's mines sank British battleship AUDACIOUS. 1914 (17/11) interned at Trondhjem, Norway. 1919 surrendered to Britain; name retained; trooping duties to India under P&O management. 1920 (Nov) sold to White Star; refitted at Portsmouth; ARABIC; 16,786 tons. 1921 (7/9) FV Southampton—Cherbourg—New York (1 voy). 1921 (20/9) FV New York—Naples—Genoa. 1923 (Oct) LV Genoa—Naples—Boston—New York. 1924 (Aug) cabin 500; III—1,200. 1924 (16/8) FV Hamburg—Southampton—Cherbourg—Halifax—New York. 1926 (11/10) LV ditto. 1926 (30/10) FV for Red Star (c), New York —Plymouth—Cherbourg—Antwerp. 1927 (Apr) funnels repainted in Red Star colours. 1929 (27/12) LV Antwerp—Southampton—Cherbourg— New York. 1930 (11/1) FV New York—Cobh—Liverpool (White Star); (cabin 177, tourist 319; III—823). 1930 (15/3) FV Liverpool—Cobh—New York. 1930 (16/7) LV ditto (5 RV); laid up. 1931 (Dec) scrapped at Genoa.

106. **1909 GEORGE WASHINGTON**

25,570. 213,07 x 23,83. (699.1 x 78.2). 2—4. 2S—Q8—18. (I—520; II—377; III—2,000). AG Vulcan, Stettin. 1908 (10/11) launched. 1909 (12/6) FV Bremen—Southampton—Cherbourg—New York. 1914 (25/7) LV ditto (New York arr 3/8). 1917 (6/4) seized by USA; GEORGE WASHING- TON (US Navy). 1919 ditto (Army transport). 1919 (Mar) carried President Wilson to France for Versailles Conference. 1920 GEORGE WASHINGTON (USSB). 1921 ditto (US Mail) (c); 23,788 tons; (I—573; II—442; III—1,485). 1921 (3/8) FV New York—Plymouth—Cherbourg— Bremen (dep 17/8)—Southampton—Cherbourg—New York (1 RV). 1921 (3/9) FV ditto for US Lines. 1926 (Jul) I; II; tourist; III. 1928 (Jan) cabin; tourist; III. 1929 (11/12) FV New York—Plymouth—Cherbourg— Hamburg. 1931 (22/9) LV ditto. 1931 (6/10) LV Hamburg—Southamp- ton—Cherbourg—New York (arr 16/10). 1932 (29/8) towed to Patuxent River, Maryland; laid up. 1940 CATLIN (US Navy transport). 1941 ditto (British); reverted to GEORGE WASHINGTON. 1942 ditto (US). 1942 (Jun)-1943 (Apr) extensively rebuilt at Brooklyn; converted to oil fuel; one funnel. 1943 US Army transport. 1947 (Mar) serious fire at New York; laid up at Baltimore. 1951 (17/1) gutted by fire at Baltimore; scrapped.

107. **(1913) KLEIST**

8,950. 141,26 x 17,52. (463.5 x 57.5). 1—2. 2S—Q8—14. (I—104; II—104; III—1,700). F. Schichau, Danzig. 1906 (3/12) launched. 1907 (17/4) MV

Bremen—Suez Canal—Australia (1 RV). 1907 (18/12) FV Bremen—Suez Canal—Far East (15 RV). 1913 (22/2) FV Bremen—New York. 1913 (9/4) LV ditto (2 RV). 1913 (7/5) resumed Bremen—Australia (1 RV). 1913 (3/9) resumed Bremen—Far East. 1914 (13/5) LV ditto (3 RV). 1919 surrendered to Britain; name unchanged. 1921 YOSHINO MARU (Jap). 1944 (1/7) sunk by Allied submarine off Luzon Island, Philippines.

COLUMBUS (I)
34,351. 1913 (17/12) launched. Never commissioned by NDL - see HOMERIC (White Star).

MÜNCHEN (II)
19,000. Never commissioned by NDL - see OHIO (RMSP).

108. 1922 SIERRA NEVADA
(1932) MADRID

8,753. 133,95 x 17,28. (439.5 x 56.7). 2—2. 2S—T6—14. (cabin 221; III—416). Vulcan Werke, Stettin. 1922 (2/5) launched for S American service. 1922 (16/9) MV Bremen—New York (2 RV). 1925 MADRID (NDL S American service). 1932 (14/7) FV Bremen—Southampton—New York (1 RV). 1935 MADRID (Hamburg S American). 1941 (9/12) sunk by air attack off Den Helder, Holland.

109. 1923 SIERRA VENTANA

11,452. 149,58 x 18,83. (490.8 x 61.8). 2—2. 2S—T6—15. (Cabin 401; III—712). Bremer Vulkan, Vegesack. 1923 (16/5) launched for S American service. 1923 (8/9) MV Bremen—New York. 1926 (May) cabin; tourist third cabin; III. 1932 (17/3) LV ditto (21 RV). 1935 SARDEGNA (Italia). 1937 ditto (Lloyd Triestino). 1940 (29/12) torpedoed and sunk by Greek submarine PROTEUS near Saseno, Albania.

110. 1923 MÜNCHEN (III)
(1931) GENERAL VON STEUBEN

13,325. 160,58 x 19,81. (526.9 x 65.0). 2—2. 2S—T6—15. (I—171; II—350; III—558). Vulcan Werke, Stettin. 1922 (25/11) launched. 1923 (21/6) MV Bremen—New York. 1930 (30/1) LV ditto (New York arr 10/2). 1930 (11/2) gutted by fire at New York; sank in Hudson River; refloated; patched up at Brooklyn. 1930 (8/5) sailed New York—Bremen in ballast; rebuilt; (cabin 214; tourist 358; III—221); converted to oil fuel; renamed GENERAL VON STEUBEN; 14,690 tons. 1931 (5/2) FV Bremen—Southampton—New York. 1934 (16/11) LV Bremen—New York. 1938 STEUBEN (NDL cruise ship). 1939 accommodation ship at Kiel. 1945 (10/2) torpedoed and sunk by Russian submarine S.13 in Baltic (3,000).

111. 1924 STUTTGART

13,367. 160,61 x 19,81. (537.0 x 65.0). 2—2. 2S—T6—15. (I—171; II—338; III—594). Vulcan Werke, Stettin. 1923 (31/7) launched. 1924 (15/1) MV Bremen—New York. 1927 (Nov) cabin; tourist third cabin; III. 1937 (Sep) LV Bremen—New York (dep 26/9)—Bremen. 1938 STUTTGART (Deutsche Arbeitsfront); (one-class 900). 1943 (9/10) destroyed during air attack at Gotenhafen (Gdynia).

112. 1924 COLUMBUS (II)

32,354. 228,46 x 25,33. (749.6 x 83.1). 2—2. 2S—T8—19. (I—478; II—644; III—602). F. Schichau, Danzig. 1914 laid down as HINDENBURG. 1922 (17/6) attempted launching as COLUMBUS; stuck on ways. 1922 (12/8) launching completed. 1924 (22/4) MV Bremen—New York. 1924 (29/5) FV Bremen—Southampton—New York. 1927 (2/8) starboard engine broke down; returned light New York—Bremen; temporarily fitted with replacement from NDL cargo steamer; 16 knots. 1928 (Mar) I; II; tourist third cabin; III. 1929 (21/6) LV Bremen—Southampton—Cherbourg—New York. 1929 re-engined by Blohm & Voss with ST(SR); 23 knots; shorter funnels of greater diameter. 1929 (14/12) resumed Bremen—Southampton—Cherbourg—New York. 1932 (Apr) I; tourist; III. 1936 (Apr) cabin; tourist; III. 1939 (Jun) LV Bremen—New York (arr 28/6). 1939 (Jun-Aug) five cruises from New York. 1939 (Sep-Dec) sheltered at Vera Cruz, Mexico. 1939 (19/12) intercepted by HMS HYPERION 300 miles east of Norfolk, Virginia; scuttled to avoid capture.

113. 1925 BERLIN (III)

15,286. 167,41 x 21,09. (549.3 x 69.2). 2—2. 2S—T6—16. (I—220; II—284; III—618). Bremer Vulkan, Vegesack. 1925 (24/3) launched. 1925 (26/9) MV Bremen—Southampton—New York. 1929 (Oct) cabin 257; tourist third cabin 261; III—361. 1938 (Oct) LV Bremen—New York; laid up at Bremen. 1939 two cruises as 'Strength through Joy' ship. 1939 (17/7) boiler explosion at Swinemünde (17); repaired at Hamburg; hospital ship. 1944 accommodation ship. 1945 (1/2) sunk by mine off Swinemünde. 1948-9 refloated by Russians; renamed ADMIRAL NAKHIMOV; rebuilt at Warnemünde; 17,053 tons.

114. (1927) DRESDEN (II)

14,588. 167,63 x 20,51. (550.0 x 67.3). 2—2. 2S—Q8—15. (Cabin 200; tourist third cabin 350; III—600). Bremer Vulkan, Vegesack. 1914 (9/6) launched as ZEPPELIN (NDL). 1919 (26/3) surrendered to Britain. 1920 ORMUZ (Orient). 1927 DRESDEN (NDL). 1927 (5/8) FV Bremen—Southampton—Cherbourg—New York. 1933 (7/9) LV Bremen—Cherbourg—Galway—New York. 1934 (20/6) stranded near Haugesund, Norway, during cruise. 1934 (21/6) heeled over and sank (4).

115. (1927) SIERRA CORDOBA

    11,469. 149,49 x 18,83. (490.5 x 61.8). 2—2. 2S—T6—15. (Cabin 160; III—1,143). Bremer Vulkan, Vegesack. 1923 (26/9) launched for S American service. 1927 (22/8) FV Bremen—New York. 1928 (Jun) cabin; tourist third cabin; III. 1932 (28/5) LV ditto (4 RV). 1935 SIERRA CORDOBA (Deutsche Arbeitsfront). 1940 accommodation ship at Kiel. 1945 (May) captured by British; accommodation ship at Hamburg. 1946 (13/1) badly damaged by fire (3). 1948 (18/1) stranded and sank near Esbjerg when under tow Hamburg—Clyde.

116. (1928) CREFELD (II)

    9,573. 144,53 x 18,56. (474.2 x 60.9). 1—4. S—T3—13. (Cabin 100; III—800). Flensburger Schiffbau, Flensburg. 1921 (23/12) launched. 1928 (Jun) FV Bremen—Montreal. 1930 (24/5) LV Montreal—Bremen (9 RV). 1930 (Jun) FV Bremen—Halifax—Galveston (2 RV). 1934 rebuilt as cargo steamer; 8,045 tons. 1941 (4/4) scuttled at Massaua, Eritrea.

117. (1928) KÖLN (III)

    9,265. 144,47 x 18,50. (474.0 x 60.7). 1—4. S—T3—13. (Cabin 100; III—800). Bremer Vulkan, Vegesack. 1921 (12/11) launched. 1928 (Jul) FV Bremen—Montreal. 1930 (6/9) LV Montreal—Bremen (11 RV). 1934 rebuilt as cargo steamer; 7,881 tons. 1940 (27/6) wrecked on Swedish coast in Gulf of Bothnia.

118. 1929 BREMEN (IV)

    51.656. 273,91 [286,25] x 31,05. [898.7 [939.1] x 101.9). 2—2—C. 4S—ST (SR)—27. (I—600; II—500; tourist third cabin—300; III—600). AG Weser, Bremen. 1928 (16/8) launched. 1929 (16/7) MV Bremen—Southampton—Cherbourg—New York. 1929 (Jul) record passages Cherbourg—Ambrose and Ambrose—Eddystone. 1933 (Jul) record passage Cherbourg—Ambrose. 1934 (Apr) II became tourist. 1936 (Feb) cabin; tourist; III- 1939 (21/8)LV Bremen—Southampton—Cherbourg—New York (arr 28/8). 1939 (30/8) LV without passengers, New York—Murmansk (arr 6/9)—Bremen (arr/13/12). 1940 accommodation ship at Bremerhaven. 1941 (16-18/3) burnt out at Bremerhaven. 1952-6 scrapped.

119. 1930 EUROPA (I)

    49,746. 271,32 [285,55] x 31,12. (890.2 [936.9] x 102.1). 2—2—C. 4S—ST(SR)—27. (I—723; II—500; tourist third cabin—300; III—600). Blohm & Voss, Hamburg. 1928 (15/8) launched. 1929 (26/3) serious fire when fitting out. 1930 (19/3) MV Bremen—Southampton—Cherbourg—New York. 1930 record passage Cherbourg—Ambrose. 1934 (Mar) II became tourist. 1936 (Mar) cabin; tourist; III. 1939 (10/8) LV Bremen—

Southampton—Cherbourg—New York (dep 23/8). 1939 (Sep) laid up at Bremerhaven; accommodation ship. 1945 (8/5) seized by USA at Bremerhaven. 1945 (13/9) Bremen—Southampton—New York with 6,500 troops. 1945 (25/11) arr New York from Southampton (5,569 troops). 1945 (17/12) ditto (6,224). 1946 (15/3) New York—Bremen. 1946 (May) awarded to France. 1946 (9/12) scuttled at Havre after breaking loose during gale. 1947 (15/4) refloated. 1947 (Nov) reconstruction started at Penhoët; name LORRAINE contemplated. 1950 (17/8) FV Havre—New York as LIBERTÉ (CGT);51,839 tons; (I—553; cabin 500; tourist 444). 1954 new funnels fitted. 1961 (2/11) LV Havre—New York—Havre (arr 16/11); laid up. 1962 (25/1) sailed Havre—Spezia, where scrapped.

120. (1930) TRIER (II)
 9,415. 139,80 x 17,55. (458.7 x 57.6). 1—2. 2S—T6—13. (Cabin 100; III—800). AG Weser, Bremen. 1923 (Nov) launched. 1930 (Jun) FV Bremen—Montreal. 1930 (27/9) LV Montreal—Bremen (3 RV)- 1936 ERKIN (Turkish Navy; submarine escort ship).

121. (1954) GRIPSHOLM (M/S) (c)
 (1955) BERLIN (IV) (M/S) (c)
 (1959) BERLIN (IV) (M/S)
 18,600. 167,63 [179,78] x 22,64. (550.0 [589.9] x 74.3). 2—2. 2S—4SC. DA—16. (I—100; tourist 725). Sir W.G.Armstrong, Whitworth & Co, Walker-on-Tyne (engines Burmeister & Wain, Copenhagen). 1924 (26/11) launched as GRIPSHOLM (Swedish American). 1954 (Jan) GRIPSHOLM (Bremen—Amerika Linie, managed by NDL). 1954 (1/2) FV Bremen—Gothenburg—Halifax—New York. 1955 (7/1) BERLIN (ditto). 1955 (8/1) FV dito. 1959 BERLIN (NDL). 1966 (3/9) LV New York—Bremen. 1966 scrapped in Italy. (See Swedish American-183).

122. (1959) BREMEN (V)
 32,336. 204,96 [212,40] x 27,49. (672.5 [696.9] x 90.2). 1—2—C. 4S—ST (SR)—26. (I—216; tourist 906). Chantiers de Penhoët, St.Nazaire. 1938 (~~15/2~~) launched as PASTEUR (Cie Sud Atlantique); 29,253 tons. 1939 (Sep) scheduled MV, Bordeaux—River Plate, cancelled owing to World War II. 1940 (2/6) MV Brest—Halifax. 1940 (Aug) taken over by Ministry of War Transport; placed under Cunard-White Star management. 1945 (Jun) returned to French flag. 1957 (25/1) laid up at Brest. 1957 (Sep) BREMEN (NDL). 1957 (26/9) sailed Brest—Bremerhaven; extensively rebuilt. 1959 (9/7) FV Bremen—Southampton—Cherbourg—New York. 1970 (10/8) LV ditto. 1970 BREMEN (Hapag-Lloyd). 1970 (11/9) FV Bremen—Southampton—Cherbourg—New York. 1971 (10/9) LV ditto (7 RV). 1971 REGINA MAGNA (Chandris).

123. (1966) EUROPA (II) (M/S)

22,071. 161,53 [182,87] x 23,50. (530.0 [600.0] x 77.1). 2—2—C. 2S—2SC. SA—19. (I—176; tourist 626). De Schelde Koninklijke Maatschappij, Flushing. 1952 (18/10) launched as KUNGSHOLM (Swedish American). 1965 EUROPA (NDL). 1966 (9/1) FV Bremen—New York. 1970 (25/8) LV Bremen—Southampton—Cherbourg—New York. 1970 EUROPA (Hapag-LLoyd). 1970 (29/9) FV Bremen—Southampton—Cherbourg—New York. Detailed to cruising with occasional North Atlantic positioning voyages. (See Swedish American - 183).

M/S - Motorship.
§ - cargo steamer.

Notes;- The 8,792 ton GOEBEN, completed in 1907 for the Far East and Australian services, did not run on the North Atlantic under that name (but see ROUSSILLON (CGT)).

In spite of many examples to the contrary, even in NDL publications, the correct spelling of No 94 was PRINCESS ALICE.

FUNNEL : 1858. Black.
1881. Ditto, but express steamers buff.
1889. Buff.

FLAG   : White; blue key and anchor crossed; oak wreath in centre. (The NDL coat-of-arms consisting of a crossed blue key and anchor came into use in 1858 or earlier. It was referred to by Herr H.H.Meier during an inaugural dinner on the BREMEN (I). It has been said that the Company's well-known houseflag, consisting of the coat-of-arms on a white background, was introduced at the same time, but it seems more likely that a white pennant with 12 red and white squares beside the hoist, and with black 'N.D.Lloyd' was used until 1866, and perhaps until about 1871-3).

BRITISH & IRISH TRANSATLANTIC STEAM PACKET COMPANY

(British)

On 4 August 1858, six weeks after the first sailing of the Galway Line from Galway to New York, the 768 ton iron screw LADY EGLINTON left Galway for Quebec and Montreal. Advertisements gave her owners as the BRITISH & IRISH TRANSATLANTIC STEAM PACKET COMPANY, but this was a trade name and they were really the British & Irish Steam Packet Company, which had been founded in Dublin in 1836 and were running steamers between Dublin and London.

The LADY EGLINTON had already made two transatlantic crossings. (Chapter 38). She catered for first class passengers at 13 guineas, second class at 9 guineas and third at 6 guineas, with special through rates from Liverpool and other places, and through rates to everywhere in North America covered by the through-booking system of the Grand Trunk Railway of Canada. [1] Advertisements also pointed out that the 'American overland conveyance' started daily from St Louis for California. [2]

The LADY EGLINTON reached Quebec on 18 August 1858 with a total of 42 first and second class and 63 steerage passengers. She started a second voyage from Galway on 23 September and arrived at Quebec on 8 October with 56 first and second class and 118 steerage. These figures were not at all bad, but there was little freight moving via Galway and this was undoubtedly the principal reason why the service was not continued. Happily, however, the British & Irish Steam Packet Company is still in existence and can proudly claim to be one of the oldest steamship companies in the world.

[1] *The Times* 23/7/1858.
[2] *The Times* 12/9/1858.

1. (1858) LADY EGLINGTON
    768. 58,51 x 8,53. (192 x 28). C—1—3. I—S—?—9. Robert Napier, Glasgow. 1853 (/) launched for British & Irish SP Co. 1853 (16/6) FV for Canadian SN Co (c), Liverpool—Quebec—Montreal. 1853 (18/8) LV ditto (2 RV). 1854 became Crimean War transport. 1858 (4/8) FV for British & Irish, Galway—Quebec—Montreal. 1858 (23/9) LV ditto (2 RV). 1891-2 scrapped.

Chapter 62

1860

NORTH ATLANTIC STEAMSHIP COMPANY

(United States)

When the mail contract between New York and San Francisco came up for renewal in 1859 the United States Mail Steamship Company, which had been responsible for the section from New York to Aspinwall, retired and two new companies were formed to take it over. One was promoted by Cornelius Vanderbilt, and the other was the NORTH ATLANTIC STEAMSHIP COMPANY, of which the principal sponsors were the Panama Railroad and the Pacific Mail Steamship Company.

The North Atlantic Steamship Company bought the ex-Collins liners ATLANTIC, BALTIC and ADRIATIC on 9 July 1859 for a reported $780,000 (£156,000). The two first-named were made ready for the New York - Aspinwall service, which started in October 1859, but the ADRIATIC was held in reserve, the idea being to send her to the Pacific.

The new contract was, in fact, awarded early in 1860 to Vanderbilt, who came to an arrangement whereby he would carry the mails between New York and Aspinwall, leaving the Pacific Mail Company in charge of the leg from Panama to San Francisco.

The North Atlantic Steamship Company naturally felt obliged to seek profitable employment for the ADRIATIC. It was decided to place her in service betwen New York, Southampton and Havre, there being no question of her competing with the VANDERBILT and ILLINOIS of the Vanderbilt European Line as she invariably sailed at least a week before or after either of them.

The ADRIATIC left New York for the first time on 14 April 1860 and arrived at Southampton with 230 passengers after a voyage of 10 days 7 hours, which happened to be exactly the time taken by the VANDERBILT three weeks earlier. She made five round voyages for the Company, her eastbound passages to Southampton averaging 9 days 19 hours 13 minutes (compared with the VANDERBILT's 10 days 8 hours 19 minutes) and westbound 10 days 2 hours 30 minutes (compared with 10 days 11 hours 7 minutes). The ADRIATIC's second eastbound passage was completed in the fast time of 9 days 13 hours 30 minutes. [1]

Altogether, the North Atlantic Steamship Company was responsible for six transatlantic round voyages, the last being undertaken by the

ATLANTIC on 17 November 1860 from New York. She was advertised to make a second voyage at the end of December, but this was cancelled and she was laid up until April 1861 when, with the Civil War in full swing, she was taken up as a Federal transport. The ADRIATIC was sold to the Galway Line.

In 1865 Vanderbilt withdrew from the mail contract and the Pacific Mail Steamship Company took over both the Atlantic and Pacific parts of the Panama route. Once again the ATLANTIC and BALTIC ran to Aspinwall - for a single voyage each - until other more suitable ships could be acquired and put on the run.

[1]   *New York Herald* 1/1/1861

1. (1860) ADRIATIC
     4,145. 105,15 x 15,24. (345 x 50). S—2—2. W—P—02—13. George & James Steers, New York (engines Novelty Iron Works, New York). 1856 (7/4) launched for Collins. 1859 (9/7) bought by North Atlantic SSCo. 1860 (14/4) FV New York—Southampton—Havre. 1860 (6/10) LV ditto (5 RV). (See Collins - 25).

2. (1860) ATLANTIC
     2,860. 85,95 x 13,71. (282 x 45). S—1—2. W—P—SL2—12. Wm H. Brown, New York (engines Novelty Iron Works, New York). 1849 (1/2) launched for Collins. 1859 (9/7) bought by North Atlantic SSCo; ran New York—Aspinwall. 1860 (17/11) FV New York—Southampton—Havre (1 RV). (See Collins - 25).

Total 6 RV.

Chapter 63

1860-63

GREAT SHIP COMPANY

(British)

The prospectus of the Eastern Steam Navigation Company, issued in December 1852, stated that it intended to establish a new line of communication between England, India and China, together with a branch to Australia, by the overland route via Egypt. The necessary capital of £1,200,000 was quickly subscribed, [1] but in spite of a favourable report by a Parliamentary Committee, a seven-year mail contract was awarded to a rival, and it was evident that the Eastern Steam Navigation Company could not hope to compete with them on the overland route. Instead, they proposed to build a steamer or steamers of sufficient size and power to complete the voyage from England to Calcutta via the Cape of Good Hope in from 28 to 32 days at a speed of 15 to 17 knots, compared with the then quickest journey by the overland route of 35 days. The ships were to be capable of carrying coal for the round voyage as well as a large quantity of cargo and passengers. [2]

Isambard Kingdom Brunel, the well-known engineer of the Great Western Railway and designer of the two steamers placed in service by the Great Western Steam Ship Company (chapter 9), was commissioned to draw up plans for such a ship, which he did in co-operation with John Scott Russell, the shipbuilder of Millwall, London. He had very little data on which to work, as the largest ship afloat was the 3,500 ton Peninsular & Oriental iron screw HIMALAYA, whose tonnage was only a fraction of what he had in mind. The HIMALAYA's length was 103,62 metres (340 feet), whereas he favoured a length approximately double that figure.

The LEVIATHAN, as the ship was intended to be called, was laid down parallel with instead of at right angles to the River Thames by Scott Russell at Millwall on 1 May 1854. She was ready for launching on iron ways on 3 November 1857 but, in the presence of a vast throng of spectators. she refused to move. A sum of £120,000 was subsequently spent on getting her into the water, although she actually launched herself on 31 January 1858 during a spring tide and a strong easterly wind. Meanwhile, her name had been changed to GREAT EASTERN.

Building and launching costs had exhausted the Eastern Steam Navigation Company's funds. In due course a new concern, the GREAT SHIP COMPANY, was formed with a capital of £340,000 and the GREAT EASTERN was bought for what, at first sight, was the bargain price of

£160,000, her cost to date being about £720,000. The original intention of running her to the East was abandoned and, instead, it was decided that she should operate on the North Atlantic.

Every important feature of the ship was on an unheard of scale of size and strength. A complete double hull of iron was provided from the keel to a point about 1,83 metres (6 feet) above the waterline, the inner and outer skins being 0,91 metres (3 feet) apart. The hull was divided by nine transverse bulkheads and as most of the watertight compartments so formed were subdivided longitudinally, there was a total of 16 compartments.

1860 GREAT EASTERN 18,915 tons
The 'white elephant' of the North Atlantic.

The GREAT EASTERN had a length of 207,13 metres (679.6 feet), her length on deck being 210,91 metres (692 feet); a beam of 25,23 metres (82.8 feet); a depth of 17,68 metres (58 feet) and a gross tonnage of 18,915. She was built on the cellular principle with 30,000 iron plates and three million rivets. Propelling machinery consisted of a set of horizontal direct-acting engines having four cylinders 2,13 metres (84 inches) in diameter by 1,20 metres (4 feet) stroke, driving a single screw 7,31 metres (24 feet) in diameter. In addition, a set of oscillating engines with four cylinders 1,88 metres (74 inches) in diameter by 4,35 metres (14¼ feet) stroke drove the 17,68 metres (58 feet) diameter paddle wheels. Ten boilers were fed by over 100 furnaces.

To begin with, accommodation was provided for 300 first class only passengers. Cabins were twice as large as those of the Cunard Line. During the day, upper and lower berths folded up in pullman style. Each cabin had a washbasin and dressing table, a rocking chair and a turkey rug. A settee concealed a bath with taps for hot fresh or cold sea water. The grand salon was 19,20 metres (63 feet) long, 14,32 metres (47 feet) wide and 4,27 metres (14 feet) high.

The GREAT EASTERN had an unorthodox appearance with five funnels - two forward of the paddle wheels and three abaft - six masts and a straight stem. The mizzen was of pine so that the compass could be placed above the magnetic field, but the other five masts were of hollow sheet iron, serving as funnels for the auxiliary engines.

On 9 September 1859 the GREAT EASTERN steamed down the Thames and through the Straits of Dover into the English Channel, bound for Portland, Dorset. All went well until she was passing Hastings, when an explosion occurred in the engine room, killing six engineers and injuring a number of others. The ship herself was not seriously damaged. It had been intended that she should make a trial cruise on 17 September from Portland to Holyhead preparatory to her maiden voyage, and the Company had advertised that passengers would be carried at fares varying between £6 and £10, according to the cabin occupied. [3] Owing to the mishap it was necessary to cancel the cruise, and after proceeding on an extended trial trip to Holyhead, where she was inspected by Prince Albert and later narrowly escaped disaster during a severe storm, the GREAT EASTERN was laid up at Southampton until the following summer. It was intended at this time that her American terminal should be Portland (Maine), where the £25,000 Victoria Pier had been specially built to accommodate her. In fact, most of the principal eastern ports of the USA and Canada were competing for the ship's patronage, but it was not until almost the last minute that New York was announced as being her chosen destination, greatly to the annoyance of the people of Portland and, in particular, of the Grand Trunk Railway.

The maiden voyage of the GREAT EASTERN was scheduled to start from Southampton on 9 June 1860, but the giant ship actually left on 16 June, New York being reached in 11 days 13¼ hours at an average speed of 11.36 knots, which was below expectations although decidedly faster than the average of those days. There were only 35 fare-paying passengers at a uniform charge of £25 and 418 crew members. In New York the ship was thrown open to the public at $1 a head (reduced after a week to 50 cents), a total of 143,764 tickets being sold. Later, 2,000 passengers were booked at $10 each, excluding meals, for a two-day cruise to Cape May. As there were berths for only 300 passengers and little, if any, consideration was given for their comfort, the cruise was a complete fiasco. Homewards, the ship left New York two months after her departure from Southampton, a brief call being made at Halifax. She had the misfortune to fracture her propeller shaft in mid Atlantic and was hove to for 12 hours while temporary repairs were made. She proceeded, as arranged, to Milford Haven, where a special train was waiting to take passengers to London.

During the winter a new propeller shaft was fitted. The GREAT EASTERN sailed from Milford Haven on 1 May 1861 and as, meanwhile, the American Civil War had broken out it was no longer possible to proceed to Annapolis (Baltimore) to implement the arrangements made during the previous year, when 5,000 tons of bunker coal had been loaded as an advance consideration of the owners' agreement to make it a regular port of call. A total of 100 passengers was carried to New York, the journey time from Milford Haven to Sandy Hook being 9 days 13 hours 20 minutes.

The homeward voyage started from New York on 25 May, second class as well as first class passengers being carried for the first time. Passengers numbered 194 and, in addition, 5,000 tons of wheat in barrels were loaded.

Following the TRENT Affair, [4] the GREAT EASTERN was next chartered by the British Government to carry troops to Quebec, her complement being 46 officers, 2,079 men, 159 wives, 244 children and 40 civilians - a total of 2,568 and at that time by far the largest number carried across the North Atlantic on one voyage of any ship. Sailing from Liverpool on 27 June 1861, she reached Quebec in the fast time of 8 days 6 hours, despite the fact that she encountered thick fog, during which she narrowly escaped a serious collision with the Cunard wooden paddle steamer ARABIA off Cape Race. She returned home with 356 passengers.

On 10 September 1861 the GREAT EASTERN sailed from Liverpool for New York with over 400 fare-paying passengers - a sure indication that the public's confidence in her was increasing. Alas! On the second day out her steering gear and both paddle wheels were put out of action during a severe equinoxial gale. For 48 hours she was tossed about like a cork, much to the discomfort of all on board, but after temporary repairs to the rudder she crept into Queenstown (Cobh) under her screw engines alone. In due course she proceeded to Milford Haven, where new paddle wheels of 1,83 metres (6 feet) less diameter than the original ones were fitted.

The GREAT EASTERN made three round voyages to New York in 1862, westbound passengers numbering 135, 376 and 1,530, respectively. The first started from Milford Haven, but the others were from Liverpool and as the ship was heavily laden Captain Walter Paton, her seventh commander, decided on the second and third occasions to anchor in Long Island Sound. When passing Montauk at the end of the third voyage there was a peculiar jolt, and in due course it was discovered that she had struck an uncharted rock and had a hole in her flat bottom over 24 metres (80 feet) long by nearly 3 metres (9 feet) wide. Fortunately, the inner hull had not been penetrated, but even so it looked as if the GREAT EASTERN might well be doomed as there was no dry dock in existence nearly large enough to accommodate her. Eventually, the daring decision was taken to build a huge wooden cofferdam somewhat longer and wider than the hole, sink this in the appropriate position, fit it over the hole, make it watertight and then pump it dry. Owing to the exigencies of the Civil War, there was the further problem of finding anyone able and willing to produce a sufficient quantity of iron plates to patch the hole. However, all difficulties were finally overcome, the plates were affixed to the outside of the hull from the floor of the cofferdam and the GREAT EASTERN sailed for home early in January

1863. The repairs had cost £70,000. [5]

Advertisements in May 1863 stated that in future the GREAT EASTERN would carry first class passengers at £20-£28, second at £12, intermediate at 8 guineas and steerage at 5 guineas. [6] Sailings took place from Liverpool on 16 May, 30 June and 12 August, and on each occasion the ship anchored in Flushing Bay, Long Island Sound. The satisfactory totals of 904, 1,024 and 1,114 passengers were landed. Nevertheless, a substantial loss had been incurred on the season's working, and this, added to previous losses, was responsible for the Great Ship Company going into liquidation in December 1863.

In the following February Daniel Gooch, locomotive superintendent of the Great Western Railway, and two colleagues bought the GREAT EASTERN at an auction for £25,000, the true cost being £95,000 as they had already acquired £70,000 worth of Great Ship Company bonds.

Before dealing with the subsequent history of the GREAT EASTERN, it should be mentioned that the first transatlantic cablegram had been despatched from Valentia (Ireland) to Newfoundland on 6 August 1858, and that the service was only in operation until 1 September of the same year, when the line failed. It was not until 1864 that the Telegraph Construction & Maintenance Company put in hand the manufacture of a new cable. Meanwhile, the GREAT EASTERN had been chartered as a cable ship. She left Liverpool for Sheerness in July 1864, and in preparation for her new duties ten of her boilers and one of her funnels were removed, besides some cabins and saloons, to make way for three large tanks capable of storing the cable, which took six months to splice and coil.

The GREAT EASTERN left the MEDWAY on 4 June 1865 with 4,600 tons of cable and 7,000 tons of coal. Operations began at Valentia on 22 July, and by 1 August over 1,000 miles of cable had been paid out, not without many anxious moments. After two faults had been rectified a third was discovered. The cable parted and sank in water over $3\frac{1}{2}$ kilometres (2 miles) deep, all efforts at recovery failed and on 10 August the GREAT EASTERN returned to port.

A new company, the Anglo-American Telegraph Company, was formed in March 1866, arrangements having already been made for the Telegraph Construction & Maintenance Company to lay a new cable and raise the original one. The GREAT EASTERN sailed from Valentia on 13 July 1866, received the shore end of the cable from an escort ship and began to pay out. On the following day some hundreds of feet of cable became twisted, but by skilful handling it was successfully straightened. The remainder of the task was completed without incident and on 26 July the GREAT EASTERN steamed into Heart's Content Harbour, Newfoundland. The shore end of the cable was landed on the following day. On 2 September the GREAT EASTERN succeeded in recovering the 1865 cable, and six days later arrived again at Heart's Content, thereby completing a second transatlantic cable.

The GREAT EASTERN was next chartered by the Société des Affréteurs du GREAT EASTERN, of Paris, for a series of voyages between New York and Brest, catering for passengers proceeding to and from the Paris Exhibition of 1867. She received new boilers, steam steering gear (the first to be installed on any ship) and a thorough refit at the hands of G.Forrester & Co of Liverpool, the cost incurred being about £50,000. She sailed from Liverpool for New York with 123 passengers on her tenth and last transatlantic passenger voyage on 26 March 1867, returning from New York on 16 April direct to Brest. Her passenger complement totalled only 191, and included the young French science-fiction writer Jules Verne, author of 'Round the World in Eighty Days' and other well known books. A heavy loss was incurred and instead of completing the series of voyages she returned to Liverpool.

In 1869 the GREAT EASTERN was engaged in a spell of cable-laying from France to North America, followed by one from Bombay to Aden. For many years subsequently she was laid up at Milford Haven. From time to time attempts were made to find profitable employment, and it was announced in 1883 that a company had been formed to purchase and employ her in carrying coal between the Firth of Forth and the Thames, the intention being to load 20,000 tons of coal in sacks on each southbound voyage. [7] The scheme fell through.

In 1886 the GREAT EASTERN was chartered to Lewis' GREAT EASTERN Exhibition Company Limited and became an exhibition ship at Liverpool. Later, she was employed in a similar capacity at Dublin and finally at Greenock. She was sold by auction in October 1887 for £26,000, the intention being to employ her as a coal hulk at Gibraltar. This fell through, however, and a month later she was resold to Henry Bath & Sons, ship-breakers, for £16,000. She left the Clyde on 22 August 1888 for Birkenhead, where she was scrapped.

So ended the career of a 'white elephant' which did, however, manage to break one record in that, during the whole of her existence, she remained by far the largest ship in the world. It was not until 1899 that another ship equalled her in length, and 1901 that her tonnage was first exceeded. Many experts have expressed the opinion that she might have been a success on the Far Eastern service, and possibly even on the North Atlantic, if she had dispensed with her paddles and had been fitted with twin or preferably triple screws combined with compound or triple-expansion engines. An important reason for her failure was undoubtedly the undeveloped state of marine engines and boilers at the time she was built.

[1] *The Times* 8/12/1852
[2] *The Times* 12/7/1852
[3] *The Times* 3/9/1859
[4] A blockading vessel of the Federal fleet stopped the British steamer TRENT on the high seas and took off two Confederate envoys who were on their way to Europe. This violation of Britain's rights as a neutral resulted in a state of war-tension, which was not relaxed until the eventual release of the envoys.
[5] JAMES DUGAN: *The Great Iron Ship* (Hamish Hamilton, London, 1953)
[6] *The Times* 9/5/1863
[7] *The Times* 16/7/1883.

1. 1860 GREAT EASTERN

18,915. 207,13 x 25,23. (679.6 x 82.8) . S—5—6. I—P&S—O4& H4—12. Scott Russell & Co, London (screw engines James Watt & Co, Birmingham). 1854 (1/5) laid down as LEVIATHAN. 1857 (3/11) unsuccessful attempt at launching; later renamed GREAT EASTERN. 1858 (31/1) launched. 1860 (16/6) MV Southampton—New York (11d 13h 15m). 1861 (1/5) Voy 2, Milford Haven—New York (9d 13h 20m). 1861 (27/6) Voy 3, Liverpool—Quebec (8d 6h). 1861 (10/9) sailed from Liverpool; put back in disabled condition. 1862 (7/5) Voy 4, Milford Haven—New York (10d 3h). 1862 (1/7) Voy 5, Liverpool—New York (10d 3h). 1862 (17/8) Voy 6, Liverpool—New York (11d 3h). 1862 (27/8) struck uncharted rock off Montauk; extensive repairs necessary. 1863 (6/1) sailed New York—Liverpool. 1863 (16/5) Voy 7, Liverpool—New York (11d). 1863 (30/6) Voy 8, Liverpool—Queenstown—New York (11d 11h 30m, Queenstown—Long Island Sound). 1863 (12/8) Voy 9, Liverpool—Queenstown—New York (11d, Queenstown—Long Island Sound). 1864 (Feb) sold to Daniel Gooch and colleagues. 1864 (Jul) proceeded Liverpool—Sheerness; 10 boilers and one funnel removed to make room for cable tanks. 1865-6 laid Atlantic cable. 1867 refitted by G. Forrester & Co, Liverpool (steam steering gear fitted), 1867 (26/3) Voy 10, Liverpool—New York for Société des Affréteurs du GREAT EASTERN (c). 1867 (16/4) LV New York—Brest (ditto). 1869 laid cable Brest—St Pierre-Miquelon (Newfoundland). 1870 laid cable Bombay—Aden. Later laid up in Milford Haven. 1886 became exhibition ship at Liverpool. 1887 ditto at Dublin. 1887 ditto at Greenock. 1887 sold. 1888 (22/8) sailed Clyde—Birkenhead; scrapped.

FUNNELS: 1860 Quaker Grey.

(Information about subsequent changes is conflicting. During her career, funnels were black; also red with black tops).

NAS–8 **

UNION MARITIME

(Belgian)

Of the five steamers laid down by the Société Belge des Bateaux à Vapeur Transatlantiques (Chapter 50), only three - the BELGIQUE, LEOPOLD 1 and CONSTITUTION - were placed in commission by them. Of the remainder, the DUC DE BRABANT was renamed PRINCE ALBERT and later ran for the Galway Line, but the fifth, the CONGRÈS, was left on the hands of her builders, the Société Cockerill of Antwerp, and was laid up from 1857 to 1861. Two enterprising Antwerp businessmen, Adolphe Strauss and Auguste André, decided in July 1861 to charter her for a new service between Antwerp and New York, to be known as the UNION MARITIME.

The CONGRÈS left Antwerp on 21 August 1861, called at Havre on the 24th and six days later lost her propeller during a gale, the remainder of the voyage to New York being completed under sail alone. She arrived there on 27 September with a general cargo and 154 passengers. The second voyage started on 16 November from Antwerp and the CONGRÈS put in at Southampton on the 29th with engine trouble. She did not resume the voyage until 18 January 1862, reached New York on 4 February and sailed again on 6 March, this time for London.

This was the last that was heard of the Union Maritime, but not of the two founders. In 1867 Adolphe Strauss combined with Hiller & Co of New York to inaugurate a line between Antwerp and New York (Chapter 80), mainly with steamers chartered from the British Colonial Steamship Company. In 1872 Auguste André became Antwerp loading broker of the White Cross Line (Chapter 95), one of whose steamers was named after him.

Despite the mishaps to the CONGRÈS, the principal reason for the discontinuance of the Union Maritime was that Cockerill had the opportunity of selling her to José Yglesias of London, who had already bought her four predecessors in preparation for handing them over to A.Lopez, the forerunner of the Compañía Trasatlántica Española. She was renamed CONGRESS but is unlikely to have traded for Yglesias; under the Spanish flag she became the ESPANA.

a. (1861) CONGRÈS (c)

1,963. 87,17 x 11,58. (286.0 x 38.0) C—1—3. I—S—I(2)—10. Société
Cockerill, Antwerp. 1857 (/) launched for Société Belge des Bateaux à
Vapeur Transatlantiques but left on builders' hands; laid up. 1861 (21/8)
MV for Union Maritime (c), Antwerp—Havre—New York (arr 27/9; dep
17/10)—Havre—Antwerp (arr 3/11). 1861 (16/11) LV Antwerp—Havre
—Southampton (arr 29/11; dep 1862 (18/1))—New York (arr 4/2; dep
6/3)—London (2 RV). 1862 sold to José Yglesias, London; renamed
CONGRESS. 1862 ESPANA (Lopez). 1874 compound engines by D.
Rowan, Glasgow. 1881 ESPANA (Cia Trasatlántica). 1890 sold Spanish;
name retained. 1892 scrapped.

WHITE STAR LINE
OF STEAMSHIPS

(British)

The 1,167 ton iron screw steamer MAVROCORDATOS reached Montreal from London in September 1862. She had called at 'three or four of the ports of the Lower Provinces' and was under charter to the WHITE STAR LINE OF STEAMSHIPS, [1]of which nothing previously had been heard. However, the name White Star was already well known in connection with sailing packets, the originators being John Pilkington and Henry Threlfall Wilson, who had set up in Liverpool in 1845 as shipbrokers under the style Pilkington & Wilson and, in the capacity of agents, had handled a number of sailing ships, mostly American-owned. In 1849 they bought their first ship, the 879 ton IOWA, many others following in 1852 and subsequent years. To begin with, sailings were almost entirely to and from North America, but the Australian gold rush of 1851 made them turn their thoughts very largely in that direction. John Pilkington retired from the partnership at the end of 1865, his place being taken by H.T.Wilson's brother-in-law, James Chambers, and the style of the firm changed to H.T.Wilson & Chambers. [2]

At a lunch on board the MAVROCORDATOS in Montreal, her commander, Captain Ewen, stated that the line would be permanently established provided sufficient inducement offered. One of his guests said in reply that if the trade of the port were sufficient to support a line to Liverpool, and two more to Glasgow he did not see why it should not support another direct to London. [1] However, no trace has been found of any subsequent steamship sailings between England and Canada by the line.

In fact, only one further North Atlantic steamship sailing has been discovered by H.T.Wilson & Chambers' White Star Line. This was undertaken by the 2,033 ton iron screw ROYAL STANDARD, which sailed from Liverpool on 23 May 1866 and Queenstown two days later for New York, where she arrived on 10 June with 310 passengers. [3] She was built for the partners in 1863 and had been employed in the Australian trade, to which she returned in September 1866 for one more voyage.

John Cunningham replaced Chambers in December 1865 as Wilson's partner and the name of the firm became Wilson & Cunningham. Before this change, a second steamer had been ordered, but was sold immediately upon completion in 1866; after two changes of name she eventually became well-known as the Anchor Line SCANDINAVIA.

The failure of the Royal Bank of Liverpool in October 1877 precipitated the dissolution of the Wilson & Cunningham partnership and the sale of their ships, of which the ROYAL STANDARD was converted to sail. The truth was that Wilson's extravagance and recklessness had made inevitable the early break up of the White Star Line, the flag and goodwill of which were sold at the end of 1867 for £1,000 to Thomas Henry Ismay, whose subsequent activities are described in Chapter 88.

[1]   *Mitchell's Steam Shipping Journal* 10/10/1862.
[2]   ROY ANDERSON: *White Star* (T.Stephenson & Sons Ltd, Prescot,
      . Merseyside).
[3]   *New York Herald* 11/6/1866.

a. (1862) MAVROCORDATOS (c)
        1,167. 70,94 x 10,18. (232.8 x 33.4). C—1—3. I—S—?—9. A.Leslie & Co,
        Hebburn-on-Tyne. 1860 (/) launched for S.Xenos, London. 1862 (Sep)
        arr Montreal from London under charter to White Star. 1865 GAMBIA
        (Henry Lafone). (See United States & United Kingdom - 76).

1. (1866) ROYAL STANDARD
        2,033. 77,72 x 8,38. (255.0 x 27.5). C—1—3. I—S—I(2)—9. Palmer Bros &
        Co, Howdon-on-Tyne. 1863 (1/8) launched for H.T.Wilson & Chambers.
        1863 (23/11) MV Liverpool—Melbourne. 1864 (4/4) damaged in contact
        with iceberg; repaired at Rio de Janeiro. 1866 (23/5) FV Liverpool—
        Queenstown—New York (1 RV). 1867 converted to sail. 1869 (10/10)
        wrecked on Brazilian coast.

Chapter 66

1863

GUION LINE (or GUION & CO'S LINE)

(Fernie Brothers)

(British)

The well-known Liverpool firm of Fernie Brothers acquired the 2,266 ton iron screw HUDSON, formerly belonging to the Norddeutscher Lloyd, in 1862.She had been badly damaged by fire at Bremerhaven four years previously, towed to her builder's yard on Tyneside and extensively rebuilt - so much so that, under her new name LOUISIANA, she was shown in Lloyd's Register as built in 1862.

After two or three voyages to the Mediterranean, the LOUISIANA was despatched by Fernie Brothers from Liverpool for New York on 22 March 1862. She was placed under the management of GUION & CO [1] who had made a name for themselves as managing agents of the Old Black Star Line of sailing packets between New York and Liverpool, which had been withdrawn owing to the American Civil War. The name Fernie Brothers was seldom used and the line was usually referred to as the GUION LINE or GUION & CO'S LINE. [2]

It had been Fernie Brothers' intention to enter the Liverpool - New Orleans trade, for which they had laid down the 2,870 ton iron screw GEORGIA, VIRGINIA and CAROLINA. The unexpected prolonging of the Civil War made employment of this nature impossible, and on completion the GEORGIA joined the LOUISIANA on the New York line. She sailed from Liverpool on 7 July 1863, and from Queenstown two days later, with over 500 passengers and 1,800 tons of cargo. Her homeward departure from New York on 3 August coincided with her sale - and perhaps that of the other steamers mentioned - to the British & American Southern Steam Navigation Company, [3] which reappointed Guion & Co as managers.

The GEORGIA stranded on Sable Island in dense fog a day after leaving New York and became a total loss. The VIRGINIA left Liverpool the same day with 829 passengers on her maiden voyage to New York and for the next four months she and the LOUISIANA shared the service. The third new steamer, the CAROLINA, was launched on 27 October, but by that time preparations were well in hand for the flotation of the National Steam Navigation Company Limited, which took over all three ships and laid down others.

The Guion Line was controlled by the same Stephen Barker Guion who founded the Liverpool & Great Western Steamship Company (or Guion Line) in 1866, but there was no direct connection between the two concerns.

[1]   *Liverpool Mercury* 20/3/1863
[2]   *The Times* 8/7/1863
[3]   *The Times* 23/10/1863

1. (1863) LOUISIANA
    2,266. 93,57 x 12,43. (307.0 x 40.8). C—1—3. I—S—I(2)—10. (I—70; III—750). Palmer Bros & Co, Jarrow-on-Tyne. 1858 (12/6) launched as HUDSON (NDL). 1858 (2/11) damaged by fire at Bremerhaven; towed to Tyneside; rebuilt; renamed LOUISIANA. 1863 (22/3) FV Liverpool—New York. 1863 (12/11) LV ditto (5 RV). (See National - 69).

2. 1863 GEORGIA
    2,870. 99,05 x 12,50. (325.0 x 41.0). C—1—3. I—S—I(2)—10. (I—70; III—550). Palmer Bros & Co, Jarrow-on-Tyne. 1863 (21/3) launched. 1863 (7/7) MV Liverpool—Queenstown—New York (dep 3/8). 1863 (4/8) wrecked on Sable Island (0).

3. 1863 VIRGINIA
    2,876. 99,05 x 12,59. (325.0 x 41.3). C—1—3. I—S—I(2)—10. (I—100; III—750). Palmer Bros & Co, Jarrow-on-Tyne. 1863 (18/6) launched. 1863 (4/8) MV Liverpool—Queenstown—New York. 1863 (23/11) LV ditto (3 RV). (See National - 69).

    CAROLINA
(Did not run for Guion; see National Line PENNSYLVANIA).

STOCK LINE
(British)

In May, 1863, C.R.Stock of Liverpool sold the 1,650 ton ADELAIDE and VICTORIA, which he had acquired from the Australian Steam Navigation Company, to Gustave Stricker, a foreigner resident in Liverpool, on the understanding that he would repurchase them forthwith, this being the most convenient means by which their names could be changed.

Starting operations in 1852 with the iron screw steamers AUSTRALIAN, SYDNEY, MELBOURNE, ADELAIDE and VICTORIA, the Australian Royal Mail Steam Navigation Company failed so dismally to carry out the terms of the mail contract that this was cancelled in April 1853, the words 'Royal Mail' being deleted from the Company's title. The outbreak of the Crimean War in the following year caused the service itself to be withdrawn and the steamers were taken up by the British Government as transports. The Australian Steam Navigation Company was wound up in 1860.

The ADELAIDE and VICTORIA were products of Scott Russell & Co, of Millwall, London, builders of the GREAT EASTERN, and had an unorthodox appearance with two funnels, arranged athwartships, and four masts. Both had already seen service on the North Atlantic - in 1859 the ADELAIDE was chartered by the Galway Line for two voyages between Galway and New York, and on 3 March 1863 the VICTORIA sailed from Liverpool for New York, [1] the agents being Taylor, Tipper & Co, of Liverpool. The outward passage lasted no fewer than 25 days. [2]

Some weeks later, the ADELAIDE was renamed MERSEY and the VICTORIA became the SHANNON in preparation for the introduction of a new transatlantic service. In this connection, the 'splendid Thames-built full-powered' [3]MERSEY left Liverpool on 2 June 1863 via Queenstown and Halifax, reaching New York on 26 June with merchandise and 426 passengers. [4] Applications for freight were directed to Taylor, Tipper & Co, and for passage to Sabel & Searle, also of Liverpool. The MERSEY was advertised to return from New York on 6 July to Queenstown and Liverpool, first cabin fares being $80, $95 and $110, and steerage $35. [5]

The SHANNON sailed from Liverpool on 12 June commanded by Captain Harris, who had been in charge of her when, as the VICTORIA she had crossed the Atlantic earlier in the year. She reached New York on 29

June with 385 passengers, [6] and made one further voyage from Liverpool on 5 September via Queenstown and Halifax. [7] She finally docked at Liverpool on 1 October with 49 passengers, including 17 members of the crew of the wrecked steamer PACTOLUS. [8]

Several advertisements and a number of reports have been discovered in connection with these voyages, but in no case was the name of the line mentioned - a state of affairs that was not at all unusual at that time. The writer feels justified in referring to it as the STOCK LINE, but does not guarantee that this was how it was best-known. No trace has been found of any further sailings by the MERSEY and SHANNON. Instead, it was stated in January 1864 that the 2,500 ton LONDON, WESTMINSTER, DUBLIN and NEW YORK would sail shortly from London to New York for the British & American Steam Navigation Company Limited, (Chapter 70) and it transpires that the MERSEY had been renamed NEW YORK and the SHANNON had become the LONDON. They each made one voyage from Liverpool to New York and the LONDON a final one from London. There is no further trace of either until January 1866, when the BRAZILIAN (ex-NEW YORK ex-MERSEY) and the BOLIVIAN (ex.LONDON ex-SHANNON) were scheduled to sail from Liverpool to New Orleans for the British & American Company. The further change of name is explained by the fact that the ships had been sold to the British & South American Steam Navigation Company Limited. They were resold to the Merchants' Trading Company, of London, by whom they were apparently chartered to the British & American Company.

The BRAZILIAN was lengthened by 37,33 metres (122.5 feet) in 1878 and received compound engines, running subsequently for the Warren Line, in whose service she was wrecked near Liverpool on 4 January 1881. The BOLIVIAN was scrapped in 1875-1876.

Thus, the STOCK LINE arranged only a total of three North Atlantic sailings by the MERSEY and SHANNON, but it is abundantly clear that these little-known steamers had full and interesting lives.

[1] *Liverpool Journal of Commerce 4/3/1863*
[2] *New York Herald 30/3/1863*
[3] *Liverpool Journal of Commerce 30/5/1863*
[4] *New York Herald 27/6/1863*
[5] *New York Herald 30/6/1863*
[6] *New York Herald 30/6/1863*
[7] *New York Herald 6/9/1863*
[8] *Liverpool Journal of Commerce 2/10/1863*

1. (1863) MERSEY

    1,653. 79,39 x 11,18. (260.5 x 36.7). C—2(abreast)—4.I—S—?—9. (I—80; II—120; III). Scott Russell & Co, London. 1852 (12/11) launched as ADELAIDE (Australian RMSN Co). 1859 (30/4) FV for Galway (c), Galway—New York.1859 (30/6) LV ditto (2 RV). 1859 (Dec) ADELAIDE (C.R.Stock, Liverpool). 1863 (May) ditto (Gustave Stricker, Liverpool). 1863 MERSEY (C.R.Stock). 1863 (2/6) FV Liverpool—Queenstown—New York (1 RV). 1864 NEW YORK (British & American). 1864 (8/7) FV Liverpool-New York (1 RV). 1864 BRAZILIAN (British & South American). 1866 ditto (Merchants' Trading Co, London). 1866 (10/5) FV for British & American (c), Liverpool—New York (1 RV). 1878 lengthened to 116,73 metres (383.0 feet); beam shown as 11,64 metres (38.2 feet); compound engines by Barrow Shipbuilding Co. 1879 (30/1) FV for Warren (c), Liverpool—Boston. 1881 (4/1) wrecked near Liverpool (0).

2. (1863) SHANNON

    1,650. 79,42 x 11,18. (260.6 x 36.7). C—2(abreast)—4. I—S—?—9. (I—80; II—120; III). Scott Russell & Co, London. 1853 (/) launched as VICTORIA (Australian RMSN Co). 1860 (May) VICTORIA (C.R. Stock, Liverpool). 1863 (3/3) FV Liverpool—New York (1 RV). 1863 ditto (Gustave Stricker, Liverpool). 1863 SHANNON (C.R.Stock). 1863 (12/6) FV Liverpool—Queenstown—Halifax—New York. 1863 (20/8) LV ditto (2 RV). 1864 LONDON (British & American). 1864 (12/5) FV Liverpool—Queenstown—New York—London. 1864 (16/7) FV London—Havre—New York (total 2 RV). 1864 BOLIVIAN (British & South American). 1866 ditto (Merchants' Trading Co, London). 1875-6 scrapped.

LONDON & NEW YORK STEAMSHIP LINE

(British)

The LONDON & NEW YORK STEAMSHIP LINE, the first company to operate a service of first-class screw steamers between the ports mentioned in its title, started activities in 1863. Its principal owners were Malcolmson Brothers of Waterford, Ireland, who had contemplated a North Atlantic steamship line as early as January 1856. [1] At that time, the suggested route was from Liverpool to New York via Queenstown (Cobh).

This was not, however, the first attempt to establish a steamship service between the Thames and the Hudson as an announcement was made in 1852 that 'a company with a capital of £500,000 has just been started in London entitled the London & New York Screw Steamship Company, the object of which is to establish a line of British steamers (screw propellers) between the Thames and New York touching at Cork. It is thought that they will also call at Southampton.' [2] Nothing further was heard of this project.

In fact, the London & New York Steamship Line started operations on 8 July 1863, when the 2,058 ton iron screw CELLA sailed from Liverpool for New York via Queenstown. She returned to London, sailing again from there on 1 September for New York via Havre. All subsequent voyages began at London and a sister ship, the BELLONA, built a year previously and having meanwhile made one or more voyages to Alexandria, joined her on 26 September.

The CELLA was a product of the Neptune Iron Works of Waterford, then owned by John Horn but bought by Malcolmson Brothers in 1863 or thereabouts. The BELLONA, on the other hand, was built by Smith & Rodger of Glasgow, as was a third steamer, the 2,668 ton ATALANTA, which should have been launched for Malcolmson on 28 November 1863, but at the first attempt stuck on the ways. On the same day, Malcolmson launched their own first product, the 1,988 ton IOWA, at the Neptune yard. An advertisement at this time mentioned that the Company would be commissioning the AVOCA, UNA and UNICA of approximately the same size as the CELLA and BELLONA, [3] but nothing more was heard of them.

The maiden voyage of the ATALANTA took place in May 1864 and that of the IOWA in July, the latter having the misfortune to strand near Cherbourg in December 1864 during the early stages of her third outward voyage - apparently owing to the misbehaviour of her compass. After the passengers and some of the cargo had been landed she suddenly sank in six metres (20 feet) of water and was not refloated until the following summer. Some months later still she was sold to the Anchor Line.

Advertisements during 1865 stated that the INDIANA and MANHATTAN would soon enter service and it is not unlikely that they were renamed versions of two of the projected steamers already mentioned. In due course the MANHATTAN appeared as the 2,647 ton WILLIAM PENN, her maiden voyage from London to New York via Havre starting on 10 April 1866, but although the INDIANA was launched by Malcolmson Brothers on 6 May 1867 she never ran for London & New York.

The year 1868 saw the Company at its peak with 26 arrivals at New York. Complete details are not available, but a total of 8,295 first cabin, second cabin and steerage passengers was landed from 20 of them, an average of 415 a voyage, suggesting that the total for all 26 voyages appreciably exceeded 10,000. On one occasion the WILLIAM PENN carried 680, the CELLA 526, the BELLONA 516 and the ATALANTA 497.

The WILLIAM PENN made her last voyage as such in the spring of 1869 before being sold to the Allan Line, which renamed her EUROPEAN. In her place the Company acquired a considerably smaller ship, the 1,444 ton PARAGUAY, which had previously been running to South America. The CELLA made her last voyage at the end of the same year and the ATALANTA and BELLONA in the spring of 1870, when the 1,372 ton PARANA joined her sister ship, the PARAGUAY. For over a year the service was maintained by these two ships and then withdrawn entirely, the last voyage being undertaken by the PARAGUAY, which sailed from London on 28 September 1871 and returned from New York on 4 November.

Thus, the London & New York Steamship Line closed down at a time when boom conditions were prevailing on the North Atlantic. The principal reason was that they had greatly overestimated the cargo requirements of the London - New York trade, and had acquired a fleet of steamers that were almost the equal of the best screw steamers on the North Atlantic, Cunard and Inman lines included. The IOWA, for example, was the largest unit of the Anchor Line's fleet for three years after her acquisition by them. More than one of the Company's successors found to their cost that the London - New York trade was an extremely precarious one.

In July 1888 a company calling itself the 'London & New York Steamship Line' was advertising cheap steerage, intermediate and saloon rates to New York, Philadelphia, Baltimore, Boston and Halifax; also assisted passages to Quebec costing £2 and reduced fares to Manitoba. The agents were shown as Smith, Sundius & Co, of Gracechurch Street, London, [4] who had been for many years the London agents of the Hamburg American

Line. No trace has been found of any arrivals at New York by a steamship company of this name.

[1]   *The Times* 26/1/1856
[2]   *New York Daily Tribune* 8/6/1852
[3]   *New York Herald* 2/12/1863
[4]   *The Times* 1/7/1885, etc.

1. 1863 CELLA

   2,058. 90,64 x 10,48. (297.4 x 34.4). C—1—3. I—S—GI(4)—10. (I—16; II—50; III—500). Neptune Iron Works, Waterford (engines Smith & Rodger,Glasgow). 1863 (/) launched. 1863 (8/7) MV Liverpool—Queenstown—New York. 1863 (1/9) FV London—Havre—New York. 1869 (5/12) LV ditto. 1870 CELLA (Hughes). 1875 compound engines by J.Jack, Rollo & Co. 1881 (2/2) FV Cie Bordelaise (c), Bordeaux—New York. 1881 (10/4) LV ditto (2 RV). 1887 SHARKI (Turkish). 1891 no longer listed.

2. (1863) BELLONA

   1,914. 91,52 x 10,42. (300.3 x 34.2). C—1—3. I—S—GI(2)—10. (I—20; II—50; III—500). Smith & Rodger, Glasgow. 1862 (/) launched. 1863 (26/9) FV London—Havre—New York. 1870 (29/4) LV ditto. 1870 BELLONA (Hughes). 1882 BENBRACK (British); compound engines. 1889 (23/1) wrecked off Texel, Holland.

3. 1864 ATALANTA

   2,668. 103,35 x 10,42. (339.1 x 34.2). C—1—4. I—S—GI(4)—10. (I; II; III—500). Smith & Rodger, Glasgow. Laid down as OHIO. 1863 (28/11) attempted launch; stuck on ways but floated within a few days. 1864 (11/5) MV London—Havre—New York. 1870 (20/3) LV ditto. 1870 ATA-LANTA (Hughes). 1874 compound engines. 1880 CLIFTON (British). 1888 OCEAN (Swedish). 1897 (Sep) in port damaged (three masts); scrapped.

4. 1864 IOWA

   1,998. 96,00 x 10,36. (315.0 x 34.0). C—1—4. I—S—GI(2)—10. (I; II; III—500). Malcolmson Bros, Waterford. 1863 (28/11) launched. 1864 (17/7) MV London—Havre—New York. 1864 (6/12) stranded at Omon-ville, near Cherbourg, on 3rd outward voyage (0). 1865 (25/7) refloated and towed to Cherbourg. 1866 (Mar) bought by Anchor - 55 (qv).

5. 1866 WILLIAM PENN

2,647. 96,40 x 11,06. (316.3 x 36.3). C—1—4. I—S—I(2)—10. (I; II; III—700). Malcolmson Bros, Waterford. Laid down as MANHATTAN. 1865 (10/7) launched as WILLIAM PENN. 1866 (10/4) MV London—Havre—St John's, NF—New York. 1869 (13/3) LV London—Havre—New York (18 RV). 1869 EUROPEAN (Allan); employed as extra steamer, Liverpool—Quebec—Montreal. 1872 EUROPEAN (Hughes). 1874 (Jul) FV Liverpool—Quebec—Montreal. 1874 (Oct) LV ditto (2 RV). 1875 broke her back when entering Morpeth Dock, Birkenhead; lengthened to 99,60 metres (326.8 feet); 2,659 tons; compound engines by London & Glasgow Co, Glasgow. 1884 new compound engines by Oswald Mordaunt & Co, Southampton; owner T.R. Oswald (British). 1889-94 owners Ross Line. 1897 reduced to a hulk.

INDIANA

2,700. C—1—4. Sister ship of WILLIAM PENN. 1867 (6/5) launched by Malcolmson Bros, Waterford, but never commissioned by London & New York.

6. (1869) PARAGUAY

1,444. 76,56 x 9,75. (251.2 x 32.0). C—1—3. I—S—I(2)—10. (I; II; III—500). Palmers Iron Shipbuilding Co, Jarrow-on-Tyne. Built 1864 for River Plate SS Co. 1869 (Apr) FV for London & New York, London—Havre—New York. 1871 (28/9) LV London—Havre—New York (arr 27/10; dep 4/11)—London; last voyage of line. 1873 compound engines by London & Glasgow Co, Glasgow. 1875 (or earlier) PARAGUAY (Hughes). 1891 (10/2) sunk in collision in River Scheldt.

7. (1870) PARANA

1,372. 76,62 x 9,81. (251.4 x 32.2). C—1—3. I—S—I(2)—10. (I; II; III—500). Palmer Iron Shipbuilding Co, Jarrow-on-Tyne. Built 1862 as NORMA; became PARANA (River Plate SS Co). 1870 (14/5) FV for London & New York, London—Havre—New York. 1871 (17/9) LV ditto. 1874 compound engines by London & Glasgow Co, Glasgow. 1875 (or earlier) PARANA (Hughes). 1885 ditto (Cia Trasatlántica). 1887 ditto (British). 1896 ROSINA (Italian). 1896 PAULINE H. (French). 1906 scrapped.

NB. The chartered CORDOVA (1,417 tons) sailed London—Havre—New York (1 RV) in March 1868. A further voyage scheduled for 1869 (23/10) was cancelled.

Chapter 69

1864-1914

NATIONAL LINE

(British)

1863 National Steam Navigation Company Limited
1867 National Steamship Company Limited

The NATIONAL STEAM NAVIGATION COMPANY LIMITED was founded in Liverpool in the autumn of 1863 with a nominal capital of £2,000,000, of which £700,000 was paid up. According to the Company's prospectus, its principal object was to 'accelerate the substitution of powerful screw steamers for sailing vessels in the American and other trades, and the first step will be to establish lines from Liverpool to New York, and from London to New York, of steamers of large size and great capacity, fitted for carrying grain, flour, provisions and all other kinds of freight, and also for the conveyance of passengers. Three new steamers have been provisionally purchased, and contracts have been entered into for the building of others of about 3,500 tons each.' [1] It was stated shortly afterwards that at the conclusion of the American Civil War the Company 'would send steamers for cotton to the southern ports' of the USA. and start a service to Brazil. [2]

The firm of Guion & Co had acted as passage brokers for Fernie Brothers during the few months in 1863 that their Liverpool - New York service was in existence, and before it was superseded by that of the National Line. They were well equipped for this duty as they had built up an extensive passenger organisation in their capacity of managing agents for the Old Black Star Line of sailing packets between New York and Liverpool, a business that had faded out owing to the Civil War. Guion & Co were, therefore, glad to place their organisation at the disposal first of the Fernie Brothers and before long of the National Line.

The three steamers already acquired by the Company were the 2,266 ton iron screw LOUISIANA (built in 1858 as the Norddeutscher Lloyd HUDSON and not, as quoted above, newly-built), the 2,876 ton VIRGINIA and the 2,872 ton CAROLINA. The first two had been running on the Liverpool - New York route for Fernie Brothers but the CAROLINA was not launched until 27 October 1863, [3] when preparations for the flotation of the National Line were well under way.

The Company's first voyage was undertaken by the VIRGINIA, which sailed from Liverpool on 2 February 1864 and after calling at Queenstown (Cobh) reached New York on 21 February with merchandise and 366 passengers. The LOUISIANA followed two days later and the PENNSYLVANIA (launched as the CAROLINA) on 16 February. As the Civil War showed no signs of ending it had been decided to rename her in order to indicate that there was no political bias even if her consorts did bear Southern names.

On her second voyage at the end of March, the VIRGINIA carried 951 passengers, followed by the PENNSYLVANIA with 953 and the LOUISIANA with 869. It is not surprising, therefore, that the Company was looking for suitable steamers to charter pending completion of the three ships under construction. The British & American Steam Navigation Company had been advertising for some months that the 2,500 ton LONDON, WESTMINSTER, DUBLIN and NEW YORK would shortly be starting a service from London to New York, [4]; and as the London & New York Steamship Line already had three steamers in operation on this route, with a fourth nearing completion, there was a lot to be said for coming to terms with the National Line.

The WESTMINSTER sailed from Liverpool for New York on 10 May 1864 and back to Liverpool, but the LONDON, which left the Mersey two days after her, returned to London, from where she made a second round voyage. In addition, the WESTMINSTER made a second round voyage from Liverpool and the NEW YORK her first and only. Advertisements in the *New York Herald* showed these sailings in between others of the National Line, [5] but the British & American Company were still advertising their London - New York service in *The Times*, so it is probably correct to credit only the Liverpool sailings to National. It may be added that British & American had no later sailings to New York during the year.

First of the new batch of steamers completed for the National Line was the 3,325 ton ERIN, which sailed from Liverpool on 2 August 1864. Two sister ships were launched in the following September and November but the earlier, the ONTARIO, is seldom mentioned as she was wrecked on the Norfolk coast on 16 October 1864 during a preliminary voyage from the Tyne to Alexandria with coal and iron, prior to taking up her station at Liverpool. [6] The maiden voyage of her successor, the HELVETIA, started in March 1865, after which there appeared in quick succession the 3,308 ton SCOTLAND and the 3,412 ton THE QUEEN. The latter had dimensions of 116,36 metres x 12,92 metres (381.8 feet x 42.4 feet), and was the largest screw steamer afloat with the sole exception of the GREAT EASTERN. The 3,308 ton ENGLAND was delivered early in 1866.

Apart from the loss of the ONTARIO, the first year of the Company's existence, 1864, could be considered as very successful. Including the five voyages under charter, there were 24 westbound sailings, a total of 14,633 passengers being landed at New York, an average of over 600 a voyage. The greatest number carried on any sailing was 1,008 by the VIRGINIA in May.

The Company purchased a ninth unit, the 2,870 ton CHILIAN, which had been launched for the West India & Pacific Company, renamed her DENMARK and despatched her from Liverpool for New York on 9 May 1866. Having lost her propeller a day or two later, she returned to Liverpool, from where she sailed again on 1 August. A sister ship was launched in May 1866 as the National Line GERMANY. The Allan Line were short of tonnage at this time and two months later she was sold to them before her owners had taken delivery.

Guion & Co's control of the Company's passenger traffic came to an end in 1866, when Stephen Barker Guion started a competitive service between Liverpool and New York, and the National Line now set up their own passenger department. About a year later, on 9 July 1867, an extraordinary general meeting was called for the purpose of reorganising the Company's affairs and changing its name to NATIONAL STEAMSHIP COMPANY LIMITED. [7] William Rome continued as chairman, two of his co-directors being Thomas Henry Ismay, who later founded the Oceanic Steam Navigation Company (White Star Line), and G.H.Fletcher.

The SCOTLAND was sunk in collision off Sandy Hook on 1 December 1866, fortunately without loss of life, but the fleet soon reverted to nine units when the 3,572 ton FRANCE was completed in the autumn of 1867. She wrested from THE QUEEN the distinction of being the world's largest screw steamer in regular service. Seven ships were normally required at this time to maintain a weekly service and the Company's resources were therefore stretched to the limit when, in the summer of 1867, THE QUEEN and ENGLAND were taken up by the British Government as transports during the Abyssinian Expedition. They were absent from the North Atlantic for more than a year and when they returned the LOUISIANA, oldest and smallest unit of the fleet, was laid up. In 1869 she was lengthened by 26,82 metres (88 feet), with an increase in tonnage from 2,266 to 3,847, fitted with compound engines and renamed HOLLAND to conform with the nomenclature of the modern units of the fleet and, as likely as not, to give the impression that she was a new ship. She sailed from Liverpool on 20 April 1870 with 890 passengers and picked up a further 345 at Queenstown on the following day. [8] Apart from the Anchor Line INDIA, a lone steamer named BRANDON (Chapter 43) and two small steamers running from Liverpool to Charleston, she was the first steamship with compound engines on the North Atlantic. It is evident that the conversion was a success as the PENNSYLVANIA and VIRGINIA were lengthened and compounded in 1872, when they became the CANADA and GREECE, respectively.

The 4,169 ton ITALY, commissioned in 1869, was a straight-stemmed and compound-engined version of the FRANCE, but the 4,512 ton SPAIN and the 4,670 ton EGYPT, which followed in 1871, differed further from the

1870 HOLLAND 3,847 tons
Built as NDL HUDSON. In 1863 became
National Line LOUISIANA and in 1870
renamed HOLLAND.

1870 ITALY 4,169 tons
First straight-stemmed National liner.

1871 SPAIN 4,512 tons
First of the National Line two-funnellers.

earlier units in that they both had two funnels and four masts. During her trials the SPAIN reached a speed of 14¼ knots, and on one occasion in 1872 steamed from Queenstown to New York in the fast time of 9 days 1 hour 17 minutes. She made an even faster eastbound voyage of 8 days 19 hours 53 minutes. In April 1873 the EGYPT carried the record number of 1,767 passengers to New York.

1871 EGYPT 4,670 tons
For a time the largest ship in the world apart from
the GREAT EASTERN.

During 1870 the Company was at the height of its fame. It had in service 10 steamers of a total tonnage of 34,000 and two more were building. These 10 steamers made 64 round voyages on the North Atlantic and landed 2,442 first class and 33,494 steerage passengers at New York, the combined total of 35,936 being second only to that of the Inman Line, and well ahead of the Guion, Anchor and Cunard lines. During the year the Company carried no less than 370,000 tons of freight.

Nothing more was heard of the National Line's original intention of starting services to New Orleans and Brazil, but the VIRGINIA sailed from London for New York on 21 July 1870 and she, the DENMARK and the PENNSYLVANIA between them undertook four further sailings during the year, a call being made at Havre on three of these occasions. A regular London - Havre - New York service was started on 25 June 1871, steamers most frequently employed being the ERIN, HELVETIA, DENMARK and HOLLAND, although sooner or later all the others took part more than once. From 1872 onwards four or five were regularly employed, this being made possible by a quicker turn-round on the Liverpool route, five ships being able to maintain a weekly sailing instead of seven, as previously. The call at Havre was discontinued in 1875.

The successful lengthening and compounding of the HOLLAND, CANADA and GREECE was responsible for the decision to lengthen and compound the ENGLAND in 1873, compound the ERIN, HELVETIA and THE QUEEN in 1873-4 and lengthen the ERIN and HELVETIA in 1877. The DENMARK and FRANCE were fitted with compound engines in 1880. The most drastic internal alterations were those to the ERIN and

605

HELVETIA, both of which were fitted with new first class amidships accommodation for 72 passengers and a new dining saloon 15,24 metres (50 feet) long, extending the entire width of the ship.

During the early 1870s several North Atlantic lines drew attention to their safety precautions for preventing a repetition of many earlier disasters. The National Line's advertisement was perhaps the most reassuring of any and read: 'This Company takes the risk of insurance (up to £100,000) on each of its vessels, thus giving passengers the best possible guarantee for safety and avoidance of danger at sea. The most southerly route has always been adopted by this Company to avoid ice and headlands.' [9]

There had been five occasions in 1868-9 when the Company's steamers put in at Boston *en route* to New York. No further calls were made at this New England port until 1874, when a rumour got round that the Cunard Line was intending to withdraw its Liverpool - Boston service. In fact, it was contemplating no such thing, but the National Line had spare tonnage available and promptly announced that they would despatch ships every fortnight from Liverpool to Boston and New York in addition to their weekly service to New York only. The GREECE took the first sailing from Liverpool on 13 August 1874, but owing to the prevailing depression the arrangement only lasted until the following November. In 1877 the experiment was tried of inserting a fortnightly homeward call at Southampton by the New York - London steamers, but it only continued for a short time.

The EGYPT, SPAIN, FRANCE and ENGLAND were chartered by the British Government as transports during the Zulu War of 1879. A year later, on 13 June 1880, THE QUEEN when approaching New York in dense fog collided with the homeward bound Anchor liner ANCHORIA, which was badly damaged and at one time seemed likely to founder. THE QUEEN suffered minor damage to her bows.

Another attempt was made in 1882 to start a Boston service, this time from London, and the twin-screw TOWER HILL was chartered to take the first sailing on 5 August. [10] Instead, she was taken up by the British Government as a transport for the Egyptian Expedition and a year later was one of four sister ships running between London and New York for the Twin Screw Line. The London - Boston project was abandoned, but in its place the National Line started a service between London and Philadelphia in October 1883. [11] It was withdrawn after one sailing by the DENMARK and two more by chartered steamers. It was also in 1883 that the EGYPT made a round voyage between Liverpool and New York for the Inman Line following the loss of their steamer CITY OF BRUSSELS, and shortly afterwards the SPAIN made two more.

The Company's only attempt to win the 'Blue Riband' was made in 1884. They had been encouraged to take this step by the apparent success of the

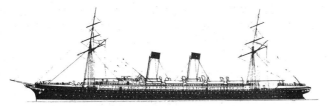

1884 AMERICA 5,528 tons
Record-breaker in point of time but not of speed.

Guion Line's record-breakers ARIZONA and ALASKA, combined with the fact that drastic action of some kind was imperative as the newest National Line ship was 13 years old and the majority of the fleet about 20. The newcomer was the 5,528 ton steel single-screw AMERICA, which was a product of J. & G. Thomson of Glasgow, was propelled by three-cylinder compound engines working at a steam pressure of 95 pounds per square inch, and had a pleasing appearance with two tall elliptical funnels, two masts and a clipper bow. Accommodation was provided for 300 first class passengers and 700 steerage, the cargo capacity being limited to about 2,000 tons. On her maiden voyage starting from Liverpool on 29 May 1884 she made a fast passage of 6 days 15 hours 22 minutes from Queenstown to New York, but her average speed was appreciably less than that of the Guion OREGON a few weeks earlier. Homewards she did even better by averaging 17.78 knots during a trip lasting 6 days 14 hours 18 minutes, but although this was a record in point of time it did not approach the OREGON'S 18.09 knot average, again a few weeks earlier. Hitherto, this passage of the AMERICA has invariably been regarded as a record one, but that is not so.

It was arranged for the AMERICA and another lone ship, the Anchor (ex-Inman) Line CITY OF ROME, to undertake a joint express service between Liverpool, Queenstown and New York during the 1885 season, it being a well-known fact that a one-ship service seldom, if ever, paid. Instead, the Russian war scare was responsible for the AMERICA being taken up as an auxiliary cruiser, but although £36,000 was said to have been spent on her in addition to the charter price she did not set sail from Liverpool. However, the joint service did come into operation in 1886 and was to have been resumed in 1887, but early in that year the AMERICA was sold to the Italian Government at a price not appreciably less than her original cost. The Company had found that her coal consumption of 190 tons a day made her too expensive to run. It may be added that whereas the saloon fare by the other National Line steamers varied between 8 and 12 guineas, the AMERICA's range was 12 to 25 guineas. The steerage fare was £4 compared with £3.16.0 by the other steamers and when required included, as customary, a rail ticket from New York to Boston,

607

Philadelphia or Baltimore.

In February 1884 the ITALY made an experimental call at Southampton *en route* from London to New York. The arrangement was not repeated, but later in the year several outward calls were made at Plymouth and there were one or two more in 1885. They had been made largely for passenger purposes, and when they ceased the carriage of steerage passengers on the London - New York service also ceased. This decision came as no great surprise as the HOLLAND and DENMARK had discontinued carrying saloon passengers in 1880 and most of the other steamers of the London service followed suit in 1881.

The year 1887 was a reasonably good one for the Company's Liverpool service, and 2,506 saloon and 17,888 steerage passengers were landed at New York in the course of 40 voyages. The rot set in during 1889, when the numbers dwindled to 1,347 and 8,120 respectively, although voyages had increased to 44. A year later the Liverpool steamerrs stopped carrying saloon passengers.

The National Line piers at New York were destroyed by fire in 1889, a cash loss of £40,000 being suffered by the Company. Worse was to follow as the ERIN went missing in January 1890 with her crew of 72 and a valuable cargo. Only six months later the EGYPT was destroyed by fire at sea, and although no human lives were lost on this occasion 600 head of cattle perished. These disasters completely exhausted the Company's insurance fund.

Having by this time decided to confine their future activities to the carriage of freight and cattle, the Company placed orders for the 5,000 ton cargo steamers AMERICA (11) and EUROPE, which were completed in 1891 to run between London and New York.

The Liverpool - New York service was to all intents and purposes withdrawn following the sailing of the ITALY from Liverpool on 2 December 1892, but there was one further sailing by THE QUEEN on 22 February 1894.

The HELVETIA made her last voyage from London in September 1892, the HOLLAND in November, the CANADA in December and the ITALY in February 1893, all four being laid up for a time in the River Medway. This was the beginning of the end of the old-timers as the DENMARK and THE QUEEN were withdrawn during 1894 and the ENGLAND, FRANCE, SPAIN and GREECE, in that order, in 1896. The only survivors were the two new cargo steamers.

Meanwhile there had been stormy meetings of the shareholders, and a take-over bid was received from the group that afterwards became the Wilson's & Furness - Leyland Line. Rather stupidly it was refused, and not long afterwards the shareholders had no alternative but to accept a less favourable offer from the Atlantic Transport Line, which decided to continue the National Line's London - New York cargo service under its existing name. Early in 1896 two members of Williams, Torrey & Field, managers of ATL joined the Board and by the end of the year all the old National directors had been replaced.

The AMERICA and EUROPE were augmented by the 3,722 ton Atlantic Transport MICHIGAN,which was transferred to the Company in time to start her first voyage from London on 22 March 1896, only a few weeks after the last voyage of the GREECE. A sister ship, the MISSISSIPPI, entered the Company's service on 25 January 1898, but both were sold to the USA in June of the same year, following the outbreak of the Spanish - American War.

During the next few months the AMERICA and EUROPE were partnered by three chartered steamers - the 4,670 ton PORT MELBOURNE, the 6,394 ton KNIGHT BACHELOR and the 5,088 ton Wilson's & Furness - Leyland GEORGIAN, pending completion of the 8,004 ton twin-screw MANHATTAN, which made a preliminary voyage from Liverpool to New York before sailing from London on 28 February 1899. The West India & Pacific Line AMERICAN and EUROPEAN also made a number of voyages in the service.

The maiden voyage of the 9,510 ton MICHIGAN (11) , laid down by Harland & Wolff as the Hamburg American BELGIA, started from Belfast direct to New York on 14 December 1899. She had been bought by ATL for their own use, but owing to the recent chartering of the AMERICA and MANHATTAN as Boer War transports her next voyage took place under National Line auspices on 4 February 1900 and she remained in their charge for the time being. All told, the MANHATTAN made seven trooping voyages to South Africa, of which the first was extended to Australia, and it seems likely that these activities may have contributed to the decision to discontinue the National Line's London - New York service. At any rate, the last sailing for some years was undertaken by the MICHIGAN on 28 September 1900. In due course this ship was transferred by her owners, ATL, to the Dominion Line, which renamed her IRISHMAN (11). In 1903 the 8,001 ton IRISHMAN (1) completed in 1898 as the Elder Dempster MONMOUTH and a sister ship of the MANHATTAN, was acquired by the National Line and renamed MICHIGAN (111), but there is no evidence that she or the MANHATTAN ran for the National Line between London and New York. From 1911 until the outbreak of World War 1 in August 1914 they took part in the Phoenix Line's service between Antwerp and New York.

In 1906 the AMERICA and EUROPE did revive the National Line's London - New York service, but this was only a short-term arrangement as they were absorbed into the ATL fleet in 1907 as the MEMPHIS and MOBILE. This seems to have marked the close of a separate service by the

National Line, but the MANHATTAN and MICHIGAN nominally belonged to the Company until completion of their Phoenix Line duties in the autumn of 1914, when they too were absorbed by ATL. The National Line then went into voluntary liquidation.

Such is the outline story of a company which met with no little success during its early years, built a series of steamers that succeeded one another as the largest on the North Atlantic, was among the first to introduce the compound engine to that trade and even if their steamer AMERICA never actually gained the'Blue Riband', she did for a few weeks hold the record for the fastest eastbound voyage in point of time. She was, in fact, long regarded as a record breaker, the time factor being then of prime importance. The National Line was worthy of a better fate.

[1] *The Times* 31/10/1863
[2] *Mitchell's Steam Shipping Journal* 11/12/1863
[3] *Mitchell's Steam Shipping Journal* 6/11/1863
[4] *The Times* 6/1/1864
[5] *New York Herald* 2/6/1864
[6] *Illustrated London News* 29/10/1864
[7] *The Times* 10/7/1867
[8] *The Times* 22/4/1870
[9] *The Times* 1874 many dates
[10] *Shipping & Mercantile Gazette* 18/7/1882
[11] *Shipping & Mercantile Gazette* 16/10/1883

1. (1864) VIRGINIA
(1872) GREECE

>   2,876. 99,05 x 12,59. (325.0 x 41.3). C—1—3.I—S—I(2)—10. (I—100; III—750). Palmer Bros & Co, Jarrow-on-Tyne. 1863 (18/6) launched for Fernie Bros. 1863 (4/8) MV Liverpool—Queenstown—New York. 1863 (23/11) LV ditto (3 RV). 1863 VIRGINIA (National). 1864 (2/2) FV of National, Liverpool—Queenstown—New York. 1870 (21/7) FV of National, London—New York (3 RV). 1872 lengthened to 119,07 metres (390.7 feet); 4,310 tons; compound engines by Laird Bros, Birkenhead; renamed GREECE. 1872 (22/8) FV Liverpool—Queenstown—New York. 1874 (13/8) LV ditto. 1874 (1/10) FV London—New York. 1896 (16/2) LV ditto. 1896 scrapped.

2. (1864) LOUISIANA
   (1870) HOLLAND

   2,266. 93,57 x 12,43. (307.0 x 40.8). C—1—3. I—S—I(2)—10. (I—70;
   III—750). Palmer Bros & Co, Jarrow-on-Tyne. 1858 (12/6) launched as
   HUDSON (NDL). (I—70; II—100; III—450). 1858 (11/9) MV Bremen—
   New York (1 RV). 1858 (2/11) damaged by fire in dock at Bremerhaven;
   towed to Palmer's yard, where rebuilt; funnels reduced from two to one.
   1862 LOUISIANA (Fernie Bros). 1863 (22/3) FV Liverpool—New York.
   1863 (12/11) LV ditto (5 RV). 1863 LOUISIANA (National). 1864 (4/2)
   FV Liverpool—Queenstown—New York. 1869-70 lengthened to 120,42
   metres (395.1 feet); 3,847 tons; compound engines by J.Jack & Co,
   Liverpool; renamed HOLLAND; III increased to 1,300. 1870 (20/4) FV
   Liverpool—Queenstown—New York. 1871 (19/11) FV London—New—
   York (1 RV). 1872 (11/9) LV Liverpool—Queenstown—New York. 1872
   (31/10) resumed London—New York. 1891 (10/3) LV ditto. 1891 (7/5)
   resumed Liverpool—Queenstown—New York. 1892 (12/11) LV
   Liverpool—New York (7 RV). 1893 sold to France. 1894 scrapped.

3. 1864 PENNSYLVANIA
   (1872) CANADA
   2,872. 99,05 x 12,56. (325.0 x 41.2). C—1—3. I—S—I(2)—10. (I—100;
   III—750). Palmer Bros & Co, Jarrow-on-Tyne. 1863 (27/10) launched as
   CAROLINA (Fernie Bros). 1863 PENNSYLVANIA (National). 1864
   (16/2) MV Liverpool—Queenstown—New York. 1866 trooping voyage,
   Liverpool—Malta—Quebec—Liverpool. 1872 lengthened to 119,35
   metres (391.6 feet); 4,276 tons; compound engines by Laird Bros,Birken-
   head; renamed CANADA. 1872 (24/4) FV Liverpool—Queenstown—
   New York. 1874 (15/9) LV ditto. 1874 (8/11) FV London—New York.
   1893 (17/12) LV ditto. 1894 scrapped.

4. 1864 ERIN
   3,325. 112,89 x 12,53. (370.4 x 41.1). C—1—3. I—S—I(2)—10. Palmer
   Bros & Co, Jarrow-on-Tyne. 1864 (18/6) launched. 1864 (2/8) MV
   Liverpool—Queenstown—New York. 1871 (25/6) FV London—Havre—
   New York. 1872 tonnage 3,956. 1873 compound engines by J.Penn & Son,
   London. 1876 (24/9) LV London—New York. 1876-7 lengthened to
   127,64 metres (418.8 feet); 4,577 tons; saloon cabins rebuilt amidships.
   (I—72; III—1,200). 1877 (4/7) resumed Liverpool—Queenstown—New
   York. 1879 (28/10) LV ditto. 1879 (17/12) resumed London—New York.
   1889 (31/12) left New York for London; went missing. (72).

   ONTARIO
   3,325. 112,77 x 12,50. (370 x 41). C—1—3. I—S—I(2)—10. Palmer Bros &

611

Co, Jarrow-on-Tyne. 1864 (3/9) launched. 1864 (16/10) sailed Newcastle—Alexandria. 1864 (16/10) wrecked on Happisburgh (Haisbro') Sands (0). (Did not run on North Atlantic).

5. 1865 HELVETIA

3,318. 113,22 x 12,56. (371.5 x 41.2). C—1—3. I—S—I(2)—10. Palmer Bros & Co, Jarrow-on-Tyne. 1864 (16/11) launched. 1865 (28/3) MV Liverpool—Queenstown—New York. 1871 (25/5) LV ditto. 1871 (11/7) FV London—Havre—New York. 1872 tonnage 3,982. 1873-4 compound engines by J.Penn & Sons, London. 1874 (14/10) resumed Liverpool—Queenstown—New York. 1877 lengthened to 127,70 metres (419.0 feet); 4,588 tons; saloon cabins rebuilt amidships. (I—72; III—1,200). 1877-86 Liverpool—New York. 1886-91 Liverpool or London—New York. 1891 (26/3) LV Liverpool—Queenstown—New York. 1891 (6/8) resumed London—New York. 1892 (8/9) LV ditto. 1893 sold to France. 1894(Apr) abandoned off Cape Finisterre on voyage to shipbreakers.

6. 1865 SCOTLAND

3,308. 114,29 x 12,80. (375 x 42). C—1—3. I—S—I(2)—10. (I—80; III—800). Palmer Bros & Co, Jarrow-on-Tyne. 1865 (11/2) launched. 1865 (2/8) MV Liverpool—Queenstown—New York. 1866 (7/11) LV ditto. 1866 (1/12) sunk in collision off Sandy Hook with bark KATE DYER (US) (0).

7. 1865 THE QUEEN

3,412. 116,15 x 12,92. (381.1 x 42.4). C—1—3. I—S—I(2)—10. Laird Bros, Birkenhead. 1865 (29/4) launched. 1865 (23/8) MV Liverpool—Queenstown—New York. 1867 served as Abyssinian campaign transport. 1872 tonnage 4,441. 1872 (21/5) FV London—Havre—New York. 1873 (16/1) LV ditto. 1873-4 compound engines by G.Forrester & Co, Liverpool. 1874 (22/4) resumed Liverpool—Queenstown—New York. 1880-6 Liverpool or London—New York. 1886 (14/4) onwards, Liverpool—New York. 1889 (25/7) LV ditto with cabin passengers. 1892 (12/3) LV ditto with III. 1894 (22/2) LV of line Liverpool—New York (cargo only). 1894 (13/4) resumed London—New York. 1894 (23/12) LV ditto. 1896 sold; scrapped.

8. 1866 ENGLAND

3,308. 114,44 x 12,95. (375.5 x 42.5). C—1—3. I—S—I(2)—10. (I—80; III—800). Palmer Bros & Co, Jarrow-on-Tyne. 1865 (24/6) launched. 1866 (7/2) MV Liverpool—Queenstown—New York. 1867 served as Abyssinian campaign transport. 1873-4 lengthened to 133,46 metres (437.9 feet); 4,898 tons; compound engines by G. Forrester & Co, Liverpool. 1874 (26/8) resumed Liverpool—Queenstown—New York. 1891 (2/1) LV

Liverpool—New York. 1891 (1/3) FV London—New York. 1896 (10/1) LV ditto. 1896 sold; scrapped in Italy.

9. (1866) DENMARK

2,870. 104,50 x 12,86. (342.9 x 42.2). C—1—3. I—S—I(2)—10. (I—70; III—200 (later 850)). Pearse & Lockwood, Stockton (engines Fossick, Blair & Co, Stockton). 1865 (7/9) launched as CHILIAN (West India & Pacific). 1866 DENMARK (National). 1866 (9/5) sailed Liverpool—Queenstown—New York, but lost propeller and returned to Liverpool. 1866 (1/8) voyage resumed. 1870 (11/11) FV London—New York. 1872-90 mainly London—New York. 1874 tonnage 3,723. 1880 compound engines by J. Jones & Sons, Liverpool. 1891 (26/4) resumed Liverpool—New York. 1892 (26/3) LV ditto. 1892 (7/12) resumed London—New York. 1894 (30/3) LV ditto. 1895 scrapped.

GERMANY

(Not commissioned by National). 1866 (16/5) launched by Pearse & Lockwood, Stockton. 1866 (Jul) sold to Allan - 44 (qv).

10. 1867 FRANCE

3,572. 117,52 x 12,92. (385.6 x 42.4). C—1—3. I—S—I(2)—10. (I—80; III—1,000). T. Royden & Sons, Liverpool (engines J. Jack & Co, Liverpool). 1867 (4/6) launched. 1867 (13/10) MV Liverpool—Queenstown—New York. 1874 (4/2) FV London—New York. 1874-96 London—New York apart from 5 voyages from Liverpool. 1875 tonnage 4,281. 1880 compound engines by J. Jones & Sons, Liverpool. 1896 (17/1) LV London—New York. 1896 sold.

11. 1870 ITALY

4,169. 118,56 x 12,89. (389.0 x 42.3). S—1—3. I—S—C2—11. J. Elder & Co, Glasgow. 1870 (2/4) launched. 1870 (13/7) MV Liverpool—Queenstown—New York. 1875 (20/5) FV London—New York. 1875-92 Liverpool or London—New York. 1892 (2/12) LV Liverpool—New York. 1893 (11/2) LV London—New York. 1894 scrapped.

12. 1871 SPAIN

4,512. 129,65 x 13,16. (425.4 x 43.2). S—2—4. I—S—C2—13. (I—120; III—1,400). Laird Bros, Birkenhead. Built in dry dock. 1871 (9/5) floated. 1871 (16/8) MV Liverpool—Queenstown—New York. 1883 (20/2) FV ditto for Inman (c) (2 RV). 1890 (11/2) FV London—New York. 1890 (23/11) LV Liverpool—New York. 1896 (31/1) LV London—New York. 1896 scrapped.

13. 1871 EGYPT
   4,670. 135,02 x 13,50. (443.0 x 44.3). S—2—4. I—S—C2—13. (I—120; III—1,400). Liverpool Shipuilding Co, Liverpool (engines J. Jack, Rollo & Co, Liverpool). 1871 (9/2) launched. 1871 (10/11) MV Liverpool— Queenstown—New York. 1883 (18/1) FV for Inman (c) ditto (1 RV). 1889 (8/11) LV Liverpool—New York. 1890 (2/1) FV London—New York. 1890 (18/6) LV ditto. 1890 (10/7) left New York for Liverpool. 1890 (19/7) destroyed by fire at sea (0).

14. 1884 AMERICA (I)
   5,528. 134,65 x 15,60. (441.8 x 51.2). C—2—2. S—S—C3—17. (I—300; III—700). J. & G. Thomson, Glasgow. 1883 (29/12) launched. 1884 (28/5) MV Liverpool—Queenstown—New York. 1885 taken up as auxiliary cruiser but remained at Liverpool. 1886 (31/3) resumed Liverpool— Queenstown—New York. 1886 (26/5) sailed for New York but returned with engine trouble. 1886 (13/10) LV Liverpool—Queenstown—New York (10 RV). 1887 TRINACRIA (Italian Navy - employed as cruiser, transport, torpedo school, royal yacht and exhibition ship). 1925 scrapped.

15. 1891 AMERICA (II) (x)
   5,158. 132,58 x 14,11. (435.0 x 46.3). S—1—4. S—S—T3—11. Gourlay Bros & Co, Dundee. 1890 (26/11) launched. 1891 (12/2) MV London— New York. 1907 MEMPHIS (ATL). 1907 (6/4) FV Leith—London—New York (2 RV). 1908 scrapped.

16. 1891 EUROPE (x)
   5,302. 132,58 x 14,14. (435.0 x 46.4). S—1—4. S—S—T3—11. Palmers Co Ltd, Jarrow-on-Tyne. 1890 (27/11) launched. 1891 (16/5) MV London— New York.1907 MOBILE (ATL).1907 (20/4) FV Leith—Antwerp—New York (2 RV). 1911 THÖGER (Norwegian). 1913 GUVERNOREN (Norwegian). 1915 (22/1) destroyed by fire off South Shetland Islands.

17. (1896) MICHIGAN (I) (x)
   3,722. 113,01 x 13,47. (370.8 x 44.2). S—1—4. S—S—T3—11. Harland & Wolff, Belfast. 1890 (19/4) launched for ATL. 1896 (22/3) FV for National, London—New York. 1898 (27/6) LV ditto. 1898 KILPATRICK (US Govt); two masts. (See ATL - 123).

18. (1898) MISSISSIPPI (x)
   3,732. 113,01 x 13,47. (370.8 x 44.2). S—1—4. S—S—T3—11. Harland & Wolff, Belfast. 1890 (29/8) launched for ATL. 1898 (25/1) FV for National, London—New York. 1898 (14/6) LV ditto (5th RV). 1898 BUFORD (US Govt). 1929 scrapped in Japan. (See ATL - 123).

18a. (1898) PORT MELBOURNE (c) (x)

4,670. 109,84 x 14,63. (360.4 x 48.0). S—1—2. S—S—T3—11. R. & W. Hawthorn, Leslie & Co, Hebburn-on-Tyne. 1892 (8/9) launched for Anglo-Australasian SN Co. 1898 (26/7) FV for National (c) Liverpool— New York—London. 1898 (6/9) FV London—New York. 1899 (27/1) sailed New York—London; went missing (52).

18b. (1898) KNIGHT BACHELOR (c) (x)

6,394. 137,15 x 15,91. (450.0 x 52.2). S—1—4. S—S—T3—11. C.Connell & Co, Glasgow (engines Dunsmuir & Jackson, Glasgow). 1894 (6/6) launched for Knight SS Co. 1898 (23/10) FV for National (c) London— New York (3 RV). 1907 SPANISH PRINCE (Prince). 1914 (Nov) sunk as blockship at Dover.

19. 1898 MANHATTAN (x)

8,004. 149,49 x 17,16. (490.5 x 56.3). 1—4. 2S—T6—13. Harland & Wolff, Belfast (engines Fawcett, Preston & Co, Liverpool). 1898 (13/9) launched for ATL; transferred to National. 1898 (31/12) MV Liverpool—New York —London. 1899 (28/2) FV London—New York. 1900 (25/1) FV London —S Africa as Boer War transport (7 RV). 1911 (5/1) FV for Phoenix (c), Antwerp—New York. 1914 (6/8) LV ditto. 1914 MANHATTAN (ATL). 1927 scrapped in Italy.

19a. 1899 MICHIGAN (II) (c) (x)

9,510. 152,60 x 19,02. (500.7 x 62.4). 1—4. 2S—Q8—13. Harland & Wolff, Belfast. Laid down as BELGIA (Hapag). 1899 (5/10) launched for ATL as MICHIGAN; chartered to National. 1899 (14/12) MV Belfast—New York—London. 1900 (4/2) FV London—New York. 1900 (28/9) LV ditto. 1904 IRISHMAN (Dominion). 1924 scrapped.

20. (1903) MICHIGAN (III) (x)

8,001. 149,49 x 17,16. (490.5 x 56.3). 1—4. 2S—T6—13. Harland & Wolff, Belfast (engines Fawcett, Preston & Co, Liverpool). 1897 (23/12) launched as MONMOUTH (Elder Dempster). 1898 IRISHMAN (Dominion). 1903 MICHIGAN (National). 1911 (22/3) FV for Phoenix (c), Antwerp—New York. 1914 (18/7) LV ditto. 1914 MICHIGAN (ATL). 1926 scrapped in Italy. (See ATL - 123).

(x) - cargo steamer.

FUNNEL: White; black top.

FLAG: Red with blue-edged white cross; 'Union Jack' in centre.

Chapter 70

1864-66

BRITISH & AMERICAN STEAM NAVIGATION COMPANY

(British)

Advertisements stated that the BRITISH & AMERICAN SOUTHERN STEAM NAVIGATION COMPANY's iron screw MALACCA and RANGOON would start a passenger and cargo service between Liverpool and New Orleans in August 1861, and that sailings would be increased to fortnightly as soon as other steamers then under construction were completed. [1]

The opening of the service was indefinitely postponed owing to the continuance of the American Civil War, and alternative employment was found for the steamers mentioned. Two years later, on 3 August 1863, the Company bought the 2,870 ton GEORGIA from Fernie Brothers, [2] who had been running a service between Liverpool and New York since the previous spring. It was popularly known as the Guion Line (or Guion & Co's Line) after the firm to whom its operation was entrusted.

Unfortunately, the GEORGIA was wrecked on Sable Island only one day after the transfer took place. It is not clear whether the other steamers of the service - the 2,266 ton LOUISIANA and the 2,876 ton VIRGINIA - were acquired from the same source at the same time but, at any rate, it could not have been for long as two or three months later this pair, together with a newly-launched sister ship of the VIRGINIA, were bought by the National Line, which continued to employ them on the Liverpool - New York route.

The British & American Southern Steam Navigation Company was still anxious to start a service to New Orleans, but the Civil War showed no signs of coming to an early conclusion. They decided, therefore, to operate a new line between London and New York and to drop the word 'Southern' from their title. Advertisements between January and June 1864 stated that the 2,500 ton LONDON, WESTMINSTER, DUBLIN and NEW YORK would start sailing from London to New York at an early date; it was announced before the end of June that the LONDON would leave Victoria Docks on 15 July. [3]

It transpires, however, that on 10 May 1864 the WESTMINSTER was responsible for starting the first of two round voyages between Liverpool and New York, and that the LONDON followed her from Liverpool two days later. They carried 662 and 677 passengers respectively. The WESTMINSTER started her second voyage from Liverpool on 5 July, but the LONDON returned from New York to London, from where she sailed again on 16 July for Havre and New York, one day later than advertised. A third steamer, the NEW YORK, made one round voyage from Liverpool to New York starting on 8th July, and that was the sum total of the Comapny's New York activities during the year, there being no evidence that the DUBLIN was employed at all. An important reason for the abandonment of the service was undoubtedly the progress of the London & New York Steamship Line. It should be added that advertisements in the *New York Herald* showed the WESTMINSTER, LONDON and NEW YORK under the heading National Line, but the British & American Company continued to advertise their London - New York service until 16 July. It may perhaps be correct to credit the Liverpool sailings as under charter to the National Line and the London sailing to the British & American.

It was announced in May 1865 that the British & American Steam Navigation Company would shortly be starting a passenger and cargo service between Liverpool and New Orleans. [4] The first sailing was taken by the ALABAMA (ex-RANGOON) on 23 September, followed by the GAMBIA, FLORIDA (ex-MALACCA), MISSISSIPPI, BOLIVIAN, BRAZILIAN and PERUVIAN, the three last-mentioned having been the LONDON, NEW YORK and WESTMINSTER, respectively. They had been bought and renamed in 1864 by the British & South American Steam Navigation Company (which seems to have had no connection with the British & American Steam Navigation Company), and in turn sold without further change of name to the Merchants' Trading Company, of London, which had chartered them to the British & American. This New Orleans service, also, was of short duration, the last sailing being taken by the ALABAMA, which left Liverpool in June 1866.

Meanwhile, the BRAZILIAN and PERUVIAN were responsible for two British & American sailings from Liverpool to New York on 10 and 14 May 1866, respectively.

The BRITISH & AMERICAN STEAM NAVIGATION COMPANY closed down after a strange and frustrated career.

[1]   *The Times* 14/5/1861
[2]   *The Times* 23/10/1863
[3]   *The Times* 25/6/1864
[4]   *The Times* 18/5/1865

1. (1864) WESTMINSTER
   (1866) PERUVIAN (c)
        1,713. 85,64 x 11,58. (281.0 x 38.0) C—1—3. I—S—I(2)—10. (I—90; III).
        M. Pearse & Co, Stockton (engines Fossick & Hackworth, Stockton).

1863 (7/3) launched as THE SOUTHERNER (Fraser, Trenhorne & Co, Liverpool). 1864 WESTMINSTER (British & American). 1864 (10/5) FV Liverpool—Queenstown—New York. 1864 (5/7) ditto (2 RV) (see text). 1864 PERUVIAN (British & South American). 1866 ditto (Merchants' Trading Co, London). 1866 (14/5) FV for British & American (c), Liverpool—New York (1 RV). 1866 (10/10) FV for Warren (c), Liverpool—Boston. 1867 (May) LV ditto. 1870 CASTILLO (Spanish). 1890 AMERICA (Stefano Rapello (Italian)). 1898 scrapped at Genoa.

2. (1864) LONDON

1,650. 79,42 x 11,18. (260.6 x 36.7). C—2(abreast)—4. I—S—?—9. (I—80; II—120; III). Scott Russell & Co, London. 1853 (/) launched as VICTORIA (Australian RMSN Co). 1863 SHANNON (Stock). 1864 LONDON (British & American). 1864 (12/5) FV Liverpool—Queenstown—New York—London (see text). 1864 (16/7) FV London—Havre—New York (dep 20/8)—London (total 2 RV). 1864 BOLIVIAN (British & South American). (See Stock - 67).

3. (1864) NEW YORK
   (1866) BRAZILIAN (c)

1,653. 79,39 x 11,18. (260.5 x 36.7). C—2(abreast)—4. I—S—?—9. (I—80; II—120; III). Scott Russell & Co, London. 1852 (12/11) launched as ADELAIDE (Australian RMSN Co). 1863 MERSEY (Stock). 1864 NEW YORK (British & American). 1864 (8/7) FV Liverpool—New York (1 RV) (see text). 1864 BRAZILIAN (British & South American). 1866 ditto (Merchants' Trading Co, London). 1866 (10/5) FV for British & American (c), Liverpool—New York (1 RV). (See Stock - 67).

DUBLIN

(Advertised to sail London—New York, but no trace that she did so).

Chapter 71

1864

COMPAGNIE GÉNÉRALE TRANSATLANTIQUE

(French Line)

(French)

The pioneer French-owned North Atlantic steamship service (Chapter 21), started in 1847, had been a dismal failure and a second attempt in 1856 (Chapter 51) was not much more successful.

Meanwhile, on 14 October 1854, the brothers Émile and Isaac Péreire founded the COMPAGNIE GÉNÉRALE MARITIME, which was registered on 24-25 February 1855 with a capital of 30 million francs (£1,200,000), an important ambition even at that early date being for the Company eventually to enter the transatlantic steamship business.

Almost at once the Compagnie Générale Maritime obtained control of the Société Terreneuvienne of Granville, Normandy, founded two years previously and already owners of 27 sailing ships as well as two small iron screw steamers, the 280 ton DIANE and VESTA, built in 1854 and employed in carrying stores and provisions to the Society's fishing stations in the French-owned islands of St Pierre and Miquelon, off the Newfoundland coast. The VESTA had become notorious on 27 September 1854 by colliding with and sinking the 2,860 ton Collins Line wooden paddle steamer ARCTIC near Cape Race. The French steamer was homeward bound at the time with a passenger complement of 147 and a crew of 50, of whom 13 were lost. She was able to proceed under her own steam to St John's, Newfoundland, for repairs.

By the end of May 1856 CGM had accumulated a massive fleet of 76 sailing ships, departures taking place from Havre or Bordeaux to many parts of the world including Australia, Réunion, the West Indies, Mexico, Argentina, Chile, Peru and California. Four additional steamers had been completed - the 650 ton DANUBE, REINE MATHILDE, MARIE STUART and SEINE ET RHONE, which were placed in service between Antwerp, Havre, Bordeaux, Spanish and Portuguese ports, Algiers and Marseilles. Two further steamers, the 427 ton PARIS and HAMBOURG, were detailed to a new line between Havre and Hamburg.

In 1858 Michel Victor Marziou, of Havre, backed by members of the Rothschild family, formed L'Union Maritime with a nominal capital of 50 million francs to run a service of five 750 horse-power steamers to New York and seven of 600 horse-power to the West Indies. A mail subsidy of

9,300,000 francs (£372,000) a year was promised by the French Government.

Two years later Monsieur Marziou realised that he would be unable to get together the large amount of capital necessary for the venture and it was arranged on 20 October 1860 for the concession to be transferred to the Compagnie Générale Maritime which, with the approval of Emperor Napoléon 111, changed its name on 25 August 1861 to COMPAGNIE GÉNÉRALE TRANSATLANTIQUE. But a lot had been going on behind the scenes before this happened as the fortunes of the Compagnie Générale Maritime had sunk to a low ebb. In 1859, therefore, having written down its capital from 30 to 24 million francs, the total was increased to 40 million by the issue of 32,000 new shares of 500 francs each. In addition, a loan of 13,600,000 francs was floated and the French Government advanced a sum equivalent to two years' subsidy - that is to say, 18,600,000 francs - on interest-free basis for a period of 20 years. Thus, the Company had the imposing sum of 72,200,000 francs (nearly £3,000,000) at its disposal to lay down the agreed number of steamers and build up the necessary organisation. It should be added that the Company's two European steamship lines were withdrawn within a year or two, although the last of the CGM sailing ships was not sold until 1873.

The new transatlantic steamship services were not scheduled to start until the summer of 1864, but the despatch of the French Expedition to Mexico in 1861 made it desirable to put forward the inaugural date of the Mexican service to 14 April 1862, when the 1,900 ton iron screw LOUISIANE sailed from St Nazaire for Vera Cruz. The TAMPICO followed on 14 May, the FLORIDE on 14 June and the VERA CRUZ on 14 July. The LOUISIANE and FLORIDE were products of Caird & Co of Greenock and had been laid down for other owners. The 1,700 ton TAMPICO and VERA CRUZ had been completed for the short-lived South American & General Steam Navigation Company in 1854 as the IMPERADOR and IMPERATRIZ, respectively, the former having made one round voyage between Liverpool and South America for that concern before being taken up as a Crimean War transport.

The agreement of 20 October 1860 stipulated that five 11½ knot steamers would be built for the New York service and six of 660 horse-power and 10½ knots for that to the Antilles, in addition to three smaller feeder steamers. After a careful study of the Cunard fleet, Émile Péreire considered that CGT ought to increase both the power and speed of their ships. He succeeded in winning over the French Postmaster-General to his views and it was decided to build eight paddle steamers of 850 horse-power, six to serve the West Indies and Central America and two to undertake the winter service to New York. The service to the latter destination between the months of March and October inclusive was to be undertaken by three steamers of 1,000 horse-power and 108 metres (355 feet) in length, comparable with the Cunard paddle steamer PERSIA.

The French authorities considered that the entire fleet should be built in France, but after Émile Péreire had pointed out the impossibility of building 11 large steamers there within three years, it was decided that six of them should be built abroad and the remainder in France. Several British, Belgian and Dutch builders were invited to submit tenders for the first three ships, the contract eventually going to John Scott & Co of Greenock, who quoted £78,000 for each hull and £25,000 for each set of engines. The total individual cost, including customs duty, amounted to £121,000, which was £27,000 less than the cheapest price quoted in France or the Low Countries.

1864 WASHINGTON 3,408 tons
North Atlantic pioneer of the French Line.

The first of the British-built ships, the 3,408 ton WASHINGTON, was launched on 17 June 1863 and sailed on her maiden voyage from Havre to New York on 15 June 1864. After a second voyage, she was joined by the LAFAYETTE, sailings taking place every 28 days. The third British-built ship, the EUROPE, entered service on 3 May 1865, enabling the WASHINGTON to be transferred to the Panama service. From mid 1865 onwards the steamers called at Brest.

Unable to obtain a cheaper French quotation than that already mentioned, the Péreire brothers were determined to establish a shipbuilding yard of their own. They succeeded in buying a strip of land near the mouth of the River Loire at St Nazaire, known locally as Penhoët, four slipways each over 91 metres (300 feet) in length being prepared. The yard was placed under the control of John Scott, the Greenock shipbuilder, who sent a dozen or more craftsmen from Scotland to superintend the 500-600 French workmen recruited from neighbouring towns and villages. A considerable quantity of machinery and fittings was imported from the United Kingdom, but nearly all the raw materials for the ships were supplied in France. Contracts for the engines of the five steamers were placed with Schneider of Creuzot.

1866 PANAMA 3,200 tons
One of four French-built paddle steamers. In 1876
rebuilt as single-screw CANADA.

The first of the French-built ships was laid down on 15 October 1862 as the ATLANTIQUE, but was launched on 23 April 1864 as the IMPÉRATRICE EUGÉNIE and sailed from St Nazaire for Vera Cruz on 16 February 1865. She was followed by the FRANCE, NOUVEAU MONDE and PANAMA, but the fifth unit, the SAINT LAURENT, was modified during construction and launched as a single-screw steamer. This change was largely due to the fact that the 2,638 ton single-screw mail steamer CHINA had preceded the 3,871 ton Cunard paddle steamer SCOTIA by a few weeks in 1862, her running costs showing a considerable economy in comparison with the latter. Three of the former CGM steamers were also converted to act as feeder steamers for the West Indies service - the MARIE STUART became the CARAIBE, the DANUBE became the CARAVELLE and the SEINE ET RHONE the CACIQUE.

The three larger paddle steamers intended for the summer service to New York were ordered from British yards in 1863. They were designed by the well-known French enginers Clapeyron and Eugène Flachat, largely in accordance with dimensions and details of the Cunard paddle steamer SCOTIA. The first, named NAPOLÉON 111, was ordered from the Thames Ironworks of London and the others, the PÉREIRE and VILLE DE PARIS, from Robert Napier of Glasgow, builder of the Cunarders SCOTIA and CHINA. During construction, plans of the Scottish pair were modified and they were completed with single screws. Unlike the CGT paddle steamers, they had clipper bows. Moreover, they had one funnel instead of two.

The maiden voyage of the PÉREIRE from Havre on 29 March 1866 coincided with an increase of sailings from monthly to fortnightly. The NAPOLÉON 111 sailed on 26 April and the VILLE DE PARIS on 24 May, the paddle steamer being a great disappointment to the Company from the point of view of speed. During 1866 she completed only three round voyages to New York, none in 1867, two in 1868 and was then laid up until 1871. The Havre-Brest-New York sailing of 10 February 1866 was undertaken by the third of the French-built paddle steamers, the NOUVEAU MONDE, which had to put back to Yarmouth, Isle of Wight, with 'rudder unshipped'. She

1866 NAPOLÉON III 3,376 tons
Lengthened 1871-2, converted to single-screw
and renamed VILLE DU HAVRE.

sailed again from Havre on 18 February, but this was her only New York voyage as a paddle steamer.

From the autumn of 1866 onwards, steamers normally responsible for the New York mail service were the PÉREIRE, VILLE DE PARIS, SAINT LAURENT and EUROPE, the NAPOLÉON 111 being held in reserve. In 1868 the PÉREIRE is believed to have proceeded from New York to Brest in 8 days 10½ hours at an average speed of 14½ knots. Two years later, after leaving Brest at 4 pm on 13 August 1870 she was stated to have arrived at Sandy Hook at 3 am on 22 August 'thus making the passage in 8 days 11 hours, being the quickest westbound passage ever made between the two ports.' [1] It is evident, however, that difference of time was not taken into consideration, and that the actual duration of the voyage was approximately 8 days 16 hours.

The WASHINGTON and her immediate successors had accommodation for 128 first class, 54 second and only 29 third class passengers. Full details are not available, but during five of the first ten westbound passages in 1864-65 the average number of passengers landed at New York was the surprisingly low one of 80. Thus, virtually no provision had been made for carrying steerage passengers to New York, but following a considerable decrease in the demand for passages and freight to Mexico, the VERA CRUZ was despatched to New York on 30 June 1866 with a total of 473 passengers, most of them steerage. All told, she made three voyages to New York, the TAMPICO two and the FLORIDE one, the last-named having to postpone her sailing from Havre by a fortnight as on the day before her scheduled departure she heeled over and sank at her berth. Some of these intermediate sailings were extended from New York to Vera Cruz.

By 1867 it was possible, in addition to the fortnightly service to New York, to arrange departures on the 8th of each month from St Nazaire to Santa Martha (Colombia), Colon and Aspinwall (Panama) and Martinique; and on the 16th of each month to Havana, Vera Cruz and Puerto Rico.

Considerable savings in fuel and increased cargo capacity of the three

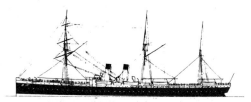

1864 WASHINGTON 3,408 tons
After conversion in 1868 from paddle to twin-screw.

screw steamers were responsible, towards the end of 1867, for the Company sending the WASHINGTON to Robert Napier, builder of the PÉREIRE and VILLE DE PARIS, for conversion from paddle to screw, this being the first time that such a conversion had taken place to a transatlantic steamer. But this was by no means all as the WASHINGTON was, in fact, fitted with twin-screws [2] and was the first example of the kind on the North Atlantic (apart from the American steamer MARMORA of 1845, which can be regarded as a freak and was not designed for the North Atlantic). It may be added that there is no truth in the statement sometimes made, that when the WASHINGTON was a paddle steamer the two paddle wheels worked independently of each other and that each was driven by a separate engine. The two wheels of this and the other CGT steamers were connected by the customary shaft, and it should also be pointed out that Robert Napier was responsible for providing the two sets of screw engines, the original paddle machinery being discarded.

In 1868 the LAFAYETTE, also, was converted to twin-screw, but this time at St Nazaire, new machinery being provided by Schneider of Creuzot. It will be convenient to mention at this stage that the twin-screw VILLE DE BORDEAUX, VILLE DE BREST and VILLE DE SAINT NAZAIRE were completed in France in 1871 for a short-lived CGT service between Panama and Valparaiso.

The Franco-Prussian War of 1870 resulted in the Company's headquarters being temporarily transferred from Paris to St Nazaire, and

1874 AMÉRIQUE 4,585 tons
In 1876 fitted with 'the lighthouse and electric light'
(external only).

1876 CANADA 4,054 tons
Built 1866 as paddle steamer PANAMA.

from 7 October the New York steamers made Southampton their terminal instead of Havre. They were extensively used for carrying arms and ammunition from the United States to France as well as French reservists returning to the colours. After the Armistice a number of ships were sent to Germany to repatriate prisoners of war. The normal Havre-Brest-New York service was resumed by the PÉREIRE on 1 April 1871.

On 16 September 1871 the NAPOLÉON III proceeded to A. Leslie & Co of Hebburn-on-Tyne to be lengthened from 111,51 to 128,52 metres (365.9 to 421.7 feet), with a consequent increase of tonnage from 3,376 to 3,950. Paddle-wheel propulsion was discarded and replaced by two-cylinder compound engines driving a single screw. In addition, the fall of the French Empire was responsible for a change of the name to VILLE DU HAVRE, the first sailing as such taking place on 13 March 1873 from Havre via Brest for New York. The EUROPE, IMPÉRATRICE EUGÉNIE (renamed AMÉRIQUE) and FRANCE were similarly lengthened and re-engined in 1873-4 by the same British firm. The last named had made one round voyage to New York in August 1872 and started another on 29 September, but had a breakdown off Cherbourg and returned to Havre under sail, with only one paddle wheel in operation. The August voyage turned out to be the last completed one on the North Atlantic by any of the Company's paddle steamers. It remains to add that in 1875 the NOUVEAU MONDE was lengthened, fitted with compound engines driving a single screw and renamed LABRADOR, but when the PANAMA was converted to single screw in 1876 and renamed CANADA she was not lengthened.

In 1873 the WASHINGTON and LAFAYETTE were refitted with four-cylinder compound engines, bringing a saving of 30 per cent in coal consumption compared with the single-expansion engines fitted previously. The question has often been asked why the other converted steamers were given single and not twin screws. The answer is simple - it was discovered that the extra cost of twin-screws was not compensated for by a sufficient increase in speed or saving in fuel. It was at approximately the same time that the PÉREIRE and VILLE DE PARIS received compound engines and had a second funnel .added.

On 22 November 1873 the VILLE DU HAVRE collided in the English Channel with the British sailing ship LOCH EARN, and sank almost at once with the loss of no fewer than 226 lives. On 3 April 1874 the EUROPE was abandoned in the Channel in a sinking condition, her passengers and crew being rescued by the National Line steamer GREECE, [3] while less than a fortnight later the AMÉRIQUE was abandoned near the French coast. She was towed to Plymouth, where it was discovered that her trouble was due to some valves having been left open and she was soon back in service. Not unnaturally, these three disasters following so soon after one another gave rise to rumours that the ships had been weakened by lengthening. This proved to be without foundation, several of the ships being successfully and profitably employed until well into the present century. The Company was undoubtedly unfortunate in having laid down a large fleet of ships just before the full advantages of screw propulsion compared with paddle had been determined, and also only a few years before the compound engine superseded the single-expansion type on the North Atlantic.

CGT was awarded a new mail contract in December 1873, under which the number of sailings to New York was increased to 40 a year, calling for weekly departures except during the months of November to March inclusive, when they remained at fortnightly. The first weekly sailing was taken on 1 April 1876 by the SAINT LAURENT, which proceeded to New York via Philadelphia in order to cater for visitors to the Philadelphia Exposition, a similar call being made on two earlier and two or three later occasions. A few months previously, in December 1875, the PÉREIRE had instituted a regular call at Plymouth in each direction to replace that at Brest, discontinued in October 1874. The number of passengers availing themselves of this new facility was, however, disappointing and the last westbound call at Plymouth was made by the LABRADOR on 6 January 1878.

To begin with, seven steamers were often required to maintain the weekly service, but the number was soon reduced to six and occasionally to five. Those employed included the AMÉRIQUE, CANADA, FRANCE, LABRADOR, PÉREIRE, SAINT LAURENT, VILLE DE PARIS and SAINT GERMAIN, the last-named, originally the Adler Line KLOPSTOCK, having been bought from the Hamburg American Line in 1876. She made only three round voyages for the Company on the North Atlantic at this time and was conspicuous by an outstandingly tall pair of funnels.

In the hope of regaining the confidence of the travelling public the Company gave wide publicity to the introduction of a number of safety precautions. In 1876 they advertised the provision of 'the lighthouse and electric light' to minimise the risk of collision, and a year later 'patent steam fog horns'. In addition, the amenities of the ships were improved by fitting electric bells in the cabins. The AMÉRIQUE was the first of the ships to be fitted with the 'lighthouse and electric light' and was, in fact, the first steamer on the North Atlantic (possibly in the world) to be lighted by electricity. Although the installation was purely external, it created a lot of interest at Plymouth when she called there on 25 March 1876, [4] and at New York. Unfortunately, the AMÉRIQUE had a second serious mishap on 7 January 1877, when she stranded at Seabright, New Jersey, but was refloated three months later and back in service within seven months.

On 10 December 1878 the MARTINIQUE (ex-VERA CRUZ)

inaugurated a new service from Marseilles to Havana and New Orleans via Barcelona, Cadiz, Teneriffe and Puerto Rico. The CALDÉRA and GUADELOUPE (ex-TAMPICO) followed at four-weekly intervals, but in May 1879 a monthly service to Panama was substituted, steamers taking part being the GUADELOUPE, VILLE DE MARSEILLE, CALDÉRA and FERDINAND DE LESSEPS. The 2,110 ton CALDÉRA, built in England in 1868, had just been acquired as had the 2,714 ton VILLE DE MARSEILLE (formerly the KNSM STAD AMSTERDAM) and the 2,865 ton FERDINAND DE LESSEPS (formerly the STAD HAARLEM). The last of these sailings took place in the autumn of 1881, but on 15 April of that year the CALDÉRA inaugurated a new service from Marseilles to New York via Cadiz. Until the following August sailings were approximately fortnightly and then became monthly, ports of call being extended to include Naples, Palermo, Malaga, Gibraltar and Cadiz, the homeward itinerary being New York - Cadiz - Gibraltar - Marseilles. In April 1882 sailings were increased to every three weeks, a further steamer, the 1,371 ton PICARDIE, being detailed to the service from time to time. She took the last sailing on 14 November 1882 and foundered off Newfoundland on 18 January 1883 during the homeward voyage. The Fabre Line had started a regular service from Marseilles to New York in 1882 and were undoubtedly delighted to learn of the rival company's withdrawal.

CGT had been awarded a mail contract in 1879 for a service from Marseilles to Algiers and Tunis. This was started on 30 June 1880 by the 1,751 ton MOISE, one of a dozen steamers built for the purpose.

An Act was passed in 1881 to encourage and subsidise French shipbuilding. Its critics pointed out that it enabled French builders to put up their prices, but on the whole it undoubtedly had beneficial results and prompted CGT to enlarge the Penhoët yard, which had fallen somewhat into a decline.

A new 15 year contract was drawn up well in advance of 1885, when the New York contract was due to expire, and called for weekly sailings at a minimum average speed of 15 knots. As a preparatory measure the Company went to the Barrow Shipbuilding Company for the 6,283 ton iron single-screw NORMANDIE, which in May 1883 completed her maiden voyage in the fast time of 8 days 11 hours 30 minutes. Three years later she was renamed LA NORMANDIE. Propelled by six-cylinder compound engines, she had accommodation for 205 first class, 76 second and 1,000 steerage passengers and on her maiden voyage carried a record number of 1,069. It seems that between 1871 and 1879 the Company was not authorised to carry steerage passengers on the New York mail steamers. In 1880, for the first time, some high figures were recorded - for examples, a total of 960 passengers on the LABRADOR, 939 on the AMÉRIQUE, 794 on the CANADA, 737 on the SAINT LAURENT and 702 on the

FRANCE.

The 7,087 ton LA CHAMPAGNE and the 7,112 ton LA BRETAGNE were built of steel at Penhoët in 1886, and the 7,395 ton LA BOURGOGNE and LA GASCOGNE of iron and steel by the Forges & Chantiers de la Méditerranée at La Seyne. A further difference between the ships was that the Penhoët pair was propelled by six-cylinder triple-expansion engines whereas the other two had six-cylinder compound ones. The best passage of LA NORMANDIE was completed in 8 days 3 hours, but LA BOURGOGNE, usually considered to be the fastest of the French-built quartette, on one occasion steamed from Havre to New York in 7 days 12 hours. The five newcomers were easily capable of maintaining a weekly service, and enabled the SAINT LAURENT, SAINT GERMAIN (which had recently been extensively employed on the North Atlantic) and the ex-paddle steamers AMÉRIQUE, CANADA, FRANCE and LABRADOR to be transferred to the West Indies service. The WASHINGTON had made her last North Atlantic voyage in 1874 and the LAFAYETTE in 1876, after which they, too, were detailed to the West Indies route.

1886 LA BOURGOGNE 7,395 tons
Sunk in collision in 1898 with heavy loss of life.

Two former Hamburg American steamers - the 2,989 ton RHENANIA and the 3,029 ton FRANCONIA - had been bought by CGT in 1878 and renamed SAINT SIMON and OLINDE RODRIGUES, respectively. The former made eight round voyages on the North Atlantic between 1883 and 1888 and the latter four between 1883 and 1885. The PÉREIRE and VILLE DE PARIS were sold in 1888 and converted to sail. A year later the 3,969 ton Hapag HAMMONIA was bought and became the VERSAILLES. She was not employed by the Company on the North Atlantic, being at first detailed to the St Nazaire - Vera Cruz service, and later ran between Bordeaux and Casablanca.

The 8,893 ton twin-screw LA TOURAINE was completed for the New York service in 1891. At that time she was the fifth largest steamer in the world and had no difficulty in beating the fastest passages of her consorts, her maiden voyage being completed at an average speed of 18½ knots.

During the late summer of 1892 a German steamer arrived at New York

1891 LA TOURAINE 8,893 tons
An early view. Her three masts were later
reduced to two.

with a number of cases of cholera. The United States authorities imposed stringent restrictions on immigration from Europe and for seven weeks from the beginning of September the weekly CGT mail steamers sailed from Cherbourg instead of Havre, carrying first and second class passengers but no steerage, the latter being debarred from the ships for a further three or four weeks.

In order to bring the New York fleet more in line with LA TOURAINE, the others were sent in turn to Penhoët to be refitted. First to be taken in hand was LA NORMANDIE, which resumed sailings on 23 June 1894 with two pole masts instead of four masts carrying a barquentine rig. Her engines were converted to triple-expansion and various improvements made in the passenger accomodation. In due course LA GASCOGNE, LA BRETAGNE, LA CHAMPAGNE and LA BOURGOGNE, in that order, were similarly dealt with except that they received quadruple-expansion engines.

In 1895 the Company was able to advertise a departure from Havre to New York every Saturday, one from Havre via Bordeaux to Haiti on the 17th of each month, and from the same ports to Colon starting on the 22nd of each month, as well as from St Nazaire to Colon on the 9th and to Vera Cruz on the 21st. A year later, a fortnightly service from New York to the West Indies was inaugurated by the twin-screw VILLE DE BREST, VILLE DE BORDEAUX and VILLE DE SAINT NAZAIRE of 1871 vintage. The last-named foundered in March 1897 while so employed.

The Company experimented in June 1898 with a pigeon post between LA BRETAGNE and the shore. Strong winds hampered the project on the outward voyage, but pigeons were released at intervals during the last 250 miles of the homeward voyage. Most arrived at Havre or Rouen the same day and all by the third day, but within a few months Marconi's successful experiments with wireless telegraphy made the pigeon post a thing of the past. [5]

In February 1896 LA BOURGOGNE had the misfortune to sink the Atlas Line steamer AILSA off the American coast. Two years later, on 23 February 1898, LA CHAMPAGNE was sighted by the Warren Line ROMAN with a broken propeller shaft and was towed by her into Halifax, salvage of £15,000 being awarded. She did not sail again from Havre until August 1898, and the 6,648 ton twin-screw LA NAVARRE, built in 1893 for the West Indies service and responsible for a round voyage to New York during the alterations to LA NORMANDIE, was detailed to replace her. LA BOURGOGNE was an unlucky ship as on 4 July 1898 she was rammed amidships and sunk in dense fog off Cape Sable by the British sailing ship CROMARTYSHIRE. She was carrying 85 first class, 125 second and 296 steerage passengers, together with a crew of 220, of whom 549 passengers and crew perished.

Owing to the spectacular increase in the amount of cargo carried by the CGT ships to and from New York, the 3,521 ton WOOLLOOMOOLOO was chartered from Lund's Blue Anchor Line and started the first of five round voyages on 5 May 1899 from Havre via Pauillac (Bordeaux) to New York. [6] The 3,462 ton CHATEAU LAFITE of the Compagnie Bordelaise was also taken up for six voyages as from 31 May, both steamers carrying steerage passengers as well as merchandise on the first few occasions. In November 1899 the BORDEAUX (formerly the Wilson Line FRANCISCO) took the place of the WOOLOOMOOLOO, and in December the PAUILLAC (formerly the Johnston Line SEDGEMORE) undertook her one and only voyage for the Company and disappeared without trace on the homeward leg. Subsequently, the cargo service was maintained for some time by the BORDEAUX, ALEXANDRE BIXIO, FOURNEL and the chartered MASSAPEQUA. The 1,934 ton ALEXANDRE BIXIO and the 1,872 ton FOURNEL had been built in Britain in 1880 for CGT.

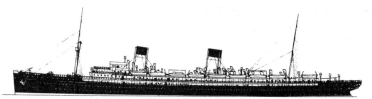

1901 LA SAVOIE 11,168 tons
Havre—New York service. Sister ship: LA LORRAINE.

Arrangements were made in 1898 for the renewal of the New York mail contract which, although it did not come into operation until 1901, necessitated the immediate building of two 20 knot steamers, which were launched on 20 November 1899 and 31 March 1900 as LA LORRAINE and LA SAVOIE, respectively. They were twin-screw ships of 11,150 tons, and it was unfortunate that neither was ready to share in the greatly-increased traffic produced by the Paris Exhibition of 1900. Moreover, they were badly needed to offset the activities of a new competitor, the American Line, whose New York - Southampton express steamers began in March 1899 to call at Cherbourg in each direction. CGT did, however, augment their service in November 1899 with the 8,242 ton twin-screw L'AQUITAINE, originally the three-funnelled Hamburg American NORMANNIA, whose services were badly required owing to the loss of LA BOURGOGNE and the increasingly frequent detailing of LA NORMANDIE to the West Indies line. In addition, the SAINT GERMAIN, whose funnels had been reduced to more normal height, made three round voyages between Havre and New York in 1900.

At a special meeting of shareholders in 1900 it was decided to sell the Penhoët shipyard. The Chairman pointed out that with the completion of the two new ships some considerable time was likely to elapse before CGT placed further substantial orders, and that the works would stand a better chance of obtaining outside orders if they were placed under independent ownership. The only apparent alternative to a sale was to pay off a large number of workers, then numbering close on 5,000.

The principal North Atlantic event of 1902 was the formation of the International Mercantile Marine Company. The attitude of CGT towards this giant combine was at first the subject of much speculation, but in the end it stood aloof, largely because of CGT's many interests not connected with the North Atlantic, and the considerable say of the French Government in the Company's activities.

During 1902-4 CGT cargo sailings to New York were maintained exclusively by the BORDEAUX, but the passenger service was augmented from time to time by the despatch of two mail steamers on the same day, partly to carry additional cargo and partly to cope with the greatly-increased number of steerage passengers, for which provision on LA GASCOGNE and her two sisters had been increased to 1,500. The capacity of L'AQUITAINE was even greater, so much so that she arrived at New York on 4 May 1903 with the Company's then record of four second class and 1,965 steerage, her small second class complement being due to the fact that she sailed from Havre on the same day as LA SAVOIE.

The *paquebots mixtes* QUÉBEC, MONTRÉAL and HUDSON were bought second hand in 1905, while the 5,104 ton LOUISIANE and the 5,152 ton CALIFORNIE were newly-built for the Company, all having accommodation for 600-700 steerage passengers and the last three for 60 second class in addition. They were followed in 1906 by the 5,607 ton SAINT LAURENT (11) and in 1907 by the 4,885 ton MEXICO and the 6,624 ton FLORIDE. The QUÉBEC and MONTRÉAL were quickly transferred to the Haiti line, but the remainder undertook a considerable number of voyages between Havre and New York. From 1908 onwards some of the ships sailed from Dunkirk to New York, with calls at Bordeaux and Coruña. Each spring one of them put in additionally at St Malo, where about 1,000 fishermen embarked for St Pierre (Miquelon), the French island off the coast of Newfoundland.

The appointment of Charles Roux in 1904 as president of CGT led to many changes. Under his *régime* the building of new ships proceeded even more vigorously than during the 1860s, and between 1905 and 1911 no fewer than 17 steamers, totalling about 125,000 tons, were completed, while several others were bought second hand. The most important new unit was the 13,753 ton LA PROVENCE, completed at Penhoët in 1906, and not only was she considerbly larger than any predecessor but she had a trial speed of 23 knots compared with the 21 knots of LA SAVOIE. On her second westbound voyage she steamed from Havre to New York in the record time of 6 days 3 hours 35 minutes at an average speed of 21.70 knots, and two voyages later she improved on this time by 25 minutes. The New York service was thenceforth entrusted to the newcomer, together with LA SAVOIE, LA LORRAINE and LA TOURAINE, and with LA BRETAGNE and LA GASCOGNE as extra steamers, enabling L'AQUITAINE to be scrapped. LA CHAMPAGNE had already been transferred to the Mexican service, but made two New York voyages in 1906. The LAFAYETTE, last of the ex-paddlers, also went to the shipbreakers.

The 11,127 ton twin-screw CHICAGO, commissioned during 1908, a year of serious slump, was interesting in that she catered for 358 second class and 1,250 steerage. She was one of the first large 'cabin' steamers to be built for one of the major New York lines, but the description 'cabin' was not, however, introduced officially until World War 1.

The 8,481 ton NIAGARA, the 13,500 ton ESPAGNE and the 12,678 ton ROCHAMBEAU followed in 1910-1, the ESPAGNE being built for the West Indies trade although she made many New York voyages. In addition, two smaller steamers, the 6,693 ton CAROLINE and the 5,330 ton VIRGINIE, the latter bought second hand, were extensively employed on the North Atlantic. The ROCHAMBEAU, also a 'cabin' steamer, had quadruple screws propelled by a combination of triple-expansion engines and low-pressure steam turbines. She became extremely popular and reached New York on 12 October 1912 with 423 second class and 1,674 steerage passengers.

In 1912 the NIAGARA, FLORIDE and CAROLINE made six round voyages between Havre, Quebec and Montreal, carrying second and third class passengers and cargo, and after the closure of the St Lawrence to navigation a call was made at Halifax *en route* to New York. A short-lived cargo service to Canada had been established as far back as 1900, and as about 90 per cent of the population of the Province of Quebec was of French origin it is not surprising that the Company made another attempt to· establish a permanent line. St Lawrence sailings in 1913 were increased to nine, including two by the mail steamer LA TOURAINE, which on those occasions carried second and third class only. Early and late in the year several calls were made at Halifax by New York steamers. In 1914 LA TOURAINE made three Quebec and Montreal voyages and the CAROLINE one, the service being brought to an abrupt conclusion by the outbreak of World War 1. It will be seen from Chapter 189 that in 1919 the

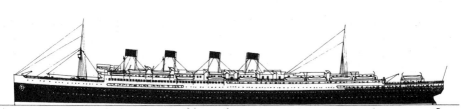

1912 FRANCE 23,666 tons
Nearest rival in speed of the LUSITANIA and
MAURETANIA.

Compagnie Canadienne Transatlantique, in which CGT had an important interest, started a passenger and cargo service between Havre, Quebec and Montreal, at first with steamers chartered from CGT and in 1920 with other chartered steamers. It did not survive beyond these two years.

The 23,666 ton quadruple-screw, four-funnelled FRANCE, laid down as LA PICARDIE and sometimes incorrectly referred to as LA FRANCE, was launched on 20 September 1910, and on trials recorded a mean speed of more than 25 knots, making her the fastest ocean going liner apart from the LUSITANIA and MAURETANIA. Her propelling machinery consisted of four sets of direct-acting steam turbines; accommodation was provided for 535 first class, 440 second and 950 third class passengers. Her maiden voyage to New York started on 20 April 1912 and occupied 6 days and 49 minutes.

Soon after the outbreak of World War 1 in August 1914 many of the Company's ships were taken up by the French Government for long or short periods and for a variety of duties. They included the FRANCE (renamed FRANCE 1V), LA PROVENCE (renamed PROVENCE 11), LA LORRAINE (renamed LORRAINE 11), LA SAVOIE, LA TOURAINE and ROCHAMBEAU. During the later stages of the war, several of the largest steamers were employed in carrying American troops to France. The PROVENCE 11 was torpedoed and sunk in the Mediterranean in 1916 while acting as an auxiliary cruiser. The *paquebots mixtes* LOUISIANE, SAINT LAURENT (11), FLORIDE, QUEBEC and MONTRÉAL were lost during the war as well as 23 other steamers, many of them normally employed in the Company's Mediterranean services.

In April 1915, owing to the invasion of part of France by the Germans, it was considered desirable to change the Company's principal terminal from Havre to Bordeaux. Steamers employed on the Bordeaux - New York route included the ROCHAMBEAU, LA TOURAINE, CALIFORNIE, HUDSON, ESPAGNE, NIAGARA, CHICAGO, LA GASCOGNE and the 11,953 ton quadruple-screw LAFAYETTE (11), which was launched on

635

1915 LAFAYETTE 11,953 tons
A wartime addition; sailed Bordeaux—
New York.

27 May 1914 as the ILE DE CUBA and started her maiden voyage from Bordeaux on 31 October 1915. LA CHAMPAGNE was wrecked near St Nazaire when on the point of being transferred back to the North Atlantic; LA GASCOGNE had been sold to the Compagnie Sud Atlantique in 1912 but was chartered by CGT for a few North Atlantic voyages.

The first CGT sailing to New York after the Armistice was taken by the ESPAGNE, which left Bordeaux on 16 November 1918. The CHICAGO followed on 26 November, LA LORRAINE on 2 December, the NIAGARA on 17 December and the ESPAGNE on 21 December. Meanwhile, the FRANCE sailed from Brest on 17 December with 3,865 troops. On her next voyage from Bordeaux on 2 February 1919 she carried no fewer than 516 first class and 56 second class passengers in addition to 4,167 troops. From February 1919 onwards LA TOURAINE, ROCHAMBEAU, LA LORRAINE, ESPAGNE and LA SAVOIE sailed from Havre instead of Bordeaux.

The first addition to the New York fleet was the 12,350 ton former Hamburg American BLÜCHER, which was seized by Brazil at Pernambuco in 1917, renamed LEOPOLDINA and in 1920 chartered to CGT, for whom her first voyage from New York to Havre started on 11 March 1920. The 6,757 ton SANTAREM, formerly the NDL EISENACH, was also seized at Pernambuco and made two round voyages for the Company on the North Atlantic at about this time. On 28 September 1920 the 8,800 ton ROUSSILLON (ex-NDL GOEBEN) started her first CGT voyage from Marseilles to New York, returning to Havre, from where subsequent voyages started. Finally, a similar ship, LA BOURDONNAIS (ex-NDL SCHARNHORST) sailed from Havre on 2 April 1921. The LEOPOLDINA was eventually bought by CGT which renamed her SUFFREN and despatched her from Havre to New York on 9 May 1923.

Of much greater importance was the commissioning in 1921 of the 34,569 ton quadruple-screw PARIS, which had been laid down at Penhoët in 1913. She was launched on 12 September 1916, but work was then suspended and she was towed to Quiberon Bay, remaining there in an uncompleted state until after the Armistice. When she sailed on her maiden voyage from Havre to New York on 15 June 1921 she was easily the largest steamer placed in service since the war. She was propelled by four sets of direct-acting steam turbines, her service speed being 21 knots.

By this time New York sailings were taking place twice weekly. The PARIS, FRANCE, LA SAVOIE and LA LORRAINE undertook the mail service, while an intermediate service was maintained by the LAFAYETTE, ROCHAMBEAU, CHICAGO, ROUSSILLON, LA BOURDONNAIS, LEOPOLDINA and LA TOURAINE, the last six of which carried cabin and third class passengers, the LAFAYETTE being a three-class ship. To the FRANCE was afforded the privilege of carrying the largest peacetime

1921 PARIS 34,569 tons
Keel laid 1913, launched 1916, commissioned 1921.

complement of fare-paying passengers ever handled by the Company on the North Atlantic - she arrived at New York on 16 January 1921 with 170 first, 462 second and 1,959 third class, a grand total of 2,591.

An attempt was made in 1921 to maintain a passenger and cargo service between New York, Hamburg and Danzig with the NIAGARA, but results were disappointing and it was withdrawn after a handful of sailings. Instead, the 3,112 ton POLOGNE was detailed to maintain a feeder service between Havre, Hamburg and Danzig, but that too was withdrawn after an extended trial.

Throughout 1919 the CHICAGO had sailed between Bordeaux and New York, assisted at times by the HUDSON and NIAGARA. During 1920 however, a less pretentious service was maintained by the NIAGARA and CAROLINE, many of the sailings in 1921-2 being by cargo steamers.

The PARIS and FRANCE reintroduced a call at Plymouth in 1922 after an interval of 44 years. By degrees more and more of the Havre - New York ships as well as those of the West Indies service began to make the call. The post-war boom on the North Atlantic was now over and the Company sold the old-timers LA LORRAINE and LA TOURAINE. In 1923 the FRANCE was converted to burn oil fuel, the opportunity being taken to make various improvements to her passenger accommodation.

In the spring of 1923 LA BOURDONNAIS was transferred to the Bordeaux - New York service, as was the ROUSSILLON in the following autumn. At that time and for about a year many outward calls were made at Halifax for the benefit of passengers destined to Canada.

For many years previously nearly all the principal CGT ships had been built at Penhoët or elsewhere in France. An important exception was the 17,707 ton DE GRASSE, which was laid down by Cammell Laird of Birkenhead in 1920. Work was delayed to such an extent that she did not enter service until 1924, at which time she was one of the largest cabin steamers on the North Atlantic. Three years later the 43,153 ton ILE DE FRANCE was completed at Penhoët. In appearance she was an enlarged

638

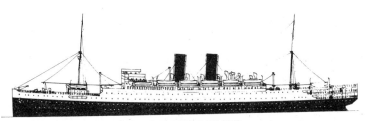
1924 DE GRASSE 17,707 tons
Reconditioned after World War II with one funnel.

PARIS, but had raised lifeboats which gave her greatly-increased deck space. Her public rooms were decorated in modern French style and were considered by many to be the most attractive of any ship afloat. She was so popular that for several years she carried more first class passengers than any other ship on the North Atlantic. In 1928 she was fitted with a catapult for releasing an aeroplane when she was about 500 miles short of her westbound and eastbound terminals, enabling passengers in a hurry and urgent mail to reach their destination many hours before the ship.

In 1929-30 the 8,400 ton DE LA SALLE, completed by Barclay Curle of Glasgow in 1921 and normally running to New Orleans, made three voyages to or via New York. She was a sister ship of the Fabre Line SINAIA.

Fire broke out on the PARIS at Havre in August 1929. Damage was confined to public rooms and was largely due to water from the fire hoses. She did not re-enter service until January 1930, the 11,337 ton West Indies steamer CUBA undertaking the first of her cancelled voyages and the MÉXIQUE two more. The latter was no newcomer to the North Atlantic as she was none other than the LAFAYETTE of 1915 under a new name, the change having taken place in 1928 when she was detailed to the Verz Cruz service.

A new service had been established in 1919 to the Pacific Coast of North America via the Panama Canal. From 1929 onwards the 7,700 ton motor ships OREGON, WYOMING and WASHINGTON and the steamship WISCONSIN, carrying a limited number of passengers, were substituted for the cargo steamers previously employed.

The 25,178 ton quadruple-screw motorship LAFAYETTE (III), whose maiden voyage Havre-Plymouth-New York started on 17 May 1930, differed greatly in appearance from any ship that preceded her. She had one huge squat funnel and a single mast. An even more remarkable ship, the 28,124 ton twin-screw geared-turbine CHAMPLAIN, was commissioned in June 1932 and could be readily distinguished from the LAFAYETTE by her rounded stem, squat pear-shaped funnel with smoke-deflecting cowl and two masts, of which the mainmast was much shorter than then

639

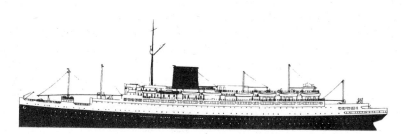

1930 LAFAYETTE 25,178 tons
Only passenger motorship built for CGT New York
service.

1932 CHAMPLAIN 28,124 tons
The 'new look' of the 1930s, with decks free from
unnecessary obstructions.

customary. The CHAMPLAIN had flush hatches and these, combined with raised lifeboats and the almost complete absence of ventilators and winches, gave her an exceptional amount of unobstructed deck space. Another interesting innovation was tiled rubber flooring on the lower promenade deck to prevent disturbance to passengers occupying cabins on the deck below.

When the ILE DE FRANCE was commissioned in 1927 she was the sixth largest liner in the world, but during the next two years the Norddeutscher Lloyd completed their 50,000 ton record-breakers BREMEN and EUROPA, and soon afterwards the Italian lines laid down two ships of similar size. In May 1930 Cunard announced that they would build a giant ship, which materialised as the QUEEN MARY but, not to be outdone, CGT had made arrangements as early as 1929 for preparation of a huge new building-berth at Penhoët. This was ready by the end of 1930, and on 26 January 1931 the keel-plate of the NORMANDIE was laid, the general belief being that she would at least equal the Cunarder in size. Excellent progress was made, the launching ceremony took place on 29 October 1932 and she was completed in 1935 - a year before the QUEEN MARY, whose construction had been interrupted for over 12 months.

The NORMANDIE was a quadruple-screw turbo-electric ship of 79,280 tons, with a rounded stem and bulbous forefoot to give added buoyancy and keep the propellers fully submerged in rough weather. The forward end was protected by a 'whale-back' under which the deck machinery and capstans were concealed. The three rather squat funnels were streamlined and receded progressively in height, the aftermost being a dummy. The foremast was stepped from the bridge and the mainmast from the superstructure abaft the funnels. The stern was of a special semi-counter type. Accommodation was of a magnificent character, nearly all the first class cabins having their own bathroom and toilet. Most imposing of the public rooms was the first class dining saloon, which seated 700 and was 93 metres (305 feet) long by 14 metres (46 feet) wide, the central portion being no less than 7,62 metres (25 feet) high. Four turbo-alternator sets generated the electricity required to drive the four electric propulsion motors coupled to the propeller shafts. On her trials, the NORMANDIE maintained an average speed of 31 knots for several hours. A remarkable feature was that at 29 knots the consumption of oil was no greater that that of the ILE DE FRANCE at $23\frac{1}{2}$ knots.

In January 1935 the ILE DE FRANCE had inaugurated an outward call at Southampton instead of Plymouth, and this became a regular feature although the homeward itinerary was still New York - Plymouth - Havre. When, therefore, the NORMANDIE started her maiden voyage from Havre on 29 May 1935 she called at Southampton to embark a large proportion of her full complement of passengers. On leaving Southampton she was slowed down by fog, but this soon cleared and she steamed from Bishop Rock to Ambrose Light in 4 days 3 hours 2 minutes at an average speed of 29,98 knots. On a slightly longer homeward course she took 4 days 3 hours 25 minutes between the same points, average speed being 30.35 knots. The NORMANDIE had broken all existing records. A good deal of prominence was given to her vibration at these high speeds, but the trouble was soon mitigated by the substitution of four-bladed for three-bladed propellers. At a later date, further improvement was effected by certain structural alterations, which increased her tonnage to 83,423.

In addition to the NORMANDIE, principal CGT North Atlantic units at this time were the ILE DE FRANCE, PARIS, CHAMPLAIN, LAFAYETTE and DE GRASSE. Within eight years the Company had commissioned four new liners of a total tonnage of 180,000 and had, meanwhile, disposed of a number of surplus ships, including the FRANCE, ROCHAMBEAU, ESPAGNE, NIAGARA, ROUSSILLON, LA BOURDONNAIS, SUFFREN and several cargo steamers. Withdrawal of the ROUSSILLON and LA BOURDONNAIS meant the closing down of the Bordeaux - New York service.

641

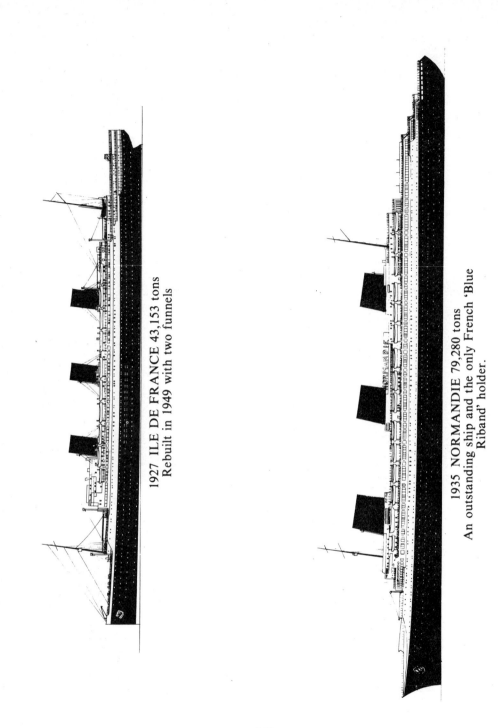

1927 ILE DE FRANCE 43,153 tons
Rebuilt in 1949 with two funnels

1935 NORMANDIE 79,280 tons
An outstanding ship and the only French 'Blue
Riband' holder.

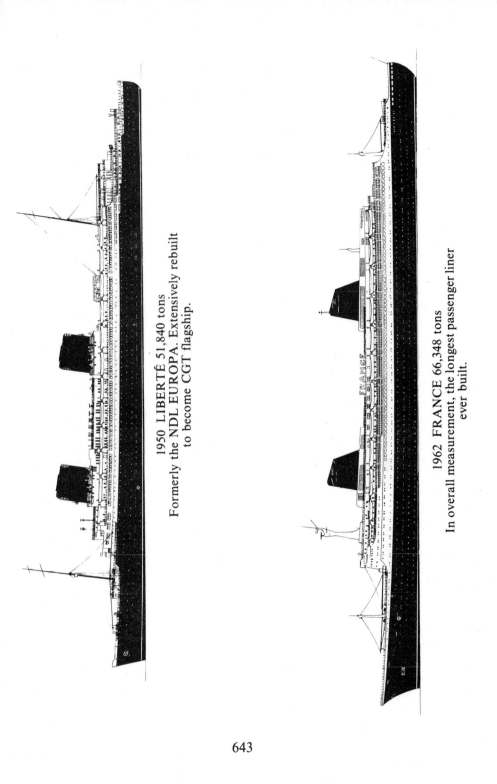

1950 LIBERTÉ 51,840 tons
Formerly the NDL EUROPA. Extensively rebuilt
to become CGT flagship.

1962 FRANCE 66,348 tons
In overall measurement, the longest passenger liner
ever built.

The world depression which started in the late 1920s played havoc with the Company's finances. A loss of 31 million francs was incurred in 1930 and no less than 369 million francs in 1931. Not surprisingly, there was a drastic reorganisation in 1933 and the French Government became the largest shareholder.

The QUEEN MARY succeeded in regaining the 'Blue Riband' from the NORMANDIE in August 1936, but a year later the NORMANDIE established new records of 30.58 knots westbound and 31.20 knots eastbound. It seemed for about a year that this would not be surpassed, but in August 1938 the QUEEN MARY improved slightly on both records. It has been shown time and time again that the publicity value of a speed record is incalculable, but from most other points of view it has little value. An increase of average speed from 30 to 31 knots, for instance, reduces the time for the crossing to New York by a mere three hours.

CGT suffered a grievous loss in May 1938, when the LAFAYETTE was seriously damaged by fire in dry dock at Havre and had to be scrapped. Worse, the PARIS was gutted by fire at her berth in Havre in April 1939, the immense quantities of water pumped into her causing her to capsize and sink. The outbreak of World War 11 a few months later rendered salvage operations impossible.

It was announced in May 1939 that work on a consort to the NORMANDIE would start in 1940, that she would be named BRETAGNE and would be faster than her predecessor. Three months later it was stated that Vladimir Yourkevitch, designer of the NORMANDIE, had prepared plans for a ship of 100,000 tons, with a length of 350 metres (1,148 feet) and a speed of 34 knots. Many considered it improbable that a steamer of this immense size would be built, a more likely proposition being one slightly larger and faster than the NORMANDIE. In the event, the outbreak of World War 11 caused cancellation of the project.

The NORMANDIE was laid up at New York from the outbreak of hostilities until 12 December 1941, when she was seized by the US Government. On 9 February 1942, during conversion to the troopship LAFAYETTE, sparks from a blow-lamp set fire to a quantity of bedding that had been place on board prematurely. She was soon well ablaze, thousands of tons of water which was played on her made her top-heavy and finally she heeled over and sank. Salvage operations took well over a year, but as by then the ship had become little more than a hulk it was decided that expenditure of further time and money was not in the nation's interest. In September 1946 the once-proud ship was towed to a nearby yard to be dismantled.

The ILE DE FRANCE sailed from Havre on 1 September 1939 and upon arrival at New York was laid up until 1 May 1940, when she proceeded to Marseilles. Before long she left for Cape Town and Saigon but was diverted to Singapore, where she was seized by the British in July 1940, after the collapse of France, and rendered splendid service as a troopship until 3 February 1946, when she was handed back to CGT. She subsequently made five round voyages betwen Southampton, Cherbourg and Halifax as a troopship, calling at Boston on the return journey to embark a limited number of civilian passengers. In July 1946 she proceeded to French Indo-China to embark French repatriates. Her first post-war westbound commercial voyage started from Cherbourg for New York on 22 October 1946, when a total of 1,689 civilian passengers was carried in austerity accommodation, many of her priority passengers having to share a cabin with seven or eight others. The ILE DE FRANCE had undoubtedly earned a respite and in April 1947 was sent to Penhoët. Reconstruction lasted over two years.

The CHAMPLAIN was sunk by a magnetic mine off La Pallice on 17 June 1940 when carrying evacuees from St Nazaire. She had made five round voyages to New York since the outbreak of hostilities. The DE GRASSE was intended to take part in the Norway Expedition in April 1940 but got no further than Greenock. In the following month she acted as a troop transport between North Africa and Marseilles. Eventually, she was seized by the Germans at Bordeaux and used as a submarine depot ship. Returned to the Company in June 1942, she was anchored below Bordeaux and became a training ship for merchant navy officers. On 30 August 1944 she was depth-charged by a German E-boat and sank in shallow water. Twelve months later she was refloated and extensively rebuilt.

The Company's Havre - New York service was reopened on 23 May 1945 by the 7,706 ton motorship OREGON, built in 1929 for the North Pacific coast service and originally having a capacity of 38 first class passengers, temporarily increased to 76 by the simple expedient of doubling the number of occupants in each cabin. She sailed again from New York on 23 June and was described as 'the first passenger liner whose departure from New York has been made public since the USA entered the war'. [7]

CGT acted as New York agents for the 11,732 ton Messageries Maritimes MARÉCHAL JOFFRE, which made three transatlantic round voyages during the second half of 1945; the 6,500 ton motorship INDOCHINOIS, owned by the French Government, which had accommodation for 12 passengers and made six round voyages in 1945-6; and the 15,276 ton ATHOS 11, also owned by Messageries Maritimes, with four round voyages, the last two between Marseilles and New York.

The 8,061 ton WISCONSIN, which had similar dimensions to the motorship OREGON but was propelled by triple-expansion engines, had been seized by the USA at Los Angeles in December 1941 and returned to the French flag on 13 November 1945. Like the OREGON, her passenger accommodation for 38 was increased to 76. She sailed from Havre on 12

645

December 1946, reached New York on 25 December, left on 5 January for Philadelphia and arrived back at Havre on 29 January 1957. From then until the autumn of 1948 she and the OREGON sailed from Havre about every six weeks for New York, thence to Norfolk, Baltimore or Philadelphia and back.

The 13,391 ton US hospital ship ALEDA E. LUTZ arrived at New York on 16 March 1946 from Hawaii with 152 patients. A day or two previously 158 French merchant seamen reached New York from La Pallice on the Chargeurs Réunis GROIX, in order to sail the ALEDA E. LUTZ - alias the COLOMBIE of CGT's pre-war Havre - West Indies service - back to France, as she was on the point of reverting to her original name and flag. The COLOMBIE was again detailed to the West Indies trade, but made two round voyages between Havre and New York, arriving there on 16 September 1946 and 14 July 1947. On the former occasion she was carrying the crews for the 19 LIBERTY ships handed over to France.

The DE GRASSE left Havre on 12 July 1947 on her first post-war sailing to New York. She had been completely reconditioned to carry 360 first class and 360 cabin passengers, her tonnage was increased to 19,918 and her funnels were reduced from two to one.

After the war the 49,746 ton ex-Norddeutscher Lloyd EUROPA made two North Atlantic voyages under the American flag before being handed over to the French Government which, in turn, allocated her to CGT. She was laid up at Havre pending reconstruction. In December 1946 she broke adrift from her berth during a gale, was blown on to the wreck of the PARIS and had to be scuttled. A year later she was towed to St Nazaire, to be strengthened and rebuilt.

The OREGON and WISCONSIN made their last New York voyages in September and November 1948, respectively, before being detailed to run between Havre and New Orleans. The DE GRASSE took full charge of the New York passenger service from then until 21 July 1949, when the ILE DE FRANCE joined her. Reconstruction included installation of new boilers and substitution of two new funnels for the original three. Completely redecorated and refurnished, her tonnage was now 44,356. Passenger capacity became 541 first class, 577 cabin and 227 tourist.

It was originally intended that the EUROPA would be renamed LORRAINE, but the final choice was LIBERTÉ. Her new tonnage was 51,840, accommodation was provided for 553 first class, 500 cabin and 444 tourist class passengers, and she sailed from Havre on 17 August 1950 for Southampton and New York.

The 20,464 ton FLANDRE and the 19,828 ton ANTILLES were laid down for the West Indies trade, which the latter entered upon completion in 1953, but it had been decided that the FLANDRE would run to New York in company with the LIBERTÉ and ILE DE FRANCE. She sailed from

1949 ILE DE FRANCE 44,356 tons
As rebuilt after World War II with funnels
reduced from three to two.

1952 FLANDRE 20,464 tons
First French post-World War II North Atlantic
liner.

Havre on 23 July 1952, but was unfortunate enough to be delayed by electrical faults and other trouble and arrived at New York in tow of a tug. Her second westbound voyage did not start until April 1953, but from then onwards she met with a full measure of success. The DE GRASSE made her last North Atlantic voyage, as such, in September 1951 and for a time acted as a consort to the COLOMBIE in the West Indies service, but in February 1953 was sold to the Canadian Pacific to replace their burned-out EMPRESS OF CANADA.

Prolonged discussions between the Company and the French Government culminated in the placing of an order on 26 July 1956 with Chantiers de l'Atlantique (successors to Chantiers de Penhoët) for a steamer of over 50,000 tons to be named FRANCE (111). First keel plate was laid on 7 September 1957.

By this time the ILE DE FRANCE had been in service for over 30 years. For another 12 months she continued to act as consort to the LIBERTÉ and FLANDRE and then, in November 1958, was laid up. Soon afterwards she was sold to Japan to be scrapped, and sailed from Havre on 26 February 1959 as the FURANSU MARU. Meanwhile, however, negotiations had been taking place between the shipbreakers and Metro-Goldwyn Mayer and upon arrival in Japan preparations were made for her to play the leading role in the film 'The Last Voyage'. For this purpose she was renamed CLARIDON after protests from the Greek Line, owners of the OLYMPIA, about an earlier choice of OLYMPUS. To add to the realism, there were fires and explosions on board, resulting in the collapse of the forward funnel and, in due course, she sank in shallow water. After this rather disgraceful episode, a much-loved ship was salvaged and finally broken up at Osaka.

The LIBERTÉ and FLANDRE were jointly responsible for the New York service until November 1961 when, over 31 years since her maiden North Atlantic voyage, the LIBERTÉ was withdrawn. She was scrapped at Spezia in the following year.

The FRANCE was launched by Madame de Gaulle, wife of the French President, on 11 May 1960, and sailed from Havre on 3 February 1962 on her maiden voyage to Southampton and New York, having undertaken an eight-day 'shakedown' cruise to the Canary Islands during the previous month. On an overall length of 315,52 metres (1,035.2 feet), she had a tonnage of 66,348, making her the third largest liner in service in the world, her tonnage being exceeded only by that of the QUEEN ELIZABETH and QUEEN MARY. And her overall length (but not her length between perpendiculars) was greater than that of any passenger liner ever built or likely to be built. Her quadruple screws were propelled by four sets of double-reduction geared turbines, which on her trials gave her an average speed of 34.13 knots. This despite the fact that she had only eight boilers, whereas the NORMANDIE had 29, and that her fuel consumption was 40 per cent less than that of her famous predecessor. The FRANCE had accommodation for 500 first class and 1,550 tourist passengers. Originally scheduled to make 23 North Atlantic round voyages each year, she thus offered an annual total of 92,000 berths - a figure greater than that of the LIBERTÉ and FLANDRE combined. Cost of the ship was in excess of £22 million, substantial assistance being received from the French Government. A conspicuous feature were the wings on her two funnels, being, in fact, tunnels to permit the emission of smoke instead of through the tops. During the summer of 1962 two of her four-bladed propellers were replaced by five-bladed.

The FLANDRE remained on the New York service until November 1962, when she joined the ANTILLES on the West Indies service. She returned temporarily to the North Atlantic in 1967, when she made two round voyages between Havre, Southampton, Quebec and Montreal in connection with the Montreal Exhibition. She was sold in 1968 to the Italian-owned Costa Line, and looking back this was unfortunate as the ANTILLES was destroyed by fire in the Caribbean in January 1971.

The FRANCE made a round voyage from Havre and Southampton to Quebec in May 1967, followed in July and October by two calls there *en route* to New York, and another in October 1968.

Following the withdrawal of the Hapag-Lloyd passenger service between Bremen and New York and the sale of the BREMEN, the FRANCE arrived at Bremerhaven on 14 October 1971 from New York, Southampton and Havre and sailed again the same day for Havre, Southampton and New York. During the 1972 summer season approximately every other voyage was made to and from Bremerhaven.

The 18,739 ton BERGENSFJORD was bought from the Norwegian America Line and placed in service in November 1971 as the DE GRASSE (11) between Havre, Southampton and the West Indies as a replacement for the ANTILLES. She was sold less than two years later, having latterly been used almost exclusively for cruising.

The withdrawal of the QUEEN ELIZABETH in 1968 made the

FRANCE the largest liner in active service in the world, and when the UNITED STATES was laid up in the autumn of 1969 she also became the fastest, although no exceptionally rapid passage was attempted. In fact, owing to escalating oil fuel prices 1974 voyages were undertaken at reduced speed, thereby adding a day to her voyage times. It was evident by then that her active career was coming to an end as there had been an operating deficit of over £6 million in 1973 and 1974 losses were likely to be appreciably greater. It was announced during the summer of 1974 that her last transatlantic voyage would start from New York on 18 October. However, when she arrived off Havre on 12 September her crew refused to let her enter the port and she anchored in the entrance channel. She eventually berthed on 10 October and was laid up. It is sad that this should happen to such a popular ship after only 12 years of service, the more so as it is extremely doubtful whether she will ever be recommissioned.

Although the Compagnie Générale Transatlantique is no longer responsible for a passenger service on the North Atlantic, it owns two of the containerships running in the Atlantic Container Line pool, the 15,351 ton ATLANTIC CHAMPAGNE and ATLANTIC COGNAC, both of which entered the trade in 1970.

In conclusion, it is interesting to note that the Compagnie Générale Transatlantique and the Messageries Maritimes were merged by official decree dated 21 December 1972, to become the COMPAGNIE GÉNÉRALE MARITIME. This name was doubly appropriate as not only did it bear some resemblance to those of its two constituents but it revived the name borne by CGT prior to August 1861. It is satisfactory that at present both CGT and MM retain their names, houseflags and funnel colours. The former also retains its two branch lines, the Compagnie Générale Transméditerranéenne and Compagnie Générale Transbaltique.

[1]   New York Herald 23/8/1870
[2]   Mitchell's Steam Shipping Journal 1/5/1868
[3]   The Times 27/4/1874
[4]   Western Morning News 27/3/1876
[5]   Syren & Shipping 4/7/1951
[6]   New York Herald 24/5/1899
[7]   New York Herald - Tribune 24/6/1945

1. 1864 WASHINGTON
        3,408. 105,62 x 13,36. (346.6 x 43.8). S—2—2. I—P—SL2—12. (I—128; II—54; III—29). Scott & Co, Greenock (engines Greenock Foundry Co). 1863 (17/6) launched. 1864 (15/6) MV Havre—New York. 1865 (8/3) LV ditto (5 RV); subsequently St Nazaire—Colon. 1868 converted to twin-

screw by Robt Napier, Glasgow; new two-cylinder single-expansion engines; mizzen mast added. 1871 (8/1) FV Brest—New York. 1873 (25/4) LV Havre—Brest—New York. 1873 engines converted to four-cylinder compound by Schneider, Creuzot. 1874 (19/6) resumed Havre—Brest—New York. 1874 (14/8) LV ditto. (Total 19 RV on N Atlantic); subsequently St Nazaire—W Indies. 1899 sold. 1900 scrapped at Marseilles.

2. 1864 LAFAYETTE (I)

3,375. 105,62 x 13,36. (346.6 x 43.8). S—2—2. I—P—SL2—12. (I—128; II—54; III—29). Scott & Co, Greenock (engines Greenock Foundry Co). 1863 (15/10) launched. 1864 (24/8) MV Havre—New York. 1866 (2/8) LV ditto (12 RV). 1866 (11/10) FV St Nazaire—Panama. 1868 converted to twinscrew at Penhoët; new two-cylinder single-expansion engines by Schneider, Creuzot; mizzen mast added. 1869 (23/4) resumed Havre—Brest—New York. 1871 (18/8) LV ditto (15 RV). 1871 (23/9) damaged by fire in dock at Havre; repaired; engines converted to four-cylinder compound by Schneider. 1873 (7/7) resumed St. Nazaire—Panama. 1874 (22/5) resumed Havre—Brest—New York. 1876 (12/2) LV ditto (3 RV); subsequently St Nazaire—Panama service. 1905 (20/3) FV St Nazaire—Fayal—New York (1 voy). 1906 scrapped at Brest.

3. 1865 EUROPE

3,400. 105,62 x 13,36. (346.6 x 43.8). S—2—2. I—P—SL2—12. (I—128; II—54; III—29). Scott & Co, Greenock (engines Greenock Foundry Co). 1864 (22/7) launched. 1865 (3/5) MV Havre—New York. 1869 (12/3) LV ditto (18 RV). 1873 lengthened to 120,08 metres (394 feet) by A. Leslie & Co, Hebburn-on-Tyne; 4,600 tons; converted to single-screw; compound engines; mizzen mast added. 1873 (28/8) resumed Havre—New York. 1874 (3/4) abandoned in N Atlantic (0); foundered about three weeks later.

4. (1866) NOUVEAU MONDE
(1875) LABRADOR

3,200. 105,62 x 13,36. (346.6 x 43.8). S—2—2. I—P—SL2—12. (I—128; II—54; III—29). Chantier de Penhoët (under supervision of Scott & Co), St Nazaire (engines Schneider, Creuzot). 1865 (27/1) launched. 1865 (16/10) MV St Nazaire—Vera Cruz. 1866 (10/2) sailed Havre—New York; put back. 1866 (18/2) FV Havre—New York (1 RV). 1866-74 St Nazaire—W Indies. 1875 lengthened to 120,35 metres (394.9 feet) by A. Leslie & Co, Hebburn-on-Tyne; 4,612 tons; converted to single-screw; compound engines by Maudslay, Sons & Field, London; mizzen mast added; renamed LABRADOR. 1875 (20/11) resumed Havre—New York. 1886 (22/10) FV Havre—Panama. 1889 triple-expansion engines by CGT, St Nazaire. 1904 sold. 1905 scrapped at Genoa.

5. 1866 PÉREIRE

    3,150. 105,15 x 13,26. (345.0 x 43.5). C—1—3. I—S—I(2)—13. (I—200; II—120). R. Napier & Sons, Glasgow. 1865 (4/11) launched. 1866 (29/3) MV Havre—Brest—New York. 1872 (10/5) LV ditto. 1872-3 engines converted to three-cylinder compound by builders; second funnel added. 1873 (14/2) resumed Havre—Brest—New York. 1883 (7/4) LV Havre—New York; subsequently Central American service. 1888 sold; became sailing ship LANCING (British; later Norwegian). 1925 scrapped at Genoa.

6. 1866 VILLE DE PARIS

    3,014. 105,15 x 13,22. (345.0 x 43.4). C—1—3. I—S—I(2)—13. (I—200; II—120). R. Napier & Sons, Glasgow. 1865 (Dec) launched. 1866 (24/5) MV Havre—Brest—New York. 1873 (3/7) LV ditto. 1873-4 engines converted to four-cylinder compound by Société de Fives Lille, Fives Lille; second funnel added. 1874 (7/5) resumed Havre—Brest—New York. 1876 (7/6) FV St Nazaire—Panama. 1878 (21/9) LV Havre—New York; subsequently Panama service. 1888 H. BISCHOFF (German sailing ship). 1900 (27/10) stranded in R Elbe; broke in two.

7. 1866 NAPOLÉON III
  (1873) VILLE DU HAVRE

    3,376. 111,50 x 13,98. (365.9 x 45.9). S—2—2. I—P—SL2—11. (I—170; II—100; III—50). Thames Ironworks, London (engines Ravenshill & Salked, London). 1865 (11/2) launched. 1866 (26/4) MV Havre—Brest—New York. 1868 (30/8) LV ditto (5 RV). 1871 (16/9) sailed Havre—Tyneside. 1871-2 lengthened to 128,52 metres (421.7 feet) by A. Leslie & Co, Hebburn-on-Tyne; 3,950 tons; converted to single-screw; compound engines; mizzen mast added; renamed VILLE DU HAVRE. 1873 (29/3) resumed Havre—Brest—New York. 1873 (22/11) sunk in collision with ship LOCH EARN (Br) in English Channel (226).

8. (1866) VERA CRUZ

    1,700. 80,77 x 11,15. (265.0 x 36.6). C—1—3. I—S—D2—10. John Laird, Birkenhead, (engines Fawcett, Preston & Co, Liverpool). 1854 (7/10) launched as IMPERATRIZ (S American & General). 1854 (Dec) Crimean War transport. 1862 VERA CRUZ (CGT). 1866 (30/6) FV Havre—New York. 1867 (22/6) LV ditto (3 RV). 1869 compound engines by John Elder, Glasgow; renamed MARTINIQUE (CGT) 1892 scrapped.

9. (1866) TAMPICO

    1,700. 80,77 x 11,12. (265.0 x 36.5). C—1—3. I—S—D2—10. John Laird, Birkenhead (engines Fawcett, Preston & Co, Liverpool). 1854 (13/7) launched as IMPERADOR (S American & General). 1854 (24/10) MV

Liverpool—S. America (1 RV). 1855 (Jan) Crimean War transport 1862
TAMPICO (CGT). 1866 (12/8) FV Havre—New York—Vera Cruz—
Havre. 1867 (11/5) LV Havre—New York (2 RV). 1869—70 compound
engines by John Elder, Glasgow; renamed GUADELOUPE (CGT). 1889
SORRENTO (Norwegian). 1890 (Aug) foundered in North Sea.

10. 1866 SAINT LAURENT (I)
3,413. 108,20 x 13,41. (355.0 x 44.0). S—2—3. I—S—H2—12. Chantier de
Penhoët (under supervision of Scott & Co), St Nazaire (engines Schneider,
Creuzot). Laid down as paddle steamer. 1866 (19/4) launched. 1866
(11/10) MV Havre—Brest—New York. 1875-6 four-cylinder compound
engines by Schneider. 1886 (10/7) LV Havre—New York. 1886 (22/9) FV
Havre—Panama. 1887-8 tonnage 3,945; triple-expansion engines by CGT,
Penhoët. 1902 scrapped at Genoa.

11. (1866) FLORIDE
1,859. 85,34 x 11,89. (280.0 x 39.0). C—1—3. I—S—I(2)—10. (I—100;
II—60; III). Caird & Co, Greenock. 1862 (Jan) launched as COLOÏD (Fr).
1862 bought by CGT when fitting out; renamed FLORIDE. 1862 (14/6)
MV St Nazaire—W Indies. 1866 (5/10) listed and sank at her berth at
Havre; refloated. 1866 (23/10) FV Havre—New York—Vera Cruz—St
Nazaire (1 voy). 1867 refitted at St Nazaire. 1874 rebuilt with additional
deck; straight stem; compound engines by SA de Construction Navale,
Havre; renamed COLOMBIE. 1875 (20/10) resumed St Nazaire—W
Indies. 1897 (Dec) scrapped at Marseilles.

12. (1872) FRANCE (I)
3,200. 105,63 x 13,41. (346.6 x 44.0). S—2—2. I—P—SL2—12. Chantier
de Penhoët (under supervision of Scott & Co), St Nazaire (engines Schneider, Creuzot). 1864 (1/10) launched. 1865 (/   ) MV St Nazaire—Vera
Cruz. 1872 (2/8) FV Havre—Brest—New York (1 RV) (last North Atlantic voyage by CGT paddle steamer). 1872 (29/9) sailed Havre—New York
but engines disabled off Cherbourg; returned to Havre. 1874 lengthened to
120,45 metres (395.2 feet) by A. Leslie & Co, Hebburn-on-Tyne; 4,648
tons; converted to single-screw; compound engines by Maudslay, Sons &
Field, London; mizzen mast added; (I & II—279; III—510). 1874 (7/11)
resumed Havre—New York. 1884 (22/3) LV ditto. 1884 (6/12) FV St
Nazaire—Panama. 1886 (20/12) damaged by fire at sea. 1886 (24/12) arr
Fort de France, Martinique. 1887 (Feb-Jun) reconditioned at St Nazaire.
1895 triple-expansion engines by CGT, Penhoët. 1910 (Jul) scrapped at
Cherbourg

13. (1874) AMÉRIQUE

4,585. 121,91 x 13,41. (400.0 x 44.0). S—2—3. I—S—C4—12. Chantier de Penhoët (under supervision of Scott & Co), St Nazaire. Laid down as ATLANTIQUE. 1864 (23/4) launched as IMPÉRATRICE EUGÉNIE (CGT); 3,200 tons; 105,63 x 13,41. (346.6 x 44.0); S—2—2; I—P—SL2—12; engines Schneider, Creuzot. 1865 (16/2) MV St Nazaire—Vera Cruz. 1865-73 ditto. 1873 lengthened by A. Leslie & Co, Hebburn-on-Tyne; converted to single-screw; compound engines by Maudslay, Sons & Field, London; mizzen mast added; renamed AMÉRIQUE. 1874 (16/1) FV Havre—New York. 1874 (14/4) abandoned near French coast; towed to Plymouth. 1875 (13/3) resumed Havre—New York. 1876 (Mar) fitted with 'the lighthouse and electric light' (external only). 1877 (7/1) stranded at Seabright, NJ. 1877 (10/4) refloated. 1877 (11/8) resumed Havre—New York. 1886 (1/5) LV ditto. 1886 (22/9) FV Havre—Panama. 1888 internal electric light installed. 1892 triple-expansion engines. 1895 (28/1) wrecked at Savanilla.

14. (1876) CANADA

4,054. 108,32 x 13,34. (355.4 x 43.8). S—2—3. I—S—C4—12. Chantier de Penhoët (under supervision of Scott & Co), St Nazaire. 186 (/) launched as PANAMA (CGT): 3,400 tons; S—2—2; I—P—SL2—12; engines Schneider, Creuzot. 1866 (/) MV St Nazaire —Vera Cruz. 1866-75 ditto. 1875-6 rebuilt (but not lengthened) by A. Leslie & Co, Hebburn-on-Tyne; converted to single-screw; compound engines by Maudslay, Sons & Field, London; mizzen mast added; renamed CANADA (CGT). 1876 (22/4) FV Havre—Plymouth—New York. 1886 (15/5) LV Havre—New York. 1886 (22/8) FV Havre—Panama. 1896 triple-expansion engines by CGT, Penhöet. 1908 scrapped at St Nazaire.

15. (1876) SAINT GERMAIN

3,554. 115,02 x 12,28. (377.4 x 40.3). S—2—2. I—S—C2—13. (I—90; II—100; III—800). J & G Thomson, Glasgow. 1874 (30/6) launched as KLOPSTOCK (Adler). 1875 ditto (Hapag). 1876 SAINT GERMAIN (CGT). 1876 (3/6) FV Havre—Plymouth—New York. 1876 (9/9) LV Havre—Plymouth—St John's, NF (for repairs)—New York (arr 8/10) (3 RV). 1876 (7/12) FV St Nazaire—Panama. 1881 (27/8) resumed Havre—New York. 1886 (10/4) LV ditto (28 RV). 1886 (8/6) resumed St Nazaire—Panama. 1900 (3/4) resumed Havre—New York. 1900 (20/10) LV ditto (3 RV). 1907 scrapped at Glasgow. (see Hapag - 53).

16. (1880) FERDINAND DE LESSEPS

2,865. 106,67 x 11,98. (350.0 x 38.3). S—1—3. I—S—C2—12. (I—45; III—500). A. & J. Inglis, Glasgow. 1875 (23/1) launched as STAD HAARLEM (KNSM). 1879 (5/2) FV London—Cape Town—New

Zealand (1 RV for NZS Co and SSA joint). 1879 sold to CGT; intended name VILLE DE MADRID but renamed FERDINAND DE LESSEPS. 1879 (14/9) FV Marseilles—Panama. 1880 (30/10) FV Havre—New York (3 RV). 1881 (28/4) FV Marseilles—New York. 1882 (10/6) LV ditto (7 RV). 1911 scrapped at Dunkirk.

17. (1880) VILLE DE MARSEILLE

2,714. 106,58 x 11,70. (349.7 x 38.4). S—1—3. I—S—C2—12. (I—45; III—500). A. & J. Inglis, Glasgow. 1874 (10/12) launched as STAD AMSTERDAM (KNSM). 1879 VILLE DE MARSEILLE (CGT). 1879 (14/6) FV Marseilles—Panama. 1880 (13/11) FV Havre—New York (4 RV). 1881 (14/5) FV Marseilles—New York. 1882 (24/9) LV ditto (8 RV). 1902 scrapped at Genoa. (See KNSM - 121).

18. (1880) CALDÉRA

2,110. 108,35 x 10,51. (355.5 x 34.5). 1—2. I—S—C4—10. Wm Denny & Bros, Dumbarton. Laid down as ASSAM (P&O). 1868 (25/6) launched as CALDÉRA; 1,741 tons; I(2) by builders. 1870 (May) engines compounded by builders (first Denny compounds). 1870 (Aug) bought by PSN. 1875 lengthened from 83,66 metres (275.4 feet); new compound engines by Laird Bros, Birkenhead. 1879 CALDÉRA (CGT). 1880 (27/11) FV Havre New York (1 RV). 1881 (15/4) FV Marseilles—New York (FV of service). 1882 (14/10) LV ditto (8 RV). 1886 sold; name retained. 1887 (15/5) sunk in collision with ss GOORKA (British India) near Suakin, Sudan.

19. (1881) PICARDIE

1,371. 92,96 x 9,75. (305.0 x 32.0). C—1—3. I—S—C2—10. (I—28; II—55; III—356). J. Laing & Sons, Sunderland. 1865 (11/1) launched as ALBANY (Fr). 1867 PICARDIE (SGTM). 1876 ditto (Valery) (Fr). 1881 ditto (CGT). 1881 (6/2) FV Marseilles—Panama. 1881 (28/5) FV Marseilles—New York. 1882 (14/11) LV ditto (4½ RV). 1883 (18/1) foundered off Newfoundland after being taken in tow by LABRADOR (CGT).

20. (1883) SAINT SIMON

2,989. 106,67 x 11,95. (350.0 x 39.2). S—1—2. I—S—C2—11. Caird & Co, Greenock. 1874 (18/4) launched as RHENANIA (Hapag). 1878 SAINT SIMON (CGT). 1883 (3/3) FV Havre—New York. 1886 (16/1) LV ditto (8 RV); subsequently West Indies service. 1905 (29/8) scrapped at Genoa.

21. 1883 NORMANDIE (I)
    (1886) LA NORMANDIE
    6,283. 139,99 x 14,99. (459.3 x 49.2). S—2—4. I—S—C6—16. (I—205; II—76; III—1,000). Barrow Shipbuilding Co, Barrow. Laid down as VILLE DE NEW YORK. 1882 (28/10) launched as NORMANDIE. 1883 (5/5) MV Havre—New York. 1886 renamed LA NORMANDIE. 1886 (24/4) FV as such, Havre—New York. 1894 triple-expansion engines by CGT, St Nazaire; masts reduced to two. 1894 (21/4) FV St Nazaire— Havana—Vera Cruz. 1894 (23/6) resumed Havre—New York. 1901 (27/7) LV ditto; subsequently St Nazaire—Havana—Vera Cruz. 1908 St Nazaire —Panama. 1911 (11/9) LV ditto. 1912 scrapped at Bo'ness.

22. (1883) OLINDE RODRIGUES
    3,029. 106,67 x 11,89. (350.0 x 39.0). S—1—2. I—S—C2—11. (I—150; II—70; III—164). Caird & Co, Greenock. 1873 (22/9) launched as FRAN-CONIA (Hapag). 1878 (12/4) OLINDE RODRIGUES (CGT). 1883 (8/12) FV Havre—New York. 1885 (13/6) LV ditto (4 RV); subsequently W Indies service. 1905 (Aug) scrapped at Cherbourg.

23. 1886 LA CHAMPAGNE
    7,087. 150,38 x 15,78. (493.4 x 51.8). S—2—4. S—S—T6—17. (I—390; II—65; III—600). CGT, St Nazaire. 1885 (15/5) launched. 1886 (22/5) MV Havre—New York. 1887 (7/8) seriously damaged in collision with VILLE DE RIO JANEIRO (Chargeurs Réunis) near Havre; latter sunk. 1896 quadruple-expansion engines by builders; two masts; III increased to 1,500. 1898 (17/2) fractured propeller shaft. 1898 (23/2) sighted by ROMAN (Warren); towed to Halifax. 1905 (21/1) LV Havre—New York. 1905 extra promenade deck added; transferred to Mexican service. 1906 (10/3) resumed Havre—New York. 1906 (7/4) LV ditto (2 RV); resumed Mexican service. 1913 St Nazaire—Panama. 1915 (28/5) stranded at St Nazaire; broke her back.

24. 1886 LA BOURGOGNE
    7,395. 150,68 x 15,91. (494.4 x 52.2). S—2—4. I&S—S—C6—17. (I—390; II—65; III—600). Forges & Chantiers de la Méditerranée, La Seyne. 1885 (8/10) launched. 1886 (19/6) MV Havre—New York. 1896 (Feb) collided with and sank ss AILSA (Atlas) off US coast. 1897-8 quadruple expansion engines by CGT, St Nazaire; two masts. 1898 (4/7) sunk in collision with' ship CROMARTYSHIRE (Br) off Cape Sable (549).

25. 1886 LA BRETAGNE
    7,112. 150,99 x 15,78. (495.4 x 51.8). S—2—4. S—S—T6—17. (I—390; II—65; III—600). CGT, St Nazaire. 1885 (9/9) launched. 1886 (14/8) MV Havre—New York. 1895 quadruple-expansion engines by builders; two

masts; III increased to 1,500. 1912 (8/6) LV Havre—New York. 1912 LA BRETAGNE (Cie Sud Atlantique). 1919 ALESIA (ditto). 1923 (Dec) sold for scrap in Holland; broke her tow near Texel Island; ran ashore; became total loss.

26. 1886 LA GASCOGNE
(1915) LA GASCOGNE (c)
7,395. 150,99 x 15,91. (495.4 x 52.2). S—2—4. I&S—S—C6—17. (I—390; II—65; III—600). Forges & Chantiers de la Méditerranée, La Seyne. Laid down as L'ALGERIE. 1886 (5/1) launched as LA GASCOGNE. 1886 (18/9) MV Havre—New York. 1894 quadruple-expansion engines by CGT, St Nazaire; two masts; III increased to 1,500. 1911 (4/3) LV Havre—New York. 1912 LA GASCOGNE (Cie Sud Atlantique). 1915 (26/2) FV for CGT (c), Bordeaux—New York. 1915 (16/7) LV ditto (3 RV). 1919 (1/7) arr Genoa to be scrapped.

27. 1891 LA TOURAINE
8,893. 158,55 x 17,07. (520.2 x 56.0). S—2—3. S—2S—T6—19. (I—392; II—98; III—600). CGT, St Nazaire. 1890 (21/3) launched. 1891 (20/6) MV Havre—New York. 1900 (Nov) - 1902 (Jan) refitted at St Nazaire; bilge keels fitted; engines overhauled; two masts; tonnage 8,429; III increased to 1,000. 1903 (21/1) damaged by fire at Havre - grand staircase, first class dining saloon and de luxe cabins rebuilt. 1910 I—69; II—263; III—686. 1913 (May) FV Havre—Quebec—Montreal (II and III only). 1914 (Jun) LV ditto (5 RV). 1915 (13/3) LV Havre—New York (I; II; III). 1915 (13/4) FV Bordeaux—New York. 1919 (9/2) resumed Havre—New York; (cabin; III). 1922 (26/9) LV ditto. 1923 (Oct) scrapped at Dunkirk.

28. (1894) LA NAVARRE
6,648. 143,55 x 15,39. (471.0 x 50.5). S—2—2. S—2S—T6—15. (I—235; II—69; III—74). CGT, St Nazaire. 1892 (4/11) launched. 1893 (21/11) MV St Nazaire—Vera Cruz. 1894 (28/7) FV Havre—New York (1 RV). 1898 (12/3) resumed ditto. 1898 (8/10) LV ditto (7 RV). 1924 sold. 1925 scrapped at Dunkirk.

28a. (1899) WOOLLOOMOOLOO (c)
3,521. 109,72 x 13,53. (360.0 x 44.4). S—1—3. S—T3—12. Wigham Richardson & Co, Walker-on-Tyne. 1891 (26/5) launched for Lund's Blue Anchor Line. 1899 (9/5) FV for CGT (c), Havre—Bordeaux—New York (III only). 1899 (26/10) LV ditto (5 RV). 1901 HARMONIDES (Houston). 1902 (7/3) collision with WAESLAND (American Line) off Anglesey; latter sunk. 1919 KHARTUM (British). 1927 scrapped at Genoa.

657

28b. (1899) CHATEAU LAFITE (c)

   3,462. 111,61 x 12,53. (366.2 x 41.1). S—1—3. I—S—C2—12. Oswald Mordaunt, Southampton. 1881 (14/6) launched for Cie Bordelaise. 1899 (31/5) FV for CGT (c), Havre—Bordeaux—New York. 1899 (4/12) LV ditto (5 RV). 1902 (Jun) sold to Italy; scrapped. (See Cie Bordelaise - 120).

29. (1899) L'AQUITAINE

   8,242. 152,39 x 17,52. (500.0 x 57.5). S—3—2. S—2S—T6—19. (I—432; II—162; III—2,000). Fairfield Co Ltd, Glasgow. 1890 (8/2) launched as NORMANNIA (Hapag). 1899 L'AQUITAINE (CGT). 1899 (9/12) FV Havre—New York. 1905 (9/9) LV ditto (33 RV). 1906 scrapped at Bo'ness. (See Hapag - 53).

30. 1900 LA LORRAINE

   11,146. 171,62 x 18,29. (563.1 x 60.0). 2—2. 2S—T8—20. (I—446; II—116; III—552). CGT, St Nazaire. 1899 (20/9) launched. 1900 (11/8) MV Havre —New York. 1914 (25/7) LV ditto. 1914-7 LORRAINE II (armed merchant cruiser). 1918 reverted to LA LORRAINE. 1918 (May) FV Bordeaux—New York. 1919 (19/1) LV ditto. 1919 (22/2) resumed Havre —New Yo.k. 1922 (May) cabin; III. 1922 (1/10) LV ditto. 1922 (Dec) scrapped at St Nazaire.

31. 1901 LA SAVOIE

   11,168. 171,62 x 18,29. (563.1 x 60.0). 2—2. 2S—T8—20. (I—437; II—118; III—398). CGT, St Nazaire. 1900 (31/3) launched. 1901 (31/8) MV Havre—New York. 1914 (18/7) LV ditto. 1914-8 armed merchant cruiser. 1919 (26/4) resumed Havre—New York. 1923 (Mar) cabin 430; III—613. 1927 (24/9) LV Havre—New York (dep 7/10)—Havre. 1927 sold. 1928 scrapped at Dunkirk.

32. (1905) QUÉBEC

   3,342. 105,36 x 13,44. (345.7 x 44.1). 1—2. S—T3—12. (III—800). R.Napier & Sons, Glasgow. 1896 (22/9) launched as EBRO (RMSP). 1903 QUEBEC (Br). 1905 QUÉBEC (CGT). 1905 (6/3) FV Havre—New York (1 RV). 1905 (6/6) FV Havre—Haiti. 1917 (24/1) sunk at mouth of R Gironde by mine laid by German submarine UC.21.

33. (1905) MONTRÉAL

   3,342. 105,36 x 13,44. (345.7 x 44.1). 1—2. S—T3—12. (III—800). R.Napier & Sons, Glasgow. 1896 (14/7) launched as MINHO (RMSP). 1903 HALIFAX (British). 1905 MONTRÉAL (CGT). 1905 (25/2) FV Havre—Fayal—New York (arr 5/4). 1905 (23/9) LV Havre—New York (3 RV); subsequently Havre—Haiti. 1917 (24/3) torpedoed and sunk by German submarine U.46, 77 miles NE of Cape Ortegal, Spain.

34. 1905 HUDSON

5,558. 119,17 x 15,39. (391.0 x 50.5). 1—2. S—T3—12. (II—60; III—700). Chantiers de Normandie, Grand Quevilly. 1904 (23/11) launched as HUDSON (French). 1905 ditto (CGT). 1905 (22/4) MV Havre—New York. 1914 (Mar) LV Havre—Bordeaux—New York. 1914 (24/10) resumed ditto. 1915 (20/4) LV Bordeaux—New York. 1919 (Aug) FV for Cie Canadienne Transatlantique (c), Havre—Quebec—Montreal. 1919 (Oct) LV ditto (3 RV). 1930 scrapped at Ghent.

35. 1905 LOUISIANE

5,104. 112,73 x 14,44. (369.9 x 47.4). 1—2. S—T3—12. (II—60; III—700). Ateliers & Chantiers de France, Dunkirk (engines Caillard & Cie, Havre). 1905 (5/2) launched. 1905 (2/7) MV Havre—New York. 1909 (12/10) LV ditto (15 RV). 1912 (20/7) resumed ditto. 1914 (5/7) LV Bordeaux—New York. 1916 (9/3) torpedoed and sunk at anchor in Havre roads by German submarine UB.18.

36. 1905 CALIFORNIE

5,152. 112,73 x 14,44. (369.9 x 47.4). 1—2. S—T3—12. (II—60; III—900). Ateliers & Chantiers de France, Dunkirk (engines Caillard & Cie, Havre). 1905 (20/7) launched. 1905 (5/11) MV Havre—New York. 1915 (13/4) LV Bordeaux—Vigo—New York (31 RV on N Atlantic); occasional later voyages to New York as cargo steamer. 1919 (Jul) FV for Cie Canadienne Transatlantique (c), Havre—Quebec—Montreal. 1919 (Nov) LV ditto (3 RV). 1934 scrapped.

37. (1906) SAINT LAURENT (II)

5,607. 119,53 x 15,42. (392.2 x 50.6). 1—2. S—T3—12. (II—25; III—700). Chantiers de Normandie, Grand Quevilly. 1905 (19/5) launched. 1906 (10/2) FV Havre—New York. 1914 (3/1) LV ditto (37 RV). 1917 (5/2) caught fire in Malta harbour when loaded with explosives; sunk by torpedo to avoid explosion.

38. 1906 LA PROVENCE

13,753. 183,57 x 19,81. (602.3 x 65.0). 2—2. 2S—T8—21. (I—422; II—132; III—808). Chantiers & Ateliers de St Nazaire, St Naziare. 1905 (21/3) launched. 1906 (21/4) MV Havre—New York. 1914 (6/6) LV ditto. 1914 PROVENCE II (armed merchant cruiser). 1916 (16/2) torpedoed and sunk by German submarine U.35 in Mediterranean (830).

39. (1907) MEXICO

4,885. 107,98 x 14,50. (354.3 x 47.6). 1—2. S—T3—12. (II—180; III—756). Forges & Chantiers de la Méditerranée, Havre. 1905 bought on stocks. 1905 (3/8) launched. 1907 (24/8) FV Havre—New York. 1913 (4/9) LV

Bordeaux—Coruña—Vigo—New York (11 RV). 1920 (1/2) resumed Havre—New York. 1920 (22/8) LV ditto (3 RV). 1925 scrapped.

40. 1907 FLORIDE

6,624. 125,94 x 15,91. (413.2 x 52.2). 1—2. S—T3—13. (II—125; III—785). Chantiers & Ateliers de Provence, Port de Bouc. 1907 (14/7) launched. 1907 (30/11) MV Havre—New York. 1912 (9/2) LV ditto. 1912 (Aug) FV Havre—Quebec—Montreal. 1913 (Sep) LV ditto (4 RV). 1914 (25/11) LV Havre—New York. 1915 (19/2) sunk off Dakar by German raider PRINZ EITEL FRIEDRICH when under charter to Cie Sud Atlantique.

41. 1908 CHICAGO

10,501. 154,95 x 17,61. (508.4 x 57.8). 2—2. 2S—T6—15. (II—358; III—1,250). Chantiers & Ateliers de St Nazaire, St Nazaire. 1907 (5/11) launched. 1908 (30/5) MV Havre—New York. 1915 (22/3) LV ditto. 1915 (16/5) FV Bordeaux—New York. 1920 (31/1) LV ditto. 1921 (3/2) resumed Havre—New York. 1926 (Aug) cabin; tourist; III. 1928 (9/6) LV Bordeaux—New York. 1928 reconstructed; renamed GUADELOUPE; West Indies service. 1936 scrapped at St Nazaire.

42. 1909 CAROLINE

6,693. 125,94 x 15,88. (413.2 x 52.1). 1—2. 2S—T6—14. (II—50; III—46, but soon increased to II—150; III—750). Chantiers & Ateliers de Provence, Port de Bouc. 1908 (14/7) launched. 1908 (26/12) MV Havre—New York. 1912 (27/4) LV Havre—New York (25 RV). 1912 (Aug) FV Havre—Quebec—Montreal. 1914 (Jul) LV ditto (6 RV). 1920 (31/7) FV Bordeaux—New York; (cabin; III).1921 (12/4) LV ditto. 1929 JACQUES CARTIER (CGT) (officer cadets' training ship). 1929 (1/12) FV Havre—New York (cargo only). 1931 (Dec) laid up at Brest. 1934 scrapped at Genoa.

43. (1910) NIAGARA

8,481. 147,88 x 17,10. (485.2 x 56.1) 1—2. 2S—T6—15. (II—182; III—960). Ateliers & Chantiers de la Loire, St Nazaire. 1908 (16/5) launched as CORSE (Chargeurs Réunis). 1910 NIAGARA (CGT). 1910 (26/3) FV Havre—New York. 1912 (4/4) LV ditto. 1912 (11/5) FV Havre—Quebec—Montreal (3 RV). 1915 (1/4) LV Havre—New York. 1915 (8/5) FV Bordeaux—New York. 1919 cabin; III—. 1920 (31/7) LV ditto. 1920 (9/9) resumed Havre—New York. 1921 (20/4) FV Hamburg—New York (3 RV). 1922 (7/5) resumed Bordeaux—New York. 1922 (10/11) LV ditto. 1922 (Dec) FV Havre—Houston. 1929 (9/6) FV Havre—New York —Havana—Houston—Havre (1 RV). 1930 (17/3) LV Havre—New York. 1931 scrapped.

44. (1911) VIRGINIE

5,330. 109,17 x 14,99. (358.2 x 49.2). 1—2. S—T3—12. (II—50; III—300).
Forges & Chantiers de la Méditerranée, La Seyne. 1903 (30/7) launched as
MALOU (French). 1907 VIRGINIE (CGT). 1911 (7/1) FV Havre—New
York. 1914 (Jun) FV Havre—Quebec—Montreal (1 RV). 1917 (4/1) LV
Bordeaux—New York (15 or more RV). 1934 scrapped in Holland.

45. (1911) ESPAGNE

11,155. 163,91 x 18,53. (537.8 x 60.8).2—2. 2S—T8—15. (I—296; II—106;
III—500). Chantiers & Ateliers de Provence, Port de Bouc. 1909 (19/12)
launched. 1910 (5/10) MV St Nazaire—W Indies. 1911 (11/2) FV Havre—
New York. 1919 (27/1) LV ditto (35 RV). 1919 (2/3) resumed Havre—New
York; (cabin; III). 1919 (5/7) LV ditto (4 RV). 1934 scrapped at St Nazaire.

46. 1911 ROCHAMBEAU

12,678. 170,49 x 19,41. (559.4 x 63.7). 2—2. 4S—T8 & ST—15. (II—428;
III—1,700). Chantiers & Ateliers de St Nazaire, St Nazaire. 1911 (2/3)
launched. 1911 (16/9) MV Havre—New York. 1915 (7/3) LV ditto. 1915
(4/4) FV Bordeaux—New York. 1919 (9/1) LV ditto. 1919 cabin 475;
III—1,450. 1919 (18/2) resumed Havre—New York. 1926 (Aug) cabin;
tourist. 1927 (Dec) cabin; tourist; III. 1933 (Jul) LV Havre—Vigo—New
York. 1934 scrapped at Dunkirk.

47. 1912 FRANCE (II)

23,666.210,33 x 23,04. (690.1 x 75.6). 4—2. 4S—ST—24. (I—535; II—440;
III—950). Chantiers & Ateliers de St Nazaire, St Nazaire. Laid down as
LA PICARDIE. 1910 (20/9) launched as FRANCE. 1912 (20/4) MV
Havre—New York.1914 (27/9) LV ditto. 1914 FRANCE IV (transport;
hospital ship; transport). 1918 reverted to FRANCE. 1918 (17/12) FV
after Armistice, Brest—New York as troopship (1 RV). 1919 (2/2) FV
Bordeaux—New York (1 RV). 1919 (6/8) resumed Havre—New York.
1923 (29/9) LV Havre—Plymouth—New York. 1923-4 converted to oil
fuel; (I—517; II—444; III—660). 1924 (10/5) resumed Havre—
Plymouth—New York. 1932 (Jun) I; tourist; III. 1932 (13/8) LV ditto.
1932 (9/9) LV New York—Plymouth—Havre. 1935 scrapped at Dunkirk.

48. 1915 LAFAYETTE (II)
   (1929) MÉXIQUE

11,953. 166,62 x 19,50. (546.7 x 64.0). 2—2. 4S—C8 & ST—16. (I—500;
II—350; III—1,500). Chantiers & Ateliers de Provence, Port de Bouc. 1914
(27/5) launched as ILE DE CUBA (CGT); completed as LAFAYETTE.
1915 (31/10) MV Bordeaux—New York. 1916 (8/10) LV ditto (9 RV).
1917 (Feb) hospital ship. 1919 (8/11) FV Havre—New York. 1924 (10/9)
LV Havre—Plymouth—New York. 1924 (Nov) FV St Nazaire—W Indies.

1927 (Jan) cabin; III. 1927 (22/1) LV Bordeaux—New York (1 RV). 1928 renamed MÉXIQUE (Vera Cruz service). 1929 (4/9) FV Havre—New York (1 RV) in lieu of PARIS. 1940 (19/6) sunk by mine at Le Verdon, R Gironde.

49. (1920) LEOPOLDINA (c) (Brazilian)
(1923) SUFFREN
12,350. 160,19 x 18,99. (525.6 x 62.3) 2—2. 2S—Q8—15. (I—390; II—230; III—550). Blohm & Voss, Hamburg. 1901 (23/11) launched as BLÜCHER (Hapag). 1917 seized by Brazil at Pernambuco; LEOPOLDINA (Brazilian Govt). 1920 (11/3) FV for CGT (c), New York—Havre. 1920 (5/6) FV Havre—New York. 1920 (Dec) cabin 500; III—250. 1923 SUFFREN (CGT). 1923 (9/5) FV Havre—New York. 1928 (22/9) LV ditto; laid up. 1929 scrapped at Genoa. (See Hapag - 53).

49a. (1920) SANTAREM (c) (Brazilian)
6,757. 127,88 x 16,61. (419.6 x 54.5). 1—2. S—Q4—14. (Cabin 50;III—900). Bremer Vulkan, Vegesack. 1908 (/) launched as EISENACH (NDL). 1917 seized by Brazil at Pernambuco; SANTAREM (Brazilian Govt). 1920 (13/12) FV for CGT (c), Marseilles—New York. 1920 (29/3) FV New York—Danzig—Hamburg. 1920 (18/5) FV Havre—York (2 RV on N Atlantic). 1962 scrapped.

50. (1920) ROUSSILLON
8,800. 140,84 x 17,55. (462.1 x 57.6). 1—2. 2S—Q8—14. (Cabin 281; III—1,333). AG Weser, Bremen. 1906 (11/12) launched as GOEBEN (NDL). 1914 (Aug) interned at Vigo. 1919 ROUSSILLON (CGT). 1920 (28/9) FV Marseilles—New York. 1920 (3/12) FV Havre—New York. 1923 (18/9) LV ditto. 1923 (1/11) FV Bordeaux—New York. 1930 (24/8) LV ditto. 1931 (Feb) scrapped at Pasajes, Spain.

51. (1921) LA BOURDONNAIS
8,287. 138,22 x 17,00. (453.5 x 55.8). 1—2. 2S—T6—14. (Cabin 122; III—500). J.C. Tecklenborg, Geestemünde. 1904 (14/5) launched as SCHARNHORST (NDL). 1919 seized by France at Cherbourg when in prisoner exchange service. 1921 LA BOURDONNAIS (CGT). 1921 (2/4) FV Havre—New York. 1923 (20/1) LV ditto. 1923 (3/3) FV Bordeaux—New York. 1931 (31/1) LV Bordeaux—Vigo—Halifax—New York. 1933 sold. 1934 scrapped at Genoa. (See NDL - 60).

52. 1921 PARIS
34,569. 224,14 [232,94] x 25,99. (735.4 [764.3] x 85.3). 3—2. 4S—ST—21. (I—565; II—480; III—1,100). Chantiers & Ateliers de St Nazaire, St Nazaire. 1913 keel laid. 1916 (12/9) launched; work suspended; towed to

Quiberon Bay. 1921 (15/6) MV Havre—New York. 1929 (Aug) damaged by fire at Havre. 1930 (15/1) resumed Havre—Plymouth—New York. 1932 (May) I; tourist; III. 1939 (31/3) LV Havre—Southampton—New York. 1939 (19/4) caught fire at Havre; capsized and sank at her berth; wreck disposed of after World War II.

53. 1924 DE GRASSE

17,707. 168,27 [174,94] x 21,76. (552.1 [574.0] x 71.4). 2—2. 2S—ST(SR) —16. (Cabin 399; III—1,712). Cammell, Laird & Co Ltd, Birkenhead. 1920 (23/3) laid down as SUFFREN (CGT); building suspended until 1923. 1924 (23/2) launched as DE GRASSE. 1924 (21/8) MV Havre— New York. 1927 (2/2) cabin 536; tourist; III—410. 1939 (18/8) LV (peace-time) Havre—New York. 1940 seized by Germans; became accommodation ship near Bordeaux. 1942 (Jun) returned to CGT; training ship. 1944 (30/8) depth-charged by German 'E' boat; sank in shallow water. 1945 (30/8) salvaged; reconditioned; one funnel; tonnage 19,918; (I—360; cabin 360). 1947 (12/7) resumed Havre—New York. 1951 (30/9) LV ditto. 1952 (24/4) FV Havre—W Indies. 1953 EMPRESS OF AUSTRALIA (Can Pac); 19,379 tons; (I—220; tourist 444). 1953 (28/4) FV Liverpool— Quebec—Montreal. 1955 (5/12) LV Quebec—Liverpool (38 RV); laid up in Gareloch. 1956 VENEZUELA (Grimaldi); 18,567 tons; (I—180; tourist 500; dormitory 800). 1956 (11/6) FV Naples—Palermo—Malaga—Vigo —La Guaira—Curaçao—Jamaica—Vera Cruz—Havana—Port Ever-glades (8/7)—Bermuda—Coruña—Southampton—Rotterdam (only North Atlantic voyage). 1960 new clipper bow; length OA 187,20 metres (614.2 feet); 18,769 tons. 1962 (16/3) beached after striking rocks off Cannes. 1962 (Apr) refloated; towed to Genoa. 1962 scrapped at Spezia.

54. 1927 ILE DE FRANCE

43,153. 230,96 [241,66] x 27,97. (757.8 [792.9] x 91.8). 3—2. 4S—ST—23. (I—537; II—603; III—646). Chantiers & Ateliers de St Nazaire, St Nazaire. 1926 (14/3) launched. 1927 (22/6) MV Havre—Plymouth—New York. 1928 (Jul) catapult fitted in stern. 1928 (13/8) seaplane catapulted from ship when 400 miles from New York. 1930 (30/10) last seaplane landing in Havre harbour. 1930-1 catapult removed. 1932 (15/3) I—670; tourist 408; III—508). 1935 (9/1) FV Havre—Southampton—New York. 1936 (Mar) cabin; tourist; III. 1939 (1/9) LV Havre—New York, where laid up. 1940 (1/5) sailed New York—Marseilles. 1940 (1/6) sailed Marseilles—Cape Town—Saigon but diverted to Singapore. 1940 (6/7) seized by British Navy. 1940 (8/11) requisitioned as troopship. 1941 (10/3) conversion completed; sailed Singapore—Sydney. 1945 (22/9) reverted to French flag; Cunard management. 1946 (3/2) reverted to CGT. 1946 (22/10) FV (commercial) Cherbourg—New York. 1947 (Apr)-1949 (Jul) reconditioned; 44,356 tons; two funnels; (I—541; cabin 577; tourist 227). 1949 (21/7) resumed Havre—Southampton—New York. 1956 (26/7) rescued 750 survivors from sinking liner ANDREA DORIA. 1958 (10/11) LV New York—Plymouth—Havre (arr 17/11). 1959 (26/2) sailed Havre—Osaka as FURANSU MARU (Jap) preparatory to scrapping. 1959 renamed CLARIDON and scuttled during filming of 'The Last Voyage'; refloated and scrapped at Osaka.

55. (1929) DE LA SALLE

8,400. 134,10 x 17,28. (440.0 x 56.7). 2—2—C. 2S—T6—14. (Cabin 163; III—128). Barclay, Curle & Co Ltd, Glasgow. 1921 (9/2) launched. 1921 (18/10) MV St Nazaire—New Orleans. 1929 (9/3) FV Havre—Vigo—New York. 1929 (21/5) 2nd voy Havre—New York—New Orleans—Havre. 1930 (Mar) LV Havre—New York—Havana—Houston—Havre (3 voyages on N Atlantic). 1943 (9/7) torpedoed and sunk by German submarine U.508 in Gulf of Benim, West Africa.

56. 1930 LAFAYETTE (III) (M/S)

25,178. 175,92 x 23,65. (577.2 x 77.6). 1—1. 4S—2SC.DA—17. (Cabin 591; tourist 334; III—142). Chantiers & Ateliers de St Nazaire, St Nazaire. 1929 (9/5) launched. 1930 (17/5) MV Havre—Plymouth—New York. 1935 (22/5) FV Havre—Southampton—New York. 1938 (8/2) LV ditto. 1938 (4-5/5) destroyed by fire in dry dock at Havre; scrapped at Rotterdam.

57. 1932 CHAMPLAIN

28,124. 184,85 x 25,30. (606.5 x 83.0). 1—2. 2S—ST(SR)—19. (Cabin 623; tourist 308; III—122). Chantiers & Ateliers de St Nazaire, St Nazaire. 1931 (15/8) launched. 1932 (18/6) MV Havre—Plymouth—New York. 1935 (22/1) FV Havre—Southampton—New York. 1940 (Jun) LV New York—St Nazaire—La Pallice (arr 16/6). 1940 (17/6) sunk by magnetic mine at La Pallice.

58. 1935 NORMANDIE (II)

79,280. 299,12 [313,75] x 35,93. (981.4 [1029.4] x 117.9). 3—2. 4S—ST(EM)—29. (I—828; tourist 670; III—454). Chantiers & Ateliers de St Nazaire, St Nazaire (engines Société Générale Als Thom, Belfort). 1931 (26/1) keel laid. 1932 (29/10) launched. 1935 (29/5) MV Havre—Southampton—New York. 1935 (May) record passage Bishop Rock—Ambrose. 1935 (Jun) ditto Ambrose—Bishop Rock. 1936 (Mar) tonnage 83,423. 1936 (May) cabin; tourist; III. 1937 (Mar; Aug) record passages Ambrose—Bishop Rock. 1937 (Jul) ditto Bishop Rock—Ambrose. 1939 (23/8) LV Havre—Southampton—New York; laid up at New York. 1941 (12/12) seized by USA; LAFAYETTE. 1942 (9/2) gutted by fire and sank in New York harbour; eventually refloated. 1946 (Dec) towed to Newark, NJ; scrapped.

59. (1939) COLOMBIE

13,391. 148,73 [155,13] x 20,29. (488.0 [509.0] x 66.6). 2—2. 2S—ST(SR) —16. (I—201; II—146; III—144). Ateliers & Chantiers de France, Dunkirk (engines Ateliers & Chantiers de Penhoët, St Nazaire). 1931 (18/7) launched for CGT (West Indies service). 1939 (13/8) FV Havre—New York—Montreal—Quebec—Havre (1 RV). 1939 'X-10' (armed merchant cruiser). 1940 laid up in Martinique. 1942 (Dec) US troopship. 1945 ALEDA E. LUTZ (US Army hospital ship). 1946 (16/3) arr New York from Hawaii; reverted to COLOMBIE. 1946 (29/5) FV New York—Marseilles. 1946 (7/9) FV Havre—New York. 1947 (Jul) LV ditto (2 RV). 1948 rebuilt by De Schelde, Flushing; one funnel; 13,808 tons; (I—192; cabin 140; tourist 246)- 1964 ATLANTIC (Typaldos (Greek)). 1964 ATLANTICA (Typaldos). 1970 laid up at Perama. 1974 scrapped at Barcelona.

60. (1945) OREGON (M/S)

7,706. 144,28 x 18,65. (473.4 x 61.2). 1—2. 2S—2SC.DA—13. (I—38; temporarily increased to 76). Bremer Vulkan, Vegesack. 1929 (7/8) launched. 1929 (20/10) MV Havre—Baltimore; subsequently Havre—Panama—North Pacific Coast. 1945 (23/5) FV after World War II, Havre —New York. 1948 (6/10) LV New York—Havre. 1949 (20/1) FV Havre—Central America. 1950 ran for Messageries Maritimes (c). 1955 PACIFIC HARMONY (Panamanian).

61. (1946) WISCONSIN

8,061. 144,28 x 18,65. (473.4 x 61.2). 1—2. S—T4—14. (I—38; temporarily increased to 76). Bremer Vulkan, Vegesack. 1929 (Dec) launched. 1941 (Dec) seized by USA at Los Angeles. 1945 (13/11) reverted to French flag. 1946 (12/12) FV Havre—New York—Philadelphia—Havre. 1948 (Nov) LV Havre—New York—Havre; transferred to Havre—New Orleans service. 1951 FRYDERYK CHOPIN (Polish Ocean). 1957 KASZUBY (ditto).

62. (1950) LIBERTÉ

51,840. 271,32 [285,55] x 31,12. (890.2 [936.9] x 102.1). 2—2—C. 4S—ST(SR)—27. (I—553; cabin 500; tourist 444). Blohm & Voss, Hamburg. 1928 (15/8) launched as EUROPA (NDL); 49,746 tons. 1945 (8/5) seized by USA at Bremerhaven. 1946 (May) awarded to France. 1946 (9/12) scuttled at Havre after breaking loose in a gale. 1947 (15/4) refloated. 1947 (9/11) sailed Havre—St Nazaire; reconditioned at Penhoët; name LORRAINE contemplated. 1950 (17/8) FV Havre—New York as

LIBERTÉ (CGT); 51,840 tons. 1954 new funnels fitted. 1961 (2/11) LV Havre—New York—Havre (arr 16/11); laid up. 1962 (25/1) sailed Havre —Spezia, where scrapped. (See NDL - 60).

63. 1952 FLANDRE
20,464. 173,11 [182,75] x 24,47. (568.0 [599.7] x 80.3). 1—2—C. 2S— ST(DR)—22. (I—402; cabin 389; tourist 97). Ateliers & Chantiers de France, Dunkirk. 1951 (31/10) launched. 1952 (23/7) MV Havre—New York; arrived at New York in tow of tug owing to electrical faults. 1953 I—339; tourist 285 (100 interchangeable). 1953 (17/4) 2nd voyage Havre— New York. 1955 (Apr) I—232; tourist 511. 1955 (29/4) Resumed Havre— New York. 1962 (24/10) LV Havre—Southampton—New York (dep 2/11)—Southampton—Havre; joined ANTILLES on Havre—West Indies service. 1967 (4/8) FV Havre—Southampton—Quebec—Montreal. 1967 (22/8) LV ditto (2 RV). 1968 CARLA C (Costa). 1969 (13/10) FV Port Everglades—Genoa—Naples (1 voy).

64. 1962 FRANCE (III)
66,348. 290,00 [315,52] x 33,79. (951.5 [1035.2] x 110.9). 2—1—C. 4S— ST(DR)—34. (I—500; tourist 1,550). Chantiers de l'Atlantique, St Nazaire. 1956 (26/7) order placed. 1957 (7/9) keel laid. 1960 (11/5) launched. 1962 (3/2) MV Havre—Southampton—New York. 1962 (28/7-10/8) four-bladed propellers replaced by five bladed. 1967 (4/5) FV Havre— Southampton—Quebec (for International Exhibition) (1 RV). 1967 (13/7) FV Havre—Southampton—Quebec—New York. 1967 (21/10) 2nd voyage ditto. 1968 (4/10) LV ditto (3 voy). 1971 (14/10) FV Bremen— Havre—Southampton—New York. 1974 (5/9) LV New York—South- ampton—Havre. 1974 (12/9) anchored outside Havre owing to refusal of crew to enter port. 1974 (10/10) entered Havre. 1974 (7/12) officially laid up.

FUNNEL: Red, black top.

FLAG: White, red ball in corner and red 'Cie Gle Transatlantique'.

Note;- It seems likely that during the 1860s or early 1870s some or all of the Company's steamers had yellow or buff funnels with black tops, and for a time, perhaps, plain black funnels. In those days there were slight variations in the design of the houseflag.

Chapter 72

1864-72

BRITISH COLONIAL STEAMSHIP COMPANY LIMITED

1872-93

TEMPERLEY LINE

(British)

The BRITISH COLONIAL STEAMSHIP COMPANY LIMITED started operations on 30 June 1864 between London (Victoria Docks), Quebec and Montreal with the 1,364 ton iron screw THAMES, newly-built at Sunderland. She was stated to have very superior accommodation for chief cabin, second cabin and steerage passengers. [1] Pending completion of a sister ship, the 1,600 ton HECTOR and the 840 ton SEA QUEEN (formerly the VENEZUELAN of the West India & Pacific Line) were each chartered for one round voyage. The THAMES proceeded to St John's (Newfoundland), Halifax and St John (New Brunswick) in March 1865 owing to the winter closure of the St Lawrence River to navigation.

The 1,398 ton ST. LAWRENCE started her maiden voyage from London to Quebec and Montreal on 26 April 1865, the 1,810 ton OTTAWA following on 16 August. Her builders were Laird Brothers of Birkenhead, she had accommodation for 25 cabin and several hundred steerage passengers and soon proved to be larger than prevailing cargo requirements justified. After making two round voyages from London to Quebec and Montreal, one from London to New York and one from Copenhagen, Gothenburg and Christiansand to New York with a cargo of iron and 399 passengers, she was chartered to Hiller & Strauss for three round voyages between Antwerp and New York. She was sold in 1868 to Allan Line.

The 985 ton ACHILLES was chartered for two round voyages during the temporary absence of the THAMES in 1866, but she and the ST.LAWRENCE were in sole charge of the service during 1867 and until 5 July 1868, when the ST.LAWRENCE foundered near Montreal during the early stages of her fifteenth homeward voyage. The 1,012 ton CLEOPATRA, built in 1865 was bought in October 1868 to take her place, but she also was wrecked less than a year later on the Newfoundland coast.

The THAMES made her last voyage for the line in the autumn of 1868 and in her place the 1,517 ton DACIA was chartered in 1869 for three voyages as consort to the CLEOPATRA, pending purchase of the 1,823 ton MEDWAY in time to sail from London on 29 July, a few days before the CLEOPATRA was wrecked. It is interesting to note that the MEDWAY's

667

dimensions were much the same as those of the OTTAWA, sold on account of her large size.

Sailings in 1870 were undertaken by the MEDWAY and three chartered steamers - the 1,440 ton AVON, the 1,108 ton ATLAS and the 1,304 ton TWEED. A year later, the MEDWAY was assisted by the 1,442 ton NIGER, the 1,271 ton SEVERN and the 1,687 ton THAMES (II). Both the NIGER and SEVERN were chartered but the THAMES (II) was newly-built for the service by A. McMillan & Son of Dumbarton. From July 1871 westbound steamers called at Plymouth to embark chief cabin and steerage passengers.

The satisfactory progress made by the line was manifested in 1872 by the purchase of the 2,146 ton SCOTLAND, built in 1869 by John Key of Kinghorn, Scotland. She was assisted by the MEDWAY and THAMES as well as by the chartered NILE, NIGER, HECTOR and EMPEROR. The NILE and NIGER were sister ships, the HECTOR had already made a voyage for the line in 1864 and the EMPEROR was a ship of 1,501 tons, dating back to 1849; she survived under a variety of owners until 1889. Thus, a service at approximately weekly intervals was possible for the first time.

After 1868 the name British Colonial Steamship Company was dropped from advertisements and no other name was substituted for several years, enquiries being invited to the brokers, Temperley's, Carter & Darke, who in or about 1871 moved from 3 White Lion Court, Cornhill, London EC to 21 Billiter Street. A sufficient reason for dropping the name British Colonial was that the Provinces of Ontario and Quebec combined with New Brunswick and Nova Scotia in 1867 to become the Dominion of Canada, and it was not appropriate for the Company's name to imply that it was connected with the former Colony of Canada.

In September 1872, for the first time, the description TEMPERLEY'S LINE appeared in advertisements, [2] but at the beginning of October was shortened to TEMPERLEY LINE. [3] As the continuity of the service was not affected and as the same brokers were involved it seems preferable to deal with the British Colonial Steamship Company and the Temperley Line in the same chapter.

The chartered steamer SEVERN was bought by the Company in 1873 when, in addition, they acquired the 1,974 ton DELTA, built in the previous year and having accommodation for 16 chief cabin, 12 second cabin and a good complement of steerage passengers. It was in April 1873 that the Company first advertised: 'CANADA. Assisted passages from London to Quebec are granted by the Dominion Government to passengers by the fine steamships of the Temperley Line, who will have to pay only £4.15s. each person over 8 years; £2.7s.6d one to 8 years; and 14s 2d for infants.' Two more chartered steamers - the 1,870 ton NYANZA and the 1,908 ton

TAGUS, each made three round voyages during the year.

Sailings from London to Quebec and Montreal numbered 24 between April and October 1872 inclusive, when trading conditions were at their zenith. In 1873 the number dropped to 19 and in 1874, when a severe recession had set in, only 13.

The MEDWAY was wrecked in the Straits of Belle Isle on 6 September 1873 with the loss of four lives and the DELTA near Cape Chat on 5 November 1874, fortunately without fatal casualties. The 2,220 ton ST.LAWRENCE (II) was commissioned in July 1874, but was wrecked only two years later near Table Bay when engaged as a troop transport. In 1874, also, the SCOTLAND was lengthened from 92,68 to 108,65 metres (304.1 to 356.5 feet), with an increase of tonnage from 2,146 to 2,645, and her engines were compounded. Owing to the recession, she returned to the North Atlantic only sparingly before 1879.

The outward call at Plymouth was discontinued in August 1876. Two months previously the Allan Line MANITOBAN (originally the British Colonial OTTAWA) made a round voyage from London to Quebec and Montreal under charter to Temperley.

Another short-lived acquisition was the 2,288 ton City Line CITY OF POONAH, which was placed in service as the CLYDE and within a year was, like the ST.LAWRENCE (II), wrecked on the coast of Cape Colony when on transport duty.

The King Line (Wm Ross & Company) advertised sailings in 1879 between London, Quebec and Montreal by the OCEAN KING, VIKING and ERL KING. [4] Very soon the description King Line was dropped and it seems that the only sailing under their auspices was undertaken by the OCEAN KING on 19 April 1879. Instead, the steamers began to run in a joint service with the SCOTLAND and THAMES under the name Temperley Line. This arrangement continued until 1885, when the THAMES was incorporated into the Ross Line fleet, followed by the SCOTLAND four years later. The Ross Line Canadian service continued until 1893, but sailings were considerably reduced in 1890-1, when most of the steamers were transferred to the New Orleans trade. The firm subsequently went into liquidation.

Although the Temperley Line no longer owned its own steamers, the firm of Temperley's, Carter & Darke continued to be interested in the Canadian trade until 1893, when they advertised sailings under the description Temperley Line from London to Montreal by the chartered MacIver Line LYCIA, [5] later owned by Elder Dempster.

The downfall of the Temperley and Ross lines can be attributed largely to the Allan Line, which started a London-Quebec-Montreal service in 1884 with appreciably larger steamers.

[1] *The Times* 25/5/1864 and 1/7/1864
[2] *Shipping & Mercantile Gazette* 20/9/1872
[3] *Shipping & Mercantile Gazette* 3/10/1872
[4] *Shipping & Mercantile Gazette* 28/3/1879
[5] *The Times* 25/8/1893

1. 1864 THAMES (I)

1,364. 77,62 x 9,84. (254.7 x 32.3). C—1—3. I—S—I(2)—10. (I; II; III). T.R. Oswald & Co, Sunderland. 1864 (/) launched. 1864 (30/6) MV London—Quebec—Montreal. 1867 (14/10) FV for Hiller & Strauss (c), Antwerp—New York (1 RV). 1868 (25/9) LV London—Quebec— Montreal. 1874 no longer listed.

1a. (1864) HECTOR (c)

1,979. 86,68 x 10,60. (284.4 x 34.8). C—1—3. I—S—I(2)—10. J. Laing, Sunderland (engines G. Clark, Sunderland). 1863 (Apr) launched for E.T. Gourley, Sunderland. 1864 (30/7) FV for Br Colonial (c) (1 RV). 1872 (May) resumed ditto (3 RV). 1888 sold. 1900 scrapped at Genoa.

2. 1865 ST LAWRENCE (I)

1,398. 78,02 x 9,75. (256 x 32). C—1—3. I—S—I(2)—10. (I; II; III). T.R. Oswald & Co, Sunderland. 1865 (/) launched. 1865 (26/4) MV London—Quebec—Montreal. 1868 (17/6) LV ditto. 1868 (5/7) foundered off Farianto Point, Montreal, on voyage Montreal—London (0).

3. 1865 OTTAWA
(1876) MANITOBAN (c)

1,810. 87,47 x 10,73. (287.0 x 35.2). C—1—3. I—S—I(2)—10. (I—25; III). Laird Bros, Birkenhead. 1865 (13/5) launched. 1865 (16/8) MV London— Quebec—Montreal (2 RV). 1865 (14/12) FV London—New York (1 RV). 1866 (15/9) FV Copenhagen—Gothenburg—Christiansand—New York (1 RV). 1868 OTTAWA. (Allan). 1872 lengthened to 103,25 metres (338.8 feet); 2,395 tons; compound engines; renamed MANITOBAN (Allan). 1876 (7/6) FV for Temperley (c), London—Quebec—Montreal (1 RV). (See Allan - 44).

3a. (1866) ACHILLES (c)

1,426. 83,75 x 9,81. (274.8 x 32.2) C—1—3. I—S—I(2)—10. J. Laing, Sunderland. 1865 (Feb) launched for E.T. Gourley, Sunderland. 1866 (18/5) FV for Br Colonial (c), London—Quebec—Montreal (2 RV). 1867 (24/5) FV for Hiller & Strauss (c), Antwerp—New York. 1867 (12/8) LV ditto (2 RV). 1903 scrapped.

4. (1868) CLEOPATRA

 1,012. 69,61 x 9,14. (228.4 x 30.0). C—1—?. I—S—I(2)—10. W. Pile, Hay & Co, Sunderland. 1865 (Jul) launched for Pile & Co. 1867 (22/7) FV for Hiller & Strauss (c), Antwerp—New York (1 RV). 1868 CLEOPATRA (Br Colonial). 1868 (12/10) FV London—Quebec—Montreal. 1869 (7/7) LV ditto. 1869 (8/8) wrecked at Trepassey Bay, NF (0).

4a. (1869) DACIA (c)

 1,856. 74,18 x 10,57. (243.4 x 34.7). C—1—3. I—S—I(2)—10. J. Laing, Sunderland (engines G.Clark, Sunderland). 1867 (Nov) launched as STELLA for Norwood & Co, London. 1869 (22/4) FV for Temperley (c), London—Quebec—Montreal (3 RV). 1870 lengthened to 86,25 metres (283.0 feet); 1,856 tons; DACIA (cable steamer). 1875 compound engines. 1916 (3/12) torpedoed and sunk by German submarine off Madeira.

5. (1869) MEDWAY

 1,823. 86,92 x 10,79. (285.2 x 35.4). C—1—2.I—S—H2—10. T.R.Oswald & Co, Sunderland. 1865 (Mar) launched. 1867 (Apr) FV for Hiller & Strauss (c), Antwerp—New York. 1867 (9/9) LV ditto (3 RV). 1869(29/7) FV for Temperley, London—Quebec—Montreal. 1873 (6/9) wrecked in Straits of Belle Isle (4).

5a. (1870) AVON (c)

 1,594. 79,33 x 10,24. (260.3 x 33.6). 1—2. I—S—I(2)—10. T.R.Oswald & Co, Sunderland (engines Thos Clark & Co, Newcastle). 1870 (2/2) launched. 1870 (11/5) FV for Temperley (c), London—Quebec— Montreal (3 RV). 1872 VESUVIUS (KNSM). 1872 (1/9) FV Antwerp— Plymouth—New York (1 RV). 1876 (8/4) sunk in collision with ss SAVERNAKE (Br) off Hastings. (0).

5b. (1870) ATLAS (c)

 1,108. 76,56 x 9,66. (251.2 x 31.7). C—1—2. I—S—I(2)—10. J.Laing, Sunderland (engines T.Richardson & Sons, Hartlepool). 1861 (Oct) launched for E.T.Gourley, Sunderland. 1869 lengthened. 1870 (9/7) FV for Temperley (c), London—Quebec—Montreal (2 RV). 1875 (Oct) wrecked on Swedish coast.

5c. 1870 TWEED (c)

 1,304. 74,97 x 9,23. (246.0 x 30.3). 1—2. I—S—I(2)—10. J.Laing, Sunderland (engines North Eastern Marine Engineering Co, Sunderland). 1870 (Feb) launched for J.Morrison, Newcastle. 1870 (18/8) MV for Temperley (c), London—Quebec—Montreal (2 RV). 1876 MARIA VITTORIA (Italian). 1900 JOSÉ MONTEYS (Spanish). 1902 ALESANDRIA (Spanish). 1903 JOSEFINA (Spanish). 1908 coal hulk. 1920 scrapped.

5d. (1871) NIGER (c)

1,442. 76,40 x 9,26. (250.7 x 30.4). 1—2. I—S—I(2)—10. Mounsey & Co, Sunderland, (engines G.Clark, Sunderland). 1868 (Jul) launched for C.M. Norwood, London. 1871 (11/5) FV for Temperley (c), London—Quebec —Montreal. 1872 (14/8) LV ditto (6 RV). 1877 (Nov) wrecked at S.Haaks, Holland.

6. (1871) SEVERN (c)
(1873) SEVERN

1.271. 74,73 x 9,17. (245.2 x 30.1).1—2. I—S—I(2)—10. J.Laing, Sunderland (engines G.Clark, Sunderland). 1870 (24/11) launched for E.T.Gourley, Sunderland. 1871 (3/6) FV for Temperley (c), London— Quebec—Montreal. 1873 SEVERN (Temperley). 1881 (Sep) LV London—Quebec—Montreal. 1883 SEVERN (Br). 1885 (26/3) sunk in collision with ss INDUS in Havre Roads.

7. 1871 THAMES (II)

1,687. 86,01 x 10,39. (282.2 x 34.1). 1—2. I—S—C2—11. A.McMillan & Son, Dumbarton (engines J. & J.Thomson, Glasgow). 1871 (Mar) launched. 1871 (29/6) MV London—Quebec—Montreal. 1882 (Sep) LV ditto. 1885 THAMES (.Ross, Quebec). 1895 (21/11) wrecked near North Sydney, Cape Breton.

7a. (1872) NILE (c)

1,442. 73,45 x 9,26. (241.0 x 30.4). 1—2. I—S—I(2)—10. Iliff, Mounsey & Co, Sunderland (engines G.Clark, Sunderland). 1868 (Jan) launched for C.M.Norwood, London. 1872 (21/4) FV for Temperley (c), London— Quebec—Montreal (2 Rv). 1879 (Apr) wrecked on coast of Spain.

8. (1872) SCOTLAND

2,146. 92,68 x 11,55. (304.1 x 37.9). 1—2. I—S—I(2)—10. John Key, Kinghorn. 1869 (Sep) launched for J.Key, Leith. 1872 SCOTLAND (Temperley). 1872 (1/5) FV London—Quebec—Montreal. 1874 lengthened to 108,65 metres (356.5 feet); 2,645 tons; compound engines by builders. 1876 (2/8) .resumed London—Quebec—Montreal. 1889 SCOTLAND (F.Ross, Quebec). 1893 ditto (London owners); scrapped.

9. (1873) DELTA

1,974. 85,70 x 10,48. (281.2 x 34.4). 1—2. I—S—C2—11. (I—16; II—12; III). Earle's Shipbuilding & Engineering Co, Hull. 1872 (8/8) launched for Smith, Hill & Co, Hull. 1873 DELTA (Temperley). 1873 (13/5) FV London—Quebec—Montreal. 1873 (21/11) FV for.South Wales Atlantic (c), Cardiff—New York (2 RV). 1874 (23/10) sailed London—Quebec— Montreal for Temperley. 1874 (5/11) wrecked near Cape Chat, Quebec (0).

9a. (1873) NYANZA (c)

    1,870. 79,88 x 10,12. (262.1 x 33.2). 1—2. I—S—I(2)—10. London & Glasgow Co, Glasgow. 1867 (1/11) launched for J.A.Dunkerly & Co. 1873 (23/5) FV for Temperley (c), London—Quebec—Montreal (3 RV). (See Mercantile - 94).

9b. (1873) TAGUS (c)

    1,908. 81,59 x 10,18. (267.7 x 33.4). 1—2. I—S—I(2)—10. London & Glasgow Co, Glasgow. 1868 (31/10) launched for J.A. Dunkerly & Co. 1873 (14/9) FV for Temperley (c), London—Quebec—Montreal. 1876 (16/9) LV ditto (3 RV). (See Mercantile - 94).

10. 1874 ST. LAWRENCE (II)

    2,220. 92,41 x 10,85. (303.2 x 35.6). S—1—2. I—S—C2—11. J.Laing, Sunderland (engines Thompson, Boyd & Co, Newcastle). 1874 (19/1) launched. 1874 (15/7) MV London—Quebec—Montreal. 1876 (29/9) sailed London S Africa as troop transport. 1876 (10/11) wrecked 90 miles N of Table Bay (0).

10a. (1875) GAMMA (c)

    1,852. 94,42 x 10,02. (309.8 x 32.9). 1—2. I—S—C2—11. (I—24). Humphrys & Pearson, Hull. 1872 (27/2) launched for Smith, Hill & Co, Hull. 1875 (30/7) FV for Temperley (c), London—Quebec—Montreal. 1878 (24/7) LV ditto (8 RV). 1888 (19/12) stranded in R Humber; later broke in two.

11. (1878) CLYDE

    2,288. 99,26 x 11,03. (325.7 x 36.2). S—1—2. I—S—C2—11. C.Connell & Co, Glasgow (engines J.Howden & Co, Glasgow). 1870 (24/11) launched as CITY OF POONAH (City). 1878 CLYDE (Temperley). 1878 (9/5) FV London—Quebec—Montreal (4 RV). 1879 (7/4) wrecked at Dyers Point, Cape Colony, when on transport duty.

11a. (1878) ERL KING (c)

    2,193. 93,14 x 10,39. (305.6 x 34.1). C—1—2. I—S—C2—10.(I—40; II & III—400). A, & J.Inglis, Glasgow. 1865 (9/9) launched for Robertson & Co, London; 1,671 tons; length 76,19 metres (250 feet); single-expansion engines. 1874 lengthened; compound engines by J, & J.Thomson, Glasgow. 1878 (26/6) FV for Temperley (c), London—Quebec—Montreal. 1878 (17/8) Fv for Donaldson (c), Glasgow—Quebec—Montreal. 1878 (9/10) LV ditto (2 RV). 1878 (6/12) sailed Glasgow—Montevideo-Buenos Aires for ditto. 1881 new compound engines by D.Rollo & Sons, Liverpool. 1891 (15/12) wrecked on Long Reef, Key West, Florida.

11b. (1878) VIKING (c)

   2,588. 106,94 x 11,34. (350.9 x 37.2) 1—2. I—S—C2—10. Aitken &
   Mansel, Glasgow (engines J. & J.Thomson, Glasgow). 1874 (30/6)
   launched for Wm Ross & Co. 1878 (18/9) FV for Temperley (c), London—
   Quebec—Montreal. 1883 (8/8) LV ditto. 1883 (Sep) wrecked on Anticosti
   Island.

11c. (1879) OCEAN KING (c)

   2,449. 106,76 x 10,97. (350.3 x 36.0). 1—3. I—S—C2—10. J.E.Scott,
   Greenock (engines J. & J.Thomson, Glasgow). 1878 (Jan) launched for
   Wm Ross & Co. 1879 (19/4) FV for King Line (Wm Ross & Co),
   London—Quebec—Montreal. 1879 (7/6) FV for Temperley (c),
   London—Quebec—Montreal. 1891 wrecked on Spiekeroog, East Frisian
   Islands.

FUNNEL: Black.

FLAG: White, blue cross.

WARREN LINE

(British)

1865. George Warren & Company
1898. White Diamond Steamship Company Limited
1912. George Warren & Company (Liverpool) Limited
1922. Warren Line (Liverpool) Limited
1935. Johnston-Warren Lines Limited
1947. Furness-Warren Line.

The WARREN LINE owed its existence to the WHITE DIAMOND LINE of sailing packets, which was founded by a Boston merchant, Enoch Train, whose first ship, the 814 ton ST.PETERSBURG, was despatched from Boston to Liverpool in 1839.

At first, the firm of Enoch Train & Company was represented in Liverpool by Baring Brothers, but in 1848 a Mr Thayer was sent over from Boston to open an office. He was succeeded in 1853 by George Warren. Four years later Enoch Train & Company failed during a period of great financial difficulty, but many of the White Diamond ships were bought by Warren, who continued to run them in the Liverpool - Boston trade under the description 'George Warren & Co's Line of Liverpool and Boston Packets'. [1]

The American Civil War was responsible for the downfall of many of the United States sailing packet companies, whose ships were an easy prey for the Confederate cruisers, but by this time most of the Warren ships safely flew the British flag. Nevertheless, the steamship was fast superseding the sailing ship on the North Atlantic, and in February 1865 advertisements announced that Warren was establishing a line of first-class screw steamers between Liverpool, Boston and Philadelphia, calling at Queenstown (Cobh). [2]

The 2,132 ton PROPONTIS, built a year previously for the Mediterranean trade and the first steamer launched by the London & Glasgow Engineering & Iron Shipbuilding Company at Glasgow, was chartered to take the first sailing on 8 April 1865 from Liverpool. [3] After several postponements, she actually sailed on 3 May, the 1,661 ton GAMBIA following on 20 May. The PROPONTIS made a second voyage in June, the 2,045 ton BOSPHORUS sailed in July and during the next year or two the service was maintained by the PROPONTIS, BOSPHORUS, DELAWARE, MELITA and PERUVIAN, which carried saloon passengers at fares of £13 - £15 to Boston, and £15 - £17 to Philadelphia in addition to steerage passengers at six guineas. From 1867 onwards their voyages usually ended at Boston instead of Philadelphia. One round voyage was undertaken in 1866 by the chartered United States steamer CONCORDIA, completed four years earlier as the Anchor Line CALEDONIA, but sold after stranding near Cape Cod, Massachusetts. The MELITA, originally a Cunarder, was destroyed by fire at sea in September 1868, but fortunately two sailing ships were at hand to take off her 114 passengers and crew.

The Warren Line's sailing packets were still, in the autumn of 1868, leaving every week or ten days but, apart from one final voyage by the DELAWARE, the chartered steamers were withdrawn after the loss of the MELITA, and although the PROPONTIS was scheduled to sail in November, cancellation took place some days beforehand. Instead, the 2,266 ton National Line LOUISIANA made a round voyage in October 1868 from Liverpool to Boston and New York with the co-operation of the Warren Line, and the 2,876 ton VIRGINIA made one in December, followed by a second in March 1869, the 2,872 ton PENNSYLVANIA being responsible for a final voyage in October 1869. Two further voyages by National steamers were projected in November and December 1869, but at short notice they proceeded direct to New York - presumably because insufficient passengers and cargo were offering for Boston. All these voyages were sponsored by the National Line and are, therefore only of limited interest insofar as the present chapter is concerned.

For a time the Warren steamship service was withdrawn altogether, but by 1871 it was in full swing again - still by chartered steamers, and all of them owned by the Mercantile Steamship Company Limited (Chapter 94), the Queenstown call being omitted. They were the 1,800 ton TAGUS, TRENT, NYANZA and TIBER, [4] 1872 additions being the SHANNON, SIR FRANCIS and GANGES, of which the SIR FRANCIS stranded on Hampton Beach in January 1873 and became a total loss. For a second time a drastic curtailment of sailings followed, due partly to the fact that a slump had set in and partly to competition from the Dominion Line, which had started a seasonal service from Liverpool to Boston and Portland in November 1872 and had decided to continue it during the spring and summer of 1873. The Cunard Line, too, ran a frequent service to Boston. One of the few sailings arranged by Warren during the second half of 1873 took place in September by the 1,832 ton POTOMAC, but during 1874 and the greater part of 1875 not one was advertised.

This, as it happened, was the turning point in the Company's career. The sailing ships were withdrawn and instead of making use only of chartered steamers, as hitherto, the 3,231 ton MANHATTAN was bought from the Guion Line and placed in service as the MASSACHUSETTS, having received compound engines a year previously. A sister ship, the MINNESOTA was also bought and fitted with compound engines; she retained her name. In addition, the Company arranged a long charter of the 2,867 ton PALESTINE, formerly of the Cunard Line, and in the autumn of 1876 of the 3,985 ton VICTORIA, originally the Guion Line's NEBRASKA. These steamers carried cabin, intermediate and steerage passengers. [5] This vast increase in the Company's activities coincided with the inauguration of the Leyland Line's Liverpool - Boston service, but time was to show that there was ample room for both.

In the autumn of 1877 the 2,696 ton Cunard JAVA made a few voyages under charter to the Warren Line before being sold to Red Star. Others chartered in 1878 included the 2,802 ton CANOPUS, the 2,010 ton NEPTHIS and the 2,410 ton PEMBROKE. The last-named had started her career with the short-lived South Wales Atlantic Steamship Company, and was joined in 1880 by her sister ship, the GLAMORGAN, which foundered on 16 February 1883 when bound for Boston. The 3,496 ton BRAZILIAN, built in 1852 as the ADELAIDE of the Australian Royal Mail Steam Navigation Company, after being lengthened by 37,33 metres (122.5 feet) - the greatest increase in the case of any steamer employed on the North Atlantic - was chartered in 1880 but was wrecked near Liverpool on 4 January 1881.

Until 1879 the Company had to be content with ships bought second hand or chartered tonnage. Business had grown to such an extent, however that an order was placed for the 4,329 ton IOWA (I), which was delivered during that year. The 5,146 ton MISSOURI followed in 1881 and a slightly larger ship, the KANSAS, in 1882. The last-named had 'accommodation for passengers unsurpassed'. The only fare quoted was £4.10s, [6] but in all probability she carried a handful or two of first class passengers as well as steerage. Building of these ships resulted in the sale of the MASSACHUSETTS and MINNESOTA, both of which still had many more years of useful service before them.

George Warren died in 1880 at a time when the Company was at the height of its fame, and was succeeded by his son. During the year, there were 84 sailings under the Company's auspices from Boston to Liverpool, 20,000 tons of merchandise, 28,000 oxen, 11,000 swine and 18,000 sheep being carried as well as some thousands of passengers.

In conjunction with an associated concern, Richards, Tweedy & Company of London, the Liverpool firm of Richards, Mills & Company placed orders for the 4,386 ton NORSEMAN, which was delivered in 1882 and was followed in 1884 by the 4,491 ton ROMAN, both of which were registered in the name of the British & North Atlantic Steam Navigation Company Limited and placed under Warren management in the Liverpool - Boston trade, although sometimes they proceeded on from Boston to New

677

York. The chartered VICTORIA, CANOPUS and PEMBROKE were withdrawn, but the PALESTINE remained and the 4,740 ton BORDERER was added.

The MISSOURI was wrecked on the Welsh coast in 1886, but was replaced in the following year by the 4,979 ton MICHIGAN, first of the fleet to be built of steel and first to have triple-expansion engines.

Three further '-MAN' ships - the 4,843 ton OTTOMAN, the 4,892 ton ANGLOMAN and the 6,059 ton CAMBROMAN - were commissioned by British & North Atlantic during 1890-2 and also placed under Warren management. The IOWA foundered in February 1891 after steaming through a thick icefield off the American coast. The PALESTINE made her last voyage for the Company in 1892.

Apart from the five '-MAN' steamers, the Company's fleet was now reduced to the KANSAS and MICHIGAN, but the 5,036 ton SAGAMORE was completed in 1892 and the 5,204 ton SACHEM in 1893, neither of which carried passengers.

In December 1894 the firm of Richards, Mills & Company became managers of the Dominion Line, and in December 1896 started a Dominion Line passenger service between Liverpool and Boston. In general, their arrangements with Warren were not affected, although from time to time various '-MAN' ships were diverted to the Dominion Line for shorter or longer periods. In 1895 a new unit, the SCOTSMAN, was fitted with passenger accommodation as was the CAMBROMAN in 1899. The latter ran for the Dominion Line for a number of years and no doubt the former would also had she not been wrecked in 1899. The ANGLOMAN was wrecked in 1897 when running for Warren.

On 19 July 1898 a limited liability company, the WHITE DIAMOND STEAMSHIP COMPANY LIMITED, was registered with a capital of £200,000. Soon afterwards the 6,824 ton twin-screw cargo and cattle steamer BAY STATE was completed by Harland & Wolff of Belfast, but had a very short life as she was wrecked on the coast of Newfoundland on 2 October 1899.

The 8,370 ton twin-screw IOWA (II) was commissioned in 1902, at about the time when the last of the '-MAN' steamers was withdrawn from Warren management and either transferred to the Dominion Line or sold. She was by far the largest steamer ever owned by the Company and although probably designed for the Liverpool - Boston trade, her maiden voyage was to Galveston, as were most if not all succeeding ones, homeward cargoes consisting mainly of cotton. She was sold in 1913.

Apart from the sale of the KANSAS in 1906 there was no other event of particular importance until 1912, when Furness, Withy & Company Limited, in conjunction with one of their subsidiaries, the British Maritime Trust, acquired a controlling interest in the White Diamond Steamship

Company Limited. A new company, GEORGE WARREN & COMPANY (LIVERPOOL) LIMITED, was formed.

An important development of 1913 was the fitting of the SAGAMORE and SACHEM with accommodation for about 60 second class passengers. They continued to ply between Liverpool and Boston in company with the MICHIGAN, whose passenger complement was limited to 12.

The MICHIGAN was sold to the Admiralty soon after the outbreak of war in August 1914, and became the dummy battleship HMS COLLINGWOOD. The SAGAMORE was lost by enemy action during the war as was the 5,000 ton BAY STATE (II), commissioned in 1915. She was later replaced by a similar ship, the RHODE ISLAND.

After the war the 3,960 ton Furness Withy DIGBY joined the SACHEM in a new passenger and cargo service between Liverpool, St John's (Newfoundland), Halifax and Boston. Several cargo steamers were acquired.

During the summer of 1920 the 7,784 ton FORT VICTORIA of the Quebec Steamship Company (another Furness Withy subsidiary) made four round voyages between Liverpool and Boston carrying first class passengers and cargo. Contemporary advertisements of these sailings referred to the FURNESS - WARREN LINE and, therefore, anticipated by 27 years a description that came into use in 1947.

The firm of George Warren & Company (Liverpool) Limited was liquidated in 1922, 10 years after its formation by Furness Withy; a new concern WARREN LINE (LIVERPOOL) LIMITED was substituted.

The 6,791 ton NEWFOUNDLAND and the 6,796 ton NOVA SCOTIA were completed for the Liverpool - St John's NF - Halifax - Boston trade in 1925-6, and although of modest size in comparison with most contemporary North Atlantic passenger liners, became very popular. They catered for 105 cabin and 80 third class passengers. The SACHEM was scrapped in 1927, but the DIGBY had many more years of service before her and in 1925 was transferred to the Furness Line service between New York and the West Indies as the DOMINICA. In 1934 she became the United Baltic Corporation's BALTROVER.

At the end of 1934 the Warren Line (Liverpool) Limited took over the assets of two other members of the Furness group - the Johnston Line Limited and the Neptune Steam Navigation Company Limited, both of which had gone into liquidation, and in turn changed its name to JOHNSTON - WARREN LINES LIMITED.

The outbreak of World War II in September 1939 had no immediate effect on the Liverpool - St John's - Halifax - Boston sailings of the NEWFOUNDLAND and NOVA SCOTIA, which were soon joined by the 5,583 ton NERISSA of the allied Bermuda & West Indies Steamship Company and the 3,960 ton BALTROVER, formerly the DIGBY and back with the Company after an interval of 14 years. The NEWFOUNDLAND was taken up as a hospital ship in September 1940, and the NOVA SCOTIA became a troopship in January 1941. Three months later, on 30 April, the NERISSA was torpedoed and sunk with heavy loss of life by a German submarine 200 miles west of Inishtrahull.

The 10,900 ton motor-ships WESTERN PRINCE, EASTERN PRINCE and NORTHERN PRINCE, employed in pre-war days in the Prince Line passenger service between New York and South America, each made several Johnston - Warren voyages between Liverpool and Canada in 1940, and the WESTERN PRINCE was torpedoed and sunk on 14 December 1940 when so engaged.

The NOVA SCOTIA was sunk by a Japanese submarine on 4 December 1942 near Lourenço Marques when carrying a large complement of Italian prisoners, many of whom were drowned. The NEWFOUNDLAND, still a hospital ship, was badly damaged by German bombers off Salerno on 13 September 1943. She was deliberately sunk by gunfire two days later.

1947 NOVA SCOTIA 7,438 tons
Liverpool—St John's (NF)—Halifax—Boston
service. Sister ship: NEWFOUNDLAND.

The 7,438 ton NOVA SCOTIA (II) and the 7,437 ton NEWFOUNDLAND (II) were built on the Tyne in 1947-8 to replace their lost namesakes. They were propelled by a combination of double and single reduction geared turbines, which gave them a service speed of 15 knots and enabled the voyage from Liverpool to St John's to be completed in six days, Halifax in nine and Boston in twelve. They had accommodation for 75 first class and 80 tourist passengers. Although nominally owned by Johnston - Warren Lines, the Liverpool - Boston service from 1947 onwards was appropriately advertised under the trade name of FURNESS - WARREN LINE.

In 1957 the NEWFOUNDLAND and NOVA SCOTIA embarked a total of 878 first class and 1,756 tourist passengers for North America during the course of 21 voyages, an average of 125 passengers a voyage. In each subsequent year the number was appreciably lower and the 1961 total, spread over 15 voyages, was no more than 318 first class and 933 tourist, an average of only 83 a voyage. It was decided, therefore, that from the beginning of 1962 onwards the ships should cater only for 12 one-class passengers. Unfortunately, this was only a temporary expedient and later in the year the ships were sold to the Dominion Navigation Company to run between Australia, Manila, Hong Kong and Japan.

In their places, the 6,950 ton cargo motorships NEWFOUNDLAND (III) and NOVA SCOTIA (III) were delivered in 1964-5, were products of the Burntisland Shipbuilding Company, followed the modern trend of having their engines aft and were owned by Furness Withy - not Johnston-Warren Lines. From July 1971 onwards sailings took place from Manchester instead of Liverpool.

There was a serious decline in traffic in 1972 and at the end of the year the NOVA SCOTIA was time chartered to Shaw Savill under the name TROPIC. In 1973 the NEWFOUNDLAND was assisted by four chartered vessels, which made a total of nine voyages, but with a further decline in traffic the NEWFOUNDLAND, also, was chartered to Shaw Savill in the autumn and renamed CUFIC.

The CUFIC and TROPIC were transferred from Furness Withy to Johnston–Warren Lines ownership in December 1973. In March and September 1974, respectively, they reverted to their original names with Messageries Maritimes as the new charterers, and the NOVA SCOTIA made one outward voyage from Liverpool to St John's, NF, Halifax and Boston. Otherwise, the service was maintained from Liverpool by chartered vessels, with some additional calls at Bermuda and Nassau.

Sad to relate, the last Furness-Warren Line sailing took place on 14 January 1975 by the chartered SUSANN BENTSEN. In a final notice to shippers, dated 6 March 1975, the Company pointed out that they had endeavoured during recent years to provide a service to St John's, NF, Halifax and Boston with conventional ships to cater for those who could not or did not wish to use containers. During the early stages of container development they were reasonably successful, but latterly the amount of available cargo had dwindled to unremunerative levels so there was no alternative but to close down the service. Although they did not say so, it was almost 110 years since the first Warren Line steamer was despatched from Liverpool. There was this in common between the first and the last sailing that each was undertaken by a chartered ship.

All North Atlantic operations of the Furness Withy Group are now handled by Manchester Liners.

[1]   *Liverpool Journal of Commerce* 1/1/1864
[2]   *Glasgow Herald* 22/2/1865
[3]   *Glasgow Herald* 17/3/1865
[4]   *Liverpool Journal of Commerce* 13/7/1871
[5]   *Glasgow Herald* Sept 1876
[6]   *Glasgow Herald* 8/5/1882

NAS–14 **

a. (1865) PROPONTIS (c)

2,132. 97,04 x 11,06. (318.4 x 36.3).C—1—3. I—S—I(2)—10. London & Glasgow Engineering & Iron Shipbuilding Co, Glasgow. 1864 (18/8) launched. 1865 (3/5) FV for Warren (c), Liverpool—Queenstown—Boston—Philadelphia. 1868 (17/6) LV Liverpool—Boston. 1874 triple-expansion engines by John Elder & Co, Glasgow (first set ever built). 1893 PROPONTIS (Hong Kong). 1901 scrapped.

b. (1865) BOSPHORUS (c)

2,045. 97,22 x 10,97. (319.0 x 36.0). C—1—3. I—S—I(2)—10- London & Glasgow Engineering & Iron Shipbuilding Co, Glasgow. 1864 (7/12) launched. 1865 (16/7) FV for Warren (c), Liverpool—Queenstown—Boston—Philadelphia. 1867 (Jun) LV Liverpool—Boston. 1873—4 removed from Register.

c. (1866) DELAWARE (c)

2,200. 98,75 x 11,06. (324.0 x 36.3). C—1—3. I—S—I(2)—10. Isle of Man Shipbuilding Co. 1865 (Aug) launched. 1866 (15/1) FV for Warren (c), Liverpool—Boston—Philadelphia. 1869 (28/5) LV Liverpool—Boston. 1869 lengthened to 115,81 metres (380 feet). 1871 (20/12) wrecked on Scilly Isles on voyage Liverpool—Calcutta.

d. (1866) MELITA (c)

1,254. 71,01 x 8,84. (233.0 x 29.0). C—1—2. I—S—GO2—9. Alexander Denny, Dumbarton (engines Macnab & Clark, Greenock). 1853 (27/3) launched for Cunard Mediterranean service. 1866 (2/6) FV for Warren (c), Liverpool—Queenstown—Boston—Philadelphia. 1868 (28/7) LV ditto. 1868 (27/8) sailed Boston—Liverpool—. 1868 (5/9) destroyed by fire at sea (0); passengers and crew rescued by sailing ships JACOB A. STAMLER and MONEQUASH. (See Cunard - 13).

e. (1866) CONCORDIA (c) (US)

1,348. 79,64 x 10,09). (261.3 x 33.1). C—1—3. I—S—I(2)—10. Tod & McGregor, Glasgow. 1862 (3/2) launched as CALEDONIA (Anchor). 1862 (31/12) stranded near Cape Cod, Mass; sold; salvaged; CONCORDIA (US). 1866 (5/7) FV for Warren (c), Liverpool—Boston (1 RV). 1872 wrecked.

f. (1866) PERUVIAN (c)

1,713. 85,64 x 11,58. (281.0 x 38.0). C—1—3. I—S—I(2)—10. (I—90; III). M.Pearse & Co, Stockton (engines Fossick & Hackworth, Stockton). 1863 (7/3) launched as THE SOUTHERNER (Fraser, Trenhorne & Co, Liverpool). 1864 WESTMINSTER (British & American). 1864 PERUVIAN (British & South American). 1866 ditto (Merchants' Trading Co, London).

1866 (10/10) FV for Warren (c), Liverpool—Boston. 1867 (May) LV ditto.
1870 CASTILLO (Spanish). 1890 AMERICA (Stefano Rapello) (Italian).
1898 scrapped at Genoa. (see British & American - 70).

The following chartered steamers were running in 1871-3;-

TAGUS	(1,899)
TRENT	(1,410)
NYANZA	(1,859)
TIBER	(1,739)
SHANNON	(1,250)
GANGES	(1,410)
CHESAPEAKE	(1,239)
POTOMAC	(1,832),

owners in each case being Mercantile SS Co Ltd (Chapter 94).

g. 1872 SIR FRANCIS (c)
   1,833. 80,03 x 10,09. (262.6 x 33.1). S—1—2. I—S—C2—10. London &
   Glasgow Co,, Glasgow. 1872 (Jul) launched for Mercantile. 1872 (8/8) MV
   for Warren (c), Liverpool—Boston. 1873 (3/1) wrecked on Salisbury
   Beach, New Hampshire (0).

1. (1876) MASSACHUSETTS
   3,231. 102.10 x 12,95. (335.0 x 42.5). C—1—2. I—S—C2—10. (I—72; III—
   800). Palmer Bros, Jarrow-on-Tyne (engines Fawcett & Preston, Liverpool). 1866 (15/5) launched as MANHATTAN (Guion). 1874 compound
   engines. 1875 MASSACHUSETTS (Warren). 1876 (1/1) FV Liverpool—
   Boston. 1881 CITY OF LINCOLN (Thistle). 1902 wrecked near Cape
   Town (0). (See Guion - 78).

1a. (1876) PALESTINE (c)
   2,867. 107,31 x 11,00. (352.1 x 36.1). C—1—3. I—S—C2—10. R.Steele &
   Co, Greenock (engines J. & J.Thomson, Glasgow). 1858 (/) launched
   for Cunard Mediterranean service. 1872 sold. 1876 (24/6) FV for Warren
   (c), Liverpool—Boston. 1892 (23/11) LV ditto. 1896 scrapped. (See
   Cunard - 13).

2. (1876) MINNESOTA
   3,008. 102,22 x 12,95. (335.4 x 42.5). C—1—2. I—S—C2—10. I—72; III—
   800). Palmer Bros, Jarrow-on-Tyne (engines J.Jack Rollo & Co, Liverpool). 1867 (Feb) launched for Guion. 1875 MINNESOTA (Warren);
   compound engines. 1876 (19/8) FV Liverpool—Boston. 1882 VINUELAS
   (Spanish). 1886 SAN IGNACIO DE LOYOLA (Cia Trasatlántica). 1908

scrapped. (See Guion - 78).

2a. (1876) VICTORIA (c)

3,985. 112,00 x 12,89. (367.5 x 42.3). C—1—2. I—S—C2—10. Palmer Bros, Jarrow-on-Tyne. 1867 (Apr) launched as NEBRASKA (Guion). 1876 VICTORIA (Br). 1876 (4/11) FV for Warren (c), Liverpool—Boston. 1887 scrapped (See Guion - 78).

2b. (1877) JAVA (c)

2,696. 102,74 x 13,07. (337.1 x 42.9). C—1—3. I—S—C2—10. (I—300; III—800). J. & G.Thomson, Glasgow. 1865 (24/6) launched for Cunard. 1877 compound engines. 1877 (20/10) FV for Warren (c), Liverpool—Boston. 1878 (12/3) LV ditto. 1878 ZEELAND (Red Star). (See Cunard - 13).

2c. (1878) PEMBROKE (c)

2,410. 97,95 x 11,15. (321.4 x 36.6). S—1—2. I—S—C2—11. W.Simons & Co, Renfrew. 1873 (15/2) launched for South Wales Atlantic. 1878 (19/1) FV for Warren (c), Liverpool—Boston. 1881 (20/5) sank off Boston after collision with ss GANOS; salved. 1883 MURCIANO (Spanish). (See South Wales Atlantic - 96).

2d. (1878) CANOPUS (c)

2,802, 117,27 x 11,28. (384.8 x 37.0).S—1—4. I—S—C2—11. C. & W. Earle, Hull. 1870 (22/10) launched for Moss Line, Liverpool. 1873 compound engines. 1878 (30/1) FV for Warren (c), Liverpool—Boston. 1880 (26/9) stranded on Mull of Kintyre; refloated. 1896 scrapped.

2e. (1878) NEPTHIS (c)

2,010. 94,48 x 10,39. (310.0 x 34.1). S—1—2. I—S—C2—10. C.Mitchell & Co, Walker-on-Tyne (engines R. & W.Hawthorn, Newcastle). 1877 (Jun) launched for Moss Line, Liverpool. 1878 (13/7) FV for Waren (c), Liverpool—Boston. 1896 NEPTHIS (Brazilian). 1896 (17/10) sank at moorings at Para; refloated; reduced to hulk.

2f. (1879) BRAZILIAN (c)

3,496. 116,73 x 11,64. (383.0 x 38.2). C—1—3. I—S—C2—10. Scott Russell & Co, London (engines Barrow Shipbuilding Co). 1852 (12/11) launched as ADELAIDE (Australian RMSN Co). 1863 MERSEY (Stock). 1864 NEW YORK (British & American). 1864 BRAZILIAN (British & South American). 1866 ditto (Merchants' Trading Co, London). 1878 lengthened from 79,39 metres (260.5 feet); compound engines. 1879 (30/1) FV for Warren (c), Liverpool—Boston. 1881 (4/1) wrecked near Liverpool (0). (See Stock Line - 67 - MERSEY).

2g. (1879) GLAMORGAN (c)

    2,411. 97,56 x 11,15. (320.1 x 36.6). S—1—2. I—S—C2—11. W.Simons &
    Co, Renfrew. 1872 (4/9) launched for South Wales Atlantic. 1879 (8/4) FV
    for Warren (c), Liverpool—Boston. 1883 (16/2) foundered at sea (7). (See
    South Wales Atlantic - 96).

3. 1880 IOWA (I)

    4,329. 115,26 x 13,37. (378.2 x 43.9). S—1—4. I—S—C2—11. R. &J.
    Evans & Co, Liverpool (engines J.Jack & Co, Liverpool). 1879 (18/9)
    launched. 1880 (10/1) MV Liverpool—Boston. 1891 (22/2) foundered
    after steaming through icefield (0).

4. 1881 MISSOURI

    5,146. 129,71 x 13,28. (425.6 x 43.6). S—1—4. I—S—C2—11. C. Connell
    & Co, Glasgow (engines J. & J.Thomson, Glasgow). 1881 (15/2) launched.
    1881 (30/5) MV Liverpool—Boston. 1886 (1/3) wrecked in Caernarvon
    Bay, Wales (0).

5. 1882 KANSAS

    5,276. 133,04 x 13,34. (436.5 x 43.8). S—1—4. I—S—C2—11. C.Connell &
    Co, Glasgow (engines J. & J.Thomson, Glasgow). 1882 (19/1) launched.
    1882 (21/5) MV Liverpool—Boston. 1906 (Nov) scrapped at Spezia.

5a. 1882 NORSEMAN (c) §

    4, 386. 119,47 x 13,41. (392.0 x 44.0). S—1—4. I—S—C2—11. Laird Bros,
    Birkenhead. 1882 (31/8) launched for British & North Atlantic SN Co.
    1882 (16/12) MV for Warren (c), Liverpool—Boston. 1899 (29/3) wrecked
    near Boston(0).

5b. 1884 BORDERER (c) §

    4,740. 121,91 x 13,47. (400.0 x 44.2). S—1—4. I—S—C2—11. Barrow
    Shipbuilding Co, Barrow. 1884 (30/1) launched. 1884 (17/4) MV for
    Warren (c), Liverpool—Boston. 1897 RIOJANO (Spanish); quadruple-
    expansion engines. 1916 YUTE (Spanish). 1920 (17/11) in distress 240
    miles S of Cape May, since when nothing heard of her.

5c. 1884 ROMAN (c) §

    4,491. 123,44 x 13,28. (405.0 x 43.6). S—1—4. I—S—C2—11. Laird Bros,
    Birkenhead. 1884 (20/9) launched for British & North Atlantic. 1884
    (29/10) MV for Warren (c), Liverpool—Boston. 1895 onwards ran for
    Dominion. 1910 scrapped. (See Dominion -93).

6. 1887 MICHIGAN

    4,979. 122,03 x 14,38. (400.4 x 47.2). S—1—4. S—S—T3—11. (I—12).
    Harland & Wolff, Belfast. 1887 (5/7) launched. 1887 (29/10) MV Liver-

pool—Boston. 1914 sold to Br Admiralty; became dummy battleship HMS COLLINGWOOD. 1915 beached near Dardanelles to act as break-water; later salved.

6a. 1890 OTTOMAN (c) §
    4,843. 123,07 x 13,89. (403.8 x 45.6) S—1—4. S—S—T3—11. Laird Bros, Birkenhead. 1890 (2/9) launched for British & North Atlantic). 1890 (8/12) MV for Warren (c), Liverpool—Boston. 1896 transferred to Dominion. 1911 scrapped at Preston. (See Dominion - 93).

6b. 1892 ANGLOMAN (c) §
    4,892. 123.07 x 13,89. (403.8 x 45.6). S—1—4- S—S—T3—11. Laird Bros, Birkenhead. 1892 (6/2) launched for British & North Atlantic. 1892 (12/4) MV for Warren (c), Liverpool—Boston. 1896 (7/5) FV for Dominion, Liverpool—Quebec—Montreal. 1896 (24/9) LV ditto (5 RV); reverted to Warren, Liverpool—Boston. 1897 (9/2) wrecked near Holyhead (0).

6c. 1892 CAMBROMAN (c) §
    6,059. 131,02 x 14,11. (429.9 x 46.3). S—1—4. S—S—T3—11. Laird Bros, Birkenhead. 1892 (6/10) launched for British & North Atlantic. 1892 (1/12) MV for Warren (c), Liverpool—Boston. 1899 transferred to Dominion. 1910 scrapped. (See Dominion - 93).

7. 1892 SAGAMORE §
   (1913) SAGAMORE
    5,036. 131,18 x 14,08. (430.4 x 46.2). S—1—4. S—S—T3—11. Harland & Wolff, Belfast. 1892 (8/9) launched. 1892 (7/12) MV Liverpool—Boston. 1913 II—60 added. 1917 (3/3) torpedoed and sunk by German submarine 150 miles WNW of Fastnet (52).

8. 1893 SACHEM §
   (1913) SACHEM
    5,204. 135,78 x 14,08. (445.5 x 46.2). S—1—4. S—S—T3—11. Harland & Wolff, Belfast. 1893 (22/6) launched. 1893 (1/11) MV Liverpool—Boston. 1913 II—58 added. 1927 (Mar) LV Liverpool—St John's, NF—Halifax—Boston. 1927 scrapped.

9. 1898 BAY STATE §
    6,824. 149,43 x 15,91. (490.3 x 52.2). S—1—4. S—2S—T6—12. Harland & Wolff, Belfast. 1898 (4/6) launched. 1898 (3/9) MV Liverpool—Boston. 1899 (2/10) wrecked near Cape Ballard, Newfoundland (0).

686

10. 1902. IOWA (II) §

8,370. 152,54 x 17,77. (500.5 x 58.3). 1—5. 2S—T6—12. Harland & Wolff, Belfast. 1902 (5/7) launched. 1902 (Nov) MV Liverpool—Galveston. 1913 (Oct) BOHEMIA. (Hapag - 53). (qv).

11. 1913 DIGBY
(1939) BALTROVER (c)

3,960. 106,91 x 15,24. (350.8 x 50.0). 1—2. S—T3—12. (I—58; II—32). Irvine's Shipbuilding & Dry Dock Co, West Hartlepool(engines Richardsons, Westgarth & Co Ltd, Hartlepool). 1912 (27/11) launched for Furness. 1913 (Apr) MV Liverpool—St John's, NF—Halifax. 1914 attached to Tenth Cruiser Squadron. 1915—7 temporarily renamed ARTOIS (French). 1918 reverted to DIGBY. 1919 (20/3) Liverpool—ST John's, NF—Halifax—Boston; (cabin 90). 1925 DOMINICA (Furness). 1934 BALTROVER (United Baltic Corporation). 1939 ran Liverpool—St John's, NF—Halifax (Furness management). 1944 LV ditto. 1946 IONIA (Greek); tonnage 4,916). 1965 IONIAN (Panamanian); scrapped in Far East.

12. (1920) FORT VICTORIA

7,784. 125,48 x 17,28. (411.7 x 56.7). 2—2. 2S—Q8—14. (I—400). W.Beardmore & Co Ltd, Glasgow. 1912 (14/8) launched as WILLOCHRA (Adelaide SS Co). 1919 FORT VICTORIA (Bermuda & West Indies). 1920 (10/7) FV Liverpool—Boston (4 RV). 1929 (18/12) sunk in collision with ss ALGONQUIN (US) in Ambrose Channel on voyage New York—Bermuda.

13. 1925 NEWFOUNDLAND (I)

6,791. 123,77 x 16,88. (406.1 x 55.4). 1—2—C. S—Q4—14. (Cabin 105; III—80). Vickers-Armstrong Ltd, Barrow. 1925 (24/1) launched. 1925 (Jun) MV Liverpool—St John's NF—Halifax—Boston. 1940 (Sep) hospital ship. 1943 (13/9) bombed and set on fire by German aircraft at Salerno, Italy (21). 1943 (15/9) sunk by gunfire.

14. 1926 NOVA SCOTIA (I)

6,796. 123,77 x 16,88. (406.1 x 55.4). 1—2—C. S—Q4—14. (Cabin 105; III—80). Vickers-Armstrong Ltd, Barrow. 1926 (29/1) launched. 1926 (May) MV Liverpool—St John's. NF—Halifax—Boston. 1941 (Jan) troopship. 1942 (4/12) torpedoed and sunk by Japanese submarine near Lourenço Marques.

14a. (1939) NERISSA (c)

5,583. 106,52 x 16,55. (349.5 x 54.3). 1—2—C. S—T4—14. (I—162; II). W.Hamilton & Co Ltd, Port Glasgow (engines D.Rowan & Co Ltd,

Glasgow). 1926 (31/3) launched for New York, Newfoundland & Halifax SS Co. 1929 NERISSA (Bermuda & West Indies). 1939-41 ran UK—Canada. 1941 (30/4) torpedoed and sunk by German submarine 200 miles west of Inishtrahull on voyage Halifax—Liverpool (207).

14b. (1940) WESTERN PRINCE (M/S) (c)

10,926. 151,23 x 19,74. (496.2 x 64.8). 1—2—C. 2S—4SC.DA—16. (I—100). Napier & Miller Ltd, Glasgow (engines J.G.Kincaid & Co Ltd, Greenock. 1929 (20/6) launched for Prince Line. 1940 7 RV UK—Canada. 1940 (14/12) torpedoed and sunk by German submarine U.96, 500 miles west of Orkney Islands on voyage New York—Liverpool (14).

14c. (1940) EASTERN PRINCE (M/S) (c)

10,926. 151,23 x 19,74. (496.2 x 64.8). 1—2—C. 2S—4SC.DA—16. (I—100). Napier & Miller Ltd, Glasgow (engines J.G.Kincaid & Co, Greenock. 1929 (29/1) launched for Prince Line. 1940(Nov) - 1941(Jun) 7 RV UK—Canada. 1943 accommodation for 2,150 troops fitted at Baltimore. 1950 EMPIRE MEDWAY (Br). 1953 scrapped at Faslane.

14d. (1940) NORTHERN PRINCE (M/S) (c)

10,917. 151,23 x 19,77. (496.2 x 64.9).1—2—C. 2S—4SC.DA—16. (I—100). Lithgows Ltd, Port Glasgow (engines J.G.Kincaid & Co Ltd, Greenock). 1928 (27/11) launched for Prince Line. 1940 7 RV, UK—Canada. 1941 (3/4) bombed and sunk by German aircraft in Antikithera Channel, Greece. (0).

15. 1947 NOVA SCOTIA (II)

7,438. 129,07 [134,24] x 18,65. (423.5 [440.5] x 61.2). 1—2—C. S—ST(DR&SR)—15. (I—75; tourist 80). Vickers-Armstrong Ltd. Walker-on-Tyne. 1946 (8/11) launched. 1947 (2/9) MV Liverpool St John's, NF—Halifax—Boston. 1961 (28/10) LV ditto; after which passengers restricted to 12. 1962 FRANCIS DRAKE (Dominion Navigation Co of Australia). 1971 scrapped at Kaohsiung.

16. 1948 NEWFOUNDLAND (II)

7,437. 129,07 [134,25] x 18,65. (423.5 [440.5] x 61.2). 1—2—C. S—ST(DR&SR)—15. (I—75; tourist 80). Vickers-Armstrong Ltd, Walker-on-Tyne. 1947 (22/5) launched. 1948 (14/2) MV Liverpool—St John's, NF—Halifax—Boston. 1961 (15/11) LV ditto; after which passengers restricted to 12. 1962 GEORGE ANSON (Dominion Navigation Co of Australia). 1971 scrapped at Kaohsiung.

17. 1964 NEWFOUNDLAND (III) (M/S) §
    6,950. 120,75 [130,75] x 18,74. (396.2 [429.0] x 61.5). 1—1—C. (engines aft).S—2SC.SA—16. Burntisland Shipbuilding Co Ltd. 1964 (9/7) launched. 1965 (14/1) MV Liverpool—Halifax—Boston. 1973 (6/11) CUFIC (Shaw Savill (c)). 1974 (13/3) NEWFOUNDLAND (Messageries Maritimes (c)).

18. 1965 NOVA SCOTIA (III) (M/S) §
    6,950. 120,75 [130,75] x 18,74. (396.2 [429.0] x 61.5). 1—1—C. (engines aft).S—2SC.SA—16. Burntisland Shipbuilding Co Ltd. 1964 (19/11) launched.1965 (29/4) MV Liverpool—Halifax—Boston. 1973 (5/2) TROPIC (Shaw Savill (c)). 1974 (12/9) NOVA SCOTIA (Messageries Maritimes (c).

§   cargo steamer.

FUNNEL: Black
FLAG : Red; white diamond.
Note: For post-1921 funnel and flag details see Furness (Chapter 111).

BALTIMORE & LIVERPOOL STEAMSHIP COMPANY

(United States)

In 1862, the year following the outbreak of the American Civil War, the New York shipbuilding firm of J.B. & J.D. Van Dusen received an order from the Neptune Line, presided over by William P.Williams, for five wooden screw steamers each of about 1,250 tons for a new service between New York and Boston. [1] Upon completion in 1863, they were bought by the United States Navy for $160,000 (£32,000) each and retained their names of NEPTUNE, NEREUS, PROTEUS, GLAUCUS and GALATEA.

On 12 July 1865, shortly after the ending of the Civil War, all except the GALATEA were sold by auction and bought at less than half the earlier price by nominees of the Baltimore & Ohio Railroad, which decided to place them in service between Baltimore and Liverpool under the description BALTIMORE & LIVERPOOL STEAMSHIP COMPANY. They were renamed ALLEGANY (ex-NEPTUNE), CARROLL (ex-PROTEUS), SOMERSET (ex-NEREUS) and WORCESTER (ex-GLAUCUS).

The service was opened by the SOMERSET, which left Baltimore on 30 September 1865 for Liverpool with the United States' mails, seven passengers and a small quantity of cargo. It was the first attempt after the Civil War to start a regular transatlantic service under the American flag. The voyage to Liverpool took 16 days, as did the homeward one starting on 9 November, 20 passengers being carried on this occasion. The SOMERSET and her sisters had accommodation for 20 first class passengers, about the same number of second class and some 300 steerage; when the service became better known the ships often attracted 200 or more passengers.

The only other voyage during 1865 was by the WORCESTER, which left Baltimore on 29 November but returned a fortnight later with engine trouble. She sailed again on 23 December, and after a very rough crossing turned up at Liverpool on 8 January minus funnel and foremast. After undergoing repairs she started her westbound voyage on 7 February with 30 passengers and again experienced rough weather, which made it necessary to call at Halifax for coal. She did not reach Baltimore until 1 March.

It had been decided that the CARROLL and ALLEGANY should run

690

1865 CARROLL 1,244 tons
One of the few wooden screw steamers regularly
employed on the North Atlantic.

between Baltimore and New York until the transatlantic service had had time to settle down, and on 5 December 1865, while so employed, the ALLEGANY stranded on Long Island in fog and became a total loss.

After two further transatlantic voyages by the SOMERSET and one by the WORCESTER, the CARROLL started her first voyage from Baltimore to Liverpool on 25 April 1866. All told, 12 voyages were undertaken during the year and all the ships had some anxious moments - the WORCESTER stranded on 10 May near the mouth of the Chesapeake but was refloated the following day; the SOMERSET struck a submerged pile when leaving her pier at Baltimore on 29 September and was delayed for repairs; and on 4 October the CARROLL, with no fewer than 250 passengers aboard, collided with and sank the schooner DORAS in the Mersey, although she herself was undamaged.

The WORCESTER was advertised to sail from Liverpool on 28 November 1866, but as there was no sign of her arrival there the 1,800 ton British iron screw MEXICAN was chartered for one round voyage and advertised to sail on 5 December. [2]

In 1867 there were only nine departures from Baltimore, the last on 26 September, after which there was a gap until February 1868. By that time the 2,321 ton iron screw BALTIMORE, operated by the Norddeutscher Lloyd and owned 50/50 by them and the Baltimore & Ohio Railroad, was on the point of starting her maiden voyage from Bremen and Southampton to Baltimore, and as it had become abundantly clear that the ships employed on the Baltimore - Liverpool service were totally unsuited to the rigours of the North Atlantic it would not have been surprising if they had been withdrawn there and then. Instead, the WORCESTER left Baltimore on 26 February as planned and during the next few months she and her sister ships undertook a total of seven round voyages, after which the service was closed down for good. The WORCESTER took the last sailing from Baltimore on 15 September and arrived back there on 1 November.

From then onwards the Baltimore & Ohio Railroad was content to leave its transatlantic affairs entirely in the hands of Norddeutscher Lloyd, its chief consideration being, of course, to get the rail haul of passengers and freight arriving at and leaving Baltimore by sea. During the winter of 1868-9 the three ships ran for a time for their owners between Baltimore and New York, but were soon laid up and three or four years elapsed before a buyer was found. Subsequently they ran for many years between Boston, Halifax and Prince Edward Island. All told they were undoubtedly a great credit to their builders, and are interesting as the only fleet of wooden screw steamers to obtain regular employment on the North Atlantic

[1] *New York Herald* 6/10/1862
[2] *Liverpool Journal of Commerce* 3/12/1866

1. (1865) SOMERSET

    1,244. 63,70 x 10,51. (209.0 x 34.5). S—1—2. W—S—I(2)—10. (I—20; II—20; III—300). J.B. & J.D. Van Dusen, New York (engines Atlantic Works, New York). 1863 (21/3) launched as NEREUS (Neptune); bought by US Navy. 1865 (12/7) bought by Baltimore & Liverpool; renamed. 1865 (30/9) FV Baltimore—Liverpool. 1868 (15/8) LV Baltimore—Liverpool (dep 16/9)—Baltimore (10 RV). 1873 sold to Boston owners; ran Boston—Halifax—Prince Edward Island- 1886 or 1887 scrapped at Boston.

2. (1865) WORCESTER

    1,244. 63,85 x 10,82. (209.5 x 35.5). Other details as (1). 1863 (11/2) launched as GLAUCUS (Neptune); bought by US Navy. 1865 (12/7) bought by Baltimore & Liverpool; renamed. 1865 (29/11) sailed Baltimore—Liverpool but returned 12/12 with engine trouble. 1865 (23/12) FV Baltimore—Liverpool. 1867 (29/5) sailed Liverpool—Baltimore; lost propeller; returned to Queenstown 4/6; towed to Liverpool for repairs. 1868 (15/9) LV Baltimore—Liverpool (dep 14/10)—Baltimore (arr 1/11) (12 RV). LV of line. 1873 sold to Boston owners; ran Boston—Halifax—Prince Edward Island. 1894 scrapped at Boston.

3. (1866) CARROLL

    1,244. 63,70 x 10,82. (209.0 x 35.5). Other details as (1). 1863 (11/4) launched as PROTEUS (Neptune); bought by US Navy; 1865 (12/7) bought by Baltimore & Liverpool; renamed. 1866 (25/4) FV Baltimore—Liverpool. 1866 (4/10) collided with and sank schooner DORAS in R Mersey. 1868 (23/7) LV Baltimore—Liverpool (dep 19/8)—Baltimore (7 RV). 1874 sold to Boston owners; ran Boston—Halifax—Prince Edward Island. 1894 scrapped at Boston.

    ALLEGANY

1,244 - details as (1). 1863 (11/2) launched as NEPTUNE (Neptune); bought by US Navy. 1865 (12/7) bought by Baltimore & Liverpool; renamed; ran Baltimore—New York. 1865 (5/12) stranded on Long Island (0). 1865 (9/12) back broken; total loss. (Did not run on N Atlantic).

Total 30 RV (including one by British iron screw MEXICAN (c)).

NORTH AMERICAN LLOYD

(United States)

It was announced in January 1866 that the NORTH AMERICAN LLOYD would be starting a service between New York, Southampton and Bremen on 17 March with the 2,250 ton wooden paddle steamer WESTERN METROPOLIS, applications for freight and passage being invited to Ruger Brothers, of New York, founders of the line.

The WESTERN METROPOLIS did not, in fact, take the first sailing as, meanwhile, the Company had bought the ex-Collins Line wooden paddle steamers ATLANTIC and BALTIC, the former leaving New York at short notice on 22 February 1866. Neither the BALTIC nor the WESTERN METROPOLIS was ready to follow so the next sailing was taken by the chartered wooden paddle steamer ERICSSON, built in 1853 and by no means a stranger to the North Atlantic (Chapter 48) . The BALTIC entered service on 26 April and like her consorts carried cabin, second cabin and steerage passengers. It was a new development for the ex-Collins ships to carry steerage.

With the WESTERN METROPOLIS still unavailable, the 2,000 ton MISSISSIPPI and MERRIMAC were each chartered for one round voyage and are interesting as the first American-built iron screw steamers to be employed in transatlantic service. Customs House records at US National Archives show the latter as MERRIMAC, and must therefore be considered as correct. To begin with, she was advertised in this way both in America and England, but later advertisements in America gave the name as MERRIMACK.

The WESTERN METROPOLIS eventually left New York on 28 June, but many of her paddle floats worked loose and she had to put back to Boston on 6 July. Sailing again four days later, she experienced further trouble and eventually returned to New York.

The departure of the ATLANTIC from New York on 19 July 1866 on her fourth voyage marked the beginning of the Company's end. The BALTIC was scheduled to follow on 2 August, but her departure was postponed successively to the 9th, 16th, 18th, 25th and to a further date not then stated. After that, the WESTERN METROPOLIS was advertised to leave on 30 August but was unable to do so. Finally it was stated that the BALTIC would 'positively sail' on 20 September. She failed to do so and the only subsequent event of importance was the arrival of the ATLANTIC at New

York on 25 September with 1,156 passengers.

One of the reasons for the downfall of the line was undoubtedly lack of capital. In this connection, an advertisement in May 1866 stated: 'For subscriptions to the stock of this company, offering a safe, dividend-paying investment, apply to V.Precht, Secretary, office of the North American Lloyd, 45 Beaver Street, New York.'[1] This also shows that the commonly-used version 'North American Lloyds' is incorrect.

A strange mistake was made in September 1866 when, for two or three weeks on end, advertisements in the *New York Herald* under the heading North American Lloyd stated that the AMERICA would sail from New York on 8 September and the HERMANN on 22 September. These steamers were both owned by the North German Lloyd (Norddeutscher Lloyd), whose representatives, Oelrichs & Co, were mentioned at the foot of the announcements, thereby ruling out any likelihood of some special arrangement between the two concerns. But this mistake shows how easy it was for the two titles to be confused and suggests that the incident may have been partly responsible, following strong protests by the Norddeutscher Lloyd, for a very different name - New York & Bremen Steamship Company - being given to the American owned line that ran between the same ports in 1867.

No evidence has been found that Ruger Brothers were in any way connected with the 1867 concern and it seems safe to assume that the North American Lloyd sold out in full to the New York & Bremen Company. If the Rugers had retained any major interest they would undoubtedly have acted as agents for the ships and thus kept an increased share of the profits in the family.

It will be convenient to refer here to two voyages made by the 1,387 ton iron screw CIRCASSIAN with Ruger Brothers acting as agents, although neither was sponsored by the North American Lloyd. Before the American Civil War the CIRCASSIAN had been employed on the North Atlantic under the red ensign. She became a blockade runner, was captured by USS SOMERSET in May 1862, seized and transferred to American registry. On 19 August 1865, approximately four months after the surrender of General Lee and his army to General Grant, she was detailed to undertake the first post-war North Atlantic steamship sailing under the American flag - from New York to Southampton and Bremen. During the later stages of the homeward voyage she went ashore at Arichat, Cape Breton Island, was refloated some days later and managed to proceed under her own steam to New York, where she arrived on 20 November, her complement of 475 passengers having put in an appearance there about a fortnight earlier on the Cunard KARNAK.

The CIRCASSIAN's second voyage under Ruger auspices started from

New York on 2 August 1867. Homewards, she left Bremen on 5 October, returning to New York via Falmouth. The fact that advertisements of this sailing made no mention of the New York & Bremen Steamship Company is further indication that Ruger Brothers had no financial interest in that concern.

[1]   *New York Herald* 10/5/1866

1. (1866) ATLANTIC
      2,845. 86,56 x 13,98. (284.0 x 45.9). S—1—2. W—P—SL2—12. Wm H. Brown, New York (engines Novelty Iron Works, New York). 1849 (1/2) launched for Collins. 1866 ATLANTIC (North American Lloyd). 1866 (22/2) FV New York—Southampton—Bremen. 1866 (19/7) LV New York—Southampton—Bremen (dep 6/9)—Southampton—New York (arr 25/9) (4 RV). (See Collins - 25).

1a. (1866) ERICSSON (c)
      1,902. 77,26 x 12,10. (253.5 x 39.7). C—2x2—2. W—P—SL2—10. Perrine, Patterson & Stack, Williamsburg, NY. 1852 (15/9) launched. 1866 (15/3) Fv for NA Lloyd (c), New York—Southampton—Bremen. 1866 (23/6) LV ditto (2 RV). (See Chapter 48).

2. (1866) BALTIC
      2,123. 86,10 x 13,71. (282.5 x 39.7). S—1—2. W—P—SL2—12. Jacob Bell, New York (engines Allaire Iron Works, New York). 1850 (5/2) launched for Collins. 1866 BALTIC (North American Lloyd). 1866 (26/4) FV New York—Southampton—Bremen (2 RV). (See Collins - 25).

2a. (1866) MISSISSIPPI (c)
      2,008. 83,60 x 11,89. (274.3 x 39.0). C—1—3. I—S—I(2)—10. Harrison, Loring & Co, Boston. 1861 (19/9) launched for Union SS Co (two masts). 1862-5 American Civil War transport. 1866 MISSISSIPPI (NY Mail SS Co). 1866 (10/5) FV for NA Lloyd (c), New York—Southampton—Bremen (1 RV). 1867 (Mar) FV for NY & Havre SN Co (c), New York—Falmouth—Havre. 1867 (29/5) LV Havre—Falmouth—New York (2 RV). 1867 MISSISSIPPI (US & Brazil Mail SS Co). 1869 (11/5) wrecked off Martinique.

2b. (1866) MERRIMAC (c)
      1,991. 82,90 x 11,89. (272.0 x 39.0). C—1—3. I—S—I(2)—10. Harrison, Loring & Co, Boston. Built 1862 for Union SS Co (two masts). 1862-5 American Civil War transport. 1866 MERRIMAC (NY Mail SS Co). 1866 (17/5) NA Lloyd (c), New York—Southampton—Bremen (1 RV). 1868

bought by US & Brazil Mail SS Co. 1887 (10/7) wrecked on Little Hope Island, Nova Scotia (0).

3. (1866) WESTERN METROPOLIS

  2,269. 86,95 x 12,40. (285.3 x 40.7). C—1—2. W—P—B(1)—12. F.D. Tucker, New York (engines Morgan Iron Works, New York). 1864 (/) launched. 1866 (28/6) sailed New York—Bremen for NA Lloyd. 1866 (6/7) put back to Boston with damage to paddle floats; sailed again 10/7; further trouble; put back to New York 19/7 for repairs; laid up. (See NY & Bremen SS Co - 79).

Total 10 RV.

FUNNEL: Black.

(See text for details of two voyages for Ruger Brothers by iron screw CIRCASSIAN. Also for comment on spelling of the name MERRIMAC).

Chapter 76

1866

UNITED STATES & UNITED KINGDOM STEAMSHIP LINE

(British)

The UNITED STATES & UNITED KINGDOM STEAMSHIP LINE was founded in Liverpool in 1866 by Henry Lafone, who bought the 1,093 ton iron screw ASIA, the 1,167 ton MAVROCORDATOS and the 1,174 ton PALIKARI, previously owned by Stephanos Xenos, of London, instigator of the unsucessful Greek & Oriental Steam Navigation Company. The ASIA retained her name, but the other two became the GAMBIA and CAROLINA respectively. The MAVROCORDATOS had already made a transatlantic crossing in 1862 under charter to the 'White Star Line' (Chapter 65).

The service was opened by the ASIA, which sailed from Liverpool on 12 April 1866 and did not reach New York until 12 May as she experienced rough weather and had to put in at Halifax for coal. [1] In consequence, the GAMBIA, which left Liverpool on 19 April, docked at New York three days before her. [2] Each was advertised as carrying first, second and third class passengers, the total numbers actually booked being 205 and 373 respectively.

The third sailing was undertaken by the 1,386 ton UNION, newly-built by T.R.Oswald & Co, of Sunderland. She left Liverpool on 12 May, and the CAROLINA followed on the 19th.

An advertisement of 4 May [3] stated that the fleet consisted of the UNION, CAROLINA, ASIA, GAMBIA, PACIFIC, UNITED STATES (building) and UNITED KINGDOM (building). No tonnages were given, and no further trace has been found of the two last-mentioned. The first four were stated to be sailing at weekly intervals starting on 10 May but the sailing of the CAROLINA, already mentioned, was the last of the line, the total number of round voyages being, therefore, only four.

It is interesting to find that after being sold by the Galway Line in 1861, the 1,469 ton iron screw paddle steamer PACIFIC had another change of owner before coming into the possession, in 1865, of Henry Lafone, who had her converted to screw propulsion. She did not sail to New York for the United States & United Kingdom Steamship Line, but left Liverpool on 4 October 1866 for New Orleans, her agents being shown as Boult, English & Brandon, [4] who earlier that year had acted in a similar capacity for the British & American Steam Navigation Company.

[1] *New York Herald* 13/5/1866
[2] *New York Herald* 10/5/1866
[3] *Liverpool Journal of Commerce* 4/5/1866
[4] *Liverpool Journal of Commerce* 4/9/1866 and 5/10/1866

1. (1866) ASIA

 1,093. 68,88 x 10,02. (226.0 x 32.9). C—1—3. I—S—I(2)—9. (I; II; III). J. Laing, Sunderland (engines Morrison & Co, Newcastle). 1858 (Mar) launched for builders. 1859 ASIA (Stephanos Xenos, London). 1866 ditto (Henry Lafone). 1866 (12/4) FV Liverpool—Halifax (for coal)—New York (arr 12/5) (1 RV). 1868 sold; rebuilt with two masts; tonnage 1,365. 1871 (5/6) stranded on Faro Islands; refloated; compound engines. 1877 MALCOLM (Br). 1880 destroyed by fire; scuttled.

2. (1866) GAMBIA

 1,167. 70,94 x 10,18. (232.8 x 33.4). C—1—3. I—S—I(2)—9. (I; II; III). A. Leslie & Co, Hebburn-on-Tyne. 1860 (/) launched as MAVRO-CORDATOS (Stephanos Xenos, London). 1862 (Sep) arr Montreal from London for White Star (c). 1865 GAMBIA (Henry Lafone). 1866 (19/4) FV Liverpool—New York (arr 9/5) (1 RV). 1871 (Jul) wrecked in Algoa Bay.

3. 1866 UNION

 1,386. 73,08 x 10,18. (239.8 x 33.4). C—1—2. I—S—I(2)—9. (I; II; III). T. R. Oswald & Co, Sunderland. 1866 (Jan) launched. 1866 (12/5) MV Liverpool—New York (arr 29/5) (1 RV).

4. (1866) CAROLINA

 1,174. 74,30 x 9,69. (243.8 x 31.8). C—1—3. I—S—I(2)—9. (I; II; III). Richardson, Duck & Co, Stockton. 1860 (Dec) launched as PALIKARI (Stephanos Xenos, London). 1865 CAROLINA (Henry Lafone). 1866 (19/5) FV Liverpool—New York (arr 6/6) (1 RV). 1868 sold to Peter Denny.

  UNITED STATES
(building; never commissioned by Company).

  UNITED KINGDOM
(building; never commissioned by Company).

  PACIFIC
(never sailed for Company on North Atlantic; see Galway Line - 59).

Chapter 77

1866

CONTINENTAL MAIL STEAMSHIP COMPANY

(United States)

The newly-established CONTINENTAL MAIL STEAMSHIP COMPANY announced in June 1866 [1] that they would despatch the iron screw CIRCASSIAN , which had had an extremely varied career since she entered service for the North Atlantic Steam Navigation Company in 1857, from New York for Antwerp direct on 18 July 1866, first cabin, second cabin and steerage passengers being carried. She duly sailed as scheduled and a few weeks later another advertisement [2] stated that the wooden paddle steamer ERICSSON, built in 1853 as a caloric ship, would sail for Havre on 23 August, two later sailing dates for each steamer being also given. In fact, the CIRCASSIAN did make a second voyage, but the ERICSSON made only the one and the next we hear of her, in 1867, is that her engines had been removed, as were the CIRCASSIAN's in 1874. Meanwhile, the latter had made four North Atlantic sailings for other lines.

The New York - Antwerp trade was a tricky one during the 1850s and 1860s and no steamship company succeeded for long in maintaining a service, but it will be seen from later chapters that from the 1870s onwards it increased out of all recognition.

[1]   *New York Herald* 30/6/1866 (advt).
[2]   *New York Herald* 18/8/1866 (advt).

a. (1866) CIRCASSIAN (c)
    1,387. 77,72 x 11,92. (255.0 x 39.1). C—1—3. I—S—GB2—9. Robert Hickson & Co, Belfast (engines Randolph, Elder & Co, Glasgow). 1856 (18/7) launched. 1866 (18/7) FV for Continental (c), New York—Antwerp. 1866 (11/10) LV New York—Havre—Antwerp (2 RV). (See North Atlantic SN Co - 56).

b. (1866) ERICSSON (c)
    1902. 77,26 x 12,10. (253.5 x 39.7). C—2x2—2. W—P—SL2—10. Perrine, Perrine, Patterson & Stack, Williamsburg, NY. 1852 (15/9) launched. 1866 (23/8) FV for Continental (c), New York—Havre—Antwerp (1 RV). (See Chapter 48).

Total 3 RV.

GUION LINE

(Liverpool & Great Western Steamship Company Limited)

(British)

The GUION LINE, known officially as the LIVERPOOL & GREAT WESTERN STEAMSHIP COMPANY LIMITED, owed its existence to Stephen Barker Guion, born in the USA in 1819, who at an early age became a partner in Williams & Guion, managing owners of the Old Black Star Line of sailing packets between New York and Liverpool. In 1851 he proceeded to Liverpool to establish a branch office under the style Guion & Co, and the business prospered so much that during subsequent summer seasons it was by no means unusual for his ships to carry 1,000 emigrants a week to America.

The American Civil War was responsible for the withdrawal of all North Atlantic sailing packets wearing the Stars and Stripes so that, by 1862, Guion & Co were seeking an outlet for the extensive organisation they had built up to handle westbound emigrant traffic. In 1863 they were placed in charge of the Cunard Line's recently-established steerage passenger business and were made passenger and freight agents for a new line of steamers between Liverpool and New York, shortly to be reconstituted as the National Line, although at first it was usually referred to as Guion & Co's Line or the Guion Line. These activities continued until 1866, but long before then Guion realised that they were likely to be only temporary and that the certain way to safeguard his long-term interests was to enter the North Atlantic steamship trade on his own account. He therefore formed a private company known as the LIVERPOOL & GREAT WESTERN STEAMSHIP COMPANY ·LIMITED, and ordered four iron screw steamers of 2,869 tons and upwards from Palmers on Tyneside. The Company was invariably known as the GUION LINE,

First unit of the new fleet was the 2,869 ton MANHATTAN, which sailed on 8 August 1866 on her maiden voyage from Liverpool and Queenstown (Cobh) to New York, took 20 days to get there and carried 703 passengers in addition to a satisfactory cargo. The CHICAGO followed on 18 December, the MINNESOTA on 14 April 1867 and an appreciably larger steamer, the 3,985 ton NEBRASKA, on 6 June. The last-named was probably bought on the stocks as the 2,927 ton COLORADO, with dimensions approximately similar to the first three, was commissioned more than six months after her. Apart from the 20 day passage already mentioned, the westbound average

701

1866 MANHATTAN 2,869 tons
Pioneer of the Guion Line. In 1875 became Warren
Line MASSACHUSETTS.

was about 13½ days.

Approaching Queenstown in dense fog on her eighth homeward voyage in January 1868, the CHICAGO stranded near Roche's Point and became a total loss, though without casualties. The COLORADO sailed for the first time only two days later, and when the NEVADA and IDAHO appeared in 1869 it was possible to increase the service to weekly.

1870 WYOMING 3,238 tons
Sister ship: WISCONSIN. Among the first North
Atlantic liners with compound engines.

A seventh unit, the 3,238 ton WISCONSIN, left Liverpool on 6 July 1870 on her maiden voyage to New York, and was notable as the first steamer designed for the North Atlantic trade to be fitted with compound engines from the outset. A sister ship, the WYOMING, was commissioned later in the year.

The introduction of the compound engine marked a turning point in the history of North Atlantic shipping. In 1871 the White Star Line started operations with a fleet of compound-engined ships which were second to none in size, speed and comfort. But more particularly, it was the advent of the National Line's 4,500 ton SPAIN and EGYPT in the same trade which made the Guion Line decide to lay down a pair of would-be record breakers, the 4,300 ton MONTANA and DAKOTA, in addition to the 3,400 ton CALIFORNIA and UTAH, the intention being to run a twice-weekly service between Liverpool, Queenstown and New York.

With eight steamers available in 1871, the NEBRASKA and

MANHATTAN were responsible for a few 'extra' sailings over and above the weekly service, but in February 1872 the COLORADO sank in collision in the Mersey with the loss of six lives, and as the short boom which succeeded the Franco-Prussian War of 1870 had already passed its peak the NEBRASKA - the misfit and 'lame duck' of the service - was laid up. The extra sailings ceased and in due course, when it was evident that a serious depression had set in, the orders for the CALIFORNIA and UTAH were cancelled.

The MONTANA was launched by Palmers on 14 November 1872, her maiden voyage being scheduled for 23 July 1873. She and her sister ship had a number of unusual features, one of which was a pronounced 'tumble home' - that is to say, the hull receded inwards to the extent of 2½ metres (8 feet) from the waterline upwards. Their three-cylinder compound engines had one vertical high-pressure cylinder 1,52 metres (60 inches) in diameter and two horizontal low-pressure cylinders 2,87 metres (113 inches) in diameter, the stroke being 1,07 metres (42 inches). There were 10 water-tube boilers with a working pressure of 100 pounds per square inch. On the trip from the Tyne to Liverpool five of the MONTANA's boilers were put out of action by tube blow-outs, with resulting injuries to some of the firemen, and the ship put in at Portsmouth for temporary repairs. Upon arrival at Liverpool the Board of Trade inspector refused to pass her until she took a six-day trial, during which further trouble was experienced so that it was decided to replace the boilers by ordinary tubular ones working at 80 pounds pressure. The outcome of these difficulties was that the MONTANA did not sail on her maiden voyage from Liverpool until 17 June 1874, nearly a year later than intended. Fortunately for the Company, both her departure on that date and her return to Liverpool with engine trouble only four days later received very little publicity. Eventually, she sailed again on 7 July 1875, almost two years behind schedule, and reached New York 10 days later with a disappointing complement of only 106 passengers.

The DAKOTA was launched on 12 June 1873 and ordinary type boilers were substituted before she put to sea. She had engine trouble on the way round to Liverpool and eventually sailed for New York on 21 July 1875, a fortnight after the MONTANA. Neither fulfilled the Company's expectations, their speed being no greater than that of the earlier ships. Meanwhile, the MINNESOTA and the pioneer MANHATTAN had been withdrawn and were sold in 1875 to the Warren Line.

For nearly two years the MONTANA and DAKOTA took turns with the WISCONSIN, WYOMING, IDAHO and NEVADA in the weekly service. Two disasters then followed, the DAKOTA being wrecked on the coast of Anglesey in May 1877 and the IDAHO on the Irish coast in June 1878. This left the Company with only four ships and in June 1878 the Inman CITY OF

1879 ARIZONA 5,147 tons
First of three Guion Line record breakers.

NEW YORK was chartered for two round voyages.

Despite the failure of the MONTANA and DAKOTA as record breakers, the Company decided to place an order with John Elder & Co of Glasgow for the 5,147 ton ARIZONA, which left Liverpool on 31 May 1879 on her maiden voyage to New York. Her time of 7 days 11 hours 22 minutes from Queenstown onwards was the fastest maiden voyage to date, but did not equal the best westbound passage of the White Star GERMANIC in 1877. Homewards, she did even better with a time of 7 days 9 hours 23 minutes, but this again did not top the White Star record. However, on her second eastbound voyage in July 1879 she completed a course of 2,810 miles in 7 days 8 hours 11 minutes at an average speed of 15.96 knots, which was 0.02 knots better than the previous best.

The ARIZONA's fifth homeward voyage ended in disaster when, travelling at full speed in misty weather off the Newfoundland Banks, she collided head-on with an iceberg. Fortunately, the forward bulkhead remained intact, the ship was cautiously backed away and when the decks were cleared of ice it was discovered that there was no more serious damage than a badly-crumpled bow. The ARIZONA proceeded to St John's, Newfoundland, under her own steam for a false wooden bow to be fitted and was then able to resume her voyage to Liverpool. She was soon back in service with her popularity increased rather than diminished owing to this practical demonstration of her great strength.

The ARIZONA did not succeed in beating the record again, but in September 1881 was responsible for completing a westbound passage in what one newspaper gave as 7 days 6 hours 9 minutes and another as 7 days 8 hours 30 minutes. A few days later she split the difference by requiring no more than 7 days 7 hours 36 minutes for the eastbound leg from New York to Queenstown. Both outwards and homewards, the time taken was the shortest to date, but as the distances covered were shorter than usual no record speeds were involved.

The MONTANA stranded in March 1880 within a few miles of the spot where her sister ship succumbed three years earlier, and the Company's fleet was again reduced to four - the ARIZONA, WISCONSIN, WYOMING and NEVADA. In consequence, the ex-Cunarder ABYSSINIA joined them in November 1880 and was regularly employed until April 1884, a few more voyages being undertaken between July 1885 and March 1886, after which she spent four years on the Pacific.

The success of the ARIZONA, the considerable volume of new business she was attracting and the fact that one express steamer could hardly be expected to pay her way made the Company decide to build a consort. The newcomer was the 6,932 ton ALASKA, which was more or less similar in appearance but exceeded her in length by 15,24 metres (50 feet). Only the Inman CITY OF ROME and the Cunard SERVIA had a greater tonnage

1881 ALASKA 6,932 tons
First 'greyhound' of the North Atlantic. Consort of
the ARIZONA and OREGON.

and neither was notable for outstanding speed. From the first, it was clear that the ALASKA would comfortably improve upon the ARIZONA's records, her fastest effort being in September 1882 when she steamed from Sandy Hook to Queenstown on a course of 2,781 miles in 6 days 18 hours 37 minutes at an average speed of 17.10 knots. In April 1883 she improved upon her own westbound record by a passage of 6 days 23 hours 48 minutes at an average of 17.05 knots.

Owing to the comparatively slow speed of the WISCONSIN, WYOMING and NEVADA and the Company's desire to maintain a regular weekly sailing, the ALASKA and ARIZONA were restricted, like the other three, to one voyage every five weeks, which meant that they were not being fully employed as a turnround every four weeks was perfectly feasible and one every three weeks just about possible. It was decided, therefore, to build a third 'greyhound', and the 7,375 ton OREGON left Liverpool on 6 October 1883 on her maiden voyage to New York. She was similar in most respects to the ALASKA and like her was lighted throughout by electricity. A surprising feature was her iron construction as by that time the use of steel had become fairly common.

In April 1884 the OREGON steamed from Sandy Hook to Queenstown at an average speed of 18.09 knots. Three months later she improved somewhat on this record but, meanwhile, had been bought by Cunard owing to Guion's inability to pay outstanding instalments to her builders. Thus, Cunard regained the 'Blue Riband' after a long interval thanks to Guion enterprise.

The sale of the OREGON was the first outward sign of the Company's decline. It had been in low water financially for some time owing to a succession of bad trading years, and the building of the ARIZONA and her consorts was a last unsuccessful bid to put the Company back on its feet. A further blow came in 1885 with the death of its founder, Stephen Barker Guion, to whom most of the credit was due for its front-rank position among North Atlantic lines and its temporary leadership in speed. A year later the Liverpool & Great Western Steamship Company Limited became a public company.

1883 OREGON 7,375 tons
Transferred in 1884 from Guion to Cunard, for
whom she regained the 'Blue Riband'.

Like their former consort, the OREGON, both the ARIZONA and ALASKA were taken up for several months by the British Government during the Russian war scare of 1885, but neither played any active part in their intended functions as armed cruisers. During their absence from the North Atlantic, the BRITISH KING and BRITISH EMPIRE of the British Shipowners Company were each chartered for one round voyage.

The ABYSSINIA temporarily re-entered the Company's service from Liverpool on 29 November 1891. Homewards, she left New York on 13 December and five days later was sighted, on fire, by the NDL SPREE, which took off all passengers and crew. She became a total loss.

There was a serious cholera outbreak at Hamburg in August 1892 so that, following the arrival at New York of more than one steamer with victims, the United States authorities imposed drastic quarantine restrictions. As a result, the WYOMING and NEVADA were both detained off New York for about 10 days and on at least seven other occasions the ALASKA, ARIZONA, WISCONSIN and NEVADA carried saloon and second cabin passengers only. In addition to the loss of the normally brisk steerage traffic, freight business was extremely poor and, consequently, the WISCONSIN sailed from Liverpool for the last time on 22 October 1892 and the WYOMING on 19 November. Both had completed 21 years' service without re-engining. The NEVADA, which was two years their senior and had been converted from single-expansion to compound in 1881, was sold to the Dominion Line in 1893.

There were no Guion sailings from Liverpool between 19 November 1892 and 8 April 1893, but from then until 14 October the ARIZONA and ALASKA sailed at fortnightly intervals, after which there was a second long gap - this time until 14 April 1894, when the service was resumed by the ARIZONA. The ALASKA followed a fortnight later and, finally, the ARIZONA sailed on 12 May, after which the Company closed down for good. Further sailings by both ships had been widely advertised.

The 1890s were extremely difficult for the British-flag North Atlantic lines and most were in trouble of one sort or another. Moreover, by 1894 the ALASKA and ARIZONA were well past their prime and heavy coal consumption made them uneconomical to run except when booked to capacity. There was no alternative but to wind up the Company.

1. 1866 MANHATTAN
2,869. 102,10 x 12,95. (335.0 x 42.5). C—1—2. I—S—I(2)—10. (I—72; III—800). Palmer Bros & Co, Jarrow-on-Tyne. 1866 (15/5) launched. 1866 (8/8) MV Liverpool—Queenstown—New York. 1874 compound engines by Fawcett & Preston, Liverpool; tonnage 3,231. 1875 (20/1) FV for American Line (c), Liverpool—Philadelphia (1 RV). 1875 (14/4) resumed Liverpool—Queenstown—New York. 1875 (3/6) LV ditto. 1875 MASSA-CHUSETTS (Warren). 1876 (1/1) FV Liverpool—Boston. 1881 CITY OF LINCOLN (Thistle). 1881 (7/9) FV Liverpool—New York—London. 1881 (29/10) FV London—New York. 1881 (23/12) LV ditto (2 RV). 1884 SOLIS (Spanish). 1885 CITY OF LINCOLN (Cassels, Liverpool); triple-expansion engines. 1902 (15/8) wrecked near Cape Town (0).

2. 1866 CHICAGO
2,869. 102,10 x 12,95. (335.0 x 42.5). C—1—2. I—S—I(2)—10. (I—72; III—800). Palmer Bros & Co, Jarrow-on-Tyne. 1866 (11/10) launched. 1866 (18/12) MV Liverpool—Queenstown—New York. 1868 (12/1) wrecked near Roche's Point, Queenstown (0).

3. 1867 MINNESOTA
3,008. 102,22 x 12,95. (335.4 x 42.5). C—1—2. I—S—I(2)—10. (I—72; III—800). Palmer Bros & Co, Jarrow-on-Tyne. 1867 (Feb) launched. 1867 (14/4) MV Liverpool—Queenstown—New York. 1874 (18/11) LV ditto. 1875 (10/2) FV for American Line (c), Liverpool—Philadelphia (1 RV). 1875 MINNESOTA (Warren); compound engines by J. Jack Rollo & Co, Liverpool. 1876 (19/8) FV Liverpool—Boston. 1882 VINUELAS (Spanish). 1886 SAN IGNACIO DE LOYOLA (Cia Trasatlántica). 1908 scrapped.

4. 1867 NEBRASKA
3,985. 112,00 x 12,89. (367.5 x 42.3). C—1—2. I—S—I(2)—10. (I—72; III—800). Palmer Bros & Co, Jarrow-on-Tyne. 1867 (Apr) launched. 1867 (8/6) MV Liverpool—Queenstown—New York. 1872 (4/7) LV ditto. 1875 compound engines by builders. 1876 VICTORIA (Br). 1876 (4/11) FV for Warren (c), Liverpool—Boston. 1887 scrapped.

5. 1868 COLORADO
2,927. 102,10 x 13,10. (335.0 x 43.0). C—1—2. I—S—I(2)—10. (I—72; III—800). Palmer Bros & Co, Jarrow-on-Tyne. 1867 (30/10) launched. 1868 (14/1) MV Liverpool—Queenstown—New York. 1872 (7/2) sailed Liverpool—New York. 1872 (7/2) sunk in collision with ss ARABIAN (Br) in R Mersey (6).

6. 1869 NEVADA

3,121. 105,33 x 13,22. (345.6 x 43.4). S—1—2. I—S—I(2)—11. Palmer Bros & Co, Jarrow-on-Tyne. 1868 (17/10) launched. 1869 (2/2) MV Liverpool—Queenstown—New York. 1881 compound engines by G. Forrester & Co, Liverpool; tonnage 3,617. 1884 (3/5) collided in N Atlantic with ROMANO (Wilson); latter sunk. 1893 (13/5) LV Liverpool—Queenstown—New York. 1894 HAMILTON (Dominion). 1894 (28/4) FV Avonmouth—Quebec—Montreal. 1894 (22/9) LV ditto (5 RV). 1896 scrapped in Italy.

7. 1869 IDAHO

3,132. 105,24 x 13,22. (345.3 x 43.4). S—1—2. I—S—I(2)—11. Palmer Bros & Co, Jarrow-on-Tyne. 1869 (13/2) launched. 1869 (13/4) MV Liverpool—Queenstown—New York. 1878 (1/6) wrecked on coast of Wexford, Ireland (0).

8. 1870 WISCONSIN

3,238. 111,55 x 13,16. (366.0 x 43.2). S—1—2. I—S—C2—11. (I—76; intermediate 100; III—800). Palmer Bros & Co, Jarrow-on-Tyne. 1870 (19/3) launched. 1870 (6/7) MV Liverpool—Queenstown—New York. 1874 (or earlier) tonnage 3,700. 1892 (22/10) LV ditto. 1893 scrapped.

9. 1870 WYOMING

3,238. 111,61 x 13,16. (366.2 x 43.2). S—I—2. I—S—C2—11. (I—76; intermediate 100; III—800). Palmer Bros & Co, Jarrow-on-Tyne. 1870 (30/7) launched. 1870 (25/11) MV Liverpool—Queenstown—New York. 1874 (or earlier) tonnage 3,729. 1892 (19/11) LV ditto. 1893 scrapped.

CALIFORNIA

3,300. (Ordered but not commissioned).

UTAH

3,400. (Ordered but not commissioned).

10. 1874 MONTANA

4,321. 122,03 x 13,31. (400.4 x 43.7). S—1—2. I—S—C3—11. (I—60; intermediate 90; III—900). Palmer Bros & Co, Jarrow-on-Tyne. 1872 (14/11) launched. 1874 (17/6) sailed Liverpool—New York but returned 21/6 with machinery disabled. 1875 (7/7) MV resumed, Liverpool—Queenstown—New York. 1880 (14/3) stranded on Anglesey, North Wales (0); refloated. 1880 scrapped at Sunderland.

11. 1875 DAKOTA

    4,332. 122,09 x 13,22. (400.6 x 43.4). S—1—2. I—S—C3—11. (I—60; intermediate 90; III—900). Palmer Bros & Co, Jarrow-on-Tyne. 1873 (12/6) launched. 1875 (21/7) MV Liverpool—Queenstown—New York. 1877 (9/5) wrecked on Anglesey, North Wales (0).

11a. (1878) CITY OF NEW YORK (c)

    3,499. 114,35 x 12,07. (375.2 x 39.6). C—1—3. I—S—C2—10. Tod & McGregor, Glasgow. 1865 completed for Inman. 1878 (8/6) FV for Guion (c), Liverpool—Queenstown—New York. 1878 (13/7) LV ditto (2 RV as replacement for IDAHO (See Inman - 28).

12. 1879 ARIZONA

    5,147. 137,21 x 13,83. (450.2 x 45.4). S—2—4. I—S—C3—15. (I—140; intermediate 70; III—140; steerage 1,000). John Elder & Co, Glasgow. 1879 (10/3) launched. 1879 (31/5) MV Liverpool—Queenstown—New York. 1879 record passage New York—Queenstown. 1879 (7/11) collision with iceberg; proceeded to St John's, NF, for temporary repairs. 1894 (12/5) LV Liverpool—Queenstown—New York. 1894 laid up in Gareloch. 1898 tonnage 5,305; yards removed; one funnel; triple-expansion engines; (I—40; III—1,000); placed in service San Francisco—Japan—China. 1898 HANCOCK (US Govt). 1903-14 receiving ship at Brooklyn Navy Yard. 1917-8 North Atlantic voys as US troopship. 1918 laid up at Philadelphia Navy Yard. 1926 scrapped.

13. (1880) ABYSSINIA

    3,376. 110,78 x 12,92. (363.5 x 42.4). S—1—3. I—S—I(2)—13. (I—202; III—1,068). J. & G. Thomson, Glasgow. 1870 (3/3) launched for Cunard. 1880 (20/11) FV for Guion, Liverpool—Queenstown—New York. 1882 compound engines by J. Jones & Sons, Liverpool. 1886 (27/3) LV ditto. 1887-91 ran on Pacific for Canadian Pacific (c). 1891 (28/11) resumed Liverpool—Queenstown—New York. 1891 (13/12) sailed New York— Liverpool. 1891 (18/12) destroyed by fire at sea (0); passengers and crew rescued by NDL SPREE. (See Cunard - 13).

14. 1881 ALASKA

    6,932. 152,39 x 15,24. (500.0 x 50.0). S—2—4. I—S--C3—16. John Elder & Co, Glasgow. 1881 (15/7) launched. 1881 (30/10) MV Liverpool— Queenstown—New York. 1882 (Apr) record passage, Queenstown—New York. 1882 (Jun) record passage, New York—Queenstown. 1894 (28/4) LV Liverpool—Queenstown—New York. 1894 laid up in Gareloch. 1897 MAGALLANES (Cia Trasatlántica (c)). 1898 laid up in R Clyde. 1899 sold for scrap but resold as accommodation ship at Barrow. 1902 scrapped at Preston.

15. 1883 OREGON

      7,375. 152,70 x 16,52. (501.0 x 54.2). S—2—4. I—S—C3—18. (I—340; intermediate 92; III—110; steerage 1,000). John Elder & Co, Glasgow. 1883 (23/6) launched. 1883 (6/10) MV Liverpool—Queenstown—New York. 1884 (Apr) record passage, New York—Queenstown. 1884 (10/5) LV Liverpool—Queenstown—New York. 1884 (May) sold to Cunard; name unchanged. 1884 (7/6) FV Liverpool—Queenstown—New York. 1884 (Aug) record passage Queenstown—New York. 1885 taken up by British Govt as armed cruiser. 1885 (14/11) resumed Liverpool—Queenstown—New York. 1886 (14/3) sunk in collision with unknown schooner (probably the CHARLES MORSE) 18 miles E of Long Island, NY (0); passengers and crew rescued by NDL FULDA.

N.B. The 3,559 ton BRITISH KING and the 3,361 ton BRITISH EMPIRE were each chartered in 1885 from the British Shipowners Company for one RV between Liverpool, Queenstown and New York. (See American Line - 101).

FUNNEL: Black, broad red band near top.

FLAG: Blue, black star in a white diamond.

Chapter 79

1867

NEW YORK & BREMEN STEAMSHIP COMPANY

(United States)

The NEW YORK & BREMEN STEAMSHIP COMPANY, presided over by Isaac Taylor, acquired the North American Lloyd's wooden paddle steamers ATLANTIC, BALTIC and WESTERN METROPOLIS towards the end of 1866, and placed them on the same route as before, namely, New York - Southampton - Bremen and *vice versa*. Despite many statements to the contrary, there seems to be no evidence that Ruger Brothers, founders of the North American Lloyd, were interested in the new line.

The first sailing was undertaken by the ATLANTIC, which left New York on 7 February 1867, the BALTIC and WESTERN METROPOLIS following at fortnightly intervals. This was the first completed transatlantic voyage of the last-named as she was obliged to put back on the only occasion during the previous year when she actually started a voyage.

The 1,768 ton NORTHERN LIGHT was chartered in May 1867 for two round voyages, enabling the Company to maintain a regular fortnightly sailing for the next two or three months - until, in fact, the WESTERN METROPOLIS turned up at Southampton on 8 September with a broken main shaft. Repairs delayed her for nearly a month.

The ATLANTIC undertook the 17th and last round voyage of the line from New York on 29 October. In theory the Company had done extremely well as on one westbound voyage the BALTIC had carried no fewer than 1,254 passengers, the ATLANTIC's best total being 950, the NORTHERN LIGHT's 944 and the WESTERN METROPOLIS's 921. All told, nearly 12,000 passengers were landed at New York during the course of the 17 arrivals there, an average of over 700 a voyage compared with only 580 on the same route by the iron screw steamers of the Norddeutscher Lloyd, whose comparative passenger total was 27,000 spread over 46 voyages. A disappointingly small volume of freight was, however, carried by the American paddle steamers which, in addition, were expensive to run. In other words, they were completely out of date and it is not surprising that the line was short-lived.

1. (1867) ATLANTIC
2,845. 86,56 x 13,98. (284.0 x 45.9). S—1—2. W—P—SL2—12. Wm. H. Brown, New York (engines Novelty Iron Works, New York). 1849 (1/2) launched for Collins. 1876 (7/2) FV for NY & Bremen, New York—Southampton—Bremen. 1867 (29/10) LV ditto (6 RV). (See Collins - 25).

2. (1867) BALTIC
2,123. 86,10 x 13,71. (282.5 x 45.0). S—1—2. W—P—SL2—12. Jacob Bell, New York (engines Allaire Iron Works, New York). 1850 (5/2) launched for Collins. 1867 (21/2) FV for NY & Bremen, New York—Southampton—Bremen. 1867 (2/10) LV ditto (5 RV). (See Collins - 25).

3. (1867) WESTERN METROPOLIS
2,269. 86,95 x 12,40. (285.3 x 40.7). C—1—2. W—P—B(1)—12. F.D. Tucker, New York (engines Morgan Iron Works, New York). 1864 (/) launched. 1864-5 American Civil War transport. 1866 bought by North American Lloyd. 1866 (28/6) sailed New York—Southampton—Bremen. 1866 (6/7) put into Boston with damage to paddle floats; sailed again 10/7; further trouble; put back to New York 19/7 for repairs; laid up. 1867 bought by NY & Bremen Co. 1867 (7/3) FV New York—Southampton—Bremen. 1867 (24/8) LV ditto. 1867 (8/9) arrived Cowes with broken shaft; delayed for repairs. 1867 (20/10) LV Bremen—Southampton—New York (4 RV). 1869 sold; name retained. 1878 engines removed.

3a. (1867) NORTHERN LIGHT (c)
1,768. 77,26 x 11,64. (253.5 x 38.2). S—2—2. W—P—B2—12. J. Simonson, New York (engines Allaire Iron Works, New York). 1851 (25/10) launched for Cornelius Vanderbilt. 1867 (18/5) FV for NY & Bremen (c), New York—Southampton—Bremen. 1867 (13/7) LV ditto (2 RV). (See Vanderbilt - 47).

Total 17 RV.

FUNNEL: Black.

Chapter 80

1867

HILLER & CO : ADOLPHE STRAUSS

(United States) : (Belgian)

In 1842, 1855 and again in 1861 steamship services of short duration were started under the Belgian flag between Antwerp and New York, and in 1866 under the American flag. Undeterred by these failures, Hiller & Co of New York combined in 1867 with Adolphe Strauss of Antwerp in a joint service between the same ports with chartered tonnage, mostly British. It was left to Strauss to charter all but one of the ships, and it was he who won a mail contract from the Belgian Government, although no subsidy was forthcoming.

The service was opened by the 1,810 ton iron screw OTTAWA, which sailed from Antwerp on 24 March 1867 and reached New York on 9 April with cargo and 417 passengers. The 1,823 ton MEDWAY followed in April, and during the next few months each made three round voyages, the 1,426 ton ACHILLES two and the CONCORDIA, IRON AGE, CLEOPATRA and THAMES one each. All except the CONCORDIA and IRON AGE were owned by or ran for the British Colonial Steamship Company between London and Canada; the CONCORDIA wore the 'Stars and Stripes' and was originally the Anchor Line CALEDONIA.

Advertisements did not quote the Company's name but merely stated: 'Direct steamship line between Antwerp and New York' [1] or 'New and only direct line of steamers to Antwerp'. [2] To begin with, the Company directed applications for passages to Hiller & Co, 3 Chambers Street, New York or for freight to R.M.Sloman & Edye, 19 South William Street. [1] From about July 1867 onwards applications for freight or passage were invited to Christian Bors, Exchange Place, New York or to Funch, Meincke & Wendt, 15 South William Street. [2] On the face of it, it would seem that Christian Bors had taken over from Hiller & Co, but the possibility cannot be excluded that the sailings of the ACHILLES, CLEOPATRA and THAMES and the final sailing of the MEDWAY were arranged independently of those of Hiller & Co. In any event, the last sailing of the line or lines was taken by the THAMES, which left Antwerp on 14 October 1867. Considerable numbers of passengers were carried on most of the sailings, and the few details available suggest that cargo loadings were also satisfactory, so it is surprising that the Company had such a short existence.

It will be seen from the foregoing details that in 1867 the New York firms of Funch, Meincke & Wendt and R.M.Sloman & Edye were close neighbours. Two years later, on the death of Andreas F. Meincke, Henry W.O. Edye joined forces with Christian F. Funch, the name of the firm being changed to Funch, Edye & Co, which became and still is one of the foremost New York firms of steamship agents and shipbrokers. The name Sloman referred, in fact, to Rob M. Sloman, Junr, the well-known Hamburg shipowner, whose daughter married the grandson of Henry Edye.

[1]   *New York Herald* 10/4/1867 (advt)
[2]   *New York Herald* 12/8/1867 (advt)

a. (1867) OTTAWA (c) (Br)
      1,810. 87,47 x 10,73. (287.0 x 35.2). C—1—3. I—S—I(2)—10. (I—25; III—700). Laird Bros, Birkenhead. 1865 (13/5) launched for British Colonial. 1867 (24/3) FV for Company (c), Antwerp—New York. 1867 (24/6) LV ditto (3 RV) (See Allan - 44).

b. (1867) MEDWAY (c) (Br)
      1,823. 86,92 x 10,79. (285.2 x 35.4). C—1—2. I—S—H2—10. T.R. Oswald & Co, Sunderland. 1865 (/   ) launched. 1867 (Apr) FV for Company (c), Antwerp—New York. 1867 (9/9) LV ditto (3 RV). (See British Colonial - 72).

c. (1867) ACHILLES (c) (Br)
      1,426. 83,75 x 9,81. (274.8 x 32.2). C—1—3. I—S—I(2)—10. J. Laing, Sunderland. 1865 (/   ) launched. 1867 (24/5) FV for Company (c), Antwerp—New York. 1867 (12/8) LV ditto (2 RV). (See British Colonial - 72).

d. (1867) CONCORDIA (c) (A)
      1,348. 79,64 x 10,09. (261.3 x 33.1). C—1—3. I—S—I(2)—10. Tod & McGregor, Glasgow. 1862 (3/2) launched as CALEDONIA (Anchor). 1862 (31/12) stranded near Cape Cod, Mass; sold; salvaged; became CONCORDIA (US). 1867 (8/6) FV for Company (c), New York—Antwerp (dep 10/7)—New York (1 RV). (See Anchor - 55).

e. (1867) IRON AGE (c) (Br)
      1,094. 70,82 x 9,38. (232.4 x 30.8). 1—2. I—S—I(2)—10. T.R. Oswald & Co, Sunderland. 1866 (Jan) launched. 1867 (21/6) FV for Company (c), Antwerp—New York (1 RV).

f. (1867) CLEOPATRA (c) (Br)
      1,012. 69,61 x 9,14. (228.4 x 30.0). C—1—?. I—S—I(2)—10. W. Pile, Hay

& Co, Sunderland. 1865 (Jul) launched. 1867 (22/7) FV for Company (c), Antwerp—New York (1 RV). (See British Colonial - 72).

g. (1867) THAMES (c) (Br)
1,364. 77,62 x 9,84. (254.7 x 32.3). C—1—3. I—S—I(2)—10. T.R. Oswald & Co, Sunderland. 1864 (/) launched. 1867 (14/10) FV for Company (c), Antwerp—New York (1 RV). (See British Colonial - 72).

(A) - United States flag.

(Br) - British flag.

Total 12 RV.

Chapter 81

1867-68

AMERICAN STEAMSHIP COMPANY
(United States)

The AMERICAN STEAMSHIP COMPANY, founded in Boston in July 1864 to operate between Boston and Liverpool, must not be confused with the Philadelphia company of the same name dating from 1871. Contracts were placed during the summer of 1865 for two screw steamers of 2,900 tons, wood being chosen partly because it was much cheaper but more especially because facilities in the United States for building iron steamers of this size were extremely limited.

First of the pair was the ONTARIO, which was launched by George W. Jackman of Newburyport, Massachusetts, in November 1866 and sailed from Boston on 5 August 1867 on her maiden voyage to Liverpool, where she arrived on the 18th. She sailed again on 7 September and made the westbound crossing in the satisfactory time of 10 days 6 hours. All told, she made three round voyages on the North Atlantic, both she and her sister ship, the ERIE, which had not made a single voyage, being sold by auction on 3 June 1868 for $256,000 (£51,000) each - only a fraction of their original cost. They were laid up until 1870.

The ONTARIO sailed from New York on 7 November 1870 for Havre with supplies for the French during the Franco-Prussian War, returning to New York on 29 January 1871 via Newfoundland and Boston. The ERIE sailed from New York on 28 November 1870 on a similar mission although ostensibly destined to Cowes, Isle of Wight, for orders. Her homeward voyage started from London on 21 January 1871, she called at Plymouth three days later and lost her propeller on 2 February, the remainder of the voyage to New York being completed under sail via St Thomas. She eventually reached New York on 13 March with 33 passengers. [1] Before long, both ships were sold to C.K.Garrison of the United States & Brazil Mail Steamship Company, for whom they did not run until some time later.

The ERIE was destroyed by fire 90 miles from Pernambuco on 1 January 1873 during her second homeward voyage from Rio de Janeiro to New York, but the ONTARIO continued sailings until 23 September 1875, when she undertook the last voyage from New York of the United States & Brazil Mail Company. In 1877-8 she carried out the round-the-world Woodruff Scientific Expedition, and was subsequently laid up at Boston. It was stated in 1879 that she would be broken up 'this year', but it is believed that she survived until 1885, when she was burnt for the metal in her hull.

1. 1867 ONTARIO

> 2,889. 98,59 x 13,34. (323.5 x 43.8). C—2—3. W—S—V2—11. (I—125; III—500). George W. Jackman, Newburyport, Mass (engines Harrison Loring, Boston). 1866 (Nov) launched. 1867 (5/8) MV Boston—Liverpool. 1867 (27/12) LV Liverpool—Boston (3 RV). 1868 (3/6) sold; name retained. 1870 (7/11) FV New York—Havre (1 RV). 1885 (?) burnt for the metal in her hull.

> ERIE

> 2,900. Did not run for Company. 1868 (3/6) sold. (Made one North Atlantic voyage in 1870-1 - see text).

FUNNEL: Lower half buff; upper half black.

FLAG: White pennant with red border; red 'A.S.S. Co.'.

ss SMIDT

(German)

The 1,672 ton iron screw steamer SMIDT was launched on 16 December 1867 by Johann Lange, predecessor of Bremer Vulkan, and was notable as the first oceangoing steamer turned out on the River k Weser - or, as likely as not, in Germany as a whole. The order was placed by Captain H. Raschen, who took command of her, but behind him were several partners. The builders themselves held a 60/200ths interest - probably because they wished to prove that German shipbuilders could compete with those in England and Scotland.

The SMIDT sailed from Geestemünde, a Weser port situated between Bremen and Bremerhaven, on 4 April 1868 with cargo and 766 passengers, experienced strong westely gales during the entire passage and did not reach New York until 3 May. [1] She carried three classes of passengers at fares of 80 taler (£12) first class, 45 taler (£6.15.0) intermediate and 40 taler (£6) steerage. Altogether, she landed 3,032 passengers at New York in 1868 during the course of four voyages, the last three starting from Bremerhaven. During the same year, Norddeutscher Lloyd carried over 36,000 westbound passengers to New York. They never made direct reference to the SMIDT, but their annual report for 1868 stated: 'We have during the past year had to fight a very strong competition, which we may still have to contend with in the future, but we hope to succeed even if we do not attain the splendid results achieved during recent years.'

The SMIDT's first voyage in 1869 nearly ended in disaster. She left Bremen on 11 January, Gravesend (London) on the 27th and reached New York on 5 March after experiencing a severe hurricane. She 'shipped a large quantity of water which washed the bridge overboard and filled the second cabin and engine room half full of water; lost deck stores and everything moveable about deck; the passengers suffered greatly.' [2]

In 1869 fares were increased to 100 taler (£15), 50 taler (£7.10.0) and 45 taler (£6.15.0), respectively. All told, the SMIDT made five round voyages to New York during the year and two in 1870, after which she is lost sight of for nearly two years - partly, of course, on account of the Franco-Prussian War. It would seem, however, that she changed hands as according to the *Bureau Veritas* of 1872 her owners were then the Bremer Dampfschiffahrt Gesellschaft.

The SMIDT made five round voyages between Bremerhaven and New

York in 1872 and four in 1873. By then the short-lived boom which succeeded the war had ended and a slump was well on the way. In 1874, the SMIDT was sold to Siedenburg & Wendt of Bremen, who removed her engines and ran her for more than 20 years as a three-masted barque.

[1]   *New York Herald* 5/5/1868
[2]   *New York Herald* 6/3/1869

1. 1868 SMIDT

    1,672. 64,00 x 12,04. (210.0 x 39.5). S—1—2. I—S—?—9. Johann Lange, Bremen. 1867 (16/12) launched. 1868 (4/4) MV Geestemünde—New York. 1868 (26/6) 2nd voy Bremerhaven—New York. 1873 (9/10) LV ditto (20 RV). 1874 sold; engines removed; converted to three-masted barque. 1896 (Oct-Nov) abandoned at sea; towed to Fayal, Azores; later to Hamburg; condemned. 1897 scrapped at Briton Ferry, South Wales.

RUGER'S AMERICAN LINE

(United States)

After the sale in 1866 of the North American Lloyd to the New York & Bremen Steamship Company, the New York firm of Ruger Brothers made no further attempt to establish a North Atlantic line composed of their own steamers. In 1867, however, they chartered the 1,387 ton iron screw CIRCASSIAN for one round voyage, starting on 2 August, from New York to Bremen, from where she returned on 5 October via Falmouth. It would seem that abnormally bad weather was experienced as she did not reach New York until 2 November.

The first two American-flag sailings of 1868 between New York and Bremen were undertaken on 28 April and 30 May, respectively, by the CIRCASSIAN, then owned by Ernest Fiedler, and the 1,790 ton wooden paddle QUAKER CITY, still much in the public eye because of her 'Mark Twain' yachting cruise to the Mediterranean during the previous year. Enquiries were directed to Lexow & Voigt of New York, [1] but in the case of the QUAKER CITY an amended advertisement appeared later with Ruger Brothers mentioned as the freight brokers. Immediately adjacent, was another announcement to the effect that applications for passages and freight should be made to Ruger Brothers and in this advertisement, for the first time, two later sailings were mentioned. [2] Further, both the CIRCASSIAN and QUAKER CITY were consigned to Ruger Brothers when they returned to New York on 6 June and 15 July, respectively.

It seems, therefore, that Ruger Brothers only came into the picture as an afterthought and that the first voyage of the CIRCASSIAN at any rate, cannot strictly be said to have come under their auspices. It is, however, included here for reasons of convenience and to some extent because it was announced in July 1868 that Ruger Brothers had chartered the NORTHERN LIGHT, QUAKER CITY, ARIEL and CIRCASSIAN. The ARIEL duly made two round voyages and the NORTHERN LIGHT and CIRCASSIAN one each. In addition, the ex-New York & Havre ARAGO made one, but the QUAKER CITY was not employed again. From July onwards the line was advertised as RUGER'S AMERICAN LINE [3] instead of, as previously, 'Steam direct to Bremen' or 'Only American Line to Europe'.

Although an average of about 550 passengers had been carried on each of the seven westbound voyages from Bremen to New York in 1868, it would seem that Ruger Brothers were aware that they could no longer hope to compete with the Norddeutscher Lloyd iron screw steamers on the same route. Consequently, after one round voyage by the ARAGO in 1869, subsequent voyages, seven in number, were extended to Copenhagen - one each by the ARIEL, NORTHERN LIGHT, OCEAN QUEEN, GUIDING STAR and SANTIAGO DE CUBA and two by the FULTON. The last of these, in August, terminated at Swinemünde (Stettin), calls on the return journey being made at Copenhagen and Southampton.

In 1870 the OCEAN QUEEN, RISING STAR and WESTERN METROPOLIS each made one round voyage to Havre, Bremen, Copenhagen, Stettin and Christiansand (Norway), and in all probability there would have been others but for the outbreak of the Franco-Prussian War in July. The extended service to Stettin, Copenhagen and Christiansand was one of considerable significance, being the first by transatlantic steamship to these ports and may well have been partly if not wholly responsible for the inauguration of the Baltischer Lloyd's service between Stettin and New York in 1871. The call at Christiansand may have encouraged the Norse American Line to start operations in the same year.

There were, in fact, three more round voyages by American wooden paddle steamers, but they were not made under Ruger auspices and details will be found under the North American Steamship Company (Chapter 84).

In addition, there was one further transatlantic arrival at New York consigned to Ruger Brothers - the 1,736 ton iron screw TIBER belonging to J. A.Dunkerly & Co of Hull, which sailed from Swinemünde on 5 December 1870, reaching New York on 13 January 1871 with 60 passengers. [4] It can be assumed that this voyage took place under the British flag and that Ruger Brothers were acting solely as agents.

[1]   *New York Herald* 21/4/1868
[2]   *New York Herald* 29/5/1868
[3]   *New York Herald* 20/7/1868
[4]   *New York Herald* 14/1/1871

a. (1868) CIRCASSIAN (c)
        1,387. 77,72 x 11,92. (255.0 x 39.1). C—1—3. I—S—GB2—9. Robt Hickson & Co, Belfast (engines Randolph, Elder & Co, Glasgow). 1856 (18/7) launched. 1867 (2/8) FV for Ruger (c), New York—Bremen (dep 5/10)—New York (arr 2/11) (1 RV). 1868 (25/4) resumed New York—Bremen. 1868 (25/7) LV ditto (2 RV). (See North Atlantic SN Co - 56).

b. (1868) QUAKER CITY (c)
        1,790. 69,18 x 10,97. (227 x 36). C—2—2. W—P—SL(1)—10. Vaughan & Lynn, Philadelphia (engines Merrick & Sons, Philadelphia). 1854 (2/5)

launched for Philadelphia & Charleston Line. 1868 (30/5) FV for Ruger (c), New York—Bremen (1 RV). (See Collins - 25).

c. (1868) ARIEL (c)
1,736. 76,95 x 9,90. (252.5 x 32.5). C—1—2. W—P—B(1)—11. J. Simonson, New York (engine Allaire Iron Works, New York). 1855 (3/3) launched for Vanderbilt. 1868 (13/6) FV for Ruger (c), New York—Bremen. 1869 (13/3) LV New York—Bremen—Copenhagen (3 RV). (See Vanderbilt - 47).

d. (1868) NORTHERN LIGHT (c)
1,768. 77,26 x 11,64. (253.5 x 38.2). S—2—2. W—P—B2—12. J. Simonson, New York (engines Allaire Iron Works, New York). 1851 (25/10) launched for Vanderbilt. 1868 (22/8) FV for Ruger (c), New York—Bremen. 1869 (27/3) LV New York—Southampton—Copenhagen (2 RV). (See Vanderbilt - 47).

e. (1868) ARAGO (c)
2,240. 89,91 x 12,19. (295.0 x 40.0). C—2—2. W—P—O2—12. J.A. Westervelt & Sons, New York (engines Novelty Iron Works, New York). 1855 (27/1) launched for New York & Havre. 1868 (5/9) FV for Ruger (c), New York—Bremen. 1868 (30/11) sailed ditto for North American SS Co. 1869 (16/1) arr Grimsby. 1869 (3/3) LV Bremen—Falmouth—New York (arr 29/3) for Ruger (c). (Total 1½ RV for Ruger). (See NY & Havre - 27).

f. (1869) OCEAN QUEEN (c)
2,801. 99,66 x 12,80. (327.0 x 42.0). S—2—2. W—P—B(1)—12. Stephen G. Bogert, New York (engine Morgan Iron Works, New York). 1857 (8-12/4) launched as QUEEN OF THE PACIFIC; became OCEAN QUEEN (Vanderbilt). 1869 (17/4) FV for Ruger (c), New York—Bremen—Copenhagen. 1870 (3/3) LV New York—Havre—Brouwershaven—Swinemünde—Christiansand—New York (2 RV). (See Vanderbilt - 47).

g. (1869) GUIDING STAR (c)
2,384. 91,58 x 12,34. (300.5 x 40.5). S—1—2. W—P—B(1)—12. Roosevelt, Joyce & Waterbury, New york (engine I.P. Morris & Co, Philadelphia). 1864 (13/8) launched for New York Mail. 1869 (1/5) FV for Ruger (c), New York—Southampton—Bremen—Copenhagen (1 RV). (See NY & Havre - 27).

h. (1869) FULTON (c)
2,307. 87,62 x 12,43. (287.5 x 40.8). C—2—2. W—P—O2—12. Smith & Dimon, New York (engines Morgan Iron Works, New York). 1855 (4/9) launched for New York & Havre. 1869 (28/5) FV for Ruger (c), New York—Bremen—Copenhagen. 1869 (21/8) LV New York—Stettin—Copen-

hagen—Southampton—New York (2 RV). (See NY & Havre - 27).

i. (1869) SANTIAGO DE CUBA (c)

    1,567. 69,18 x 11,58. (227.0 x 38.0). C—1—2. W—P—B(1)—12. J. Simonson, New York (engine Neptune Iron Works, New York). 1861 (2/4) launched for Valiente & Co, New York. 1867 SANTIAGO DE CUBA (North American SS Co). 1869 (17/6) FV for Ruger (c), New York—Bremen—Copenhagen (1 RV). 1869 (29/11) FV for North American, New Orleans—Bermuda—Havre (arr 29/12; dep 1870 (16/1))—New York. 1870 (3/9) LV ditto, New York—Brouwershaven (dep 28/10)—New York (arr 21/11) (2 RV). Last N Atlantic RV by wooden paddle steamer. 1878 converted to screw. 1886 MARION (coastal service).

j. (1870) RISING STAR (c)

    2,726. 92,50 x 13,31. (303.5 x 43.7). S—1—2. W—P—B(1)—12. Roosevelt, Joyce & Waterbury, New York (engine Etna Iron Works, New York). 1865 (5/4) launched for Star Line (US). 1870 (24/3) FV for Ruger (c), New York—Havre—Stettin—Copenhagen—Christiansand—New York (1 RV). 1877 scrapped.

k. (1870) WESTERN METROPOLIS (c)

    2,269. 86,95 x 12,40. (285.3 x 40.7). C—1—2. W—P—B(1)—12. F.D. Tucker, New York (engine Morgan Iron Works, New York). 1864 completed. 1870 (18/5) FV for Ruger (c), New York—Havre—Stettin—Kiel—Christiansand—New York (1 RV). (See NY & Bremen - 79).

Note: In 1865 a new basis was introduced for calculating tonnage - hence the difference between ARIEL'S tonnage when running for the Vanderbilt Line and that quoted above.

FUNNEL: Black.

Chapter 84

1869-70

NORTH AMERICAN STEAMSHIP COMPANY

(United States)

The NORTH AMERICAN STEAMSHIP COMPANY, presided over by William H. Webb, well-known shipbuilder and founder of the Webb Institute of Naval Architecture, New York, took over the fleet of the Central American Transit Company in 1867 and started sailings between New York and Aspinwall in replacement of the service hitherto operated to Nicaragua. As before, the ships employed were wooden paddle steamers.

In the following year, the ARAGO and FULTON of the recently-disbanded New York & Havre Steam Navigation Company were chartered by the North American Steamship Company to run to Aspinwall, but they were not really suitable for that service and each made a North Atlantic voyage under rather mysterious circumstances. The ARAGO sailed from New York on 30 November 1868 for Bremen. She was advertised by Godeffroy Branker & Co but sailed under the auspices of the North American Steamship Company. What happened next is far from clear as she proceeded from Bremen to Grimsby, where she arrived about 16 January 1869 and seems to have spent several weeks there. She was back in Bremen by about 3 March, sailed again on 12 March and reached New York on 29 March under the auspices of Ruger Brothers, whose Ruger's American Line has already been described in Chapter 83.

The second mysterious voyage was that of the FULTON on 21 August 1869 from New York for Copenhagen and Stettin, from where she sailed on 18 September via Copenhagen and Southampton, arriving back at New York on 23 October, the entire voyage being reported or advertised under the name of Ruger Brothers. In fact, the return voyage was originally intended to terminate at Philadelphia, the consignee being the North American Steamship Company. The ship put in at New York owing to leaking boilers.

The real justifications for this chapter were two voyages by the 1,567 ton wooden paddle steamer SANTIAGO DE CUBA for the North American Steamship Company, the first from New Orleans to Havre in December 1869, returning to New York, and the second from New York to Havre and Brouwershaven (Holland) and back in September 1870. Also one round voyage by the 2,596 ton GUIDING STAR from New York to Havre and Antwerp in August 1870, the homeward leg being made via Southampton and Bermuda (for coal).

The September voyage of the SANTIAGO DE CUBA was the last round voyage across the North Atlantic by any American wooden paddle steamer and virtually the last under the 'Start and Stripes' until the advent of the American Line in 1873, the only exceptions being one round voyage each by the wooden screw steamers ONTARIO and ERIE in 1870-1, carrying supplies to the French during the Franco-Prussian War, and two one-way trips by the Pacific Mail Steamship Company to the Pacific via the Suez Canal. But for the war it is not unlikely that there would have been further North Atlantic sailings by the North American Steamship Company. However, the wooden paddle steamer was long out of date, and not a few were affected by dry rot. The GUIDING STAR, for example, was scrapped at the early age of ten and others had even shorter lives.

1. (1869) SANTIAGO DE CUBA

    1,567. 69,18 x 11,58. (227.0 x 38.0). C—1—2. W—P—B(1)—12. J. Simonson, New York (engine Neptune Iron Works, New York). 1861 (2/4) launched for Valiente & Co, New York. 1867 bought by North American SS Co; name unchanged. 1869 (Dec) FV New Orleans—Havre—New York. 1870 (3/9) LV New York—Havre—Brouwershaven—New York (arr 21/11) (2 RV). Last N Atlantic RV by wooden paddle steamer. 1878 converted to screw. 1886 MARION (coastal service). (See Ruger's American Line - 83).

2. (1870) GUIDING STAR

    2,384. 91,58 x 12,34. (300.5 x 40.5). S—1—2. W—P—B(1)—12. Roosevelt, Joyce & Waterbury, New York (engine I.P. Morris & Co, Philadelphia). 1864 (13/8) launched for New York Mail. 1867 bought by North American SS Co; name unchanged. 1870 (25/8) FV New York—Havre—Antwerp—Southampton—Bermuda (for coal)—New York (1 RV). (See New York & Havre - 27).

LIVERPOOL & CHARLESTON STEAMSHIP LINE

(British)

Surprisingly few attempts were made during the 1860s and 1870s to start North Atlantic steamship services to destinations south of Philadelphia and Baltimore unless one includes those to the Mexican Gulf ports of New Orleans and Galveston, which cannot properly be considered to come within the North Atlantic sphere. In fact, the only line requiring mention here is the LIVERPOOL & CHARLESTON STEAMSHIP LINE, for whom the Liverpool firm of George Campbell & Co acted as managers, the first sailing being taken by the 1,172 ton DARIEN, which left Liverpool for Charleston, South Carolina, on 5 October 1869. Advertisements stated that cabin and steerage passengers were carried. [1]

The 912 ton MARMORA followed on 3 October, the 1,271 ton ADALIA on 20 November and the 1,315 ton ARRAGON on 19 December. The last-named was undertaking her maiden voyage, as was the 1,480 ton LUMSDEN, which sailed from Liverpool on 16 January 1870, and notably both were fitted with compound engines. Their only predecessors on the North Atlantic with this important new type of machinery were the BRANDON in 1854 and the Anchor Line INDIA early in 1869.

Unfortunately, the Company attracted disappointingly small cargoes and only modest numbers of passengers and after a second voyage by the ARRAGON the service was withdrawn. This ship later became well-known as the pioneer of the Great Western Steamship Line between Bristol and New York (Chapter 91).

[1]   *Glasgow Herald* 21/9/1869.

a. (1869) DARIEN (c)
    1,172. 62,32 x 9,63. (204.5 x 31.6). 1—3. I—S—I(2)—9. Pile, Spence & Co, West Hartlepool. 1863 (/) launched. 1869 (5/10) FV for Liverpool & Charleston (c), Liverpool—Charleston (1 RV). 1885 (16/1) wrecked in Riposto Roads, Sicily.

b. (1869) MARMORA (c)

912. 65,28 x 8,58. (214.2 x 28.2). I—S—I(2)—9. Denton, Gray & Co, Hartlepool. 1868 (Mar) launched. 1869 (30/10) Fv for Liverpool & Charleston (c), Liverpool—Charleston (1 RV). 1885 (12/11) wrecked at Huelva.

c. (1869) ADALIA (c)

1,271. 70,70 x 9,75. (232.0 x 32.0).I—S—?—9. Wm Doxford & Sons, Sunderland. 1864 (/) launched. 1869 (29/11) FV for Liverpool & Charleston (c), Liverpool—Charleston (1 RV). 1872 (24/6) wrecked on St Paul Island, Cape Breton.

d. 1869 ARRAGON (c)

1,315. 71,80 x 9,60. (235.6 x 31.5). S—1—2. I—S—C2—10. Barclay, Curle & Co, Glasgow. 1869 (Oct) launched. 1869 (19/12) MV for Liverpool & Charleston (c), Liverpool—Charleston. 1870 (4/3) LV ditto (2 RV). 1871 ARRAGON (Great Western SS Line - 91) (qv).

e. 1870 LUMSDEN (c)

1,480. 76,40 x 10,39. (250.7 x 34.1). 1—2. I—S—C2—10. (I—20; II—10). M.Pearse & Co, Stockton (engines C.D.Holmes & Co, Hull). 1869 (9/9) launched for Brownlow, Lumsden & Co, Hull. 1870 (16/1) MV for Liverpool & Charleston (c), Liverpool—Charleston (1 RV). 1878 (15/7) wrecked off Jutland.

MILFORD LINE

(British)

Several attempts have been made, without much success, to establish Milford Haven as a transatlantic terminal or port of call. One of these was by the MILFORD LINE, which advertised that the 2,500 ton Clyde-built steamer MINIA would sail from London for New York, calling at Milford Haven on 7 June 1870 to embark steerage passengers, for whom the ocean fare was £6. Rail fare of 12s 6d was quoted from London (Paddington) to Milford. [1]

There is no trace of the MINIA among New York arrivals for 1870, but she did arrive at New York from Antwerp (not for the Milford Line) with 291 passengers on 23 May 1872, [2] and returned to London on or about 6 June. Later in the same year, in August and again in November, she turned up at New York with cargoes of railway iron from Cardiff.

The MINIA was an iron screw steamer of 1,986 tons, built by the London & Glasgow Engineering & Iron Shipbuilding Company of Glasgow in 1866, and owned by the Anglo-American Telegraph Company of London.

[1]   *Shipping & Mercantile Gazette* 2/6/1870 (advt).
[2]   *New York Herald* 24/5/1872

PACIFIC MAIL STEAMSHIP COMPANY

(United States)

The PACIFIC MAIL STEAMSHIP COMPANY started operations in 1849 between Panama, California and Oregon with the 1,100 ton wooden paddle steamers CALIFORNIA, OREGON and PANAMA. Within a few months northbound voyages terminated at San Francisco, from where chartered sailing ships and, before long, the Company's own steamers were employed to carry mails to Columbia River and Puget Sound ports.

In 1865 Congress agreed to provide an annual subsidy of $500,000 (£100,000) for a monthly mail service between San Francisco, Yokohama and Hong Kong. The Pacific Mail Company's bid was accepted and the 3,728 ton wooden paddle steamer COLORADO was responsible for the first sailing from San Francisco on 1 January 1867. She and most succeeding steamers of the service reached San Francisco from New York via Cape Horn, but in the same year the COSTA RICA, NEW YORK and the ARIEL (formerly of the Vanderbilt European Line) proceeded across the Atlantic from New York to Cape Town and, finally, Yokohama in preparation for the opening of a branch line from Yokohama to Shanghai. It should be emphasised that these cannot be regarded as North Atlantic sailings.

With the opening of the Suez Canal in 1869 it was decided to despatch two Pacific Mail wooden paddle steamers from New York to San Francisco via the Mediterranean. The 2,793 ton ARIZONA left New York for a 'Grand Oriental Trip' on 22 December 1870 via Gibraltar, Malta, Port Said, Suez Canal, Singapore, Hong Kong and San Francisco, after which she was employed in the Company's coastal service between San Francisco and Panama. [1]

The 4,011 ton ALASKA sailed a month later, on 21 January 1871, on a similarly advertised trip and with the addition of a call for passenger purposes at Marseilles. Upon arrival at San Francisco she joined the GREAT REPUBLIC, AMERICA and CHINA in the Company's trans-pacific service between San Francisco, Yokohama and Hong Kong. [1]

This North Atlantic voyage of the ALASKA was notable as the last transatlantic crossing (albeit one-way) of a United States passenger liner prior to the commissioning of the American Line's service in 1873 between Philadelphia and Liverpool. She also had the distinction of being the largest beam-engined wooden paddle steamer ever to cross the North Atlantic.

The writer's justification for devoting a chapter to these two sailings is that the Pacific Mail Steamship Company was the forerunner on the Pacific of the Dollar Steamship Line, whose Round the World service is described in Chapter 206.

[1] PROFESSOR CEDRIC RIDGELY-NEVITT: *The Walking Beam Engine in Atlantic Service* ('Steamship Bill', journal of the Steamship Historical Society of America. No. 111, Fall 1969).

1. (1870) ARIZONA
    2,793. 98,65 x 13,62. (323.7 x 44.7). S—1—2. W—P—B(1)—13. Henry Steers, Long Island, NY (engine Novelty Iron Works, New York). 1866 (19/1) launched. 1870 (22/12) sailed New York—Gibraltar—Malta—Port Said—Suez Canal—Singapore—Hong Kong—San Francisco (one way only); ran San Francisco—Panama. 1876 laid up. Later sold to Japanese owners. 1882 still listed.

2. (1871) ALASKA
    4,011. 105,45 x 14,47. (346.0 x 47.5). S—1—2. W—P—B(1)—13. Henry Steers, Long Island, NY (engine Novelty Iron Works, New York). 1868 (Mar) launched. 1871 (21/1) sailed New York—Gibraltar—Marseilles—Malta—Port Said—Suez Canal—Singapore—Hong Kong—San Francisco (one way only); ran San Francisco—Yokohama—Hong Kong. 1879 became a hulk at Acapulco; in use as late as 1885.

FUNNEL: Black

FLAG : Burgee, Red—white—blue—white—red horizontal stripes

WHITE STAR LINE

(British)

The White Star Line of sailing packets to Australia (Chapter 65) was bought in 1867 by Thomas Henry Ismay, who had been running sailing ships to the west coast of South America and the Caribbean and in 1864 had become a director of the National Steam Navigation Company Limited, trading between Liverpool and New York. A year or so after the purchase, Ismay came into contact with Gustavus C. Schwabe, a prominent Liverpool merchant and financier and the uncle of Gustav Wilhelm Wolff, junior partner of Belfast shipbuilders Harland & Wolff. Schwabe offered to assist Ismay in raising capital to start a new line of steamers provided the ships were built and all possible repair work done by his nephew's firm. The OCEANIC STEAM NAVIGATION COMPANY LIMITED was founded on 6 September 1869 with a capital of £400,000 in shares of £1,000. Of these T.H.Ismay acquired 50, G.H.Fletcher (who played a prominent part in the formation of the line) 50 and G.C.Schwabe 12. From earliest days the Company was invariably known as the WHITE STAR LINE.

1871 OCEANIC 3,707 tons
Famous White Star pioneer. Sister ships:
ATLANTIC, BALTIC, REPUBLIC.

The first of four ships ordered from Harland & Wolff, the 3,707 ton OCEANIC, was launched on 27 August 1870, a contemporary account describing her as 'designed for the White Star Line of Australian packets'. [1] but it is evident that she was always intended to operate on the North Atlantic. She was an iron screw steamer with dimensions of 128,01 x 12,46 metres (420.0 x 40.9 feet) and had many novel features, one of the most important being her compound engines, the first permanent examples of which had appeared on the North Atlantic only a year or two previously. Steam pressure jumped from the 30 pounds of the Inman CITY OF BRUSSELS to 65 pounds per square inch. Daily coal consumption at 14 knots was under 60 tons compared with the Inman ship's 110. Hitherto, all North Atlantic lines had followed the sailing ship tradition of placing first class passengers right aft. This was reasonable enough so long as paddles remained the means of propulsion, but with high-powered screw steamers vibration aft became a serious factor. The new company, therefore, broke with tradition by placing the first class dining saloon and cabins amidships.

The OCEANIC's ratio of length to beam - 10 to 1 instead of the then-customary 8 -1 was distinctive but has been overstressed, as the vogue for long ships was comparatively short-lived, and the generally-accepted notion that the White Star pioneer was the first ship with the increased ratio is incorrect. The Bibby (later Leyland) liners IBERIAN, ILLYRIAN and ISTRIAN of 1867 had preceded her, as had the Inman CITY OF BRUSSELS of 1869.

Innovations in the passenger accommodation were more original and lasting. The customary narrow deckhouses and high bulwarks were replaced by an iron promenade deck with open railings. Cabins were nearly double the usual size and almost every one had a porthole. The portholes themselves were much larger than any previously known on the North Atlantic. The saloon extended the entire width of the ship. The effect of these changes was an impression of lightness and airiness. Minor improvements were electric bells in the cabins and separate chairs for passengers in the dining saloon.

The OCEANIC left Liverpool for New York on 2 March 1871, overheated bearings occurring at an early stage and making it necessary to put into Holyhead and, eventually, return to Liverpool. She sailed again on 16 March, called at Queenstown a day later and, arriving at New York on the 28th, had made a disappointingly slow passage. After a few voyages she went back to Belfast for alterations which increased her boiler power and her stowage of coal.

The second ship, the ATLANTIC, entered service in June 1871, followed by the BALTIC in September. The latter had been launched on 8 March as the PACIFIC, [2] the name having been hurriedly changed after someone had drawn attention to the disaster that had befallen the Collins Line PACIFIC in 1856. The BALTIC incorporated changes that experience with the OCEANIC had shown to be desirable. The REPUBLIC, so named because she was launched on Independence Day, 4 July 1871, completed the first group of four ships. A further pair, the ADRIATIC and CELTIC (laid down as the ARCTIC but renamed owing to tragic Collins Line associations), were 5,18 metres (17 feet) longer than their predecessors and were lighted by gas generated by oil. Fractures in the piping were, however, caused by the 'working' of the ships, and after a short trial the then-customary oil-burning lamps were substituted.

At a later date Harland & Wolff engined their own ships, but at this stage lacked the necessary facilities and contracts for the six sets of engines were shared by Maudslay, Sons & Field of London and Geo Forrester & Co of Liverpool.

It so happened that the years 1871-3 were notorious for long successions of severe gales on the North Atlantic and, in consequence, over a year passed before the new company was able to break any speed records. In May 1872 the ADRIATIC completed a course of 2,778 miles from Queenstown to Sandy Hook in 7 days 23 hours 17 minutes at an average speed of 14,53 knots, [3] which was .07 knots faster than the Queenstown - New York record of the Cunard paddle steamer SCOTIA in July 1863. By this time it had become commonplace to quote voyage times as between Queenstown and Sandy Hook instead of New York, so there is full justification for applying this arrangement in the case of the ADRIATIC and, for that matter, all succeeding record passages.

In January 1873 the BALTIC made a record eastbound voyage of 7 days 20 hours 9 minutes from Sandy Hook to Queenstown at an average of 15.09 knots. During 1873 the Company's steamers averaged 11.8 knots westbound and 13.4 eastbound - in each case at least half a knot faster than their nearest rivals, Cunard and Inman.

By the autumn of 1872 all six ships were in service, but only five were required to maintain a weekly sailing to New York. Four smaller ships - the 2,000 ton TROPIC and ASIATIC, built by T. Royden & Sons of Liverpool, and the 2,650 ton GAELIC and BELGIC, built by Harland & Wolff - had been bought on the stocks. It was clear, therefore, that the Company was planning to extend its operations, but those who hoped for a White Star steamship service to Australia were soon disappointed. Instead, Ismay set out to break the Pacific Steam Navigation Company's monopoly of the steam traffic to Chile and Peru. The REPUBLIC took the first sailing in October 1872; the new vessels and chartered tonnage followed. The ATLANTIC was scheduled to sail for South America in January 1873 but unfortunately for herself this sailing was cancelled. Other sailings were repeatedly postponed and it soon became apparent that the new service was not a paying proposition. The last steamship departure took place from Liverpool in December 1873; the TROPIC and ASIATIC were sold.

The Company suffered a major disaster on 1 April 1873. The outward-bound ATLANTIC had encountered such bad weather that she ran short of coal. Her captain decided to make for Halifax, but she went on the rocks outside that port in appalling weather conditions, the after part of the ship sinking almost immediately, leaving only the bows and part of the rigging above the water. Altogether, 585 lives were lost out of 1,038 passengers and

734

crew. Had not the boatswain heroically swum through the raging surf carrying a lifeline ashore it is doubtful whether there would have been any survivors. As it was, the loss of life was the heaviest to date of any North Atlantic steamship disaster and the Company came in for much criticism - most of it completely unjustified as, for example, the statement that the ship had put to sea with insufficient coal. In any event, it was quite common in those days for steamers to put into Halifax for coal during a spell of particularly bad weather on the North Atlantic, but so far as the writer is aware this was the one and only time White Star ever had occasion to do so.

The OCEANIC and her sisters were so far ahead of other North Atlantic liners that the Inman and Cunard companies were obliged to take counter measures. Inman's redesigned their latest ship and ordered three new ones on OCEANIC lines. Cunard ordered two larger but slower steamers. Having declared that they would operate the largest and fastest steamers on the New York run, White Star felt compelled to lay down two new and still better ships, even though their original group had barely been completed. In fact, the first step towards this action had been taken in December 1872, when the Company's capital was increased to £750,000, having already been increased from £400,000 to £500,000 earlier in the same year.

1874 BRITANNIC 5,004 tons
A larger and faster edition of the OCEANIC.
Sister Ship: GERMANIC.

The newcomers, the 5,000 ton BRITANNIC and GERMANIC, were two-funnellers, but in essentials only improved editions of the OCEANIC. Speed increased from 14 to 15½ knots; daily coal consumption rose to just over 100 tons; the first class passenger complement rose from 166 to 220, and steerage from 800 to 1,500. The ships cost £200,000 each.

An interesting innovation was tried in the BRITANNIC, the centre-line of whose propeller was normally only a little above the keel, and the machinery was raked aft in order to keep the shaft in line. The purpose of this was to increase thrust and reduce the tendency of the propeller to race when the ship was pitching. A universal joint in the shaft allowed the propeller to be lifted into the orthodox position when the ship was in shallow water. The arrangement was a failure and after a few months the

BRITANNIC was sent back to Belfast for reconstruction. The GERMANIC was built on orthodox lines and on her third westbound voyage starting in July 1875 improved slightly on the ADRIATIC's 1872 record. Within three months the Inman CITY OF BERLIN had captured the record in both directions, but her success was short-lived as the GERMANIC made the fastest eastbound crossing in February 1876, while later that year the BRITANNIC, back in service after her propeller alterations, gained the record out and home. There was little to choose between the two sisters, the outcome being that the GERMANIC was responsible for the fastest westbound passage at an average speed of 15.76 knots and the BRITANNIC for the eastbound at 15.94 knots. It is remarkable that the ships became faster still with age until, in the early 1890s, they made some 16 knot crossings although, of course, they were then completely outpaced by newer vessels.

Six ships were more than ample for a weekly service to New York so the completion of the BRITANNIC and GERMANIC rendered one of the OCEANIC class redundant. Employment had also to be found for the GAELIC and BELGIC of the South American service. The former undertook eight round voyages between Liverpool and New York and in May 1874 the BELGIC one, after which each made four round voyages in an experimental service from London to New York, followed by one or two more from Liverpool. Both, together with the OCEANIC, were then chartered by the Occidental & Oriental Steamship Company to run between San Francisco, Japan and Hong Kong. This company had been incorporated in November 1874 with substantial backing from the Central Pacific (later Southern Pacific) and Union Pacific railroads for the express purpose of competing with the Pacific Mail Steamship Company, whose principal aim at that time was to route cargo destined from the Orient to New York, and *vice versa*, via Panama and rail across the isthmus, greatly to the detriment of the two railroads, whose transcontinental line had been completed in 1869.

The year 1876, like its two predecessors, was an extremely unprofitable one on the North Atlantic. White Star and Inman were unhampered by any mail contract and were able to reduce their working expenses by each agreeing to despatch only three ships every five weeks. In the following year, the two companies were allowed to share the contract with Cunard, payment being made by results - namely, 4 shillings a pound for letters and 4 pence a pound for newspapers. From the end of 1877 to the end of 1884, White Star and Inman sailings from Liverpool interchanged between Tuesdays and Thursdays, but in 1885 White Star settled down to weekly departures on Thursdays. Two years later, Inman lost their British mail contract. White Star and Cunard became the sole contractors, the latter retaining their Saturday sailing day from Liverpool and White Star changing from Thursday to Wednesday.

The 4,400 ton ARABIC (I) and COPTIC were completed in 1881 for the San Francisco - Hong Kong trade, but made two or three New York voyages before setting out for the Pacific via the Suez Canal. A slightly larger pair, the IONIC and DORIC, were completed two years later and detailed to a new service to New Zealand, which White Star ran jointly with Shaw, Savill & Albion. All four were built of steel, but were somewhat slower than the OCEANIC and had reduced passenger accommodation.

It was announced in July 1884 that the ADRIATIC would carry intermediate class passengers as well as first and steerage, [4] and in March 1887 the CELTIC did the same. During 1883 and 1885-7, the BALTIC made 17 round voyages between Liverpool and New York for Inman. When she returned to White Star service in April 1887 she made at least one voyage from Liverpool to New York with her passenger complement restricted to intermediate and steerage. During 1888 the ARABIC, which had returned from the Pacific a year previously, and the REPUBLIC both made some 'extra' sailings in which they omitted to call at Queenstown, and they, too carried intermediate and steerage only. The intermediate class was sometimes so described in advertisements, sometimes as second class and occasionally as second cabin. For example, it was stated in connection with the ARABIC's sailing on 31 March 1888 from New York to Liverpool that 'the second cabin passengers will be berthed in the saloon staterooms and have the use of the saloon deck. Rates $30 and $35. Steerage $20.' [5] There will be further examples in this and many other chapters of first class accommodation becoming second class or intermediate, and after World War I cabin; it is practically certain that the BALTIC was the originator of the arrangement in 1887 in respect of the New York lines. It was also in that year that the BRITANNIC and CELTIC had a minor collision 300 miles east of Sandy Hook, both captains being censured for excessive speed in fog.

The 4,639 ton CUFIC, first of the Company's purely cargo steamers and known as one of the 'cattle boats' owing to her special facilities for stabling live cattle was completed in December 1888 for the Liverpool - New York trade and succeeded early the following year by a sister ship, the RUNIC. They were the first ships to be designed for the cattle trade and were also the first of the White Star fleet to be fitted with triple-expansion engines, their performance being closely watched in view of the forthcoming introduction of this system in the new passenger ships then under construction.

Partial renewal of the passenger fleet was long overdue, and became urgent when the newly-revived Inman Line came out with the first of two 10,000 tonners in August 1888. The 9,984 ton twin-screw TEUTONIC appeared 12 months later, followed by the MAJESTIC (I) in the spring of 1890. In capability there was nothing to choose between either pair,

1889 TEUTONIC 9,984 tons
The silhouette of the modern liner and the
abandonment of sail power. Sister ship:
MAJESTIC.

although outwardly they were very dissimilar. The TEUTONIC and her sister were long ships of rather less tonnage than the CITY OF NEW YORK and CITY OF PARIS and were built along strictly utilitarian lines, a new development being the abandonment of sail powers. Gross tonnage was virtually double that of the BRITANNIC. And the White Star pair were the first North Atlantic liners to be built to Admiralty requirements for use as armed cruisers in times of war, the Company being paid a special retaining fee on this account.

Both ships succeeded in gaining the westbound 'Blue Riband'. The MAJESTIC reached New York on 5 August 1891 after a crossing of 5 days 18 hours 8 minutes at an average speed of 20.10 knots, and only two weeks later the TEUTONIC, on a course just one mile longer, reduced the time to 5 days 16 hours 31 minutes and increased the average to 20.35 knots. This remained a record for nearly a year.

The commissioning of these ships made it possible to dispose of the BALTIC, REPUBLIC, CELTIC and ARABIC. The ADRIATIC was retained as a reserve steamer until 1897, while the OCEANIC, after returning to Liverpool in 1879 for a refit and the installation of new boilers, continued to run for the O&O Line until 1895, when she returned to Belfast for re-engining, but instead was sold and scrapped.

Hard on the heels of the MAJESTIC appeared the first of an enlarged and improved series of cattle steamers, the 5,949 ton twin-screw NOMADIC, followed in 1892 by the TAURIC, NARONIC and BOVIC. The NARONIC left Liverpool for New York on 11 February 1893 on her seventh westbound voyage and disappeared without trace. She was replaced in 1894 by the 8,315 ton CEVIC, which had a length of 152,39 metres (500 feet) compared with the 131,27 metres (430.7 feet) of the CUFIC and RUNIC and the 143,25 metres (470 feet) of the NARONIC and BOVIC. Last of the series, the 10,077 ton GEORGIC (I) was commissioned in August 1895, her length being no less than 170,28 metres (558.7 feet).

To begin with these cattle steamers did not cater for passengers, but on

738

her maiden voyage to New York in 1891 the TAURIC carried two cabin and one steerage, and from then onwards there were numerous occasions when two or three handfuls were carried. The largest numbers noted, all westbound, were seven cabin and 11 steerage by the NOMADIC in 1891, seven cabin and 10 steerage by the TAURIC in 1893 and two cabin and 14 steerage by the CUFIC in 1892. The largest number noted on the GEORGIC was 10 cabin in 1900.

The 12,552 ton twin-screw CYMRIC was laid down as an enlarged GEORGIC, herself the world's largest cargo and cattle steamer, but with the important difference that she was fitted with accommodation for about 150 first class passengers. The idea of carrying passengers as well as cattle - a practice then much in favour with some lines - was becoming unpopular and it was decided at the last minute that the CYMRIC should cater for cargo and human beings only, much of the space originally intended for cattle being turned into steerage accommodation.

1899 OCEANIC 17,274 tons
First liner to exceed the GREAT EASTERN in
length.

The new passenger liner that had been talked about for a number of years and was so badly needed to maintain the Company's prestige was launched on 14 January 1899 as the OCEANIC (II). At one stage, no doubt, she was intended to be a record breaker, but the Norddeutscher Lloyd KAISER WILHELM DER GROSSE was completed in 1897 and before the end of that year set up a new record average speed of 22.35 knots. It seems clear that by then, if not before, White Star had abandoned any idea of regaining the 'Blue Riband', and on her maiden voyage in September 1899, the OCEANIC crossed at an average speed no greater than 19.57 knots, taking 6 days 2 hours 37 minutes from Queenstown to Sandy Hook. She had a tonnage of 17,274, dimensions of 208,98 x 20,84 metres (685.7 x 68.4 feet) and was the first steamer to exceed the GREAT EASTERN in length, although she fell slightly behind in the matter of tonnage. Her outstanding feature was the comfort of her accommodation in all three classes. She had berths for 410 first class, 300 second and 1,000 third.

The OCEANIC marked a turning point in White Star policy, and the fact that she fell some way short of being a record-breaker in no way affected her popularity. On the contrary, it rather enhanced it as experienced travellers were getting sceptical of high speed. It was well-known that the German greyhound and her successors vibrated excessively, and were having a number of minor mishaps which in some cases considerably prolonged their crossings and occasionally put them out of action for weeks on end. Moreover, it was their owners' policy to drive them at maximum speed whatever the weather, and this did not make for comfortable travel. White Star decided in the case of the OCEANIC and her successors to make comfort their first consideration. To this end they built ships of great size and exceptional steadiness, with no more than moderate speed.

T.H.Ismay, founder of the line, died on 23 November 1899, only a few weeks after the OCEANIC's maiden voyage and was succeeded by his son, Bruce. One of the nicest tributes paid to him was the naming of London & North Western Railway locomotive No. 1921 'T.H.Ismay' at the time of its completion in 1900, but this was probably in recognition of his services as a director of the railway rather than his White Star activities, although at one time or another the names of many White Star ships were borne by LNWR locomotives.

Another important event of 1899 was the opening of the first White Star steamship service to Australia via the Cape of Good Hope by the 12,000 ton MEDIC, followed by the PERSIC, AFRIC, RUNIC (II) and SUEVIC. In fact, the AFRIC was the first of the quintette, but for some reason her maiden voyage was to New York, after which she returned to Belfast for alterations and improvements. She made a further voyage to New York in August 1900, and the SUEVIC also made one 12 months later, when she carried 127 cabin passengers destined to an American exhibition. The SUEVIC became notorious in 1907 when she stranded near the Lizard. The wreck was cut in two and the stern section towed to Southampton for a new bow section, built at Belfast, to be added.

The 7,755 ton twin-screw GOTHIC had been built for the New Zealand joint service in 1893, followed by the 8,273 ton DELPHIC in 1897 the latter's maiden voyage taking place from Liverpool to New York, after which she made a voyage from London to New York. The 12,300 ton ATHENIC, CORINTHIC and IONIC (II), comparable in size with the five Australian steamers, were completed for the joint service in 1902.

Encouraged by the success of the OCEANIC, the 20,904 ton CELTIC was commissioned for the Liverpool - New York trade in 1901, being joined by the 21,035 ton CEDRIC in 1903. Although nearly 4,000 tons larger than the OCEANIC they were $1\frac{1}{2}$ metres (5 feet) shorter, a considerably greater beam being the chief reason for the tonnage increase. Despite being the world's largest ships, they really came into the intermediate category, their speed being no more than 16 knots. They had a huge cargo capacity and

1901 CELTIC 20,904 tons
First of the 'Big Four' and for a time the largest liner
in the world. Sister ship: CEDRIC.

accommodation for 350 first class, 160 second and no fewer than 2,350 third class passengers. A feature of the first class was the provision of a number of single berth cabins.

The MAJESTIC, CYMRIC, BRITANNIC and NOMADIC served as transports during the Boer War, the BRITANNIC being one of the most successful of all the ships taken up by the British Government, with at least 11 round voyages to South Africa to her credit. After the war, she was sent to Belfast for re-engining, but at the last moment it was decided that her moderate tonnage compared with that of more modern ships made the heavy cost of these alterations uneconomical and, instead, she was sold in 1903 to German shipbreakers. Her sister ship GERMANIC had had an extensive refit at Belfast in 1895, when a new deck was added above the promenade deck, her funnels were lengthened and she was fitted with triple-expansion engines. Four years later she had a curious accident at her berth in New York, snow and ice that had accumulated on her decks and upperworks during a particularly severe voyage causing her to heel over and sink. No structural damage was done and she was back in service within four months. In 1905 she became the Dominion Line OTTAWA.

The outstanding shipping event of 1902 was the formation of the International Mercantile Marine Company, which succeeded the International Navigation Company, owners of the Red Star and American lines. The capital of the new concern was increased from £3,000,000 to £24,000,000 to enable many important purchases to be made, including the entire share capital of the White Star Line and the business of Ismay, Imrie & Co, its managers. This meant, in effect, that the Company became American-owned, but there was never any intention of transferring the ships to the American flag, nor were the arrangements for converting ships into British auxiliary cruisers in times of war affected. Nevertheless, the sale to America of one of the world's best-known steamship companies was a sad blow to British pride. First president of IMM was Clement A. Griscom, who had played a leading part in founding the Red Star Line in 1871 and who resigned in 1903 owing to ill-health. Bruce Ismay was appointed in his place.

741

One of the first results of the IMM merger was that White Star took over the Dominion Line's Liverpool - Boston and Boston - Mediterranean services. This was bad luck for the Dominion Line, but was a sound move as White Star prestige stood very high. The four largest Dominion steamers - the 11,394 ton NEW ENGLAND, 12,097 ton COMMONWEALTH, 13,507 ton MAYFLOWER and 15,378 ton COLUMBUS - went with the services and were given White Star names - ROMANIC, CANOPIC, CRETIC and REPUBLIC (II), respectively, the first sailing from Liverpool to Boston being taken by the ROMANIC in November 1903. Upon arrival at Boston she opened the Mediterranean service to Naples and Genoa via the Azores and Gibraltar, her consorts being the REPUBLIC and CANOPIC. In the autumn of 1904 the CRETIC, which had been running during the year between Liverpool and Boston in conjunction with the CYMRIC, was also detailed to the Mediterranean but she, and the REPUBLIC from then onwards, terminated at New York instead of Boston. It was arranged for the REPUBLIC to run between Liverpool and Boston in summer and between New York and the Mediterranean during the remainder of the year.

The Leyland Line was one of those acquired by IMM, and in order to avoid competition with White Star they withdrew their newly-established Liverpool - New York service. During the greater part of 1903 the 8,825 ton VICTORIAN and ARMENIAN of the Leyland Liverpool - Boston service, joined the GEORGIC, CEVIC and BOVIC in White Star's New York cargo service. Their accommodation for 60 passengers was described as second class and on several occasions full complements were carried. In 1904 and subsequently, however, they normally carried cargo only. In addition, the Leyland EUROPEAN and AMERICAN became the White Star TROPIC and CUFIC (II) and were detailed to the Australasian trade. The White Star cargo steamers NOMADIC and TAURIC were transferred to the Dominion Line.

1903 ARABIC 15,801 tons
Laid down as ATL MINNEWASKA but
completed for White Star.

A further White Star acquisition was the Atlantic Transport MINNEWASKA, fourth of a series of ships carrying first class passengers and cargo. Taken over on the stocks and completed as a three-class ship of 15,801 tons, she was named ARABIC and made her first sailing from Liverpool to New York in June 1903. She was transferred to the Boston service in the spring of 1905 as a consort to the CYMRIC and REPUBLIC.

The success of the CELTIC justified the laying down of a third of the class, the BALTIC, in September 1902 - before even the name International Mercantile Marine Company had been announced - and was a sure indication that White Star was to become the showpiece of the group. The BALTIC was 8,53 metres (28 feet) longer than the earlier pair and had a tonnage of 23,876. The final unit of the 'Big Four', the ADRIATIC, whose construction was announced in December 1903, was not commissioned until 1907. Two important innovations were an indoor swimming pool and Turkish baths.

1907 ADRIATIC 24,541 tons
Last of the 'Big Four'. Sister ship: BALTIC..
Very similar: CELTIC, CEDRIC.

A rumour circulated in 1902, at the time when IMM was being formed, that the TEUTONIC, MAJESTIC and OCEANIC were to be despatched from Southampton instead of Liverpool, but this was denied and no more was heard until 1907, when the three steamers, together with the 24,541 ton ADRIATIC, inaugurated a new service from Southampton to New York - outwards via Cherbourg and Queenstown; homewards via Plymouth and Cherbourg. The ADRIATIC's maiden voyage started from Liverpool on 8 May 1907, but she returned from New York to Southampton and in this way was responsible for the first sailing of the new service. However, she was not the first White Star ship to be employed on the route as a few weeks previously the CELTIC had made two round voyages for the American Line, largely to give White Star some valuable advance experience.

On her maiden voyage the ADRIATIC carried the satisfactory total of 365 first, 335 second and 1,802 third class passengers, an aggregate of 2,502. This, however, was by no means a record number for the Company as in September 1904 the westbound CELTIC carried 310 first, 239 second and no fewer than 2,408 third class, a total of 2,957, which was the Company's peacetime record. It may be added, prematurely, that the largest number carried by White Star's largest ship, the MAJESTIC (II), was 480 first, 736 second and 1,409 third class, a total of 2,625, in 1923.

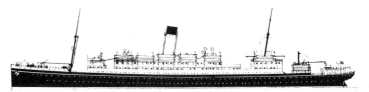

1909 MEGANTIC 14,878 tons
Near-sister: LAURENTIC. First ships completed
for White Star Canadian service.

The Dominion Line had been participating in the Liverpool - Quebec - Montreal trade since 1872. Their passenger fleet was composed of ships at least ten years old, and in consequence two much larger units were laid down as the ALBERTA and ALBANY. In view, however, of White Star prestige standing so high, they were launched in September and December 1908 as the LAURENTIC and MEGANTIC, the intention being that they would inaugurate a new joint service to Canada under the description WHITE STAR - DOMINION LINE JOINT SERVICE, their sailings to alternate with the Dominion Line's CANADA and DOMINION. The 14,892 ton LAURENTIC and the 14,878 ton MEGANTIC were the largest steamers in the Canadian trade, the White Star policy of producing large, comfortable ships of moderate speed being continued, with no attempt to rival the speed exploits of the Canadian Pacific 'EMPRESSES' and the Allan Line VICTORIAN and VIRGINIAN.

There was an interesting difference between the LAURENTIC and MEGANTIC. The latter was fitted with quadruple-expansion engines of conventional design driving twin-screws, whereas the LAURENTIC was a triple-screw steamer. The two outer screws were driven by triple-expansion engines, whose exhaust steam was used to drive a low-pressure turbine connected to the centre screw. Performances of the ships were studied closely in order to determine what motive power should be used for the mammoth White Star liner OLYMPIC, which had been laid down at Belfast in December 1908. The Harland & Wolff combination of reciprocating engines and low pressure turbine proved to be a great success and was duly adopted.

The year 1908 was one of serious slump on the North Atlantic, and the Company's Liverpool - New York cargo service was suspended for five months.

The third White Star disaster took place on 23 January 1909 when the REPUBLIC was sunk in collision with the Italian liner FLORIDA off the American coast. Her passengers and crew were rescued by the BALTIC, which was summoned to her assistance by wireless telegraphy. It was the first demonstration of the value of wireless as a life-saving device at sea.

The homeward-bound CEDRIC made the first of a series of calls at Holyhead on 20 June 1909 to land passengers and mails by tender. Three special trains, two for London and one for the Midlands, left soon afterwards and it was stated that London passengers would be comfortably settled in their hotels by the time the steamer reached Liverpool. The call was abandoned in October 1910 - apparently because the public failed to take sufficient advantage of the facilities offered.

The triple-screw OLYMPIC was launched on 20 October 1910, and took her first sailing from Southampton to New York via Cherbourg and Queenstown on 14 June 1911. Her passage from land to land occupied 5 days 16 hours, her average speed being a little over 21 knots. Like the LUSITANIA and MAURETANIA, she had four huge funnels, the aftermost being a dummy. Her tonnage was 45,324; she exceeded the CELTIC in length by 52,11 metres (171 feet) and the MAURETANIA by 27,43 metres (90 feet). The first class dining saloon was 28,04 metres (92 feet) in breadth by 34,74 metres (114 feet) long and could accommodate 532 people at one sitting. In addition, there was a first class à la carte restaurant, passengers booking without meals being allowed a small fare reduction. Other public rooms included a magnificent lounge, a reading and writing room and a smoking room. The swimming pool was nine metres (30 feet) long and adjacent to it were the Turkish baths. The OLYMPIC was a perfect example of the White Star policy of great size and extreme comfort combined with moderate speed.

Three months after her maiden voyage the OLYMPIC met with a serious mishap in the Solent when she collided with HMS HAWKE, a 7,350 ton cruiser, whose bow tore a large hole in her side near the stern. Fortunately there were no fatalities on either ship, but the OLYMPIC had to go to Belfast for repairs, and was out of service for two months.

A sister ship, the 46,329 ton TITANIC, set out on her maiden voyage from Southampton to New York on 10 April 1912 with 1,316 passengers and 890 crew. The tragedy that befell her just over four days later is still so well known that it need only be stated that the TITANIC sank 2½ hours after striking an iceberg, and that 1,503 lives were lost in what was by far the worst peacetime disaster at sea. Radar would almost certainly have prevented it; wireless should have mitigated it, but by a stroke of bad luck failed to do so.

White Star did all they could to regain their good name. During the autumn of 1912 the OLYMPIC was sent to Belfast for drastic safety-first alterations, which included the provision of a complete inner skin and a greatly increased number of lifeboats, total cost being about £250,000. Tonnage of the ship increased to 46,359. While she was out of service, some of her cancelled sailings were undertaken by the American Line ST.LOUIS, ST.PAUL and NEW YORK.

As the passenger capacities of the OLYMPIC and TITANIC have frequently been quoted incorrectly, it will be appropriate to state that the OLYMPIC's original figures were given in the midsummer 1911 special number of *The Shipbuilder* as 735 first class, 674 second and 1,026 third. The report of Lord Mersey's TITANIC enquiry gave the totals for that ship as 1,034 first class, 510 second and 1,022 third. Both sets of figures can, therefore, be considered authentic. The greatly increased first class capacity of the TITANIC was partly due to the plating in of the lower promenade deck ('B' Deck) and partly to the inclusion of many cabins that were, in fact, interchangeable between first and second class.

It had been intended that the Southampton - New York service would be carried on by the TITANIC, OLYMPIC and OCEANIC until the last-named could be replaced by a third mammoth ship. The ADRIATIC had already joined the BALTIC, CEDRIC and CELTIC on the Liverpool-New York service, and the TEUTONIC had joined the LAURENTIC, MEGANTIC and the Dominion Line's CANADA on the White Star - Dominion Line to Canada. Loss of the TITANIC made it necessary for the MAJESTIC to continue in the Southampton service. She was, however, withdrawn for scrapping early in 1914 as the BRITANNIC (II), an improved and slightly larger version of the OLYMPIC, was launched on 26 February 1914. The 52,000 ton Hamburg American IMPERATOR had entered North Atlantic service some months previously, wresting from the OLYMPIC the distinction of being the world's largest steamer.

With the return of the ADRIATIC to Liverpool in 1911, the ARABIC rejoined the CYMRIC on the Liverpool-Boston service which, since the loss of the REPUBLIC two years previously, had been undertaken by the CYMRIC and the 11,905 ton ZEELAND, the latter owned by the allied Red Star Line, another of whose steamers, the FINLAND, made three White Star round voyages between New York and the Mediterranean in the winter and spring of 1909 as a temporary replacement for the REPUBLIC. From April 1913 onwards, the ARABIC and CYMRIC carried second and third classes only.

The ROMANIC of the Boston-Mediterranean service was sold to the Allan Line in January 1912. Subsequently, the CRETIC terminated at Boston instead of New York, leaving her and the CANOPIC to take care of a trade that had been seriously affected by competition from the Italian lines. For the same reason, the New York - Mediterranean service began to function only during the winter and spring, when the ADRIATIC and

CEDRIC made some special voyages, as had the CEDRIC and CELTIC each previous year since 1906.

The BOVIC sailed from Manchester and Liverpool to New York on 21 February 1914 and was the first White Star representative of a new cargo link known as the White Star-Leyland-Lamport & Holt Joint Service. Sailings had already been undertaken by Leyland's MEMPHIAN and IBERIAN and Lamport & Holt's CANNING. The service was resumed after World War I, and the BOVIC again took part until 1921.

It was stated in Liverpool in March 1914 that White Star had ordered a 30,000 ton liner from Harland & Wolff. [6] It transpired that this was substantially correct and that the new steamer had been provisionally named GERMANIC (II). It can be assumed that she was intended to run in conjunction with the OLYMPIC and BRITANNIC (II), indicating that the Company did not feel able to order a vessel of the same mammoth size. Red Star, Holland America, Norddeutscher Lloyd and CGT all had ships on order of roughly the same size as the GERMANIC.

Following the outbreak of World War I in August 1914, the TEUTONIC, OCEANIC, CEDRIC and CELTIC were taken up as auxiliary cruisers, the OCEANIC being wrecked on the Shetlands on 8 September 1914 when a naval officer was in command. The TEUTONIC was bought by the British Government. It was fitting that the most spectacular part should be played by the giant OLYMPIC. During the early days of the war she made a gallant but unsuccessful attempt to tow into port the battleship AUDACIOUS, which had struck an enemy mine. After the United States entered the war she carried thousands of troops across the Atlantic, and on one occasion had the satisfaction of ramming and sinking a German submarine which only a few minutes previously had narrowly missed torpedoing her.

The Southampton - New York service was discontinued at once, but the ADRIATIC and BALTIC remained to carry on the Liverpool - New York service, aided by the CYMRIC, ARABIC and the Red Star Lapland. From November 1914 onwards, the White Star - Dominion service was undertaken mainly by the Red Star ZEELAND and VADERLAND which, owing to the latter's German-sounding name (actually it was Flemish), were renamed NORTHLAND and SOUTHLAND, repectively. Early in 1916 the CEDRIC and CELTIC were released from their auxiliary cruiser duties and rejoined the ADRIATIC and BALTIC on the North Atlantic. For a time all the 'Big Four' imported fuel oil to England by means of their deep tanks.

The ARABIC was torpedoed and sunk by a German submarine off the Old Head of Kinsale in August 1915 with the loss of 44 lives, but by far the most serious White Star loss was the 48,158 ton BRITANNIC (II). Completed in 1915 and commissioned as a hospital ship, she sank in the Aegean Sea in February 1916 after striking a mine laid by German submarine U.73, and never ran on the North Atlantic. The CYMRIC was torpedoed in May 1916, the GEORGIC was sunk by the German raider MOEWE in December 1916 and the LAURENTIC was mined off the Irish coast in January 1917 when carrying a vast cargo of bullion. Another ship lost was the 32,120 ton JUSTICIA, laid down at Belfast as the Holland America STATENDAM and put under White Star management after completion in 1917. The reason for her Cunard-sounding name was that she was originally intended to take the place of the torpedoed LUSITANIA, but shortage of officers and crew made this impracticable. The JUSTICIA was torpedoed in July 1918.

Several ships had narrow escapes, the CELTIC being mined in February 1917 and torpedoed in March 1918, on each occasion managing to reach port, as did the LAPLAND when mined in April 1917. The Canadian Pacific MONTREAL sank near the Mersey Bar after colliding with the CEDRIC in January 1918. The CEVIC was converted into the dummy battle cruiser QUEEN MARY at the end of 1914, but in 1916 became a fleet oil tanker.

Some idea of the immensity of the White Star contribution to the war effort will be apparent by mentioning that during the course of hostilities the Company's ships carried over half a million troops and over four million tons of cargo.

Surviving units of the White Star North Atlantic fleet at the Armistice in November 1918 were the OLYMPIC, ADRIATIC, BALTIC, CEDRIC, CELTIC, MEGANTIC, CRETIC and CANOPIC. In addition, there were several cargo steamers, the most interesting being the BELGIC, which at the outbreak of the war was under construction at Belfast as the Red Star BELGENLAND. She was hurriedly completed minus her two uppermost passenger decks and appeared with two funnels and three masts instead of the three funnels and two masts with which she made her first Red Star voyage in 1923. But after losing her wartime camouflage she always had Red Star funnel markings rather than White Star. The 9,332 ton VEDIC was completed at Belfast in July 1918 and entered trooping service forthwith. As a peacetime commercial liner she carried cargo and 1,250 third class passengers.

The Liverpool - New York service was restarted soon after the Armistice by the 'Big Four', assisted until September 1919 by the LAPLAND and until 1921 by the cargo steamer BELGIC. Many cargo steamers of other components of the IMM group lent their services when required, and in the summer of 1920 the 16,960 ton passenger liner MOBILE, formerly the Hamburg American CLEVELAND, was detailed to the Company by the Shipping Controller for two round voyages. The New York - Mediterranean service was resumed by the CRETIC and CANOPIC in July 1919, while two months later the ADRIATIC and LAPLAND reestablished the Southampton-Cherbourg-New York service. The LAPLAND reverted to Red Star after three voyages, but in July 1920, after conversion from coal to oil burning, the OLYMPIC joined the ADRIATIC at Southampton.

It was stated in February 1919 that the 33,600 ton HOMERIC was under construction for White Star. [7] In the autumn of 1919 the Company reprinted in booklet form a long article about their wartime activities that had appeared in a Liverpool newspaper, and included on the final page a detailed list of the White Star fleet, which had a tonnage of 341,127, excluding the HOMERIC and a 16,000 ton ship, both of which were stated to be building. [8] The HOMERIC was undoubtedly the steamer ordered in 1914 as the GERMANIC, but it was learnt in 1921 that this order had been cancelled. 'A beginning had been made on her at the outbreak of war, but the keel and floor were lifted to make way for urgent naval work. The keel was never re-laid and the material was dispersed.' [9]

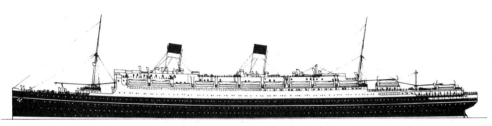

1922 HOMERIC 34,351 tons
Consort for ten years of the MAJESTIC and
OLYMPIC and largest twin-screw steamer then
afloat.

The Company's first acquisition of ex-German tonnage was the NDL BERLIN, the ship responsible for sinking HMS AUDACIOUS. She was commissioned in September 1921 as the 16,786 ton ARABIC (III) and allotted to the Mediterranean service in place of the CANOPIC, which joined the Canadian service in the spring of 1922.

Two very much more important units were commissioned in 1922 - first, the 34,351 ton twin-screw HOMERIC (II), laid down as the NDL COLUMBUS and second, the 56,551 ton quadruple-screw MAJESTIC, laid down as the Hamburg American BISMARCK. Not only was she the largest steamer in the world, but she was also by far the largest and fastest ever owned by White Star, making some of her best passages at an average speed of over 24 knots. Many experts considered that her overall length of 291,38 metres (956 feet) would never be exceeded but time has proved them wrong. The MAJESTIC had accommodation for 700 first class, 545 second

749

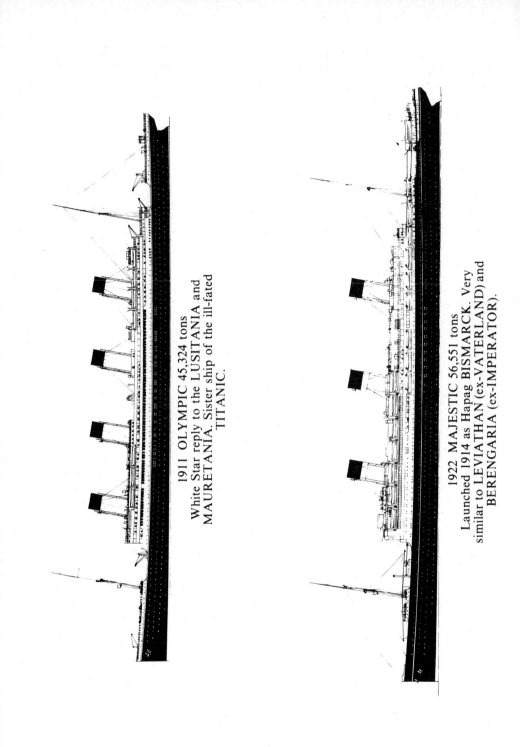

1911 OLYMPIC 45,324 tons
White Star reply to the LUSITANIA and
MAURETANIA. Sister ship of the ill-fated
TITANIC.

1922 MAJESTIC 56,551 tons
Launched 1914 as Hapag BISMARCK. Very
similar to LEVIATHAN (ex-VATERLAND) and
BERENGARIA (ex-IMPERATOR).

and 850 third class passengers, but some of the first and second class accommodation was interchangeable and, as has already been seen, the third class could be considerably augmented when necessary.

For several years subsequently the American-owned LEVIATHAN, commissioned in 1914 as the 54,282 ton Hamburg American VATERLAND, was advertised as having a tonnage of 59,956, but a different and unorthodox basis of calculation was used and there is no doubt that the MAJESTIC was the larger ship. When it suited them the American company reduced their tonnage claim to 48,943! It is important to mention that White Star and Cunard had made a joint purchase of the BISMARCK and IMPERATOR (later the BERENGARIA) from the Shipping Controller in order to avoid outbidding each other. The partnership lasted about ten years, each line taking, however, full control of its respective ship.

The MAJESTIC, OLYMPIC and HOMERIC were in charge of the Southampton - Cherbourg - New York express service for the next ten years. The MAJESTIC's claims to notability have already been mentioned. The OLYMPIC was often described as the largest British-built steamer or the largest triple-screw steamer. The Company might with some justification have referred to the HOMERIC as the world's steadiest steamer but contented themselves with calling her the largest twin-screw steamer. In the autumn of 1923, White Star and Cunard announced that they had come to a joint working agreement for one express steamer instead of two to sail each week during the winter.

After an overhaul the ADRIATIC reverted to the Liverpool service in 1922. In the spring of that year the VEDIC and POLAND started a new emigrant service from Bremen, Southampton and Cherbourg to Quebec and Montreal. The POLAND was really an Atlantic Transport ship, but had been running for Red Star. At the close of the St Lawrence season, the American destinations were changed to Halifax and New York, and the much larger PITTSBURGH and CANOPIC substituted. A year later, owing to the rapid recovery of the German lines, the European terminal was changed from Bremen to Hamburg with the result that, before long, White Star took over the American Line service that had been running between New York and Hamburg for several years. By 1926 German recovery was complete, and White Star withdrew entirely from the German trade.

The Dominion Line's 16,313 ton triple-screw REGINA, which had been completed in 1918 as a cargo steamer, made her first sailing as a passenger liner on the Liverpool - Canada service in 1922. She was joined in July 1923 by the 16,484 ton twin-screw DORIC, which was similar except as regards her propelling machinery, consisting of single-reduction geared turbines, whereas the REGINA had a combination of reciprocating engines and a low-pressure turbine on the well-known Harland & Wolff system.

751

From 1923 onwards a fortnightly call was made at Boston by two units of the 'Big Four' *en route* to New York, with the result that the Liverpool - Boston - Philadelphia service was withdrawn in 1924. This had been taken over from the American Line three years earlier and had been maintained by the HAVERFORD, assisted for a time by the PITTSBURGH, both being ex-American Line steamers. In 1924 the New York - Mediterranean service was also abandoned except for two or three special sailings each subsequent winter. Principal reasons for this withdrawal were restrictions imposed on foreign shipping by the Italian Government and US 'quota' restrictions.

Following the transfer of the Dominion Line fleet to Leyland ownership in 1921, it was only to be expected that the name 'Dominion' would gradually die out, and in 1925 the White Star - Dominion Joint Service became known as WHITE STAR LINE (CANADIAN SERVICES). The REGINA dropped her Dominion funnel colours and flag and outwardly became a White Star ship.

An announcement was made in April 1926 that IMM had received a cash offer for White Star from certain British interests. It became known in due course that a syndicate headed by Furness, Withy & Company Limited had been the party concerned, and that negotiations had been broken off. Only a few months later, in November 1926, the Royal Mail Steam Packet Company announced that they had made arrangements to acquire the entire share capital of the White Star Line (Oceanic Steam Navigation Company Limited) as from 1 January 1927. Thus, after an interval of over 20 years White Star again became a purely British concern.

RMSP had been running a passenger and freight service between Southampton and New York since 1921 and in view of White Star's major interest in the route, it was withdrawn. Two of the 'O' steamers taking part were returned to the Pacific Steam Navigation Company and the other two, the 18,940 ton OHIO and the 16,063 ton ORCA, were transferred to White Star and renamed ALBERTIC and CALGARIC for the Canadian run.

Four steamers were required to maintain a weekly sailing to Canada. The advent of this new tonnage gave the Company five - the ALBERTIC, CALGARIC, DORIC, REGINA and MEGANTIC - and when the 18,724 ton LAURENTIC (II) was commissioned in November 1927 they had two spare ships. In the spring of 1928, therefore, the ALBERTIC and MEGANTIC opened a new service from London, Havre and Southampton to Quebec and Montreal.

The sale of White Star had no noticeable effect on the Southampton - Cherbourg - New York service, but in 1928 the keel of a 60,000 ton liner, the OCEANIC (III), was laid at Belfast, the intention being that she should replace the HOMERIC, whose speed of 19 knots was too slow for the express service. The OCEANIC never progressed very far, however, and her construction was eventually abandoned with the excuse that 'the progress and development of varying types of engines are so rapid that it is naturally of the utmost importance to give the fullest and maturest consideration to the design of the propulsive machinery for so large and costly a vessel.'[10]

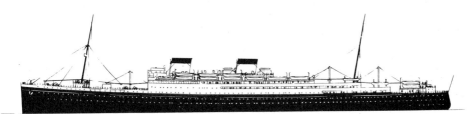

1930 BRITANNIC 26,943 tons
First British passenger motorship on North
Atlantic. Near-sister: GEORGIC.

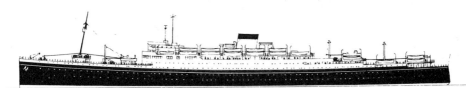

1932 GEORGIC 27,759 tons
Rebuilt in 1943-4 as one-funnelled troopship after
severe bomb damage. Ran on North Atlantic for
Cunard in 1950-4.

In her place, the 26,943 ton motorship BRITANNIC (III) was built at Belfast and entered service in June 1930 between Liverpool and New York, followed by the 27,759 ton GEORGIC (II) in June 1932. They were the first British passenger liners on the North Atlantic to be fitted with oil engines and had a service speed of 18 knots. At the time they were the largest 'cabin' ships in the world. Their arrival was opportune as the CELTIC had been wrecked near Cobh in December 1928, and the CEDRIC, BALTIC and ADRIATIC were all due for retirement. It should be added that the first class accommodation of the CELTIC and CEDRIC became cabin class in October and November 1926, similar changes taking place on the BALTIC and ADRIATIC in 1927 and 1928, respectively.

An immediate result of the loss of the CELTIC was the temporary transfer of the ALBERTIC to the Liverpool - New York service, which was in turn responsible for the CALGARIC joining the MEGANTIC in April 1929 in the London - Canada service. Owing, however, to the prevailing business recession, the MEGANTIC undertook only three round voyages on the route in 1929, two in 1930 and one in 1931, while the CALGARIC made only one St Lawrence voyage in 1929, one in 1930 and none at all in 1931. The service ceased to function in May 1931.

The Liverpool - Quebec - Montreal service also was seriously affected by the slump, the first casualty being the REGINA, which left Liverpool for the last time on 1 November 1929. Soon afterwards she was transferred to Red Star for service between Antwerp, Southampton and New York as the WESTERNLAND. The advent of the BRITANNIC in June 1930 enabled the ALBERTIC to be detailed to the Liverpool - Canada service as a consort of the LAURENTIC and DORIC. Unfortunately, business was so bad that she was withdrawn at the conclusion of her 29 August 1930 voyage and was laid up for a long spell before being sold for scrap. Two Liverpool - Canada sailings by the ARABIC in the autumn of 1930 and another by the MEGANTIC in June 1931 were also cancelled and neither ship crossed the Atlantic again. The LAURENTIC and DORIC were employed fairly consistently until May 1932, after which the latter took part exclusively in cruising. The CALGARIC did not undertake a single Atlantic crossing between September 1930 and June 1933, when she made a round voyage to Quebec and Montreal before being laid up at Milford Haven. The LAURENTIC was in sole charge of the Company's Canadian service from then onwards. She was the last North Atlantic liner to be built with reciprocating engines and as a coal-burner.

In 1930, the year of the BRITANNIC's completion, there were one or two changes in the Liverpool - Boston - New York service, and it was decided to include Galway as well as Cobh in the itinerary about once a month. In addition, Belfast and Glasgow were substituted for Cobh at similar intervals. The Liverpool - Canada steamers had been making regular calls at Belfast and Glasgow since 1928.

The CEDRIC started her last transatlantic voyage from Liverpool on 5 September 1931, the BALTIC on 17 September 1932 and the ADRIATIC on 24 February 1934. The CEDRIC was scrapped at Inverkeithing, and the BALTIC sailed to Japan for a similar purpose but the ADRIATIC undertook one or two cruises between spells of idleness. Like the DORIC, the HOMERIC was employed exclusively on cruising from the summer of 1932 onwards.

The rival Cunard Line had laid down an 80,000 ton liner in December 1930. Owing to the depression, work was suspended a year later and was not resumed until April 1934. Meanwhile, after endless discussions, agreement was reached in February 1934 between Cunard, White Star and the British Government whereby the assets of the two concerns were to be merged into a new company, CUNARD-WHITE STAR LIMITED, while the Government undertook to advance a vast sum to enable the new ship to be completed and a sister ship laid down.

During the amalgamation talks Bruce Ismay, in the twilight of his life (he died in 1937), and at the instigation of Lieut-Colonel Frank Bustard, White Star passenger traffic manager, tried unsuccessfully to save his old company from extinction by raising the necessary finance to buy it back. Incidentally, it is not generally known that as early as February 1912, two months before the TITANIC's fatal voyage, Ismay had decided, as from 30 June 1913, to retire from the chairmanship of White Star and presidency of IMM in favour of his old friend and partner, Harold Sanderson.

Activities of the combined fleet are dealt with in the Cunard chapter. Sufficient to mention here that the Cunard Steam-Ship Company Limited acquired the entire share capital of Cunard-White Star Limited in 1947, and two years later took over control of the Cunard-White Star ships and organisation. The description 'Cunard - White Star' is now no longer heard. Sad to say, the BRITANNIC, last White Star survivor, was scrapped in 1961. It is a remarkable fact that she, like every other ship ordered by White Star, was a product of Harland & Wolff of Belfast.

[1]   *Mitchell's Maritime Register* 2/9/1870
[2]   *Mitchell's Maritime Register* 10/3/1871
[3]   *New York Herald* 26/5/1872
[4]   *New York Herald* 31/7/1884
[5]   *New York Herald* 16/3/1888
[6]   *The Times* 12/3/1914
[7]   *The Times* 27/2/1919
[8]   *Liverpool Courier* 6/9/1919
[9]   *Shipbuilding & Shipping Record* 2/6/1921
[10] *The Times* 17/5/1930

1. 1871 OCEANIC (I)
    3,707. 128,01 x 12,46. (420.0 x 40.9). S—1—4. I—S—C4—14. (I—166; III—1,000). Harland & Wolff, Belfast (engines Maudslay, Sons & Field, London). 1870 (27/8) launched. 1871 (2/3) MV Liverpool—Queenstown—New York; put into Holyhead with overheated bearings; returned to Liverpool. 1871 (14/3) MV resumed; arr New York 28/3. 1875 (11/3) LV ditto. 1875 chartered to Occidental & Oriental; ran San Francisco—Yokohama—Hong Kong. 1879 returned to Liverpool for refit. 1880 (16/3) sailed Liverpool—Suez Canal—Hong Kong. 1895 returned to Belfast for re-engining but plan abandoned. 1896 scrapped at London.

2. 1871 ATLANTIC
    3,707. 128,01 x 12,46. (420.0 x 40.9). S—1—4. I—S—C4—14. (I—166; III—1,000). Harland & Wolff, Belfast (engines G.Forrester & Co, Liver-

pool). 1870 (1/12) launched. 1871 (8/6) MV Liverpool—Queenstown—
New York. 1873 (20/3) sailed from Liverpool. 1873 (1/4) wrecked near
Halifax (585).

3. 1871 BALTIC (I)
   3,707. 128,01 x 12,46. (420.0 x 40.9). S—1—4- I—S—C4—14. (I—166;
   III—1,000). Harland & Wolff, Belfast (engines Maudslay, Sons & Field,
   London). 1871 (8/3) launched as PACIFIC. 1871 (14/9) MV Liverpool—
   Queenstown—New York as BALTIC. 1873 (Jan) record passage New
   York—Queenstown. 1883 (3/4) FV for Inman (c), Liverpool—Queens-
   town—New York (2 RV). 1885 (10/3) resumed ditto. 1887 (29/3) LV ditto
   (15 more RV). 1888 (5/5) LV for W.Star, Liverpool—New York. 1888
   VEENDAM (Holland America); (I—150; III—800). 1888 (3/11) FV
   Rotterdam—New York. 1890 triple-expansion engines. 1898 (7/2)
   foundered in N Atlantic after striking submerged wreck (0).

4. 1872 REPUBLIC (I)
   3,707. 128,01 x 12,46. (420.0 x 40.9). S—1—4. I—S—C4—14. (I—166;
   III—1,000). Harland & Wolff, Belfast (engines G.Forrester & Co, Liver-
   pool). 1871 (4/7) launched. 1872 (1/2) MV Liverpool—Queenstown—
   New York. 1889 (16/1) LV ditto. 1889 MAASDAM (Holland America);
   triple-expansion engines by G.Forrester & Co, Liverpool; (I—150; II—60;
   III—800). 1890 (15/3) FV Rotterdam—New York. 1902 (6/3) Rotter-
   dam—Boulogne—New York. 1902 VITTORIA (Italian). 1902 CITTÀ DI
   NAPOLI (La Veloce); (III—1,424). 1902 (30/9) FV Genoa—Naples—
   New York. 1907 (27/4) LV ditto (30 RV). 1908 sold. 1910 scrapped at
   Genoa.

5. 1872 ADRIATIC (I)
   3,888. 133,25 x 12,46. (437.2 x 40.9). S—1—4. I—S—C4—14. (I—166;
   III—1,000). Harland & Wolff, Belfast (engines Maudslay, Sons & Field,
   London). 1871 (17/10) launched. 1872 (11/4) MV Liverpool—Queens-
   town—New York. 1872 (May) record passage Queenstown—Sandy
   Hook. 1884 II added. 1897 (17/11) LV Liverpool—Queenstown—New
   York. 1899 scrapped at Preston.

6. 1872 CELTIC (I)
   3,867. 133,25 x 12,46. (437.2 x 40.9). S—1—4. I—S—C4—14. (I—166;
   III—1,000). Harland & Wolff, Belfast (engines G.Forrester & Co, Liverpool). Laid down as ARCTIC. 1872 (8/6) launched as CELTIC. 1872
   (24/10) MV Liverpool—Queenstown—New York. 1887 (19/5) collision
   with BRITANNIC (White Star) off Sandy Hook; both damaged. 1887 II
   added. 1891 (4/2) LV Liverpool—Queenstown—New York. 1893 (6/4)
   AMERIKA (Thingvalla). 1893 (27/5) FV Copenhagen—Christiania—

Christiansand—New York. 1897 (7/9) LV ditto (8 RV). 1898 scrapped at Brest.

7. (1873) GAELIC
2,658. 112,77 x 11,06. (370.0 x 36.3). S—1—4. I—S—C2—12. (I—40). Harland & Wolff, Belfast (engines J.Jack, Rollo & Co, Liverpool); bought on stocks from J.J.Bibby. 1872 (4/10) launched for S American service). 1873 (10/7) FV Liverpool—New York. 1874 (Apr) LV ditto (8 RV). 1874 (3/6) FV London—New York. 1874 (2/11) LV ditto (4 RV). 1874 (24/12) resumed Liverpool—New York. 1875 (11/2) LV ditto (2 RV). 1875 chartered to Occidental & Oriental; ran San Francisco—Yokohama—Hong Kong. 1883 HUGO (Spanish). 1896 (24/9) stranded off Terschelling Island, Holland; scrapped at Amsterdam.

8. (1874) BELGIC (I)
2,652. 112,77 x 11,06. (370.0 x 36.3). S—1—4. I—S—C2—12. (I—40). Harland & Wolff, Belfast (engines J.Jack, Rollo & Co, Liverpool); bought on stocks from J.J.Bibby. 1873 (Jan) launched for S American service. 1874 (30/5) FV Liverpool—New York (1 RV). 1874 (10/7) FV London—New York. 1874 (25/11) LV ditto (4 RV). 1875 (28/1) resumed Liverpool—New York (1 RV). 1875 chartered to Occidental & Oriental; ran San Francisco—Yokohama—Hong Kong. 1883 GOEFREDO (Spanish). 1884 (26/12) wrecked in R Mersey.

9. 1874 BRITANNIC (I)
5,004. 138,68 x 13,77. (455.0 x 45.2). S—2—4. I—S—C4—15. (I—220; III—1,500). Harland & Wolff, Belfast (engines Maudslay, Sons & Field, London). Laid down as HELLENIC. 1874 (3/2) launched as BRITANNIC. 1874 (25/6) MV Liverpool—Queenstown—New York. 1876 (9/6) FV ditto after propeller-shaft alterations. 1876 (Nov) record passage, Queenstown—New York. 1876 (Dec) record passage New York—Queenstown. 1887 (19/5) collided with White Star CELTIC off Sandy Hook; both damaged. 1899 (16/8) LV Liverpool—Queenstown—New York. 1899 Boer War transport. 1903 scrapped at Hamburg.

10. 1875 GERMANIC (I)
5,008. 138,68 x 13,77. (455.0 x 45.2). S—2—4. I—S—C4—15. (I—220; III—1,500). Harland & Wolff, Belfast (engines Maudslay, Sons & Field, London). 1874 (15/7) launched. 1875 (20/5) MV Liverpool—Queenstown—New York. 1875 (Jul) and 1877 (Apr) record passages Queenstown—New York. 1876 (Feb) record passage, New York—Queenstown. 1895 extra deck added; tonnage 5,066; triple-expansion engines by Harland & Wolff; funnels lengthened. 1899 (13/2) capsized at New York berth; salvaged. 1899 (7/6) resumed Liverpool—Queenstown—New

York. 1903 (23/9) LV dito. 1904 (23/4) FV for American Line (c), Southampton—Cherbourg— New York. 1904 (2/10) LV ditto (6 RV). 1905 OTTAWA (Dominion); (II—250; III—1,500). 1905 (27/4) FV Liverpool—Quebec—Montreal. 1909 (2/9) LV ditto. 1911 (15/3) sailed Liverpool—Constantinople; GUL DJEMAL (Turkish). 1915 (3/5) torpedoed and sunk by British submarine E.14 in Sea of Marmora; salvaged. 1920 (6/10) FV Constantinople—New York. 1921 (21/10) LV ditto (4 RV). 1928 spelling amended to GULCEMAL. 1950 scrapped at Messina.

11. 1881 ARABIC (I)
4,368. 130,38 x 12,77. (427.8 x 41.9). S—1—4. S—S—C4—13. Harland & Wolff, Belfast (engines J.Jack & Co, Liverpool). 1881 (30/4) launched as ASIATIC. 1881 (10/9) MV Liverpool—New York as ARABIC. 1881 (2/12) LV ditto (3 RV). 1882 (4/2) sailed Liverpool—Suez Canal—Hong Kong—San Francisco; chartered to Occidental & Oriental. 1887 (30/3) London—Queenstown—New York. 1887 (12/5) resumed Liverpool—New York. 1888 (19/4) LV ditto. 1888 resumed San Francisco—Yokohama—Hong Kong. 1890 SPAARNDAM (Holland America) 1890 (29/3) FV Rotterdam—New York. 1901 (7/2) LV ditto. 1901 scrapped at Preston.

12. 1881 COPTIC
4,448. 131,12 x 12,86. (430.2 x 42.2). S—1—4. S—S—C4—13. Harland & Wolff, Belfast (engines J. Jack & Co, Liverpool). 1881 (10/8) launched. 1881 (16/11) MV Liverpool—New York (2 RV). 1882 (11/3) sailed Liverpool—Suez Canal—Hong Kong—San Francisco; chartered to Occidental & Oriental. 1884 (26/5) FV London—New Zealand. 1894 triple-expansion engines by Harland & Wolff. 1895 resumed San Francisco—Yokohama—Hong Kong. 1907 PERSIA (Pacific Mail). 1915 PERSIA MARU (Toyo Kisen Kaisha). 1925 scrapped at Osaka.

13. 1888 CUFIC (x)
4,639. 131,27 x 13,77. (430.7 x 45.2). S—1—4. S—S—T3—13. Harland & Wolff, Belfast (engines ditto). 1888 (10/10) launched. 1888 (8/12) MV Liverpool—New York. 1896 (Jul) NUESTRA SENORA DE GUADALUPE (Cia Trasatlántica (c)). 1898 CUFIC (White Star). 1901 MANXMAN (Dominion). 1915 ditto (Canadian). 1919 ditto (US). 1919 (18/12) foundered in N Atlantic (40).

14. 1889 RUNIC (x)
4,833. 131,27 x 13,77. (430.7 x 45.2) S—1—4. S—S—T3—13. Harland & Wolff, Belfast. 1889 (1/1) launched. 1889 (21/2) MV Liverpool—New York. 1895 TAMPICAN (West India & Pacific). 1899 (31/12) ditto

(Leyland). 1912 ditto (Moss (Br)). 1912 IMO (Norwegian). 1917 (6/12) collided at Halifax with MONT BLANC (French munition ship); explosion devastated the city. 1920 GUVERNOREN (Norwegian). 1921 wrecked at Port Stanley, Falkland Is.

15. **1889 TEUTONIC**

9,984. 172,44 x 17,61. (565.8 x 57.8). S—2—3. S—2S—T6—19. (I—300; II—190; III—1,000). Harland & Wolff, Belfast. 1889 (19/1) launched. 1889 (1/8) proceeded Liverpool—Spithead for Naval Review; first armed merchant cruiser. 1889 (7/8) MV Liverpool—Queenstown—New York. 1891 (Aug) record passage Queenstown—Sandy Hook. 1907 (15/5) LV Liverpool—Queenstown—New York. 1907 (12/6) FV Southampton—Cherbourg—New York. 1911 (19/4) LV ditto. 1911 (13/5) FV Liverpool —Quebec—Montreal; (II—550; III—1,000). 1914 (20/9) armed merchant cruiser, Tenth Cruiser Squadron. 1915 (16/8) bought by British Admiralty. 1918 troopship. 1921 laid up at Cowes, Isle of Wight. 1921 scrapped at Emden.

16. **1890 MAJESTIC (I)**

9,965. 172,44 x 17,61. (565.8 x 57.8). S—2—3. S—2S—T6—19. (I—300; II—190; III—1,000). Harland & Wolff, Belfast. 1889 (29/6) launched. 1890 (2/4) MV Liverpool—Queenstown—New York. 1891 (Aug) record passage Queenstown—Sandy Hook. 1899-1900 Boer War Transport (2 RV). 1902-3 refitted at Belfast; new boilers; funnels lengthened by 3 metres (10 feet); mizzen mast removed; tonnage 10,147. 1907 (29/5) LV Liverpool—Queenstown—New York. 1907 (26/6) FV Southampton—Cherbourg—New York. 1914 (14/1) LV ditto. 1914 scrapped at Morecambe.

17. **1891 NOMADIC (x)**

5,749. 140,44 x 14,96. (460.8 x 49.1). S—1—4. S—2S—T6—13. Harland & Wolff, Belfast. 1891 (11/2) launched. 1891 (24/4) MV Liverpool—New York. 1899-1900 Boer War transport (3 RV). 1903 NOMADIC (Dominion). 1904 CORNISHMAN (ditto). 1921 ditto (Leyland). 1926 scrapped at Lelant, Cornwall.

18. **1891 TAURIC (x)**

5,728. 140,44 x 14,96. (460.8 x 49.1). S—1—4. S—2S—T6—13. Harland & Wolff, Belfast. 1891 (12/3) launched. 1891 (22/5) MV Liverpool—New York. 1903 TAURIC (Dominion). 1904 WELSHMAN (ditto). 1921 ditto (Leyland). 1929 (Dec) scrapped at Bo'ness.

19. 1892 NARONIC (x)

    6,594. 143,25 x 16,18. (470.0 x 53.1). S—1—4. S—2S—T6—13. Harland & Wolff, Belfast. 1892 (26/5) launched. 1892 (15/7) MV Liverpool—New York. 1893 (11/2) sailed Liverpool—New York; went missing (74).

20. 1892 BOVIC (x)

    6,583. 143,25 x 16,18. (470.0 x 53.1). S—1—4. S—2S—T6—13. Harland & Wolff, Belfast. 1892 (28/6) launched. 1892 (26/8) MV Liverpool—New York. 1914 (21/2) FV Manchester—New York. 1922 COLONIAN (Leyland). 1928 scrapped at Rotterdam.

21. 1894 CEVIC (x)

    8,315. 152,39 x 18,29. (500.0 x 60.0). S—1—4. S—2S—T6—13. Harland & Wolff, Belfast. 1893 (23/9) launched. 1894 (12/1) MV Liverpool—New York. 1914 converted at Belfast to dummy battlecruiser QUEEN MARY. 1915 (Sep) paid off at Belfast. 1916 BAYOL (naval oiler). 1917 BAYLEAF (Lane & McAndrew). 1920 PYRULA (Anglo-Saxon Petroleum). 1925 hulked at Curaçao. 1933 scrapped at Genoa.

22. 1895 GEORGIC (I) (x)

    10,077. 170,28 x 18,38. (558.7 x 60.3). S—1—4. S—2S—T6—13 Harland & Wolff, Belfast. 1895 (22/6) launched. 1895 (16/8) MV Liverpool—New York. 1916 (10/12) captured and sunk by German raider MOEWE 600 miles from Cape Race.

23. 1898 CYMRIC

    12,552. 178,44 x 19,59. (585.5 x 64.3). S—1—4. S—2S—Q8—15. (I—150; III—1,160). Harland & Wolff, Belfast. 1897 (12/10) launched. 1898 (11/2) MV Liverpool—New York. 1900 Boer War transport (2 RV to S Africa). 1903 (6/11) LV Liverpool—New York. 1903 (10/12) FV Liverpool—Boston. 1913 I became II. 1914 (20/12) resumed Liverpool—New York. 1916 (13/4) LV ditto. 1916 (8/5) torpedoed and sunk by German submarine U.20, 140 miles from Fastnet (5).

24. 1899 OCEANIC (II)

    17,272. 208,98 x 20,84. (685.7 x 68.4). 2—3. 2S—T6—19. (I—410; II—300; III—1,000). Harland & Wolff, Belfast. 1899 (14/1) launched. 1899 (6/9) MV Liverpool—Queenstown—New York. 1907 (22/5) LV ditto. 1907 (5/6) FV New York—Plymouth—Cherbourg—Southampton. 1907 (19/6) FV Southampton—Cherbourg—Queenstown—New York. 1914 (22/7) LV ditto. 1914 (Aug) armed merchant cruiser. 1914 (8/9) wrecked on Foula Island, Shetlands.

25. 1901 CELTIC (II)

20,904. 207,52 x 22,95. (680.9 x 75.3). 2—4. 2S—Q8—16. (I—347; II—160; III—2,350). Harland & Wolff, Belfast. 1901 (4/4) launched. 1901 (26/7) MV Liverpool—New York. 1907 (6/4) FV for American Line, New York—Cherbourg—Southampton. 1907 (18/5) LV Southampton—Cherbourg—New York (2 RV). 1914 (30/9) LV Liverpool—New York. 1914 (20/10) armed merchant cruiser. 1916 (Jan) paid off. 1916 (7/3) resumed Liverpool—New York. 1917 (15/2) mined in Irish Sea; towed to Liverpool. 1918 (Mar) torpedoed in Irish Sea; repaired at Belfast. 1918 (8/12) resumed Liverpool—New York. 1920 I—347; II—250; III—1,000. 1926 (6/11) cabin; tourist; III. 1928 (17/11) LV Liverpool—New York. 1928 (10/12) wrecked at Roche's Point, Cobh (0). 1933 demolition completed.

26. 1903 CEDRIC

21,035. 207,52 x 22,95. (680,9 x 75.3). 2—4. 2S—Q8—16. (I—365; II—160; III—2,352). Harland & Wolff, Belfast. 1902 (21/8) launched. 1903 (11/2) MV Liverpool—New York. 1914 (21/10) LV ditto. 1914 (Nov) armed merchant cruiser. 1916 (18/12) resumed Liverpool—New York. 1918 (29/1) collided near Mersey Bar with MONTREAL (Can Pac); latter sank. 1918 (14/12) resumed Liverpool—New York. 1920 I—347; II—250; III—1,000). 1926 (23/10) cabin; tourist; III. 1931 (5/9) LV Liverpool—New York. 1931 sold. 1932 scrapped at Inverkeithing.

26a. (1903) VICTORIAN (c)

8,825. 156,20 x 18,04. (512.5 x 59.2). 1—4. S—T3—13. (II—60). Harland & Wolff, Belfast. 1895 (7/7) launched for Leyland. 1903 (28/2) FV for White Star (c), Liverpool—New York. 1903 (20/11) last passenger sailing ditto. 1914 (16/5) LV ditto as cargo steamer. 1914 RUSSIAN (Leyland). 1916 (14/12) torpedoed and sunk by German submarine near Malta. (See Leyland - 106).

26b. (1903) ARMENIAN (c)

8,825. 156,20 x 18,04. (512.5 x 59.2). 1—4. S—T3—13. (II—60). Harland & Wolff, Belfast. 1895 (25/11) launched as INDIAN (Leyland); commissioned as ARMENIAN (ditto). 1903 (20/3) FV for White Star (c), Liverpool—New York. 1903 (17/12) last passenger sailing ditto. 1914 (3/3) LV ditto as cargo steamer. 1915 (25/6) captured, torpedoed and sunk by German submarine U.38 off Trevose Head, Cornwall (20). (See Leyland - 106).

27. 1903 ARABIC (II)

15,801. 183,08 x 19,96. (600.7 x 65.5). 1—4. 2S—Q8—16. (I; II; III). Harland & Wolff, Belfast. Laid down as MINNEWASKA (ATL). 1902

(18/12) launched as ARABIC. 1903 (26/6) MV Liverpool—New York. 1905 (14/4) FV Liverpool—Boston. 1907 (20/6) resumed Liverpool—New York. 1911 (1/8) resumed Liverpool—Boston. 1913 I became II. 1914 (23/12) resumed Liverpool—New York. 1915 (19/8) torpedoed and sunk by German submarine U.24 off Old Head of Kinsale, Ireland (44).

28. (1903) ROMANIC

11,394. 167,72 x 18,07. (550.3 x 59.3). 1—2. 2S—T8—15. (I—200; II—200; III—800). Harland & Wolff, Belfast. 1898 (7/4) launched as NEW ENGLAND (Dominion). 1898 (30/6) MV Liverpool—Boston. 1903 (17/9) LV ditto. 1903 ROMANIC (White Star). 1903 (19/11) FV Liverpool—Boston. 1903 (5/12) FV Boston—Naples—Genoa. 1911 (Nov) LV Genoa—Naples—Boston (arr 22/11)—Naples—Genoa. 1912 (3/1) sailed Genoa—Glasgow. 1912 (Jan) SCANDINAVIAN (Allan); (II—400; III—800). 1912 (23/3) FV Glasgow—Halifax—Boston. 1912 (4/5) FV Glasgow—Quebec—Montreal. 1914 (22/8) ditto; eastbound was CEF troopship; then resumed Glasgow—Canada service. 1917 SCANDINAVIAN (CPOS). 1918 (22/8) FV Liverpool—New York. 1918 (19/11) FV Liverpool—St John, NB. 1920 (18/5) FV Antwerp—Southampton—Quebec—Montreal. 1922 (24/5) LV ditto. 1922 (Jul) laid up at Falmouth. 1923 (Jan) ditto in Gareloch. 1923 scrapped in Germany.

29. (1903) CRETIC

13,518. 177,38 x 18,38. (582.0 x 60.3). 1—4 2S—T6—15. R. & W. Hawthorn, Leslie & Co, Hebburn-on-Tyne. 1902 (25/2) launched as HANOVERIAN (Leyland); (I—260). 1902 (19/7) MV Liverpool—Boston. 1902 (27/9) LV ditto (3 RV). 1903 MAYFLOWER (Dominion); (I—260; II—250; III—1,000). 1903 (9/4) FV Liverpool—Boston. 1903 (22/10) LV ditto (7 RV). 1903 CRETIC (White Star). 1903 (19/11) FV Liverpool—Boston (10 RV). 1904 (Nov) FV Boston—Naples—Genoa—Naples—New York (arr 7/12). 1911 (21/11) LV (Genoa)—Naples—New York. 1912 (Mar) FV Genoa—Naples—Boston. 1915 (17/3) FV Genoa—Naples—Boston—New York. 1918 (Jan) LV Genoa—Naples—Boston (arr 30/1)—Liverpool. 1918 (Apr) FV Liverpool—New York. 1919 (5/9) LV ditto. 1919 (24/9) resumed New York—Naples—Genoa; (I—300; II—210; III—800). 1922 (18/10) LV Genoa—Naples—New York. 1923 DEVONIAN (Leyland); 12,153 tons; (cabin 250). 1923 (Jun) FV Liverpool—Boston (arr 24/6). 1926 (Apr) cabin became tourist third cabin. 1927 (10/12) FV for Red Star (c), New York—Plymouth—Antwerp. 1928 (9/3) LV Antwerp—Southampton—New York (3 RV). 1928 (23/3) sailed New York—Philadelphia. 1928 (15/9) LV Boston—Liverpool (2½ RV). 1929 scrapped at Bo'ness.

30. (1903) REPUBLIC (II)

15,378. 173,72 x 20,66.(570.0 x 67.8). 1—4. 2S—Q8—16. (I; II; III;). Harland & Wolff, Belfast. 1903 (26/2) launched as COLUMBUS (Dominion). 1903 (1/10) MV Liverpool—Boston. 1903 (29/10) LV ditto (2 RV). 1903 REPUBLIC (White Star). 1903 (17/12) FV Liverpool—Boston. 1904 (2/1) FV Boston—Naples—Genoa. 1904 (Apr) LV Genoa—Naples—Boston (arr 27/4). 1904 (May) FV Boston—Liverpool. 1904 (22/9) LV Liverpool—Boston. 1904 (Oct) FV Boston—Naples—Genoa—Naples—New York. Subsequent voys New York—Mediterranean in autumn and winter; Liverpool—Boston in spring and summer. 1909 (23/1) collided near Nantucket with FLORIDA (Lloyd Italiano); sank next day (4).

31. (1904) CANOPIC

12,097. 176,25 x 18.07. (578.3 x 59.3). 1—2. 2S—T8—16. (I—250; II—250; III—800). Harland & Wolff, Belfast. 1900 (31/5) launched as COMMONWEALTH (Dominion). 1900 (4/10) MV Liverpool—Boston. 1901 (16/11) LV ditto. 1901 (Nov) FV Boston—Naples—Genoa (3 RV). 1902 (10/4) resumed Liverpool—Boston. 1903 (5/11) LV ditto. 1903 CANOPIC (White Star). 1904 (14/1) FV Liverpool—Boston. 1904 (Jan) FV Boston—Naples—Genoa. 1914 (23/8) FV New York—Naples—Genoa—Boston—New York. 1918 (Mar) LV Genoa—Naples—Boston (arr 30/3). 1919 (6/2) FV Liverpool—Boston—New York. 1919 (27/2) resumed New York—Mediterranean; (I; II; III). 1921 (Oct) LV Genoa—Naples—Boston—New York. 1922 (13/4) resumed Liverpool—Halifax—Boston; (Cabin; III). 1922 (13/5) FV Liverpool—Quebec—Montreal (6 RV). 1922 (10/11) FV Bremen—Southampton—Halifax—New York. 1924 (4/5) LV Hamburg—Southampton—Halifax—New York. 1924 (Sep) FV Liverpool—Philadelphia (arr 29/9) (1 RV). 1925 (20/3) LV Liverpool—Halifax—Portland. 1925 (Oct) scrapped at Briton Ferry.

32. 1904 BALTIC (II)

23,876. 216,15 x 23,04. (709.2 x 75.6). 2—4. 2S—Q8—17. (I—425; II—450; III—2,000). Harland & Wolff, Belfast. 1903 (21/11) launched. 1904 (29/6) MV Liverpool—New York. 1909 rescued survivors of REPUBLIC-FLORIDA collision. 1918 (12/12) FV after Armistice, Liverpool—New York. 1927 (29/10) cabin 393; tourist 339; III—1,150. 1932 (17/9) LV Liverpool—New York (dep 1/10)—Liverpool. 1933 (17/2) sailed Liverpool—Osaka, where scrapped.

33. 1907 ADRIATIC

24,541. 216,15 x 23,01. (709.2 x 75.5). 2—4. 2S—Q8—17. (I—425; II—500; III—2,000). Harland & Wolff, Belfast. 1906 (20/9) launched. 1907 (8/5) MV Liverpool—New York. 1907 (22/5) FV New York—Ply-

mouth—Cherbourg—Southampton. 1907 (5/6) FV Southampton—
Cherbourg—Queenstown—New York. 1911 (26/7) LV ditto. 1911 (26/8)
resumed Liverpool—New York. 1919 (28/7) LV ditto. 1919 I—400;
II—465; III—1,300.. 1919 (3/9) resumed Southampton—New York. 1921
(14/12) LV ditto. 1922 (13/5) resumed Liverpool—New York. 1928 (Apr)
cabin 506; tourist 560; III—404. 1933 (25/2) LV Liverpool—New York;
subsequently cruising. 1933 (Aug) laid up at Liverpool. 1934 (24/2)
resumed Liverpool—Cobh—Halifax—Boston—New York (dep 9/3)—
Boston—Halifax—Galway—Cobh—Liverpool (1 RV); subsequently
cruising. 1934 (19/12) sailed Liverpool—Osaka, where scrapped.

33a. (1909) FINLAND (c)

    12,760. 170,68 x 18,35. (560.0 x 60.2). 2—4. 2S—T6—15. (I—342; II—194;
III—626). W.Cramp & Sons, Philadelphia. 1902 (21/6) launched for Red
Star. 1909 (6/3) FV for White Star (c), Naples—New York. 1909 (5/6) LV
New York—Naples (3 RV). (See Red Star - 98).

34. 1909 LAURENTIC (I)

    14,892. 167,75 x 20.51. (550.4 x 67.3). 1—2. 3S—T8 & ST—16. (I—230;
II—430; III—1,000). Harland & Wolff, Belfast. Laid down as ALBERTA
(Dominion). 1908 (9/9) launched as LAURENTIC. 1909 (29/4) MV
Liverpool—Quebec—Montreal. 1914 (13/9) commissioned at Montreal
as Canadian Expeditionary Force transport. 1917 (23/1) sunk off
Northern Ireland by mine laid by German submarine U.80 (354). (After
World War I nearly all £5 million bullion was recovered).

35. 1909 MEGANTIC

    14,878. 167,75 x 20,51. (550.4 x 67.3). 1—2. 2S—Q8—16. (I—230; II—430;
III—1,000). Harland & Wolff, Belfast. Laid down as ALBANY
(Dominion). 1908 (10/12) launched as MEGANTIC. 1909 (17/6) MV
Liverpool—Quebec—Montreal. 1914 (30/11) FV Liverpool—New York.
1915 (21/4) LV ditto. 1917 (6/4) operated under Liner Requisition
Scheme. 1918 (Apr) resumed Liverpool—New York. 1919 (1/4) LV ditto.
1919 I—325; II—260; III—550. 1919 (May) resumed Liverpool—Quebec
—Montreal. 1924 (May) cabin; III. 1928 (Mar) cabin; tourist; III. 1928
(22/3) FV London—Havre—Southampton—Halifax—New York. 1928
(19/4) FV London—Havre—Southampton—Quebec—Montreal. 1931
(16/5) LV (London—Havre)—Southampton—Quebec—Montreal;
subsequently laid up at Rothesay, Scotland. 1933 (Feb) sailed Rothesay—
Osaka, where scrapped.

35a. (1910) ZEELAND (c)
    (1915) NORTHLAND (c)

    11,905. 171,16 x 18,35. (561.6 x 60.2). 2—4. 2S—Q8—15. (I—342; II—194;

III—626). John Brown & Co Ltd, Glasgow. 1900 (24/11) launched for Red Star. 1910 (19/4) FV for White Star (c), Liverpool—Boston. 1911 (Sep) LV ditto; resumed for Red Star. 1914 (Nov) FV for White Star-Dominion (c), Liverpool—Quebec—Montreal. 1914 (Dec) FV ditto, Liverpool—Halifax—Portland. 1915 NORTHLAND (International Navigation Co) (Br). 1915 (Mar) FV Liverpool—Halifax—Portland. 1915 (Jun) LV Liverpool—Quebec—Montreal. 1915 troopship 1916 (Aug) resumed for White Star-Dominion (c), Liverpool—Quebec—Montreal. 1917 (Apr) LV Liverpool—Halifax (7 RV). (See Red Star - 98).

36. 1911 OLYMPIC
45,324. 259,83 [269,13] x 28,19. (852.5 [883.0] x 92.5). 4—2. 3S—T8&ST—21. (I—735; II—674; III—1,026). Harland & Wolff, Belfast. 1908 (16/12) keel laid. 1910 (20/10) launched. 1911 (14/6) MV Southampton—Cherbourg—Queenstown—New York. 1911 (20/9) collided with British cruiser HAWKE in the Solent; OLYMPIC held to blame; repaired at Belfast. 1911 (30/11) resumed Southampton— Cherbourg—Queenstown—New York. 1912-3 extensively rebuilt after TITANIC disaster; tonnage 46,359. 1913 (2/4) resumed Southampton—Cherbourg—Queenstown—New York. 1914 (Oct) attempted to tow British battleship AUDACIOUS to port after striking mine. 1915 (Sep) troopship. 1918 (12/5) rammed and sank German submarine U.103 near the Lizard. 1918 (8/12) FV after Armistice, Southampton—Halifax with 5,000 Canadian troops. 1919 (12/2) FV Liverpool—Brest—New York. 1919 (Jul) LV Halifax—Liverpool— as troopship (arr 21/7). 1919 (11/8) sailed Liverpool—Belfast; reconditioned; converted to oil fuel. 1920 (25/6) resumed Southampton—Cherbourg—New York. 1924 (22/3) collision with FORT ST.GEORGE (Furness) near New York; sternpost damaged. 1928 (Jan) I, II; tourist; III. 1931 (Oct) I—618; tourist 447; III—382. 1934 (16/5) rammed and sank Nantucket Lightship in fog. 1934 OLYMPIC (Cunard-White Star). 1935 (27/3) LV Southampton—Cherbourg—New York; laid up at Southampton. 1935 (Sep) sold. 1935 (13/10) arrived Jarrow for scrapping. 1937 (19/9) hulk towed to Inverkeithing for final demolition.

37. 1912 TITANIC
46,328. 259,83 x 28,19. (852.5 x 92.5). 4—2. 3S—T8 & ST—21. (I—1,034; II—510; III—1,022). Harland & Wolff, Belfast. 1911 (31/5) launched. 1912 (10/4) MV Southampton—Cherbourg—Queenstown *en route* to New York. 1912 (14/4) struck iceberg and sank in early hours of 15/4. (1,503).

GERMANIC (II)
HOMERIC (I)
33,600. Ordered from Harland & Wolff, Belfast, in 1914 as GERMANIC;

name changed to HOMERIC after outbreak of war. Little or no work done on ship. 1920 order cancelled.

37a (1914) LAPLAND (c)

17,540. 184,64 x 21,45. (605.8 x 70.4). 2—4. 2S—Q8—17. (I—450; II—400; III—1,500). Harland & Wolff, Belfast. 1908 (27/6) launched for Red Star. 1914 (29/10) FV for White Star (c), Liverpool—New York. 1917 (Apr) mined off Mersey Bar lightship but reached Liverpool. 1918 (23/11) FV after Armistice, Liverpool—New York. 1919 (2/8) LV ditto (6 RV). 1919 (16/9) Fv Southampton—Cherbourg—New York. 1919 (27/11) ditto (3 RV); subsequently for Red Star - 98. (qv).

BRITANNIC (II)

48,158. 259,68 x 28,65. (852 x 94). 4—2. 3S—T8 & ST—21. (I—790; II—830; III—1,000). Harland & Wolff, Belfast. 1911 (2/11) keel laid. 1914 (26/2) launched. Never ran on N Atlantic. 1915 (8/12) handed over; commissioned as hospital ship. 1916 (21/11) sunk in Aegean Sea by mine from German submarine U.73. (21).

37b. (1914) VADERLAND (c)
(1916) SOUTHLAND (c)

11,899. 170,92 x 18,35. (560.8 x 60.2). 2—4. 2S—Q8—15. (I—342; II—194; III—626). John Brown & Co Ltd, Glasgow. 1900 (12/7) launched for Red Star. 1914 (Dec) FV for White Star - Dominion (c), Liverpool—Halifax—Portland. 1915 (Feb) LV ditto (3 RV). 1915 renamed SOUTHLAND; taken up as troopship. 1915 (2/9) torpedoed in Aegean Sea; reached port; repaired. 1916 (Aug) FV for White Star - Dominion (c), Liverpool—Quebec—Montreal. 1917 (4/6) torpedoed and sunk by German submarine U.70 off Irish coast. (4). (See Red Star - 98).

37c. 1917 JUSTICIA (c)

32,120. 225,69 x 26,33. (740.5 x 86.4). 3—2. 3S—T8 & ST—18. Harland & Wolff, Belfast. 1914 (9/7) launched as STATENDAM (Holland America). Requisitioned before completion. 1917 (7/4) handed over as troopship JUSTICIA (White Star management). 1918 (19/7) torpedoed by German submarine UB.64, 20 miles from Skerryvore, Scotland; taken in tow. 1918 (20/7) again torpedoed by UB.124; sank. (10).

37d. (1920) MOBILE (c)

16,960. 179,48 x 19,90. (588.9 x 65.3). 2—4. 2S—Q8—16. (I—250; II—390; III—2,550). Blohm & Voss, Hamburg. 1908 (26/9) launched as CLEVELAND (Hapag). 1919 (Mar) surrendered to USA; became MOBILE (US troopship). 1920 MOBILE (White Star (c)). 1920 (25/6) sailed Liverpool—New York but put back. 1920 (6/8) FV Liverpool—New York. 1920 (17/9) LV ditto (2 RV). (See Hapag - 53).

38.(1920) VEDIC

9,332. 140,35 x 17,77. (460.5 x 58.3). 1—2—C. 2S—ST(SR)—14. (III—1,250). Harland & Wolff, Belfast. 1917 (18/12) launched. 1918 (11/7) MV Belfast—Glasgow—Boston as troopship. 1919 (Sep) repatriated British troops from Russia. 1920 refitted at Middlesbrough. 1920 (Aug) FV Liverpool—Quebec—Montreal. 1921 (22/12) FV Liverpool—Halifax—Portland. 1922 (6/4) LV ditto. 1922 (17/5) FV Bremen—Southampton—Quebec—Montreal. 1922 (11/10) LV ditto (4 RV). 1925 refitted at Belfast for Australian emigrant service. 1934 scrapped at Rosyth.

38a. (1920) HAVERFORD (c)

11,635. 161,84 x 18,04. (531.0 x 59.2). 1—4. 2S—T6—14. (Cabin 150; III—1,700). John Brown & Co Ltd, Glasgow. 1901 (4/5) launched for American Line. 1921 (1/4) FV for White Star (c), Liverpool—Philadelphia. 1921 (6/11) LV ditto (7 RV). 1922 (16/5) FV Liverpool—Boston—Philadelphia. 1924 (27/8) LV Liverpool—Belfast—Glasgow—Philadelphia. 1925 scrapped in Italy. (See American - 101).

39. (1921) ARABIC (III)

16,786. 179,88 x 21,24. (590.2 x 69.7). 2—2. 2S—Q8—17. (I—266; II—246; III—2,700). AG Weser, Bremen. 1908 (7/11) launched as BERLIN (NDL). 1920 (Nov) sold to White Star; refitted at Portsmouth; renamed ARABIC. 1921 (7/9) FV Southampton—New York (1 voy). 1921 (20/9) FV New York—Naples—Genoa. 1923 (Oct) LV Genoa—Naples—Boston—New York. 1924 (Aug) Cabin 500; III—1,200. 1924 (16/8) FV Hamburg—Southampton—Cherbourg—Halifax—New York. 1926 (11/10) LV ditto. 1926 (30/10) FV for Red Star (c), New York—Plymouth—Cherbourg—Antwerp. 1927 (Apr) repainted in Red Star colours. 1929 (Mar) cabin; tourist; III. 1929 (27/12) LV Antwerp—Southampton—Cherbourg—New York. 1930 (11/1) sailed New York—Cobh—Liverpool for White Star; (Cabin 177; tourist 319; III—823). 1930 (15/3) FV Liverpool—New York. 1930 (16/7) LV ditto (5 RV); laid up. 1931 (Dec) scrapped at Genoa. (See NDL - 60).

40. 1922 HOMERIC (II)

34,351. 228,89 [236.0] x 25,39. (751.0 [774.3] x 83.3). 2—2. 2S—T8—19. (I—529; II—487; III—1,750). F.Schichau, Danzig. 1913 (17/12) launched as COLUMBUS (NDL). 1920 handed over to British Govt; bought by White Star; renamed HOMERIC. 1922 (21/1) arr Southampton. 1922 (15/2) MV Southampton—Cherbourg—New York. 1923 (Nov)—1924 (Apr) converted to oil fuel. 1926 (Apr) I; II; tourist; III. 1930 (Apr) I—523; tourist 841; III—314. 1932 (1/6) LV Southampton—Cherbourg—New York (dep 10/6)—Cherbourg—Southampton. Subsequently cruising. 1932 (28/9) slight damage in collision when anchored at Teneriffe. 1934

HOMERIC (Cunard-White Star). 1935 (Sep) laid up off Ryde, IOW. 1936 (Mar) arr Inverkeithing; scrapped.

40a. (1922) POLAND (c)

8,282. 144,92 x 15,91. (475.5. x 52.2). 1—4. S—T3—13. (III—1,000). Furness, Withy & Co, West Hartlepool. 1897 (31/7) launched as VICTORIA (Wilson's & Furness-Leyland). 1898 MANITOU (ATL). 1921 POLAND (Red Star). 1922 (26/4) FV for White Star (c), Bremen—South - ampton —Quebec —Montreal. 1922 (Jul) LV ditto (3 RV). (See ATL - 123).

41. 1922 MAJESTIC (II)

56,551. 279,03 [291,31] x 30,51. (915.5 [955.8] x 100.1). 3—2. 4S—ST—23. (I—700; II—545; III—850). Blohm & Voss, Hamburg. 1914 (20/6) launched as BISMARCK (Hapag). 1919 handed over to British Govt; bought jointly by White Star and Cunard (as was IMPERATOR, which became Cunard BERENGARIA). 1922 (Mar) completed at Hamburg. 1922 (10/5) MV Southampton—Cherbourg—New York as MAJESTIC. 1926 (Jun) I; II; tourist; III. 1931 (Oct) I; tourist; III. 1934 MAJESTIC (Cunard - White Star). 1936 (13/2) LV Southampton—Cherbourg— New York (dep 21/2)—Cherbourg—Southampton; laid up at Southampton. 1936 (May) sold for scrapping; resold to British Admiralty; converted into boys' training ship CALEDONIA. 1937 (8/4) sailed Southampton—Rosyth. 1939 (29/9) gutted by fire at Rosyth; sank. 1940 (Mar) sold to T.W. Ward for scrapping. 1943 (17/7) refloated; scrapped at Inverkeithing.

41a. 1922 PITTSBURGH (c)

16,322. 175,06 x 20,66. (574.4 x 67.8). 2—2—C. 3S—T8 & ST—15. (Cabin 600; III—1,500). Harland & Wolff, Belfast. 1913 (Nov) laid down for American Line. 1920 (11/11) launched. 1922 (6/6) MV for White Star (c), Liverpool—Philadelphia—Boston. (Owners International Navigation Co Ltd, Liverpool). 1922 (Nov) rescued crew of MONTE GRAPPA (Navigazione Libera Triestina). 1922 (1/12) FV Bremen—Southampton— Halifax—New York. 1923 (25/11) FV Hamburg—Southampton— Halifax—New York. 1925 (20/1) FV for Red Star (c), Antwerp—South̦ ampton—Halifax—New York. 1926 (2/4) FV as PENNLAND (Red Star) ditto. 1930 (Jan) tourist; III. 1934 (16/11) LV Antwerp—Havre—South ampton—New York (arr 25/11; dep 30/11)—Havre—London—Antwerp 1935 PENNLAND (Bernstein Red Star); reconditioned at Kiel; (tourist only 486). 1935 (10/5) FV Antwerp—Southampton—New York. 1939 (Apr) LV Antwerp—Havre—Southampton—New York (dep 6/5)— Antwerp. 1939 PENNLAND (Holland America). 1939 (Jun) FV Antwerp —Southampton—New York. 1940 (10/3) sailed Antwerp—New York (dep 26/3)—Antwerp. 1940 (Apr) LV Antwerp—Dunkirk—New York. 1940 PENNLAND (Ministry of War Transport); served as British troopship. 1941 (25/4) bombed and sunk by German aircraft in Gulf of Athens.

42. 1923 DORIC

16,484. 175,40 x 20,69. (575.5 x 67.9). 2—2—C. 2S—ST(SR)—15. (Cabin 600; III—1,700). Harland & Wolff, Belfast. 1922 (8/8) launched. 1923 (8/6) MV Liverpool—Quebec—Montreal. 1926 (Jun) Cabin; tourist; III. 1932 (27/5) LV ditto; subsequently used for cruising. 1935 (5/9) collided with ss FORMIGNY (Fr) off Cape Finisterre; temporary repairs at Vigo. 1935 (7/10) sailed London—Newport, Mon; scrapped.

42a. (1926) REGINA (c)

16,313. 175,06 x 20,66. (574.4 x 67.8). 2—2—C. 3S—T8 & ST—15. (Cabin 631; III—1,824). Harland & Wolff, Glasgow (engines Harland & Wolff, Belfast). 1917 (19/4) launched for Dominion. 1925 (12/12) FV for White Star (c), Liverpool—Halifax—New York. 1926 (May) FV Liverpool—Quebec—Montreal. 1926 (Jun) cabin; tourist; III. 1929 (1/11) LV Liverpool—Belfast—Glasgow—Quebec—Montreal. 1930 WESTERNLAND (Red Star). (See Dominion - 93).

43. (1927) ALBERTIC

18,940. 180,06 x 21,94. (590.8 x 72.0). 2—2. 2S—Q8—17. (Cabin 350; tourist 400; III—690). AG Weser, Bremen. 1920 (23/3) launched as MÜNCHEN (NDL). 1923 (27/3) transferred to RMSP; renamed OHIO. 1927 ALBERTIC (White Star). 1927 (22/4) FV Liverpool—Quebec—Montreal. 1928 (31/3) LV Liverpool—New York. 1928 (14/4) FV New York—Southampton—Havre—London. 1928 (5/5) FV London—Havre—Southampton—Quebec—Montreal. 1929 (2/2) FV Liverpool—Boston—New York. 1930 (5/4) LV ditto. 1930 (9/5) resumed Liverpool—Quebec—Montreal. 1930 (29/8) LV ditto; laid up in Clyde. 1934 (Aug) sailed for Osaka, where scrapped. (See RMSP - 200).

44. (1927) CALGARIC

16,063. 167,72 x 20,51. (550.3 x 67.3). 1—2—C. 3S—T8 & ST—15. (Cabin; tourist; III). Harland & Wolff, Belfast. 1918 (Jan) launched as ORCA (PSN). 1923 ORCA (RMSP). 1927 CALGARIC (White Star). 1927 (4/5) FV Liverpool—Quebec—Montreal. 1929 (20/4) FV (London—Havre)—Southampton—Quebec—Montreal. 1930 (6/9) LV ditto (2 RV); laid up. 1933 (9/6) resumed Liverpool—Quebec—Montreal (1 RV); laid up in Milford Haven. 1934 (20/12) sailed Pembroke—Inverkeithing; where scrapped. (See RMSP - 200).

45. 1927 LAURENTIC (II)
   18,724. 176,22 x 22,98. (578.2 x 75.4). 2—2—C. 3S—T8 & ST—16. Coal burner. (Cabin 594; tourist 406; III—500). Harland & Wolff, Belfast. 1927 (16/6) launched. 1927 (12/11) MV Liverpool—New York. 1928 (27/4) Fv Liverpool—Quebec—Montreal. 1932 (3/10) collided in Belle Isle Strait with ss LURIGETHAN (Br); both damaged above waterline. 1934 (25/2) LV Boston—Halifax—Liverpool. 1934 LAURENTIC (Cunard-White Star). 1934 (Jul) FV Liverpool—Quebec—Montreal. 1934 (14/9) LV Montreal—Quebec—Liverpool (2 RV); subsequently cruising. 1935 (18/8) collided in Irish Sea with NAPIER STAR (Blue Star) (6). 1935 (Dec) laid up at Southampton. 1936 (14/9) trooping voyage to Palestine. 1938 (Apr) laid up at Falmouth. 1939 (24/8) armed merchant cruiser. 1940 (3/11) torpedoed and sunk by German submarine U.99 off Bloody Foreland, North Western Approaches (49).

   OCEANIC (III)
   60,000. 304,79 x 36,57. (1,000 x 120). 3—2—C. 4S—DE—30. 1928 (Jun) keel laid by Harland & Wolff, Belfast, but project soon abandoned.

46. 1930 BRITANNIC (III) (M/S)
   26,943. 208,38 [216,94] x 25.14. (683.7 [711.8] x 82.5). 2—2—C. 2S—4SC. DA—18. (Cabin 504; tourist 551; III—506). Harland & Wolff, Belfast. 1929 (6/8) launched. 1930 (28/6) MV Liverpool—Belfast—Glasgow—New York. 1934 BRITANNIC (Cunard-White Star). 1935 (19/4) FV London—Southampton—New York. 1939 (Aug) LV ditto. 1939 (29/8) requisitioned as troopship. 1939 (5/9) sailed Greenock—Bombay. 1947 (Mar) returned to Cunard-White Star; refitted at Liverpool; tonnage 27,650; (I—429; tourist 564). 1948 (22/5) resumed Liverpool—New York. 1950 (1/6) collided with ss PIONEER LAND (US) in Ambrose Channel, but continued voyage. 1960 (11/11) LV Liverpool—New York (dep 25/11) —Liverpool (arr 4/12). 1960 (16/12) sailed Liverpool—Inverkeithing, where scrapped. (BRITANNIC was the last ship to wear White Star colours).

47. 1932 GEORGIC (II) (M/S)
   27,759. 208,38 [216,94] x 25,11. (682.8 [711.8] x 82.4). 2—2—C. 2S—4SC. DA—18. (Cabin 479; tourist 557; III—506). Harland & Wolff, Belfast. 1931 (12/11) launched. 1932 (25/6) MV Liverpool—New York. 1933 (11/1) FV Southampton—Cherbourg—New York (2 RV). 1934 GEORGIC (Cunard-White Star). 1935 (3/5) FV London—Southampton—New York. 1939 (17/8) LV ditto; subsequently made 5 RV Liverpool—New York. 1940 (Apr) proceeded to R Clyde for conversion to troopship. 1941 (14/7) bombed and burnt out at Port Tewfik, Gulf of

Suez. 1941 (Dec) towed to Port Sudan for temporary repairs. 1942 (Mar) towed to Karachi for further repairs. 1943 (1/3) reached Liverpool under own power; rebuilt at Belfast as troopship (one funnel; one mast); 27,268 tons. 1944 (Dec) placed under Cunard-White Star management. 1948 (Jul) arrived Tyneside for refitting by Palmers Hebburn as Australian and New Zealand emigrant ship. 1950 (4/5) FV for Cunard (c), Liverpool—Cobh— New York (6 RV). 1951 (22/3) FV ditto, Southampton—Havre—Cobh— New York (7 RV). 1952 ditto (8 RV). 1953 ditto (7 RV). 1954 ditto (7 RV). 1954 (19/10) LV for Cunard, New York—Halifax—Cobh—Havre— Southampton. 1956 (Feb) scrapped at Faslane (Gareloch).

Notes: (x) - cargo steamer with limited passenger accommodation. (M/S) - Motorship
The 8,010 ton twin-screw cargo steamer BARDIC ran on North Atlantic for White Star in 1919.

FUNNEL: Buff (very pale pink); black top.
FLAG : Red swallow-tailed pennant with white star. (See Chapter 13 for details of Cunard - White Star flag).

BALTISCHER LLOYD

(German)

During 1868 no fewer than 25,000 emigrants from the States of Prussia and Bohemia passed through the port of Bremen *en route* to the USA, the majority being carried by the iron screw steamers of Norddeutscher Lloyd, although nearly 4,000 patronised the wooden paddle steamers of Ruger's American Line. A year later, Ruger's extended their service to include Copenhagen and one steamer at least proceeded as far as Stettin and back. In 1870 there were three further voyages to and from both ports, and probably there would have been others but for the outbreak of the Franco-Prussian War in July.

It was announced in December 1870 that the Stettin - American Steamship Navigation Company would start running early in 1871 between Stettin and New York, having been incorporated at the beginning of 1870 with a capital of 650,000 thalers (£100,000). [1] In fact, the correct name of the company - at any rate by the time it started operations - was BALTISCHER LLOYD (Baltic Lloyd). Orders had been placed with Oswald & Co of Sunderland for the 1,800 ton iron screw HUMBOLDT and FRANKLIN, and the former left Stettin on 27 June 1871 via Copenhagen and Christiansand, reaching New York on 16 July with merchandise and 655 passengers. New York representatives were Wendt & Rammelsberg of 40 Broadway. It will be observed that the steamers bore the same names as the New York & Havre Steam Navigation Company's first two units, which were wrecked in 1853-4 (Chapter 27).

The 2,600 ton THORWALDSEN entered service in 1872, followed by the ERNST MORITZ ARNDT and WASHINGTON in 1873. They came from the same builders, exceeded the HUMBOLDT and FRANKLIN in length by 7½ metres (25 feet) or more and were fitted with compound instead of single-expansion engines. They could accommodate 150 first and second class and 700 steerage passengers, but following the practice of the Hamburg American Line and Norddeutscher Lloyd, top classes were often referred to as first class (upper saloon) and first class (lower saloon). [2] Unfortunately, the THORWALDSEN was wrecked on the Swedish coast on 4 April 1873 during her third homeward voyage.

For more than two years, the Company was able to take advantage of the boom on the North Atlantic after the Franco-Prussian War. To begin with, the ships proceeded from Stettin to Copenhagen and Christiansand, then direct to New York via the north of Scotland, but in February 1872 the HUMBOLDT called at London and Havre, from where she proceeded via the English Channel. From July 1872 nearly all sailings were made via one or both of these ports; London agents were Westcott & Laurance of 9 Fenchurch Street. Commencing with the sailing of the ERNST MORITZ ARNDT from Stettin on 16 October 1873, however, the steamers began instead to call at Antwerp as Baltischer Lloyd had made arrangements with the White Cross Line to run a joint service from Antwerp to New York in the hope that between them they would be able to capture a considerably larger share of the German emigrant traffic, much of which was proceeding via Havre. A total of 13 calls was made at Antwerp by the Company's ships up to and including July 1874, but results were disappointing.

Until the end of 1873 Baltischer Lloyd had done quite well with passengers. Their record complement was 990 on the second westbound voyage of the ERNST MORITZ ARNDT in 1873, and on at least ten occasions one or other of the steamers carried over 600. But freights did not by any means come up to expectations, which was hardly surprising as Stettin's principal exports were agricultural products, of which the United States already had sufficient, and the only item exported from America to Stettin in large quantities was oil, which for safety reasons was normally carried by sailing ships. On 9 July 1874, therefore, the HUMBOLDT undertook the Company's last sailing when she left Stettin for New York via Antwerp. By that time a serious slump had set in on the North Atlantic and the Company was certainly wise to cut its losses.

The HUMBOLDT and FRANKLIN were sold to Raffaele Rubattino of Genoa, and the ERNST MORITZ ARNDT and WASHINGTON passed to A.Lopez y Compañía. Baltischer Lloyd went into liquidation on 25 April 1876.

[1] *Mitchell's Maritime Register* 30/12/1870
[2] *The Times* 14/2/1873.

1. 1871 HUMBOLDT
    1,801. 85,95 x 10,97- (282 x 36). C—1—2. I—S—I(2)—11. T.R.Oswald & Co, Sunderland. 1871 (Apr) launched. 1871 (27/6) MV Stettin—Copenhagen—Christiansand—New York. 1874 (9/7) LV Stettin—Antwerp—New York (arr 3/8; dep 13/8)—Stettin (15 RV). LV of line. 1874 SUMATRA (Rubattino). 1881 ditto (NGI).

2. 1871 FRANKLIN
    1,878. 85,95 x 10,97. (282 x 36). C—1—2. I—S—I(2)—11. T.R.Oswald & Co, Sunderland. 1871 (Jun) launched. 1871 (8/8) MV Stettin—Copenhagen—New York. 1874 (18/6) LV Stettin—Copenhagen—Antwerp—New York (arr 15/7; dep 22/7)—Stettin (14 RV). 1874 BATAVIA (Rubattino). 1877 (23/11) wrecked on Capy Shoals, near Marseilles.

3. 1872 THORWALDSEN
    2,600. 94,48 x 11,58. (310 x 38). S—1—2. I—S—C2—12. (I & II—150; III—700). T.R.Oswald & Co, Sunderland. 1872 (9/5) launched. 1872 (12/10) MV Stettin—Copenhagen—Havre—New York. 1873 (19/3) sailed New York—Stettin (3rd RV). 1873 (4/4) wrecked on Swedish coast (0).

4. 1873 ERNST MORITZ ARNDT
    2,597. 96,61 x 11,58. (317.0 x 38.0). S—1—2. I—S—C2—12. (I & II—150; III—950). T.R.Oswald & Co, Sunderland. 1872 (22/8) launched. 1873 (27/2) MV London—Havre—New York. 1874 (28/5) LV Stettin—Antwerp—New York (6 RV). 1879 HABANA (Lopez). 1881 ditto (Cia Trasatlántica). 1900 scrapped.

5. 1873 WASHINGTON
    2,576. 93,50 x 11,64. (306.8 x 38.2) S—1—2. I—S—C2—12. (I & II—150; III—700). T.R.Oswald & Co, Sunderland. 1873 (May) launched. 1873 (31/7) MV Stettin—Havre—New York. 1874 (2/4) LV Stettin—Copenhagen—Antwerp—New York. (4 RV). 1879 CIUDAD CONDAL (Lopez). 1881 ditto (Cia Trasatlántica). 1906 scrapped at Genoa.

Total 41 RV (plus one uncompleted).

FUNNEL: White, black top
FLAG : White, black 'BALTISCHER LLOYD, STETTIN' between two black concentric circles; in centre, black head of a bird (probably an eagle).

DET NORSK - AMERIKANSKE DAMPSKIBSSELSKAB

(Norse American Line)

(Norwegian)

Until 1869 passengers destined from Norway to North America invariably travelled either by sailing ship or by steamer with transhipment at Hamburg, Bremen or a British port, the last-mentioned option becoming increasingly popular in that year following the introduction of connecting services across the North Sea by the Anchor and Allan lines. In 1870, for the first time, there were a few direct steamship sailings from Christiansand, Norway, to New York by Ruger's American Line.

Emigration from Norway to the USA was booming and in the same year, 1870, DET NORSK - AMERIKANSKE DAMPSKIBSSELSKAB (the NORSE AMERICAN LINE) was founded under the presidency of Peter Jebsen to maintain a passenger and cargo service between Bergen and New York. Its first ship, the 1,935 ton iron screw ST.OLAF, was launched by Wigham Richardson on Tyneside in April 1871, sailed from Bergen on 7 July on her maiden voyage and, proceeding via the north of Scotland, reached New York on 23 July with 256 passengers. [1]

The 1,268 ton PETER JEBSEN and the 2,084 ton HARALD HAARFAGER, products of Backhouse & Dixon of Middlesbrough, joined the service in 1872, when there was a total of eight sailings, increased in 1873 to 20.

The 18 April 1873 sailing from Bergen was undertaken by a steamer advertised as the FRITHIOF and on one occasion stated to have a tonnage of 1,950. No trace has been found of any such ship and it is evident that she was really the 932 ton FRIDTJOF, built at Bergen in 1872 for Det Norske Lloyd, another concern in which Peter Jebsen had a substantial interest. She landed 206 passengers at New York on 6 May 1873, [2] and made two further transatlantic voyages during the year.

The 1,403 ton HAKON ADELSTEEN sailed from Bergen on 29 April 1873 and it is probable that the FRIDTJOF had joined the service owing to the late delivery of the 2,386 ton KONG SVERRE, which was launched by Backhouse & Dixon on 29 March, her maiden voyage starting on 29 June. She was easily the largest of the fleet and could carry the greatest number of passengers - 35 first class, 40 second and 650 steerage. [3] As Backhouse & Dixon were responsible for four of the six ships that ran for the Company, it

1873 **KONG SVERRE** 2,386 tons
Largest of five Norwegian consorts.

is difficult to find a satisfactory explanation for their widely differing tonnages and dimensions unless some of the ships were bought on the stocks.

As a rule, calls were made at London and Newcastle on the homeward voyage to Bergen, and in 1873 there were a number of calls at Christiania (Oslo) in addition. It had become apparent by then that at certain times of the year there was insufficient demand for a high-class service between Norway and the USA. In November 1873, therefore, the KONG SVERRE inaugurated a new service from London to New York via Havre. This only met with limited success and, starting in April 1874, sailings were advertised as being from London to New York 'with liberty to call at Christiania and Bergen'. [4] In effect, this was more or less the original arrangement except that a call was no longer made at Newcastle.

By 1874 all North Atlantic lines were feeling the effects of the trade depression that was hitting Europe and America. The Norse American Line was no exception and the New York service was withdrawn following the departure of the KONG SVERRE on 26 July 1874 from Bergen, apart from one sailing in May 1875 by the ST.OLAF and one a month later by the HAKON ADELSTEEN. Few subsequent details are available, but it would appear that there were a limited number of sailings to Philadelphia instead of New York.

The KONG SVERRE was wrecked near the entrance to Dunkirk harbour on 16 October 1875. She was only partly insured and for this and other reasons the Company was wound up and the surviving ships sold.

[1] *New York Herald* 24/7/1871
[2] *New York Herald* 6/5/1873
[3] *Mitchell's Maritime Register* 11/4/1873
[4] *Shipping & Mercantile Gazette* 18/3/1874

1. 1871. ST. OLAF
       1,935. 89,57 x 10,73. (293.9 x 35.2). S—1—2. I—S—C2—10. (I—30; III—500). Wigham Richardson & Co, Walker-on-Tyne (engines North Eastern Marine Co, Sunderland). 1871 (Apr) launched. 1871 (7/7) MV Bergen—New York. 1875 (17/5) LV ditto. 1880 sold; name unchanged. 1903 scrapped at Genoa.

2. 1872 PETER JEBSEN
       1,268. 70,70 x 9,23. (232.0 x 30.3). S—1—2. I—S—C2—10. Backhouse & Dixon, Middlesbrough (engines Maudslay, Sons & Field, London). 1872 (10/2) launched. 1872 (29/4) MV Newcastle—Bergen (dep 3/5)—New York. 1873 (6/11) LV Bergen—New York. 1881 stranded; salvaged;

became ROMANUL (Br). 1898 NINA (Italian). 1905 LUSITANIA (Italian). 1913 (20/10) put into Almeria with cargo on fire; sold; scrapped at Genoa.

3. 1872 HARALD HAARFAGER
2,084. 89,60 x 11,03. (294.0 x 36.2). S—1—2. I—S—C2—10. Backhouse & Dixon, Middlesbrough (engines North Eastern Marine Co, Sunderland). 1872 (10/4) launched. 1872 (10/7) MV Bergen—New York. 1874 (4/7) LV Havre—New York. 1891 (14/10) wrecked at Nettegrunden Utö (Baltic).

3a. 1873 FRIDTJOF (c)
932. 58,02 x 8,93. (190.4 x 29.3). 1—2. I—S—C2—10. Bergens Mekaniske Verksted, Bergen. 1872 (/) launched for Det Norske Lloyd (P.Jebsen). 1873 (18/4) MV for Norse American (c), Bergen—New York. 1873 (19/8) LV Havre—New York (3 RV). 1912 scrapped.

4. 1873 HAKON ADELSTEEN
1,403. 76,19 x 9,81. (250.0 x 32.2). S—1—2. I—S—C2—10. Backhouse & Dixon, Middlesbrough (engines North Eastern Marine Co, Sunderland). 1873 (15/2) launched. 1873 (29/4) MV Bergen—New York. 1875 (30/5) LV Newcastle—Bergen (dep 6/6)—New York (arr 24/6); last New York voyage of line. 1895 (12/7) wrecked on Brazilian coast.

5. 1873 KONG SVERRE
2,386. 94,48 x 11,28. (310.0 x 37.0). S—1—2. I—S—C2—10. (I—35; II—40; III—650). Backhouse & Dixon, Middlesbrough (engines T.Richardson & Sons, Hartlepool). 1873 (29/3) launched. 1873 (29/6) MV Bergen—New York. 1874 (26/7) LV ditto. 1875 (16/10) wrecked near entrance to Dunkirk harbour.

Note : See text for comment about FRIDTJOF.

Chapter 91

1871-87

GREAT WESTERN STEAMSHIP LINE

(British)

1871. Great Western Steamship Line
(Mark Whitwill & Son)
1881. Great Western Steamship Company Limited

Nearly 30 years elapsed between the last sailing of the pioneer wooden paddle steamer GREAT WESTERN from Bristol to New York in 1843 and the inauguration of a second steamship service between the same ports. The principal reason for this long interval was that Bristol was unable to offer dock facilities in any way comparable with those of a port such as Liverpool. In fact, it had been considered inadvisable for the GREAT WESTERN to negotiate the awkward seven mile stretch of the Avon at the beginning and end of each voyage so she normally moored at Kingroad, in the Bristol Channel, not far from the mouth of the river, her passengers being transferred by tender and her cargo by lighters. There was, of course, a loud public demand for drastic action, but it was not until 1868 that a start was made on building Avonmouth Dock, at the mouth of the river, and another nine years passed before it was completed.

One of the directors of the dock company was Mark Whitwill, head of a firm of Bristol shipbrokers, who had had wide experience of running sailing ships between Bristol, Canada and the United States. The trade boom that followed the Franco-Prussian War and the knowledge that an adequate dock system would soon be available convinced him that the time was ripe to start a new steamship service between Bristol and New York, the name Great Western being used again in the sure knowledge that it would appeal to local sentiment.

The 1,317 ton iron screw ARRAGON, which had made two round voyages for the Liverpool & Charleston Line (Chapter 85), was bought in June 1871 and sailed from Bristol on 1 July with 44 passengers and 1,000 tons of cargo, thereby inaugurating the GREAT WESTERN STEAMSHIP LINE. Meanwhile, an order was placed for the 1,541 ton GREAT WESTERN, which was launched by Wm Pile & Co of Sunderland on 7 March 1872 and sailed on 5 June from Bristol with 266 passengers on her maiden voyage to New York. Three classes were carried, namely, saloon, second cabin and steerage at fares of 13, 8½ and 5 guineas.

1871 ARRAGON 1,317 tons
Ran Bristol—New York between 1871 and 1882.

In 1873 an increased volume of business resulted in the 1,269 ton LAPLAND and the 1,833 ton LADY LYCETT being chartered for four round voyages. The LAPLAND had been running for Donald Currie's Castle Line to South Africa; the LADY LYCETT was owned by the Mercantile Steamship Company and made a further Great Western voyage in 1874.

The 1,872 ton CORNWALL replaced the chartered steamers at the end of 1873 and was followed in 1875 by the 1,923 ton SOMERSET, both being products of Richardson, Duck & Company of Stockton, a similar ship, the DEVON, being completed by Scott & Co of Greenock in 1878.

The GREAT WESTERN and ARRAGON were each chartered by Phelps Brothers & Co, managers of the Mediterranean & New York Steamship Company, for two or three voyages between the Mediterranean and New York in 1875-6. Unfortunately, the GREAT WESTERN was wrecked on Long Island on 25 March 1876, at the conclustion of her second westbound voyage.

The new Avonmouth Dock was opened on 24 February 1877, the Great Western Steamship Line being the first local concern to use it to the full. It will be seen in due course that this eagerness was largely responsible for their eventual downfall.

A new service from Avonmouth to Quebec and Montreal was started in 1879 by the chartered cargo steamers BELSIZE, GOVINO, RIVERSDALE, KATE FAWCETT and BARNARD CASTLE, the KATE FAWCETT and BELSIZE being responsible also for some voyages between Avonmouth and New York. Another steamer, the BERNINA, reached New York safely, but left for Avonmouth on 29 May 1879 and was never heard of again. In 1880-1 some of the foregoing as well as other steamers were chartered not only for the Canadian run but also for a new service from Avonmouth to Baltimore. Bad luck continued, as the BELSIZE was abandoned in mid Atlantic on 15 April 1881 and the SOUTHBOURNE was wrecked on Miquelon Island in the following August.

The 1,983 ton CITY OF VALPARAISO and the 2,004 ton CITY OF SANTIAGO were bought in 1879-80, both having been completed in 1875 by different builders for different owners. They were renamed BRISTOL and GLOUCESTER.

Hitherto, ownership of the various ships in the fleet had been based on the orthodox arrangement of dividing each into 64 shares, Mark Whitwill having an interest in all of them, but many of the other owners varied from ship to ship. In June 1881 a new concern, GREAT WESTERN STEAMSHIP COMPANY LIMITED, was floated with a capital of £300,000, with Mark Whitwill & Son named as managers. The fleet included the 125 ton REDLAND, a small coaster built a year previously to carry transhipment cargo from Swansea, Newport and other South Wales ports to Avonmouth.

The 2,638 ton DORSET was commissioned within a few weeks of these changes and the 2,527 ton WARWICK followed in 1882, being the first unit of the fleet to be built of steel. This acquisition of tonnage made it unnecessary after 1881 to use chartered steamers between Avonmouth, Quebec and Montreal and in the following year the ARRAGON, CORNWALL, SOMERSET, DEVON, BRISTOL and GLOUCESTER all made one or more round voyages to Canada, sailings taking place at fortnightly intervals. The ARRAGON stranded on Anticosti Island on 1 November 1882 in dense fog and became a total loss.

In 1881 the Company landed 1,637 passengers, including 185 first and second class, at New York during the course of 35 voyages, an average of 47 a voyage. This did not compare at all well with the year 1873, when the total was 1,698 from 15 of the 19 sailings, figures for the others being unknown. And much worse was to follow as in 1885 the total was only 35 cabin and 187 steerage during 15 voyages, a paltry average of 15 a voyage.

Even more serious was the fact that the Company's cargo carryings also dropped steeply, largely owing to the appearance on the scene in 1879 of the Bristol City Line, with the first two of a series of cargo steamers, the 1,700 ton BRISTOL CITY and NEW YORK CITY. Whereas the Great Western Company relied almost exclusively on the new Avonmouth Dock as its terminal, the Bristol City Line decided to concentrate entirely on the old City Docks and, *mirabile dictu,* this policy paid them handsome dividends.

In July 1883 the Great Western Steamers began to call at Swansea after leaving Avonmouth, with the result that the services of the coaster REDLAND were no longer required. She was sold in the following year.

No trace has been found of any Great Western Canadian sailings after the 1884 St Lawrence season, and by 1885 the Company had come to realise that the New York service would have to be drastically reduced. In October of that year they sold the CORNWALL to the Turkish Government, which also acquired the SOMERSET, DEVON and GLOUCESTER in 1886. The BRISTOL was sold in 1887 and more or less simultaneously the Company commissioned the 2,900 ton cargo steamers WORCESTER and OXFORD, which had dimensions very similar to those of the WARWICK and like her were built of steel but had triple-expansion engines instead of compound. They did not carry passengers. Between them, these newcomers made half a dozen round voyages from Avonmouth to New York via Cardiff or Newport during 1887, the WARWICK and DORSET being their only other consorts. The service was in its death throes, the last sailing being taken by the WARWICK, which arrived at New York on 23 December 1887.

The DORSET and WARWICK were sold in 1888-9, the latter to the

Donaldson Line. She had had a very near escape from total disaster on 13 July 1884 when she stranded on Fame Point, Gaspé Peninsula, during a voyage from Avonmouth to Quebec and Montreal. The WORCESTER and OXFORD went tramping, as did three new steamers, the 2,336 ton CAMBRIDGE, the 2,647 ton HEREFORD and the 2,506 ton MONMOUTH, all of which were completed in 1889-90. Another newcomer, the BRISTOL (II), was never delivered to the Company, being sold to Christopher Furness and renamed HALIFAX CITY. The CAMBRIDGE was wrecked within a year and unfortunately the others did not have much of a chance as a severe depression brought freights to such a low ebb that the Company had no alternative but to cut their losses and sell the entire fleet. The Company itself was wound up on 13 July 1895.

It is easy to be wise after the event, but if the Company had been content to continue their service from the City Docks at Bristol instead of moving to Avonmouth it is quite likely that the Bristol City Line would never have come into existence, and in that event the Great Western Steamship Company Limited might be alive to-day.

1. (1871) ARRAGON

    1,317. 71,80 x 9,60. (235.6 x 31.5). S—1—2. I—S—C2—10. Barclay, Curle & Co, Glasgow. 1869 (Oct) launched. 1869 (19/12) MV Liverpool—Charleston for Liverpool & Charleston Line. 1870 (4/3) LV ditto (2 RV). 1871 bought by Great Western. 1871 (1/7) FV Bristol—New York. 1882 (27/4) LV ditto. 1882 (Jun) FV Avonmouth—Quebec—Montreal. 1882 (1/11) wrecked on Anticosti Island.

2. 1872 GREAT WESTERN

    1,541. 84,12 x 9,99. (276.0 x 32.8). S—1—2. I—S—C2—10. (I—24; III—252). Wm Pile & Co, Sunderland (engines North Eastern Marine Co, Sunderland). 1872 (7/3) launched. 1872 (5/6) MV Bristol—New York. 1875 (14/9) LV ditto. 1875 (30/11) FV Valencia—New York. 1876 (25/3) wrecked on Long Island, NY (0), on 2nd voyage Mediterranean—New York.

2a. (1873) LAPLAND (c)

    1,269. 76,28 x 9,14. (250.3 x 30.0). S—1—3. I—S—C2—10. Barclay, Curle & Co, Glasgow. 1872 (Sep) launched for Leith, Hull & Hamburg SP Co. 1873 (10/5) FV for Great Western (c), Bristol—New York. 1873 (4/10) LV ditto (4 RV). 1903 SHUNA (Br). 1907 SOFIA M. (Greek). 1911 SCUTARI (Br). 1912 VARVARA (Greek). 1917 (19/7) torpedoed and sunk by enemy submarine in Mediterranean.

2b. (1873) LADY LYCETT (c)

1,833. 80,03 x 10,09. (262.6 x 33.1). S—1—2. I—S—C2—10. London & Glasgow Co, Glasgow. 1872 (Mar) launched for Mercantile. 1873 (28/5) FV for Great Western (c), Bristol—New York. 1874 (4/6) LV ditto (5 RV). 1891 LIFFEY (Mercantile). 1899 LIFFEY (Italian). 1901 (16/2) wrecked south of Minorca.

3. 1873 CORNWALL

1,872. 85,34 x 10,70. (280.0 x 35.1). S—1—3. I—S—C2—10. (I—34; intermediate 99; III—122). Richardson, Duck & Co, Stockton (engines Blair & Co, Stockton). 1873 (22/10) launched. 1873 (31/1) MV Middlesbrough—New York—Bristol. 1874 (15/4) FV Bristol—New York. 1885 (May) LV Bristol—Swansea (dep 11/5)—New York. 1885 (Oct) HASSAN PASHA (Turkish).

4. 1875 SOMERSET

1,923. 86,68 x 10,91. (284.4 x 35.8). S—1—3. I—S—C2—10. (I—34; intermediate 99; III—122). Richardson, Duck & Co, Stockton (engines Blair & Co, Stockton). 1875 (23/3) launched. 1875 (19/6) MV Bristol—New York. 1885 (24/2) LV Bristol—Swansea—New York. 1886 ALI SAIB PASHA (Turkish).

5. 1878 DEVON

1,856. 87,04 x 10,85. (285.6 x 35.6). S—1—3. I—S—C2—10. Scott & Co, Greenock (engines J. Howden & Co, Glasgow). 1878 (May) launched. 1878 (28/6) MV Greenock—New York—Bristol. 1878 (8/8) FV Bristol—New York. 1885 (17/3) LV ditto. 1886 KYAMIL PASHA (Turkish).

6. (1879) BRISTOL

1,983. 84,73 x 11,67. (278.0 x 38.3). C—1—3. I—S—C2—10.. M. Pearse & Co, Stockton (engines Hawks, Crawshay & Co, Gateshead). 1875 (Sep) launched as CITY OF VALPARAISO (Br). 1879 BRISTOL (Great Western). 1879 (6/6) FV Bristol—New York. 1885 (31/1) LV Bristol—New York—Bristol; laid up. 1886 (19/10) Newport—New York. 1886 (20/12) Swansea—New York. 1887 COSTA RICA (Costa Rican). 1897 BRISTOL (Canadian). 1902 (2/1) wrecked at Dixon Entrance, BC. (5).

7. (1880) GLOUCESTER

2,004. 85,24 x 11,61. (279.7 x 38.1). C—1—3. I—S—C2—10. R. Steele & Co, Greenock. 1875 (Nov) launched as CITY OF SANTIAGO (Br). 1880 GLOUCESTER (Great Western). 1880 (14/2) FV Bristol—New York. 1885 (1/1) LV ditto. 1886 SOOGOODLEE (Turkish).

8. 1881 DORSET

 2,638. 100,88 x 11,89. (331.0 x 39.0). 1—3. I—S—C2—12. J.L.Thompson
 & Son, Sunderland (engines G.Clark, Sunderland). 1881 (28/5) launched.
 1881 (11/8) MV Bristol—New York. 1887 (11/7) LV Bristol—Newport—
 Swansea—New York. 1887 (9/11) sailed Liverpool—Swansea—New
 York. 1888 DORSET (Br). 1906 CORRENTI (Norwegian). 1907 scrapped
 in Italy.

9. 1882 WARWICK

 2,527. 96,31 x 12,50. (316.0 x 41.2). C—1—3. S—S—C2—12. (I—50;
 Intermediate 30; III—380). Wigham Richardson & Co, Walker-on-Tyne.
 1882 (17/5) launched. 1882 (1/7) MV Bristol—New York. 1884 (13/7)
 stranded at Fame Point, Gaspé Peninsula; refloated; repaired. 1887 (30/6)
 LV Bristol—New York. 1887 (6/12) sailed Swansea—New York. 1889
 WARWICK (Donaldson). 1889 (Jul) FV Glasgow—Quebec—Montreal.
 1896 (Dec) LV Glasgow—St John, NB. 1896 (Dec) wrecked in Bay of
 Fundy.

In addition:

 WORCESTER (2,908) and OXFORD (2,901) carried cargo only to New
 York in 1887.
 The cargo steamers CAMBRIDGE, HEREFORD and MONMOUTH
 did not run on the North Atlantic.

FUNNEL : Black; broad red band with blue and white ball.
FLAG   : Red; large blue and white ball in centre.

785

LLOYD ITALIANO

(Italian)

The LLOYD ITALIANO was founded in Genoa on 22 July 1871 by a group of local financiers supported by the Banco di Genova, for the purpose of carrying passengers and cargo between Italian ports and the Black Sea; between Genoa, Naples, Colombo and Calcutta via the Suez Canal; and between Genoa, Naples and New York.

The North Atlantic service was never started, but by 1873 the Company had in commission the iron screw steamers FIRENZE, ROMA, TORINO, LIVORNO and GENOVA, varying between 1,014 and 1,869 tons, which were maintaining a fairly regular service to India. The FIRENZE was wrecked in the Red Sea on 7 March 1874 and the GENOVA on the coast of Ceylon in November 1876.

Owing to these losses and to the competition of the Rubattino Line, the Company withdrew its service in 1877, the three surviving steamers being sold to Raffaele Rubattino. All three came into the hands of the Navigazione Generale Italiana when the Florio and Rubattino lines amalgamated in 1881, and one of them, the BENGALA (ex-LIVORNO), was detailed to the North Atlantic, although for one round voyage only (Chapter 124).

DOMINION LINE

(British)

(1870). Liverpool & Mississippi Steamship Company
1872. Mississippi & Dominion Steamship Company Limited
1894. Mississippi & Dominion Steamship Company Limited
British & North Atlantic Steam Navigation Company Limited
1921. Frederick Leyland & Company Limited
1909. White Star - Dominion Line Joint Service

Greatly increased trade between Europe and the southern States of the USA after the American Civil War resulted in the establishment of several new steamship services to the Mississippi River port of New Orleans. One of the principal of these was undertaken by the LIVERPOOL & MISSISSIPPI STEAMSHIP COMPANY, which started operations in 1870 under the management of Flinn, Main & Montgomery of Liverpool, whose partners had had considerable experience of the sailing ship trade between the same ports.

The service was opened by the 1,827 ton iron screw ST.LOUIS, one of the first transatlantic steamers to be fitted with compound engines and possessing, therefore, increased carrying capacity combined with greatly reduced coal consumption. Accommodation was provided for 50 first class and 500 steerage passengers, her maiden voyage starting from Liverpool on 6 October 1870. The CRESCENT CITY (the nickname of New Orleans) followed on 10 November from Glasgow via Liverpool, but was wrecked on the Irish coast on 8 February 1871 when nearing the end of her homeward voyage. The 2,485 ton MEMPHIS was added in 1871, by which time three more steamers were on order.

Trading opportunities with New Orleans were found to be strictly limited during the summer months but, on the other hand, emigration from the United Kingdom to Canada was booming at that time of year, following the establishment in 1870 of Canadian immigration agents in London and elsewhere in Britain to control and regulate the flow of settlers. According to a prospectus issued in September 1872, the Liverpool & Mississippi Steamship Company was 'urged by influential Canadian friends' to extend its operations to the Quebec and Montreal trade, and decided to send a steamer there under the name DOMINION LINE. [1]

The 2,159 ton MISSISSIPPI took the first Canadian sailing on 4 May 1872 from Liverpool via Queenstown to Quebec and Montreal. She was followed by the 2,484 ton VICKSBURG, which was completed by the same builders, A. McMillan & Son of Dumbarton, at the beginning of June, and the ST.LOUIS also made one Canadian voyage. The intention was that the MISSISSIPPI, MEMPHIS and VICKSBURG would be responsible for a fortnightly service from Liverpool, with a call at Queenstown to pick up passengers from Ireland, but unfortunately the VICKSBURG stranded in the St Lawrence during the concluding stages of her second westbound voyage and was out of commission for over a year. In consequence, the 3,386 ton LORD CLIVE was chartered from G.M.Papayanni of Liverpool.

A new company, MISSISSIPPI & DOMINION STEAMSHIP COMPANY LIMITED, was registered on 29 August 1872, thus drawing attention to the extended scope of its activities. Within a short time it was invariably referred to as the DOMINION LINE. It may be added that services between Europe and New Orleans are not normally regarded as coming within the description 'North Atlantic', hence the starting date of 1872 shown at the head of this chapter.

The Allan Line had had a virtual monopoly of the Canadian trade for many years, and in retaliation for what they considered an unwarranted intrusion started a service between Liverpool and New Orleans in the autumn of 1872. It was abandoned after only one completed voyage.

The Dominion Line had to decide what to do with the Canadian service steamers between mid-November and mid-April, when the St Lawrence was closed to navigation. A newly-acquired unit, the ex-Allan Line BELGIAN (originally the Hamburg American HAMMONIA), the ST.LOUIS and the MEMPHIS were placed on the New Orleans route in the autumn of 1872, the newcomer being renamed MISSOURI at the conclusion of her second voyage. The LORD CLIVE, the MISSISSIPPI, the newly-built TEXAS and a second chartered steamer, the 2,867 ton ex-Cunarder PALESTINE, ran to Boston and sometimes to Boston and Portland, Maine. It would seem that the call at Boston was producing encouraging results as in the spring and early summer of 1873 the LORD CLIVE made two further voyages for the Company - ostensibly to Boston only but, in fact, returning via New York. She subsequently ran for some time between Liverpool and Boston under the auspices of her owner.

The TEXAS, MISSOURI and PALESTINE opened the fortnightly service to Quebec and Montreal in 1873, but after one voyage the MISSOURI was replaced by the 2,167 ton chartered steamer NEERA, and towards the end of the summer the MEMPHIS and MISSISSIPPI replaced the NEERA and PALESTINE. The MISSOURI sailed from Liverpool for New Orleans in September and was wrecked in the Bahamas a few days later.

The outward call at Queenstown by the Canadian steamers was discontinued in 1873 and, instead, they proceeded via Belfast, probably to compete with the Allan Line, whose Liverpool - Quebec - Montreal steamers put in at Moville (Londonderry). Subsequent winter sailings of the Dominion Line were to Boston.

Up to this time all units of the fleet had been allotted names appropriate to the New Orleans trade, but the 2,138 ton CITY OF DUBLIN, formerly of the Inman Line, entered service in February 1874 and before starting her second voyage in April was renamed QUEBEC, drawing attention to the Company's fast-growing Canadian interests. Within a few weeks, the newly-completed DOMINION and ONTARIO of 3,175 tons followed, both being products of McMillan. The introduction of these ships enabled the service to be increased to weekly.

The loss of the MISSOURI was followed by further misfortunes. The MISSISSIPPI stranded near Cape Florida in April 1874 and although successfully refloated was out of service for about a year. The VICKSBURG did not long profit from her narrow escape in 1872 as she sank in 1875 after colliding with an iceberg near the Newfoundland coast, 47 lives being lost.

Six steamers were required to run the weekly service to Quebec and Montreal. The loss of the VICKSBURG left the Company with seven, and in consequence there could only be occasional sailings to New Orleans during the summer of 1875. The position was temporarily improved in 1876 when Flinn, Main & Montgomery bought the 2,200 ton Hamburg American BORUSSIA and BAVARIA, which were commissioned without change of name, but the latter was burnt at sea on 6 February 1877 during the homeward leg of her first voyage to New Orleans. The BORUSSIA foundered at sea in December 1879 with heavy loss of life, having run exclusively between Liverpool and New Orleans apart from one round voyage to Quebec and Montreal - arranged at short notice in July 1878 - and a trooping voyage to South Africa in connection with the Zulu War in the spring of 1879. Meanwhile, a further Hapag unit, the TEUTONIA, was bought and ran for the Company for about five years, during which she made a number of Canadian voyages. It is a remarkable fact that four of the first six units of Hapag's steamship fleet, all products of Caird & Co of Greenock, found their way to the Dominion Line.

At the conclusion of the 1876 St Lawrence season the steamers began to run to Halifax and Philadelphia instead of Boston. The ST.LOUIS and TEXAS continued this arrangement during the summer of 1877, when the Quebec and Montreal service was being undertaken by the QUEBEC, MISSISSIPPI, MEMPHIS, ONTARIO and DOMINION. But after a final sailing by the TEXAS to Halifax and Philadelphia in November 1877, the winter service became firmly established as Liverpool - Halifax - Portland. This was a wise move as the distance by rail from Halifax to Montreal was 865 miles, whereas Montreal was only 297 miles from

Portland.

The 2,911 ton CITY OF BROOKLYN was bought from the Inman Line, renamed BROOKLYN and sailed from Liverpool for Quebec and Montreal on 4 September 1878. After her second voyage she was lengthened by 16,88 metres (55.4 feet) with a consequent increase in tonnage to 4,215. In addition, she was fitted with compound engines by J. & J. Thompson of Glasgow, from which port she sailed on 20 June 1879 for Quebec and Montreal via Liverpool.

The keel of the 3,308 ton MONTREAL was laid by C. Connell & Co of Glasgow early in May 1879, and she was launched on 18 September after being on the stocks for the incredibly short time of 4½ months, [2] her maiden voyage taking place on 27 October from Glasgow via Liverpool to New Orleans, less than six months after being laid down. She entered the Canadian trade in April 1880. A sister ship, the TORONTO, followed.

A further order was placed with the same firm for the 3,712 ton OTTAWA, which sailed from Glasgow for Quebec and Montreal on 1 November 1880 and was wrecked at Cape La Roche on 22 November, during the early stages of her maiden homeward voyage. Her saloons and staterooms for 24 passengers were stated to be 'in a house on deck aft, where no inconvenience can be experienced from cattle.' [3] The report went on to say that the steerage 'tween decks were unusually lofty and could accommodate 800 emigrants. The shipment of live cattle across the North Atlantic was started by the Anchor Line in 1872 and by 1880 had grown into a thriving business.

Soon after the loss of the OTTAWA, Connell laid down the SARNIA and OREGON, which were approximately similar to her in tonnage and dimensions, but had 'saloon amidships, music room, smoke room and all latest improvements.' [4] They accommodated 80 first class, 60 intermediate and 1,200 steerage passengers.

The completion of the SARNIA in September 1882 was opportune as the MEMPHIS had been wrecked near Coruña in 1879 on voyage from New Orleans to Liverpool, the MONTREAL and TEXAS were under charter to the British Government as transports for the Egyptian Expedition and the pioneer ST.LOUIS had been sold. The OREGON sailed from Liverpool on 15 March 1883 on her maiden voyage to Halifax and Portland, but her addition was offset by the sale of the TEUTONIA. The fleet now consisted of 10 ships. Sailings to New Orleans were much less frequent than formerly and by degrees ceased altogether. The last recorded one was taken by the TORONTO in November 1889.

An outstanding ship, the 5,141 ton VANCOUVER, was commissioned in 1884. Although slightly slower, smaller and less luxurious than the Allan Line's PARISIAN, and built of iron instead of steel, she was a valuable addition to the fleet, her passenger complement being 200 first class, 120

1884 VANCOUVER 5,141 tons
Dominion Line's reply to the Allan PARISIAN.
Rebuilt with one funnel in 1893.

intermediate and 1,500 steerage. In fact, she was the second steamer of the name as an almost exact replica was sold on the stocks to the Inman Line in the spring of 1883, when they were desperately short of tonnage.

The Company entered the Bristol - Quebec - Montreal trade on 13 June 1885, when the ONTARIO left Avonmouth with a few passengers and 2,500 tons of cargo. The TEXAS and DOMINION followed and this trio maintained a fortnightly service throughout the summer.

Having been awarded a share of the Canadian mail contract for the first time, Dominion Line advertisements in December 1885 stated :- 'Dominion Line Royal Mail steamers sailing on Thursdays, alternately from Liverpool and Bristol for Halifax and Portland, and from Bristol to New York fortnightly.' [5] There were, in fact, only three sailings from Avonmouth to New York at that time - one by the MONTREAL in November 1885 and two by the ONTARIO in December 1885 and January 1886, but the DOMINION, TEXAS and MONTREAL were responsible for some additional sailings from Avonmouth to Portland. And there were hardly any Avonmouth - New York sailings in subsequent years.

During the early months of 1888 the winter service from Liverpool ran temporarily to Halifax and Baltimore, but the customary sailings to Halifax and Portland were reinstated in the following autumn. Liverpool steamers called alternately at Belfast and Moville during the summers of 1886-90, but in subsequent years sailings were usually via the latter port.

The BROOKLYN had been wrecked on Anticosti Island, in the Gulf of St Lawrence, in November 1885, and the MONTREAL at Belle Isle in August 1889. The QUEBEC and MISSISSIPPI were sold in 1888 and this meant that the fleet was reduced to seven - the VANCOUVER, OREGON, SARNIA, TORONTO, ONTARIO, DOMINION and TEXAS. The first four plus the DOMINION or ONTARIO ran from Liverpool. It may be added that in November 1886 the TORONTO was chartered by the Inman Line for one round voyage between Liverpool, Queenstown and New York and a month later the VANCOUVER made the first of two for the same concern on the same route.

The 4,737 ton steel single-screw LABRADOR was completed by

791

1891 LABRADOR 4,737 tons
A faster but slightly smaller consort of the
VANCOUVER.

Harland & Wolff of Belfast in August 1891. She was propelled by triple-expansion engines, and although nine metres (nearly 30 feet) shorter than the VANCOUVER was appreciably faster and had greatly-improved accommodation for 100 first class, 50 second and 1,000 steerage passengers. In August 1894 she steamed from Moville to Rimouski in 6 days 8 hours, and in December of the same year from Moville to Halifax in 6 days 12 hours at an average speed of 14½ knots. [6]

This important addition to the fleet enabled the DOMINION, ONTARIO and TEXAS to devote most of their time during the summer of 1891 to the Avonmouth service, which was becoming increasingly popular with freight shippers - so much so that the 3,036 ton PEVERIL was chartered for three round voyages. She was employed again in 1892, when also the 3,176 ton PLASSEY was chartered from the African Steam Ship Company (Elder Dempster & Co) for one or more voyages. The ONTARIO sailed from Avonmouth for the last time on 23 July 1892, and upon completion of this voyage was laid up until 1896, when she was scrapped.

In 1893 a former Dominion steamer, the SICILIA (ex-MISSISSIPPI), returned to the Avonmouth service under charter for the season, and the 3,185 ton MEXICO (ex-SOBRAON) took the place of her sister ship PLASSEY, which had meanwhile been renamed MEMNON. There were further developments in 1894, when the Donaldson Line introduced a short-lived Avonmouth - Quebec - Montreal service. The most important was the purchase in March of the 3,617 ton NEVADA, formerly of the Guion Line, by H. S. Flinn, senior partner of Flinn, Main & Montgomery. She was renamed HAMILTON and within a few weeks was transferred to the Hamilton Steamship Company, starting her first Dominion voyage from Avonmouth to Quebec and Montreal on 28 April 1894 and completing a total of five during ensuing months. The MEXICO was again employed, as was a sister ship, the MEMPHIS, also owned by the African Steam Ship Company. The TEXAS was wrecked near Cape Race on 4 June 1894.

The success of the LABRADOR's triple-expansion engines prompted the Company to send the VANCOUVER to Harland & Wolff in 1893 for machinery of similar type and new boilers, her funnels being reduced from two to one. Although a great favourite with passengers she certainly had her full share of mishaps. She struck an iceberg near Belle Isle during fog in August 1890 but suffered only slight damage; her commander and a quartermaster were swept overboard and drowned during a storm in November 1890; and in November 1894 she stranded at the entrance to Lough Foyle, Northern Ireland, and had to be towed to Liverpool. [7]

The SARNIA, too, was unlucky. In March 1893 she had a machinery breakdown, but managed to reach Halifax without assistance after temporary repairs, taking six days, had been carried out at sea. In the following August she had a broken propeller shaft and was towed 1,000 miles to Queenstown by the Allan Line MONTE VIDEAN, and in December 1894 she lost her rudder in the Atlantic, being taken in tow by the Allan NORWEGIAN to Inishtrahull, and from there by tugs to Belfast. [8] She did not run again for the Company, her place being taken by the 5,305 ton twin-screw MARIPOSA, which was chartered from Elder Dempster and carried a few first class passengers. There was a happier side of the picture, however, as the OREGON towed the disabled Anchor liner ETHIOPIA to an Irish port, and the TEXAS towed the rudderless Allan Line SARDINIAN to Liverpool.

The early 1890s were extremely difficult times on the North Atlantic, and the Dominion Line was not the only one to find itself in serious financial difficulties. The outcome was the retirement of the managers. Flinn, Main & Montgomery, and the announcement on 12 December 1894 that the business had been sold to Richards, Mills & Company of Liverpool, the original £20 shares realising only £1.16.6 each, with the purchasers responsible for the Company's heavy liabilities. They were already owners of the British & North Atlantic Steam Navigation Company Limited and its fleet of five cargo steamers - the NORSEMAN (I), ROMAN, OTTOMAN, ANGLOMAN (I) and CAMBROMAN - which had been running between Liverpool and Boston under Warren Line management.

Richards Mills decided to retain the LABRADOR and VANCOUVER, but to dispose of the remaining ships - the DOMINION, ONTARIO, SARNIA and OREGON. It was intended at first to strip the passenger accommodation from the two survivors, but on second thoughts the Company decided to continue and even develop the passenger side of the business.

Ships assigned to the Liverpool . Quebec - Montreal trade in 1895 were the LABRADOR, VANCOUVER and MARIPOSA, but the last-named was wrecked in the St Lawrence on 27 September and the ex-Hamburg - American RUGIA was scheduled to replace her for one voyage in October. After several postponements, the sailing was cancelled and, instead, the RUGIA sailed for Marseilles, where she was taken over by the Fabre Line.

1895 SCOTSMAN 6,041 tons
Laid down as a cargo steamer but completed to carry three classes of passengers.

The chartered BRITISH PRINCE had made a voyage in May and the ROMAN in September.

The laying up of the ONTARIO, the loss of the TEXAS and the disposal of the HAMILTON were alone sufficient to indicate that the Avonmouth service was on its last legs. The TORONTO made her final voyage in October 1894 and was sold to Italy, leaving only the DOMINION and the chartered African Line steamers. The DOMINION sailed from Avonmouth for Quebec and Montreal on six occasions between April and October 1895, and for Portland in December. It seems that all the St Lawrence sailings were for Mississippi & Dominion, but she was sold in the autumn to E. Thirkell & Co, for whom the Portland sailing was made. This voyage, unfortunately, ended in disaster as she was wrecked on 4 January 1896 at Castletown Berehaven, Ireland, during its closing stages. It will be seen from Chapter 143 (Elder Dempster) that the African Steam Ship Company took over the service under the title DOMINION LINE (AFRICAN STEAM SHIP COMPANY) and, surprisingly, its participating steamers adopted Mississippi & Dominion funnel colours despite the fact that this company was still running a regular service from Liverpool to Canada.

As evidence of Richards Mills' determination to develop the passenger business, a newly-launched '-MAN' cargo steamer - the 6,041 ton twin-screw SCOTSMAN - was fitted with accommodation for 100 first class, 130 second and 800 steerage passengers and sailed from Liverpool on 28 November 1895 on her maiden voyage to Halifax and Portland. In the following spring the cargo steamers OTTOMAN and ANGLOMAN were temporarily transferred from the Warren Line, enabling the Company to run a weekly service to Quebec and Montreal.

The VANCOUVER met with further ill-luck, and in August 1896 was involved in a head-on collision with the Beaver Line LAKE ONTARIO in the St Lawrence. She was out of service for over two months, but the first of the new steamers laid down for the Company, the 8,806 ton twin-screw CANADA, was nearing completion and sailed from Liverpool on 1 October 1896 for Quebec and Montreal. She was by far the largest and most elaborately appointed steamer in the Canadian trade, with accommodation for 200 first class, 200 second and 800 steerage passengers. A product of Harland & Wolff, her dimensions were 152,51 x 17,74 metres (500.4 x 58.2 feet).

After two round voyages between Liverpool, Quebec and Montreal, the CANADA inaugurated a new winter service to Boston, which met with such success that it was continued indefinitely instead of her reverting to the Canadian trade in the following spring. The ANGLOMAN made her last Dominion Line voyage in September 1896, but the OTTOMAN ran again to Montreal throughout the 1897 season and from time to time thereafter.

1896 CANADA 8,806 tons
First twin-screw steamer built for the Canadian
trade.

The 5,965 ton twin-screw PRUSSIA was bought from the Hamburg American Line in 1898. She was fitted at Belfast with stalls for several hundred cattle and her passenger accommodation increased to 200 first class, 170 second and 750 steerage, her revised tonnage being 6,618. She was renamed DOMINION (II) and sailed from Liverpool on 7 May 1898 for Quebec and Montreal. A fortnight previously the 4,269 ton Bibby Line YORKSHIRE made the first of five voyages for the Company on the same route. Second of the new steamers was the 11,394 ton NEW ENGLAND, which exceeded the CANADA in length by 15 metres (50 feet) and joined her on the Boston service in June 1898.

During the winter of 1898-9 the LABRADOR, VANCOUVER and SCOTSMAN proceeded to Halifax and St John, New Brunswick, but the service reverted to Halifax and Portland in November 1899.

The Company's tenth and most serious loss to date occurred on 1 March 1899 when the LABRADOR was wrecked in the Hebrides, fortunately without casualties. As a result, the 6,059 ton single-screw CAMBROMAN was fitted with extensive passenger accommodation. She entered Dominion Line service on 28 June 1899, and had been running for less than three months when the Company suffered a further disaster. The SCOTSMAN was wrecked in the Straits of Belle Isle with a loss of 13 lives.

To help cope with a seasonal increase of business, the 6,636 ton twin-screw DERBYSHIRE (not the LANCASHIRE, as sometimes stated) was chartered from the Bibby Line for four round voyages between Liverpool and Boston during the summer of 1899. Shortly afterwards, the CANADA was taken up as a Boer War transport, serving in that capacity until several months after peace was signed in May 1902 and being responsible for 13 round voyages to South Africa, one of which was extended to Bombay.

Three second hand twin-screw cargo steamers were placed in service by the Company in 1899 - the 5,829 ton TURCOMAN (ex-LORD ERNE of the Lord Line), the 8,001 ton IRISHMAN (ex-Elder Dempster MONMOUTH) and the 6,336 ton ENGLISHMAN, which had had three previous owners and served as a transport throughout the war.

A very different type of ship was also acquired in 1899 - the 10,336 ton

BRASILIA, which the Hamburg American Line had resold to her builders, Harland & Wolff, and which, renamed NORSEMAN, started her Dominion career as transport No 80. The height of her funnel had been increased and her two masts became four. When built she had accommodation for 300 first class and 2,400 steerage passengers; on her one and only South African voyage she carried 27 officers, 1,115 men and 430 horses, her gross tonnage being then given as 11,677. She was a complete misfit in the Dominion fleet, and the fact that her tonnage was soon reduced to 9,546 implies that she discontinued carrying passengers. She made many voyages between Liverpool and Portland in summer and between Liverpool and Galveston in winter until transferred to the Aberdeen Line in 1910.

An even larger Harland & Wolff product, the 12,097 ton COMMONWEALTH, joined the NEW ENGLAND on the Boston service in October 1900. A few weeks later, at the close of the St Lawrence season, the DOMINION, CAMBROMAN and VANCOUVER began to run between Liverpool and Portland, the Halifax call being discontinued. The Company had entered into an arrangement with the Grand Trunk Railway to undertake an all-year-round service to Portland in return for specially reduced rates of inland freight. [9] During the summers of 1901-2 there were no Quebec and Montreal passenger sailings by the Dominion LIne.

There arose a new problem of what the Company should do with their large new steamers during the winter months, and as it was decided that the NEW ENGLAND could fully cope with the requirements of the Liverpool-Boston trade for the time being the COMMONWEALTH was despatched from Boston to Naples and Genoa in November 1901. She made three round voyages to the Mediterranean, of which the second was extended to Alexandria. Owing to the success of this experiment, the CAMBROMAN sailed from Liverpool on 10 March 1902 direct for Naples, followed 19 days later by the VANCOUVER. These two steamers maintained a regular service between the Mediterranean and Boston at threeweekly intervals until the autumn of 1903.

The outstanding shipping event of 1902 was the formation of the International Mercantile Marine Company, whose principals could not help but notice the rapid growth of the Dominion Line and, in particular, its successful participation in the Boston trade. Arrangements were, therefore, made to acquire the share capital of the Mississippi & Dominion Steamship Company Limited and of the British & North Atlantic Steam Navigation Company Limited, thereby bringing the Dominion Line under the same control as White Star, Red Star, American, Leyland, Atlantic Transport and other important North Atlantic lines, all of which retained their separate identities.

It was announced that in December 1902 the Dominion Line would start a fortnightly freight service between Avonmouth and Portland with the

MANXMAN, OTTOMAN and ROMAN, the first-mentioned having been acquired in the previous year from White Star, for whom she had been built in 1888 as the CUFIC. The OTTOMAN and ROMAN had already run from Liverpool for Dominion. The introduction of this service enabled the Company to withdraw their summer service between Liverpool and Portland. This had been carried on in 1902 by the 6,000 ton chartered Leyland Line steamers COLONIAN and CALIFORNIAN, which were responsible for eight and five round voyages, respectively, and had accommodation for 60 first class, and, surprisingly, 350 steerage passengers. The DOMINION (II) had been taken up as a transport to help repatriate troops from South Africa.

Everything pointed to the likelihood of the Dominion Line being expanded still further, and as a first step the Liverpool - Quebec -Montreal service was fully restored in the spring of 1903. In fact, it was considerably augmented as the steamers taking part were the CANADA and DOMINION, recently returned from their trooping activities, and the 8,600 ton twin-screw SOUTHWARK and KENSINGTON, transferred from the allied Red Star Line. The CANADA and DOMINION carried first, second and third class passengers, but the SOUTHWARK and KENSINGTON catered only for second and third.

At the same time, the 13,507 ton HANOVERIAN was acquired from the Leyland Line, sent to Harland & Wolff for 250 second and 1,000 third class berths to be added to the 260 first class already available, renamed MAYFLOWER and replaced the 11,621 ton American Line MERION on the Liverpool - Boston service, to which she had been allocated when completed in March 1902. The 15,378 ton COLUMBUS joined the MAYFLOWER, COMMONWEALTH and NEW ENGLAND in time to sail from Liverpool on 1 October 1903.

1903 COLUMBUS 15,378 tons
Became White Star REPUBLIC after only two
Dominion Line voyages.

Dominion was now at the peak of its power, but this happy state of affairs only lasted for a few weeks as White Star then took over the Liverpool - Boston and Boston - Mediterranean services, together with the

COLUMBUS, MAYFLOWER, COMMONWEALTH and NEW ENGLAND, which were renamed REPUBLIC, CRETIC, CANOPIC and ROMANIC, respectively. The COLUMBUS had only made two Dominion Line voyages and the MAYFLOWER no more than seven. In fairness, it must be pointed out that White Star was unquestionably the most important constituent of the IMM group and enjoyed a reputation second to none. But it can have been very minor consolation for Dominion to receive in part exchange the White Star cargo steamers NOMADIC and TAURIC, which became the CORNISHMAN and WELSHMAN.

Mention has already been made of the acquisition in 1899 of the Elder Dempster MONMOUTH, which was renamed IRISHMAN (I) and was sold to the National Line in 1903 to become the MICHIGAN. Soon afterwards a steamer laid down as the Hapag BELGIA, but completed as the ATL MICHIGAN, was sold to the Dominion Line and renamed IRISHMAN (II). It is hardly surprising that there has been much confusion between the two, particularly as both were of the familiar Harland & Wolff design with one funnel and four masts.

In 1904 the VANCOUVER rejoined the Canadian service, to which was added in the following year the 5,071 ton OTTAWA (II), better-known as the White Star GERMANIC, built in 1875. In both cases their first class accommodation became second.

Canadian Pacific entered the North Atlantic trade in 1903, and three years later commissioned two 'EMPRESS' steamers of over 14,000 tons. It is necessary to refer only briefly to the Dominion Line's reactions to this competition as, owing to White Star prestige being so high, it was decided that the two new 14,900 ton steamers ALBERTA and ALBANY, then under construction for Dominion, should be placed in service as the White Star LAURENTIC and MEGANTIC. They were completed in 1909, were slightly larger but slower than the 'EMPRESSES' and introduced a number of new features in their accommodation. In conjunction with the surviving Dominion ships, they established what became known as the WHITE STAR - DOMINION LINE JOINT SERVICE. The Allan Line, in particular, objected strongly to White Star's entry into the Canadian trade, and even threatened to withdraw from the Passenger Conference.

The VANCOUVER, SOUTHWARK and KENSINGTON were scrapped in 1910-1 and the OTTAWA was sold to Turkey. The DOMINION continued to run for the Company in winter, but betweeen 1908 and 1915 made 28 summer voyages for the American Line between Liverpool and Philadelphia. Thus, the CANADA was the only other survivor of the Dominion passenger fleet; she became a second and third class only carrier in November 1909. In May 1911 the 9,984 ton White Star TEUTONIC joined the LAURENTIC, MEGANTIC and CANADA in the White Star - Dominion service, the high speed of these four ships enabling them to maintain a weekly summer sailing to Quebec and Montreal.

The title Mississippi & Dominion Steamship Company Limited had survived the many changes described above, although ever since the turn of the century all but three or four of the Dominion ships had been registered in the name of the British & North Atlantic Steam Navigation Company Limited. In *Lloyd's Register* for 1914-5 the entire fleet, including the '-MAN' steamers, was shown for the first time under BRITISH & NORTH ATLANTIC STEAM NAVIGATION COMPANY LIMITED (DOMINION) LINE.

The TEUTONIC was taken up by the Admiralty soon after the otbreak of World War I in August 1914 and was sold to them a year later. The CANADA and LAURENTIC both helped to bring over the First Canadian Expeditionary Force, after which the former was used as an accommodation ship for German prisoners for some weeks, the remainder of the war being spent by her as a transport. The DOMINION ran for the American Line between Liverpool and Philadelphia until the middle of 1915. Thus, the last of the Dominion ships was temporarily withdrawn from the White Star - Dominion Joint Service, but the name was retained and for a time the service was carried on by the Red Star ZEELAND and VADERLAND, which were renamed NORTHLAND and SOUTHLAND in the spring of 1915. At a later date the SOUTHLAND became a war casualty, as did the LAURENTIC.

Two new Dominion steamers, and the only ones laid down and completed for the Company following its acquisition by IMM, the 16,313 ton triple-screw REGINA and the 9,281 ton twin-screw RIMOUSKI, were placed in service during the war. The upper promenade deck of the former was omitted at this stage and she appeared with one funnel and one mast instead of the two and two which she carried in 1922, when entering peacetime passenger service. Meanwhile, she was employed first on trooping duties and after the Armistice as a cargo steamer on one of the White Star routes. The RIMOUSKI, although used extensively as a troop carrier, was never fitted out as a passenger ship. In 1919 she was detailed to the Liverpool - Quebec - Montreal trade, but later saw much service under the White Star flag.

The passenger service was carried on in 1919-21 by the CANADA and MEGANTIC, which were joined in 1921 by the White Star VEDIC, a 9,332 ton third class only carrier of similar dimensions to the RIMOUSKI, but propelled by two sets of single-reduction geared turbines instead of quadruple-expansion reciprocating engines.

In 1921 the CANADA, DOMINION, REGINA and the '-MAN' steamers were transferred to the ownership of Frederick Leyland & Company Limited, but the change attracted little attention as the White Star - Dominion title remained in use for the passenger ships. Several of the

'-MAN' ships were employed on a resumed cargo service between Bristol and Portland or Quebec and Montreal, according to season. Two had been lost during the war. Most of the survivors were scrapped in 1926 or earlier.

1922 REGINA 16,313 tons
Last passenger ship built for Dominion Line.
In 1929 became Red Star WESTERNLAND.

The REGINA sailed from Liverpool for Halifax and Portland on 16 March 1922 on her first voyage as a passenger steamer, subsequent voyages being to Quebec and Montreal. She had accommodation for 600 cabin and 1,700 third class passengers. A fortnight later the VEDIC started her last passenger voyage from Liverpool before being transferred to a short-lived White Star service between Bremen, Southampton, Cherbourg, Quebec and Montreal. Subsequently, the REGINA, CANADA, MEGANTIC and the White Star CANOPIC (originally the Dominion COMMONWEALTH) undertook a weekly service from Liverpool to Quebec and Montreal. In the autumn the CANOPIC was transferred to a new White Star service between Bremen, Southampton, Cherbourg, Halifax and New York, but in July 1923 she was more than replaced by the 16,484 ton White Star DORIC, which was similar to the REGINA except that she had twin instead of triple screws, driven by single-reduction geared turbines.

The REGINA sailed from Montreal and Quebec for Liverpool on 21 June 1924 with a total of 572 cabin and 652 third class passengers, practically all the latter consisting of American and Canadian college students on a visit to Europe. For this reason, the description 'College Tours' was applied to the third class accommodation set aside for their benefit, other lines being quick to follow this lead and use a similar term. It soon became evident that a welcome new type of business had been created, and in April 1925 the official title 'Tourist Third Cabin' was introduced by the North Atlantic Passenger Conference and made obligatory for all conference lines until 1931 when 'Tourist Class' was substituted. Meanwhile, there had been a vast improvement in the quality of accommodation provided.

The description White Star - Dominion Line Joint Service remained in use until 1925, after which WHITE STAR LINE (CANADIAN SERVICES) was substituted. Strictly speaking, the REGINA made her last Dominion sailing on 6 November 1925 as on 12 December she left Liverpool for New York with her funnels painted in White Star colours. However, she continued until 1929 to run to Quebec and Montreal in summer, and subsequently became the Red Star WESTERNLAND. The CANADA - still, it is believed, with Dominion funnel colours - sailed for the last time on 13 August 1926 from Liverpool for Quebec and Montreal, and it is fitting that she should have been withdrawn at this time after 30 years of successful service. Only a few months later, Sidney E. Cruse, chief assistant manager of White Star, retired. He had joined the Dominion Line on 1 January 1889 as assistant accountant and secretary and before long was appointed passenger manager. To him should be given much of the credit for the spectacular revival of the line around the turn of the century.

In fact, it could be said that the Company was perhaps too successful at that time as otherwise it might not have been acquired by IMM and its best steamers transferred to White Star.

It has to be admitted that between 1870 and 1899 the Dominion Line had one of the worst safety records of all North Atlantic lines, no fewer than 12 steamers (plus two more on charter) being wrecked or lost at sea out of a total of 27. It must have been a matter of great satisfaction to Mr.Cruse and his colleagues that the only losses experienced subsequently took place during World War I and were the results of enemy action.

[1]   *Shipping & Mercantile Gazette* 11/6/1873
[2]   *Mitchell's Maritime Register* 26/9/1879
[3]   *North British Daily Mail* 3/11/1880
[4]   *The Times* 15/8/1882
[5]   *Glasgow Herald* 7/12/1885
[6]   HENRY FRY: *The History of North Atlantic Steam Navigation*
                (Sampson, Low, Marston & Co Ltd. London, 1896)
[7]   Ibid.
[8]   Ibid.
[9]   *The Times* 4/5/1901

1. 1872 MISSISSIPPI
   (1894) SICILIA (c)
        2,159. 97,68 x 10,67. (320.5 x 35.0). S—1—2. I—S—C2—11. (Cabin 80; III—600). A.McMillan & Son, Dumbarton (engines J.Jack, Rollo & Co, Liverpool). 1871 (29/11) launched. 1872 (4/5) MV Liverpool—Quebec— Montreal (first Canadian sailing of line). 1874 (20/4) stranded near Cape

Florida; refloated. 1875 (21/4) resumed Liverpool—Quebec—Montreal. 1886 (18/10) FV Avonmouth—Quebec—Montreal. 1887 (7/7) LV ditto. 1888 SICILIA (Sicilia SS Co (Br)). 1893 (11/6) FV for Dominion (c), Avonmouth—Quebec—Montreal. 1893 (7/10) LV ditto (4 RV). 1895 (3/10) wrecked near Trevose Head, Cornwall.

2. 1872 VICKSBURG

2,484. 99,63 x 11,67. (326.9 x 38.3). S—1—2. I—S—C2—11. (Cabin 80; III—600). A.McMillan & Son, Dumbarton (engines J. & J.Thomson, Glasgow). 1872 (28/3) launched. 1872 (9/6) MV Glasgow—Quebec—Montreal. 1872 (27/7) FV Liverpool—Quebec—Montreal. 1872 (8/8) stranded in St Lawrence River; refloated. 1874 (21/2) FV Liverpool—New Orleans. 1874 (13/5) resumed Liverpool—Quebec—Montreal. 1875 (28/4) LV ditto. 1875 (1/6) sunk in collision with iceberg near Newfoundland (47).

3. (1872) ST.LOUIS

1,827. 91,83 x 10,67. (301.3 x 35.0). S—1—2. I—S—C2—10. (Cabin 50; III—500). R.Clover & Co, Birkenhead (engines J.Jack & Co, Liverpool). 1870 (31/7) launched. 1870 (6/10) MV Liverpool—New Orleans. 1872 (12/6) FV Liverpool—Quebec—Montreal (1 RV). 1877 (12/5) FV Liverpool—Halifax—Philadelphia. 1877 (22/8) LV ditto (3 RV). 1882 sold; new compound engines. 1889 CHEANG CHEW (Singapore).

4. (1872) MEMPHIS

2,485. 99,66 x 11,64. (327.0 x 38.2). S—1—2. I—S—C2—11. (Cabin 80; III—600). A.McMillan & Son, Dumbarton (engines J. & J. Thomson, Glasgow). 1871 (18/9) launched. 1871 (18/11) MV Liverpool—New Orleans. 1872 (3/7) FV Liverpool—Quebec—Montreal. 1872-9 mainly Canadian service in summer; New Orleans in winter. 1879 (25/2) wrecked near Coruña, Spain.

4a. (1872) LORD CLIVE (c)

3,386. 116,12 x 12,19. (381.0 x 40.1). S—1—4. I—S—C2—12. R. & J. Evans, Liverpool (engines G.Forrester & Co, Liverpool). 1871 (28/10) launched for G.M.Papayanni, Liverpool. 1872 (15/9) FV for Dominion (c), Liverpool—Quebec—Montreal. 1872 (7/11) FV Liverpool—Boston—Portland. 1873 (9/7) LV Liverpool—Boston. 1873 (Sep) FV for G.M. Papayanni, ditto. 1875 (15/12) FV for American LIne (c), Liverpool—Philadelphia. 1888 bought by Lord Clive SS Co (American Line); British flag. 1893 (27/9) LV Liverpool—Philadelphia. 1896 CLIVE (Gastaldi & Co, Genoa (Br)). 1896 (8/11) FV for Furness (c), New York—Naples—Genoa. 1897 (1/3) LV Leghorn—Genoa—Naples—New York (3 RV). 1898 (Apr) scrapped.

5. 1872 TEXAS

   2,372. 99,20 x 11,06. (325.5 x 36.3). S—1—2. I—S—C2—11. (Cabin 80; III—600). A.McMillan & Son, Dumbarton (engines J. & J. Thomson, Glasgow). 1872 (21/8) launched. 1872 (12/12) MV Liverpool—Boston—Portland. 1873 (17/4) FV Liverpool—Quebec—Montreal. 1873-84 to Canada in summer; some winter New Orleans sailings. 1882 chartered by British Government for Egyptian Expedition. 1885 (27/6) FV Avonmouth—Quebec—Montreal. 1894 (12/5) LV ditto. 1894 (5/6) wrecked near Cape Race (0).

5a. (1873) PALESTINE (c)

   2,867. 107,31 x 11,00. (352.1 x 36.1). C—1—3. I—S—C2—10. R.Steele & Co, Greenock. 1858 (/) launched for Cunard. 1873 (27/3) FV for Dominion (c), Liverpool—Boston (1 RV). 1873 (16/5) FV Liverpool—Quebec—Montreal. 1873 (21/8) LV ditto (3 RV). (See Cunard - 13).

6. (1873) MISSOURI

   2,259. 85,34 x 11,73. (280.0 x 38.5). C—1—3. I—S—GO2—10. Caird & Co, Greenock. 1855 (5/5) launched as HAMMONIA (Hapag). 1868 BELGIAN (Allan). 1872 ditto (Dominion). 1872 (6/9) FV Liverpool—New Orleans. 1873 renamed MISSOURI. 1873 (2/5) FV Liverpool—Quebec—Montreal (1 RV). 1873 (17/9) sailed Liverpool—New Orleans. 1873 (1/10) wrecked on Bahamas Is (0). (See Hapag - 53).

6a. (1873) NEERA (c)

   2,167. 100,70 x 10,51. (330.4 x 34.5). 1—2. I—S—C4—10. A.Leslie & Co, Hebburn-on-Tyne (engines J.Jones & Co, Liverpool). 1858 (Sep) launched for Moss Line, Liverpool. 1873 (24/6) FV for Dominion (c), Liverpool—Quebec—Montreal (2 RV). 1884 (21/2) wrecked near Suakin, Red Sea.

7. (1874) CITY OF DUBLIN
   (1874) QUEBEC

   2,138. 96,92 x 11,06. (318.0 x 36.3). C—1—3. I—S—C2—11. Smith & Rodger, Glasgow. 1864 completed as CITY OF DUBLIN (Inman). 1873 CITY OF DUBLIN (Dominion); compound engines by Laird Bros, Birkenhead. 1874 (19/2) FV Liverpool—Boston (1 RV). 1874 renamed QUEBEC. 1874 (16/4) FV Liverpool—Quebec—Montreal. 1886 (30/4) FV Avonmouth—Quebec—Montreal. 1887 (16/12) LV Avonmouth—Swansea—New York. 1888 NAUTIQUE (French). 1890 (16/2) abandoned in N Atlantic. (See Inman - 28).

8. 1874 DOMINION (I)

   3,176. 102,10 x 11,70. (335.0 x 38.4). S—1—3. I—S—C2—11. (Cabin 130; III—600). A.McMillan & Son, Dumbarton (engines J.Jack, Rollo & Co,

Liverpool). 1873 (22/11) launched. 1874 (6/5) MV Liverpool—Quebec—
Montreal. 1885 (11/7) FV Avonmouth—Quebec—Montreal. 1890 triple-
expansion engines. 1895 sold to E.Thirkell & Co (Br); name retained. 1896
(4/1) wrecked at Castletown Berehaven, Eire.

9. 1874 ONTARIO

3,175. 102,31 x 11,70. (335.7 x 38.4). S—1—3. I—S—C2—11. (Cabin 130;
III—600). A.McMillan & Son, Dumbarton (engines J. & J.Thomson,
Glasgow). 1874 (5/3) launched. 1874 (3/6) MV Liverpool—Quebec—
Montreal. 1885 (13/6) FV Avonmouth—Quebec—Montreal. 1892 (23/7)
LV ditto. 1896 scrapped.

10. (1878) BORUSSIA

2,131. 85,34 x 11,73. (280.0 x 38.5). C—1—3. I—S—C2—10. Caird & Co,
Greenock. 1855 (3/7) launched as BORUSSIA (Hapag). 1876 BORUSS-
IA (Dominion). 1876 (2/9) FV Liverpool—New Orleans. 1878 (14/7) FV
Liverpool—Quebec—Montreal (1 RV). 1879 (20/11) sailed Liverpool—
New Orleans. 1879 (2/12) abandoned at sea (165). (See Hapag - 53).

BAVARIA

2,405. 1856 (30/10) launched as PETROPOLIS (Hamburg-Brasilianische). 1858 BAVARIA (Hapag). 1876 ditto (Dominion). 1877 (6/2)
destroyed by fire at sea (0). (Did not run on North Atlantic for Dominion
-see Hapag - 53).

11. (1878) TEUTONIA

2,693. 85,98 x 12,01. (282.1 x 39.4). C—1—3. I—S—C2—10. Caird & Co,
Greenock. 1856 (4/8) launched for Hamburg-Brasilianische. 1858
TEUTONIA (Hapag). 1877 ditto (Dominion). 1877 (13/3) FV Liverpool
—New Orleans. 1878 (22/8) FV Liverpool—Quebec—Montreal (several
RV). 1883 TEUTONIA (Br). (See Hapag - 53).

12. (1878) BROOKLYN

2,911. 108,01 x 12,95. (354.4 x 42.5). C—1—3. I—S—I(2)—13. Tod &
McGregor, Glasgow. 1868 (Dec) launched as CITY OF BROOKLYN
(Inman). 1878 BROOKLYN (Dominion). 1878 (4/9) FV Liverpool—
Quebec—Montreal (2 RV). 1878-9 lengthened to 121,85 metres (399.8
feet); tonnage 4,215; compound engines by J. & J.Thomson, Glasgow.
1879 (25/6) resumed Liverpool—Quebec—Montreal. 1885 (8/11)
wrecked on Anticosti Island (0). (See Inman - 28).

13. 1879 MONTREAL

3.308. 100,42 x 11,98. (329.5 x 39.3). S—1—3. I—S—C2—12. (Cabin 30;
III—1,000).C.Connell & Co, Glasgow (engines J. & J. Thomson,

Glasgow). 1879 (May) keel laid. 1879 (18/9) launched. 1879 (27/10) MV Glasgow—Liverpool—New Orleans. 1880 (23/4) FV Liverpool—Quebec—Montreal. 1882 chartered by British Govt. for Egyptian Expedition. 1889 (4/8) wrecked off Belle Isle (0).

14. 1880 TORONTO

3,316. 100,42 x 11,98. (329.5 x 39.3). S—1—3. I—S—C2—12. (Cabin 30; III—1,000). C. Connell & Co, Glasgow (engines J. & J. Thomson, Glasgow). 1880 (27/1) launched. 1880 (26/3) MV Liverpool—Halifax—Portland. 1880 (7/5) FV Liverpool—Quebec—Montreal. 1886 (16/11) FV for Inman (c), Liverpool—Queenstown—New York (1 RV). 1889 (8/2) FV Avonmouth—Portland. 1894 (3/8) LV Liverpool—Quebec—Montreal. 1894 (17/10) LV Avonmouth—Quebec—Montreal. 1894 PINA (Italian). 1897 scrapped.

15. 1880 OTTAWA (I)

3,712. 109,41 x 12,31. (359.0 x 40.4). S—1—4. I—S—C2—12. (I—24; III—800). C. Connell & Co, Glasgow (engines J. & J. Thomson, Glasgow). 1880 (23/8) launched. 1880 (1/11) MV Glasgow—Quebec—Montreal. 1880 (22/11) wrecked at Cape la Roche (0) on MV Montreal—Liverpool.

16. 1882 SARNIA

3,728. 109,93 x 12,28. (360.7 x 40.3). S—1—4. I—S—C2—12. (Cabin 80; intermediate 60: III—1,200). C.Connell & Co, Glasgow (engines J. & J. Thomson, Glasgow). 1882 (30/6) launched. 1882 (7/9) MV Liverpool—Quebec—Montreal. 1893 (Aug) broke propeller shaft; towed 1,000 miles to Queenstown by MONTE VIDEAN (Allan). 18.. masts reduced to two. 1894 (22/12) lost rudder; towed to Inishtrahull by NORWEGIAN (Allan); thence to Belfast by tugs. 1896 SARNIA (Furness). 1896 (20/6) FV for Hapag (c), Hamburg—Montreal (2 RV). 1896 (24/11) FV for Furness, Genoa—New York. 1897 (28/7) LV New York—Naples—Genoa—Leghorn (4 RV). 1897 (Sep) scrapped at Genoa.

17. 1883 OREGON

3,672. 109,93 x 12,28. (360.7 x 40.3). S—1—4. I—S—C2—12. (Cabin 80; intermediate 60; III—1,200). C.Connell & Co, Glasgow (engines J. & J. Thomson, Glasgow). 1882 (23/12) launched. 1883 (15/3) MV Liverpool—Halifax—Portland. 1883 (3/5) FV Liverpool—Quebec—Montreal. 18.. masts reduced to two. 1895 (19/6) LV ditto. 1896 OREGON (Furness). 1896 (18/7) FV for Hapag (c), Hamburg—Montreal (1 RV). 1896 (15/9) sailed Hamburg—New York. 1896 (10/10) FV for Furness, New York—Naples—Genoa—Leghorn. 1897 (8/7) LV ditto (4 RV). 1897 (Sep) scrapped at Genoa.

VANCOUVER (I)

5,202. (Did not run for Dominion; see Inman - 28 - CITY OF CHICAGO).

18. 1884 VANCOUVER (II)

5,141. 131,54 x 13,71. (430.6 x 45.0). S—2—4. I—S—C3—14. (Cabin 200; intermediate 120; III—1,500). C.Connell & Co, Glasgow (engines J. & J. Thomson, Glasgow). 1884 (12/3) launched. 1884 (19/6) MV Liverpool—Quebec—Montreal. 1886 (28/12) FV for Inman (c), Liverpool—Queenstown—New York (2 RV). 1890 (Aug) collision in fog with iceberg near Belle Isle; slight damage. 1890 (Nov) her commander and a quartermaster swept overboard and drowned. 1892 triple-expansion engines; one funnel. 1894 (Nov) stranded at entrance to Lough Foyle; towed to Liverpool. 1896 (Aug) collision in St Lawrence River with ss LAKE ONTARIO (Beaver); both damaged. 1902 (29/3) sailed Liverpool—Naples. 1902 (10/4) FV Naples—Boston. 1903 (21/11) LV Boston—Genoa—Naples. 1904 (May) resumed Liverpool—Quebec—Montreal; (II—300; III—1,500). 1909 (27/3) LV Portland—Liverpool. 1910 scrapped.

19. 1891 LABRADOR

4,737. 122,22 x 14,38. (401.0 x 47.2). S—1—4. S—S—T3—15. (I—100; II—50; III—1,000). Harland & Wolff, Belfast. 1891 (11/4) launched. 1891 (20/8) MV Liverpool—Quebec—Montreal. 1899 (1/3) wrecked at Skerryvore, Hebrides (0).

20. (1894) HAMILTON

3,617. 105,33 x 13,22. (345.6 x 43.4). S—1—2. I—S—C2—11. Palmers Co Ltd, Jarrow-on-Tyne. 1868 (17/10) launched as NEVADA (Guion). 1894 HAMILTON (Dominion), 1894 (28/4) FV Avonmouth—Quebec—Montreal. 1894 (22/9) LV ditto (5 RV). 1896 scrapped in Italy. (See Guion - 78).

20a. (1895) BRITISH PRINCE (c)

3,871. 128,04 x 12,86. (420.1 x 42.2). S—1—4. S—S—C2—12. Harland & Wolff, Belfast. 1882 (4/2) launched for British Shipowners. 1895 (1/5) FV for Dominion (c), Liverpool—Quebec—Montreal (1 RV). 1895 LES ANDES (French). (See American - 101).

21. (1895) ROMAN §

4,572. 123,44 x 13,28. (405.0 x 43.6). S—1—4. I—S—C2—12. Laird Bros, Birkenhead. 1884 (20/9) launched for British & North Atlantic; ran for Warren. 1895 (31/8) FV for Dominion, Liverpool—Quebec—Montreal (1 RV). 1901 onwards Liverpool or Avonmouth—Portland. 1910 scrapped at Troon.

RUGIA (c)

4,053. 109,11 x 12,95. (358.0 x 42.5). S—1—3. S—S—C2—12. (I—96; III—1,000). AG Vulcan, Stettin. 1882 (29/7) launched for Hapag; 3,467 tons. 1895 taken by Harland & Wolff in part payment for PENN-SYLVANIA; tonnage 4,053. 1895 (10/10) scheduled for Dominion (c), Liverpool—Quebec—Montreal but sailing cancelled after several post-ponements. 1895 PATRIA (Fabre). 1895 (28/11) FV Marseilles—Naples —New York. (See Fabre - 126).

22. 1895 SCOTSMAN

6,041. 143,46 x 14,99. (470.7 x 49.2). S—1—4. S—2S—T6—13. (I—100; II—130; III—800). Harland & Wolff, Belfast. 1894 (13/12) launched. 1895 (28/11) MV Liverpool—Halifax—Portland. 1896 (14/5) FV Liverpool—Quebec—Montreal. 1899 (29/9) wrecked in Straits of Belle Isle (13).

23. (1896) OTTOMAN §

4,843. 123.07 x 13,89. (403.8 x 45.6). S—1—4. S—S—T3—12. Laird Bros, Birkenhead. 1890 (2/9) launched for British & North Atlantic. 1890 (8/12) MV for Warren (c), Liverpool—Boston. 1896 (23/4) FV for Dominion, Liverpool—Quebec—Montreal. 1897 (2/11) LV ditto, apart from occasional sailings 1898-9. 1901 onwards Liverpool or Avonmouth—Portland. 1911 (May) scrapped at Preston.

24. (1896) ANGLOMAN §

4,892. 123,07 x 10,85. (403.8 x 45.6). S—1—4. S—S—T3—12. Laird Bros, Birkenhead. 1892 (6/2) launched for British & North Atlantic. 1896 (7/5) FV for Dominion, Liverpool—Quebec—Montreal. 1896 (24/9) LV ditto (5 RV). (See Warren - 73).

25. 1896 CANADA

8,806. 152,51 x 17,74. (500.4 x 58.2). S—1—2. S—2S—T6—15. (I—200; II—200; III—800). Harland & Wolff, Belfast. 1896 (14/5) launched. 1896 (1/10) MV Liverpool—Quebec—Montreal (2 RV). 1896 (23/12) FV Liverpool—Boston. 1899 (Nov)-1902 (autumn) Boer War transport. 1903 (19/3) Fv Liverpool—Halifax—Boston; tonnage 9,413. 1903 (22/4) resumed Liverpool—Quebec—Montreal. 1909 (Nov) II—463; III—755. 1914 (22/8) LV Liverpool—Quebec—Montreal; eastbound was Canadian Expeditionary Force transport. 1914 (autumn) accommodation ship for German prisoners. 1915-8 transport service. 1918 (Nov) FV after Armistice, Liverpool—Portland. 1926 (13/8) LV Liverpool—Quebec—Montreal. 1926 scrapped in Italy.

25a. (1898) YORKSHIRE (c)

4,269. 122,12 x 13,77. (400.7 x 45.2). S—1—4. S—S—T3—13. Harland &

Wolff, Belfast. 1889 (27/7) launched for Bibby. 1889 (12/10) MV for Anchor (c), Liverpool—New York (cargo only) (2 RV). 1898 (21/4) FV for Dominion (c), Liverpool—Quebec—Montreal. 1898 (8/9) LV ditto (5 RV). 1905 INDIEN (East Asiatic). 1907 ESTONIA (Russian American). 1907 (17/6) FV Libau—Rotterdam—New York. 1912 (18/3) LV Libau—Copenhagen—Halifax—New York; transferred to Far East service. 1913 (16/1) abandoned on fire at sea near Port Sudan. 1913 (23/1) sunk by explosion.

26. (1898) DOMINION (II)

6,618. 135,78 x 15,30. (445.5 x 50.2). S—1—4. S—2S—T6—13. (I—200; II—170; III—750). Harland & Wolff, Belfast. 1894 (10/4) launched as PRUSSIA (Hapag). 1898 DOMINION (Dominion). 1898 (7/5) FV Liverpool—Quebec—Montreal. 1908 (Dec) FV for American Line (c), Liverpool—Philadelphia; (II—370; III—750). 1915 (May) LV ditto (28 RV); some intervening Dominion sailings. 1918 (2/12) FV after Armistice, Liverpool—Portland. 1919 (autumn) cargo only. 1921 (26/2) LV Liverpool—Portland. 1922 scrapped in Germany. (See Hapag - 53).

27. 1898 NEW ENGLAND

11,394. 167,72 x 18,07. (550.3 x 59.3). S—1—2. S—2S—T8—16. (I—200; II—200; III—800). Harland & Wolff, Belfast. 1898 (7/4) launched. 1898 (30/6) MV Liverpool—Boston. 1903 (17/9) LV ditto. 1903 ROMANIC (White Star - 88) (qv).

28. (1898) IRISHMAN (I) §

8,001. 149,49 x 17,16. (490.5 x 56.3). 1—4. 2S—T6—13. Harland & Wolff, Belfast (engines Fawcett, Preston & Co, Liverpool). 1897 (23/12) launched as MONMOUTH (Elder Dempster). 1898 IRISHMAN (Dominion). 1903 MICHIGAN (National). 1914 MICHIGAN (ATL). 1926 scrapped in Italy. (See ATL - 123).

28a. (1899) DERBYSHIRE (c)

6,636. 137,76 x 15,91. (452.0 x 52.2). 1—4. 2S—T6—14. (I—140). Harland & Wolff, Belfast. 1897 (21/7) launched for Bibby. 1899 (8/6) FV for Dominion (c), Liverpool—Boston. 1899 (31/8) LV ditto (4 RV). 1931 scrapped in Japan.

29. (1899) CAMBROMAN

6,059. 131,02 x 14,11. (429,9 x 46.3). 1—4. S—T3—12. (I—100; II; III). Laird Bros, Birkenhead. 1892 (6/10) launched for British & North Atlantic (cargo only). 1892 (1/12) MV for Warren (c), Liverpool—Boston. 1899 passenger accommodation fitted. 1899 (28/6) FV for Dominion, Liverpool—Quebec—Montreal. 1902 (10/3) sailed Liverpool—Naples direct.

1902 (Mar) FV Naples—Boston. 1903 (19/9) LV Boston—Naples—
Genoa. 1907 (8/3) FV Antwerp—New York for Red Star (c); (III—1,275)
(3 RV). 1910 scrapped.

30. (1899) TURCOMAN §

5,829. 135,63 x 14,99. (445.0 x 49.2). 1—4. 2S—T6—13. Harland & Wolff,
Belfast. 1892 (29/3) launched as LORD ERNE (Irish Shipowners). 1899
TURCOMAN (Dominion). 1925 (May) scrapped in Italy.

31. (1899) ENGLISHMAN §

5,257. 131,06 x 14,32. (430.0 x 47.0). 1—4. 2S—T6—13. Harland & Wolff,
Belfast. 1891 (31/10) launched as IONIA (City of Liverpool). 1892
MONTEZUMA (Elder Dempster). 1898 SANDUSKY (Union). 1899
ENGLISHMAN (Dominion). 1900 (28/1) FV as Boer War transport (10
RV). 1916 (24/3) torpedoed and sunk by German submarine on voyage
Avonmouth—Portland (10). (See Elder Dempster - 143).

32. (1899) NORSEMAN

9,546. 152,60 x 18,99. (500.7 x 62.3). 1—4. 2S—Q8—13. (I—300; III—
2,400). Harland & Wolff, Belfast. 1897 (27/11) launched as BRASILIA
(Hapag); 10,336 tons; two masts. 1899 BRASILIA (Harland & Wolff).
1899 NORSEMAN (Dominion); four masts. 1900 (10/2) FV Liverpool—
South Africa as Boer War transport; 11,677 tons (1 RV). 1910 (7/6) FV for
Aberdeen Line (c), London—Cape Town—Australia. 1914 (30/1) LV
ditto. 1916 (22/1) torpedoed by German submarine U.39 in Gulf of
Salonika; towed to Mudros harbour; where again torpedoed; sank. 1920
refloated; scrapped. (See Hapag - 53).

33. 1900 COMMONWEALTH

12,097. 176,25 x 18,07. (578.3 x 59.3). 1—2. 2—S—T8—16. (I—250;
II—250; III—800). Harland & Wolff, Belfast. 1900 (31/5) launched. 1900
(4/10) MV Liverpool—Boston. 1901 (16/11) LV ditto. 1901 (Nov) FV
Boston—Naples—Genoa (3 RV). 1902 (10/4) resumed Liverpool—Boston. 1903 (5/11) LV ditto. 1903 CANOPIC (White Star - 88) (qv).

34. (1901) MANXMAN §

4,827. 131,27 x 13,77. (430.7 x 45.2). 1—4. S—T3—13. Harland & Wolff,
Belfast. 1888 (10/10) launched as CUFIC (White Star). 1901 MANXMAN
(Dominion). 1915 ditto (Canadian). 1919 ditto (US). 1919 (18/12) found-
ered in N Atlantic (40). (See White Star - 88).

34a. 1902 MERION (c)

11,621. 161,68 x 18,04. (530.5 x 59.2). 1—4. 2S—T6—14. (I—150; III—
1,700). John Brown & Co Ltd, Glasgow. 1901 (26/11) launched for
American Line. 1902 (8/3) MV for Dominion (c), Liverpool—Boston.

1903 (5/3) LV ditto (11 RV). 1903 (Apr) FV Liverpool—Philadelphia for American Line - 101. (qv).

34b. (1902) COLONIAN (c)

6.440. 137,30 x 16,52. (450.5 x 54.2). 1—4. S—T3—12. (I—60; III—350). R. & W. Hawthorn, Leslie & Co Ltd, Hebburn-on-Tyne (engines North Eastern Marine Engineering Co Ltd, Newcastle). 1901 (19/7) launched for Leyland. 1902 (Mar) FV for Dominion (c), Liverpool—Portland. 1902 (Dec) LV ditto (8 RV). 1917 (20/5) wrecked at south end of Bishop's Rock, Pembrokeshire.

34c. (1902) CALIFORNIAN (c)

6,223. 136,42 x 16,39. (447.6 x 53.8). 1—4. S—T3—12. (I—60; III—350). Caledon Shipbuilding & Engineering Co, Dundee. 1901 (26/11) launched for Leyland. 1902 (Apr) FV for Dominion (c), Liverpool—Portland. 1902 (Dec) LV ditto (5 RV). 1915 (9/11) torpedoed and sunk by enemy submarine off Cape Matapan, Greece (1).

35. (1903) MAYFLOWER

13,507. 177,38 x 18,38. (582.0 x 60.3). 1—4. 2S—T6—15. R. & W. Hawthorn, Leslie & Co Ltd, Hebburn-on-Tyne. 1902 (25/2) launched as HANOVERIAN (Leyland); (I—260). 1903 MAYFLOWER (Dominion); (I—260; II—250; III—1,000). 1903 (9/4) FV Liverpool—Boston. 1903 (22/10) LV ditto (7 RV). 1903 CRETIC (White Star - 88) (qv).

35a (1903) KENSINGTON (c)

8,669. 146,30 x 17,43. (480.0 x 57.2). 1—4. 2S—Q8—14. (II—250; III—929). J. & G. Thomson, Glasgow. 1893 (26/10) launched for American Line. 1903 (29/4) FV for Dominion (c), Liverpool—Quebec—Montreal. 1908 (8/11) LV Montreal—Quebec—Liverpool. 1910 scrapped in Italy. (See American - 101).

35b. (1903) SOUTHWARK (c)

8,607. 146,30 x 17,43. (480.0 x 57.2). 1—4. 2S—Q8—14. (II—250; III—929). Wm Denny & Bros, Dumbarton. 1893 (4/7) launched for American Line. 1903 (13/5) FV for Dominion (c), Liverpool—Quebec—Montreal. 1911 (May) LV ditto (Montreal arr 31/5). (See American - 101).

36. 1903 COLUMBUS

15,378. 173,72 x 20,66. (570.0 x 67.8). 1—4. 2S—Q8—16. Harland & Wolff, Belfast. 1903 (26/2) launched. 1903 (1/10) MV Liverpool—Boston. 1903 (29/10) LV ditto (2 RV). 1903 REPUBLIC (White Star - 88). (qv).

37. (1903) NOMADIC §
(1904) CORNISHMAN §

    5,749. 140,44 x 14,96. (460.8 x 49.1). 1—4. 2S—T6—13. Harland & Wolff, Belfast. 1891 (11/12) launched as NOMADIC (White Star). 1903 NOMADIC (Dominion). 1904 CORNISHMAN (ditto). 1921 ditto (Leyland). 1926 scrapped at Lelant, Cornwall. (See White Star - 88).

38. (1903) TAURIC §
(1904) WELSHMAN §

    5,728. 140,44 x 14,96. (460.8 x 49.1). 1—4. 2S—T6—13. Harland & Wolff, Belfast. 1891 (12/3) launched as TAURIC (White Star). 1903 TAURIC (Dominion). 1904 WELSHMAN (ditto). 1921 ditto (Leyland). 1929 (Dec) scrapped at Bo'ness. (See White Star - 88).

39. (1904) IRISHMAN (II) §

    9,510. 152,60 x 19,02. (500.7 x 62.4). 1—4. 2S—Q8—13. Harland & Wolff, Belfast. Laid down as BELGIA (Hapag). 1899 (5/10) launched as MICHIGAN (ATL); chartered to National. 1904 IRISHMAN (Dominion). 1924 scrapped. (See National - 69).

40. (1905) OTTAWA (II)

    5,071. 138,68 x 13,77. (455.0 x 45.2). 2—4. I—S—T3—15. (II—250; III—1,500). Harland & Wolff, Belfast. 1875 (15/7) launched as GERMANIC (White Star). 1905 OTTAWA (Dominion). 1905 (27/4) FV Liverpool—Quebec—Montreal. 1909 (2/9) LV ditto. (See White Star - 88).

40a. (1908) HAVERFORD (c)

    11,635. 161,84 x 18,04. (531.0 x 59.2). 1—4. 2S—T6—14. (II—150; III—1,700). John Brown & Co Ltd, Glasgow. 1901 (4/5) launched for American Line. 1908 (17/12) FV for Dominion (c), Liverpool—Halifax—Portland (2 RV). (See American - 101).

    ALBERTA
14,892. (Did not run for Dominion; see White Star - 88 - LAURENTIC).

    ALBANY
14,878. (Did not run for Dominion; see White Star - 88 - MEGANTIC).

41. 1918 RIMOUSKI §

    9,281. 140,29 x 17,77. (460.3 x 58.3). 1—2—C. 2S—Q8—14. Harland & Wolff, Glasgow (engines Harland & Wolff, Belfast). 1917 (30/8) launched. 1928 BOSTONIAN (Leyland). 1932 (Sep) scrapped in Italy.

42. (1922) REGINA

16,313. 175,06 x 20,66. (574.4 x 67.8). 2—2—C. 3S—T8&ST—15. Cabin 600; III—1,700). Harland & Wolff, Glasgow (engines Harland & Wolff, Belfast). 1917 (19/4) launched. 1918 completed as cargo steamer (1—1—C; minus upper promenade deck). 1920 (Aug) arr Harland & Wolff, Belfast, for completion as passenger steamer. 1922 (16/3) FV Liverpool—Halifax—Portland. 1922 (29/4) FV Liverpool—Quebec—Montreal. 1924 (21/6) FV Montreal—Quebec—Liverpool carrying 'College Tours'. 1925 (6/11) LV Liverpool—Quebec—Montreal. 1925 (12/12) FV for White Star (c), Liverpool—Halifax—New York. 1926 (Jun) cabin; tourist; III. 1929 (1/11) LV Liverpool—Belfast—Glasgow—Quebec—Montreal for White Star. 1929 WESTERNLAND (Red Star). 1930 (10/1) FV Antwerp—Southampton—Cherbourg—New York; (tourist; III). 1934 (30/11) LV Antwerp—Havre—Southampton—New York (arr 10/12; dep 12/12)—Havre—London—Antwerp. 1935 WESTERNLAND (Bernstein Red Star); (tourist 486). 1935 (29/3) FV Antwerp—Southampton—New York. 1939 (6/5) LV ditto. 1939 WESTERNLAND (Holland America). 1939 (Jun) FV Antwerp—Southampton—New York. 1940 (10/4) LV Antwerp—New York. 1942 (Nov) bought by British Admiralty; repair ship. 1947 (Aug) scrapped at Blyth.

The following African Steam Ship Company (Elder Dempster) steamers ran for the Dominion Line (see Elder Dempster fleet list - Chapter 143):-

1892	PLASSEY	(3,176 tons)	
1893-5	MEXICO	(3,185 tons)	(*)
1894-5	MEMPHIS	(3,191 tons)	
1894-5	MARIPOSA	(5,305 tons)	(*)
1895	ETOLIA	(3,270 tons)	
1895	MEMNON	(3,176 tons) (ex-PLASSEY)	
1895	LYCIA	(3,282 tons)	

(*) wrecked when running for the Dominion Line.

In addition, the CRESCENT CITY (2,017 tons; 1870-1) made one voyage to New Orleans and was wrecked on the Irish coast during the homeward leg.

§ - cargo steamer.

FUNNEL: Red with white band; black top.

FLAG: (a) Red; blue ball in large white diamond.
        (b) Red Pennant; blue ball in small white diamond.

Chapter 94

MERCANTILE STEAMSHIP COMPANY
(British)

In or about 1851 John Ashforth Dunkerly set up in business in Hull as a shipbroker under the style J.A.DUNKERLY & CO. A few years later his brother, Charles Henry Dunkerly, became a partner. The business prospered and as a result of experience gained as agents for the North of Europe Steam Navigation Company it was decided in 1864 to start a steamship service to the Baltic, orders being placed for the 970 ton iron screw NILE and NEVA. The 1,900 ton NYANZA, GANGES and TAGUS were added in 1867-8 to enable operations to be extended to the Mediterranean. Two slightly smaller ships, the 1,730 ton TRENT and TIBER appeared in 1870; the 1,210 ton SHANNON was bought on the stocks.

It was at this time that the Dunkerly brothers entered into partnership with Rudolph Steinmann, a Liverpool shipowner, the separate firm of Dunkerly & Steinmann being established with headquarters in Water Street, Liverpool. [1] The advantages of this arrangement were seen in June 1871, when the TIBER, TRENT, TAGUS and NYANZA were chartered to the Warren Line, which was thus able to resume its steamship service between Liverpool and Boston.

Prospects seemed extremely good, but the Company was suffering from a shortage of capital. On 19 August 1871, therefore, the COMMERCIAL STEAM SHIPPING COMPANY LIMITED was registered with a nominal capital of £300,000, but at the request of the Registrar this name was changed later in the same month to MERCANTILE STEAMSHIP COMPANY LIMITED owing to the possibility of confusion with another concern. Directors of the Company were the three partners of Dunkerly & Steinmann, together with John and R.R.Glover of Glover Brothers, London. Largest shareholder was Sir Francis Lycett, which accounts for the fact that two of the new steamers under construction were named SIR FRANCIS and LADY LYCETT, respectively, both being of 1,833 tons. [1] The other two were the 1,476 ton CHESAPEAKE and the 1,832 ton POTOMAC, the choice of names correctly suggesting that they would probably be employed on the North Atlantic. Earlier Dunkerly steamers were placed under Mercantile management, but were not transferred to them at this stage.

An advertisement of February 1872 [2] stated that the NYANZA of the

LIVERPOOL & MONTREAL STEAMSHIP LINE would be despatched from Liverpool to Quebec and Montreal on 13 April 1872, applications for freight or passage being invited to Wm Hunter & Co. The Company's fleet was shown as the SHANNON, LADY LYCETT, POTOMAC, TRENT, TIBER, NYANZA, GANGES and TAGUS, in that order, all owned by J.A.Dunkerly & Co, except the LADY LYCETT, which was registered in the name of the Mercantile Steamship Company. Thus, the name 'Liverpool & Montreal Steamship Line' was more a description of the route undertaken than a trade name. A later advertisement substituted the LADY LYCETT for the NYANZA, but as the former was still running for the Warren Line it was eventually necessary for the 860 ton VIKING to be chartered to take her place. After two postponements she eventually got away on 9 May. The CHESAPEAKE was intended to sail at the end of May but was replaced by the NYANZA, which left on 6 June, followed by the CHESAPEAKE on 28 June. Finally, the TIBER was advertised to sail 'shortly' - a state of affairs that continued until 3 September, when the announcement ceased as did the idea of a Canadian service. However, there was one further sailing by the SHANNON, which went missing after leaving Sydney, Cape Breton Island, on 13 November 1872 on her homeward voyage from Montreal to London. All told there had been only four sailings including the chartered one. The withdrawal can be considered as due in no small degree to the introduction of a regular service on the same route in May 1872 by the appreciably larger steamers of the Dominion Line.

Instead, it was decided to start a service between Liverpool and Philadelphia by the TAGUS on 20 July 1872. She was followed by the GANGES in August, the POTOMAC in September and the LADY LYCETT in October. Early advertisements did not mention the name of the line, application being directed to Dunkerly & Steinmann or Wm Hunter & Co, of Liverpool, or to the Philadelphia consignees, Peter Wright & Sons. Sailings continued fairly regularly until 15 April 1873, when the NYANZA was scheduled to leave Liverpool but was postponed in stages until 15 May and then cancelled outright. The final advertisement appeared under the name of the Mercantile Steamship Company, which should undoubtedly have been mentioned from the start.

This was the last that was heard of the Mercantile Line's service, but immediately underneath the final advertisement for the NYANZA there appeared on many days running one stating that the 2,554 ton ABBOTSFORD was 'in every way superior to any steamer yet despatched' from Liverpool to Philadelphia [3] and that she would sail thereto at the end of April, the agents being shown as Wm Hunter & Co. She eventually got away on 10 May and it is interesting to note that a report of her arrival at Philadelphia referred to her as 'the pioneer of the Red Star Line's Liverpool service.' [4] She sailed again from Liverpool on 26 June and on that and subsequent occasions was advertised under the International Navigation Company (Red Star Line).[5] It may well be that the Mercantile Steamship Company had decided to discontinue their Liverpool - Philadelphia service before the ABBOTSFORD came on the scene, but it is equally possible that Wm Hunter & Co were trying to serve two masters and that, as with the Dominion Line, Mercantile decided that they could not compete with a concern that had such considerable backing, particularly in the USA. [6]

Thus, the Mercantile Steamship Company, as such, undertook only four round voyages between Liverpool, Quebec and Montreal and eight between Liverpool and Philadelphia, but its activities on the North Atlantic were much more important than this suggests. Its steamers were also responsible for upwards of 20 voyages under charter to the Warren Line, one of the last being by the SIR FRANCIS, which was wrecked on Salisbury Beach, New Hampshire, on 3 January 1873 while so employed. In addition, the LADY LYCETT made five voyages between Bristol and New York for the Great Western Steamship Line, and other steamers carried out six or more voyages for the Temperly Line between London and Canada.

The North Atlantic boom which followed the Franco-Prussian War did not last beyond 1873 and the Mercantile Steamship Company wisely confined its subsequent activities to tramping. Following an increase of capital in November 1874, most of the remaining Dunkerly steamers were transferred to Mercantile ownership, periodical additions being made to the fleet from 1877 onwards. At the outbreak of World War I in 1914 the Company owned a total of 14 up-to-date ships, only three of which survived the Armistice, two others having been added during the war. Early in 1918, the P&O Company acquired control, and in 1923 the Mercantile Steamship Company went into voluntary liquidation, assets being transferred to the Hain Steamship Company, which P&O had taken over in October 1917.

[1] W.A.LAXON: *Mercantile Steamers* ('Sea Breezes' November 1965).
[2] *Glasgow Herald* 26/2/1872
[3] *Liverpool Journal of Commerce* 12/4/1873, etc.
[4] *Philadelphia North American & United States Gazette* 27/5/1873
[5] *Liverpool Journal of Commerce* 9/6/1873
[6] See Chapters 98 (Red Star) and 101 (American Line).

1. (1872) NYANZA
        1,870. 79,88 x 10,12. (262.1 x 33.2). 1—2. I—S—I(2)—10. London & Glasgow Co, Glasgow. 1867 (1/11) launched for J.A.Dunkerly & Co. 1871 (Oct) FV Liverpool—Boston for Warren (c). 1872 (6/6) Fv Liverpool—

Quebec—Montreal for Mercantile (1 RV). 1873 (23/5) FV London—
Quebec—Montreal for Temperley (c) (3 RV). 1893 (16/12) sailed Glasgow
—Leghorn; went missing.

2. (1872) CHESAPEAKE
1,474. 73,14 x 9,96. (240.0 x 32.7). 1—2. I—S—C2—10. Gourlay Bros &
Co, Dundee. 1872 (8/4) launched for Mercantile. 1872 (28/6) MV Liver-
pool—Quebec—Montreal (1 RV). 1872 (Aug) FV Liverpool—Boston for
Warren (c) (2 RV). 1892 SEEBOLD (Spanish). 1895 (16/1) foundered off
Cape Villano, Spain.

3. (1872) SHANNON
1,210. 73,14 x 9,93. (240.0 x 32.6). 1—2. I—S—C2—10. Gourlay Bros &
Co, Dundee. 1871 launched for J.A.Dunkerly & Co. 1872 (Apr) FV Liverpool—Boston for Warren (c) (3 RV). 1872 (Oct) FV Liverpool—Montreal
for Mercantile. 1872 (13/11) sailed from Sydney, CBI, on voyage
Montreal—London; went missing.

4. (1873) TAGUS
1,908. 81,59 x 10,18. (267.7 x 33.4). 1—2. I—S—I(2)—10. London &
Glasgow Co, Glasgow. 1868 (31/10) launched for J.A.Dunkerly & Co.
1871 (Jul) FV Liverpool—Boston for Warren (c). 1872 (20/7) FV Liverpool—Philadelphia for Mercantile. 1873 (27/3) LV ditto (4 RV). 1873
(14/9) FV London—Quebec—Montreal for Temperley (c). 1876 (16/9)
LV ditto (3 RV). 1898 sold to Germany. 1899 became hulk at Kiel.

5. (1873) GANGES
1,903. 81,53 x 10,18. (267.5 x 33.4). S—1—2. I—S—I(2)—10. London &
Glasgow Co, Glasgow. 1868 (3/9) launched for J.A.Dunkerly & Co. 1872
(14/8) FV Liverpool—Philadelphia for Mercantile (1 RV). 1872 (Oct) FV
Liverpool—Boston for Warren (c) (2RV). 1898 MERCURIUS (Italian).
1899 ditto (Swedish). 1899 (11/10) sunk in collision near Gothenburg;
refloated; resumed service. 1913 scrapped.

6. (1873) POTOMAC
1,832. 80,09 x 10,09. (262.8 x 33.1). 1—2. I—S—C2—10. London &
Glasgow Co, Glasgow. 1872 launched for Mercantile. 1872 (17/9) MV
Liverpool—Philadelphia for Mercantile (1 RV). 1873 (Sep) FV Liverpool
—Boston for Warren (c). 1893 (21/11) wrecked near Flamborough Head,
Yorkshire.

7. (1872) LADY LYCETT
1,833. 80,03 x 10,09. (262.6 x 33.1). S—1—2. I—S—C2—10. London &
Glasgow Co, Glasgow. 1872 launched for Mercantile. 1872 (30/10) FV

Liverpool—Philadelphia for Mercantile (2 RV). 1873 (28/5) FV for Great Western (c), Bristol—New York. 1874 (4/6) LV ditto (5 RV). 1891 LIFFEY (Mercantile). 1899 LIFFEY (Italian). 1901 (16/2) wrecked south of Minorca.

Total 4 RV Liverpool—Quebec—Montreal (including one by chartered steamer VIKING).
    8 RV Liverpool—Philadelphia.

FUNNEL : Black

FLAG : Blue, white 'MSCo'.

WHITE CROSS LINE

(Belgian)

Daniel Steinmann emigrated in 1852 from his native town of St Gallen, Switzerland, to Antwerp, where two years later he founded the firm of Steinmann & Cie, emigration agents. Soon afterwards he started an emigrant and cargo service from Antwerp to New York with chartered sailing ships, and later visited South America in preparation for the establishment of a second service to Brazil. In due course, sailings were extended to Montevideo and Buenos Aires. Steinmann & Cie adopted as their houseflag the Swiss national emblem, a white cross on a red field, so it was not to be wondered at that the Company became known as the WHITE CROSS LINE. It seems certain that this name was in use by 1860, if not before.

The Company relied entirely on chartered sailing ships until November 1863, when they decided to branch out as shipowners, the 213 ton brig HOMER being bought from Mr Le Couteur of Jersey and renamed HELVETIA in honour of Steinmann's country of birth. Two further sailing ships were acquired in 1865, one of them being sold three years later. The HELVETIA, too, was sold in 1870 and replaced in 1872 by the 1,188 ton American-built FREE TRADE, which was renamed HELVETIA (II). Meanwhile, many further sailing ships were chartered for both North and South Altantic trades. It was not uncommon for these and the Company's own vessels to make triangular voyages, Antwerp - South America - New York - Antwerp.

In 1871 a German national named Hermann Ludwig, who had been associated with Steinmann for a number of years, became a director, the style of the firm being changed to Steinmann, Ludwig & Cie. At this time, shortly after the Franco-Prussian War, trade was expanding rapidly and the number of emigrants proceeding via Antwerp increased by leaps and bounds. It was decided to place an order with Wigham Richardson & Co, on Tyneside, for an iron screw steamer, but in order to start steamship operations as soon as possible the 908 ton SELICA was chartered from Belgian owners for one round voyage from Antwerp to New York, where she arrived on 13 July 1872 with passengers and cargo after a protracted voyage of 23 days. She was consigned to Funch, Edye & Co, who acted as their brokers throughout the Company's long connection with the port of New York. (See Chapter 80).

The 1,263 ton White Cross STEINMANN was completed in time to sail from Antwerp on 12 October 1872. She undertook two further voyages before being joined by the 1,501 ton C.F.FUNCH, built in 1871 as the ALPS of the Glasgow & South American Steamship Company. She was named after Christian F. Funch, senior partner of Funch, Edye & Co, who had a one-third interest in the ship, as had both Steinmann, Ludwig & Cie and the latter's Antwerp loading broker, Auguste André. The two last-named each had a 50 per cent interest in the Company's next steamer, which was appropriately named AUGUSTE ANDRÉ and was built by Forges et Chantiers de la Méditerranée at La Seyne. She left Marseilles on 29 March 1874 for New York, returning from there to Antwerp.

Although the Engels Line had arranged for two steamship sailings from Antwerp to New York in 1871-2, they took no further part in this trade until 1876. A year previously, the only Belgian lines running steamers to New York were White Cross and Red Star. The latter first entered the Antwerp - New York trade in March 1874, and in the following year were employing one of their own steamers of 2,800 tons and a chartered British steamer of 2,500 tons, which between them were responsible for 15 arrivals at New York during the year, whereas the three White Cross steamers, whose average tonnage was only 1,400, undertook 16. Red Star carried many more passengers than its rival.

The C.F.FUNCH arrived in Flushing Roads from New York on 24 August 1876 with her cargo on fire; she was beached near the mouth of the Scheldt, was completely burnt out and a day or two later broke in two. To replace her the Company took delivery in Glasgow of the 1,505 ton ANDES, which was renamed HERMANN LUDWIG and sailed in February 1877 from Glasgow to Buenos Aires, from where she proceeded to Rio de Janeiro, Norfold (Virginia), New York and finally Antwerp. She then undertook a round voyage between Antwerp and New York and in August 1878 was advertised to proceed from London to Boston via Antwerp and Halifax. She sailed from New York for Antwerp on 28 September 1878 and went missing.

The Company acquired the 1,790 ton KHÉDIVE from A. Smyers & Cie of Antwerp in February 1877, renamed her DANIEL STEINMANN and handed over in exchange the STEINMANN, which Smyers renamed ALEXANDRE SMYERS. The KHÉDIVE had proved too large for the Antwerp - Baltic trade, in which she had been engaged, and presumably White Cross were able to strike a satisfactory bargain.

In March 1878 the 1,958 ton Engels Line MERCATOR, whose only previous activity had been a voyage to South America, was chartered by White Cross for one voyage from Antwerp to New York, after which she and the 2,280 ton DE RUYTER started a regular service on the same route. During the year they undertook nine voyages, the corresponding White

Cross total being no more than seven.

In order to avoid further wasteful competition, Daniel Steinmann announced in June 1879 that White Cross and Engels would henceforth run a joint passenger and cargo service to New York under the description White Cross line. This arrangement did not include the Engels sailing ships, nor did it affect in any way their steamship service to South America. More or less simultaneously, Auguste André ceased to be White Cross loading broker in Antwerp and, in consequence, the steamer named after him became the HELVETIA, the second sailing ship of that name having been sold. It should be added that New York voyages by Red Star increased from 15 in 1878 to 22 in 1879, when they had at their disposal six steamers varying between 2,700 and 3,700 tons. It is evident that a major reason for the formation of the White Cross - Engels joint service was to help them compete more successfully with Red Star.

The 2,417 ton HENRY EDYE started her maiden voyage for White Cross on 2 June 1879 from Sunderland, where she had been built by Doxford. She was named after one of the partners of Funch, Edye & Co, who had a half interest in the ship. Subsequently, she joined the White Cross DANIEL STEINMANN and HELVETIA and the Engels DE RUYTER and MERCATOR in the joint service, to which the 2,328 ton Engels PLANTYN was added in the following autumn. The MERCATOR was posted missing after leaving Antwerp for New York on 4 April 1880.

The 3,414 ton Engels Line JAN BREYDEL was added to the joint service during the summer of 1880 and was followed by the 3,310 ton PIETER DE CONINCK a year later, their maiden voyages starting from Newcastle and Glasgow, respectively, the ports where they were built. In addition, White Cross commissioned the 2,879 ton HERMANN in 1881, having bought her on the stocks. Unfortunately, the HENRY EDYE disappeared without trace after sailing from Antwerp on 19 November 1881.

During 1881 there were 36 joint arrivals at New York, passengers being carried on 27 of these occasions, the total number westbound being 48 cabin and 6,576 steerage. In 1882 the total was fractionally higher but in 1883, although voyages had increased to 43, passengers fell to 67 cabin and 3,157 steerage. In comparison, Red Star was running a regular weekly service on the route with six steamers varying between 3,700 and 5,700 tons, and landed 22,542 passengers at New York during 1884 in the course of 52 voyages.

From 1879 onwards, certain steamers called at London after leaving Antwerp for New York and others did so on the homeward voyage. A number of advertisements appeared in 1881 to the effect that the Company quoted a reduced rate of £4.18.0 third class from Hull and London each week to New York. There is no record of any of the steamers calling at Hull, and it would seem that these arrangements were normally made possible by

1881 HERMANN 2,879 tons
All eight White Cross steamers were lost, the
HERMANN and another under later owners.

transhipment at Antwerp.

The HELVETIA sailed from Antwerp to Quebec and Montreal during the summer of 1881. This experiment was fairly successful and further voyages to Canada were made during subsequent years. In 1883 White Cross acquired the 3,087 ton Norddeutscher Lloyd HANSA, which was renamed LUDWIG, sailed from Antwerp for Quebec and Montreal on 2 July 1883 and shortly afterwards disappeared without trace. Further voyages were made by the HELVETIA on the same route, but she foundered off the Canadian coast on 9 May 1885 after being damaged by ice, her passengers and crew being rescued by the Allan Line feeder steamer ACADIAN. This second disaster caused the abandonment of the service.

Two further losses were experienced by the joint fleet in 1883-4, the PLANTYN being abandoned at sea during a voyage from New York to Antwerp and the DANIEL STEINMANN foundering after striking a rock near Halifax *en route* from Antwerp to Halifax and New York.

In view of these losses and the continued drop in the number of passengers carried, it was decided during the early summer of 1884 that in future the steamers would cater for cargo only, the last passenger sailing being taken by the DE RUYTER, which left Antwerp on 22 July 1884 with 25 in the steerage. For another four years the White Cross HERMANN and the Engels DE RUYTER, JAN BREYDEL and PIETER DE CONINCK continued to take part in a joint Antwerp - New York cargo service, an intermediate call being usually made at Boston.

In the autumn of 1888 the nine-year-old agreement between Daniel Steinmann and Theodore Engels came to an end, and the latter again took over full responsibility for his steamers, of which the JAN BREYDEL and PIETER DE CONINCK were sold to the Thingvalla Line. The DE RUYTER was transferred to a single-ship company, the Société Anonyme du Steamer DE RUYTER, which was owned by T.C.Engels & Co, but managed by White Cross. One result of this reorganisation was that Hermann Ludwig left the firm of Steinmann, Ludwig & Cie, which reverted to the style Steinmann & Cie.

The HERMANN sailed from Antwerp for the last time on 3 December 1893 and was sold early in the following year. A few weeks later, on 12 March 1894, the DE RUYTER sailed from Antwerp for Boston and New York, passed the Lizard on the following day and was never heard of again. Thus, two of the five Engels Line steamers in the joint service went missing and another was abandoned at sea. The White Cross fleet was even more unfortunate as, between 1876 and 1885, no fewer than six of its eight steamers were lost at sea and three of the six went missing.

Neither line acquired any more ships, but it is of interest to note that the Antwerp firm of Steinmann & Cie is still in existence as shipbrokers and forwarding agents.

a. (1872) SELICA (c)

908. 68,97 x 9,38. (226.3 x 30.8). S—1—3. I—S—C2—10. A. Stephen & Sons, Glasgow (engines D. Rowan, Glasgow). 1872 (24/1) launched for F.J. Servais (Belg). 1872 (20/6) FV for White Cross (c), Antwerp—New York (1 RV). 1876 ALICE (CGT). 1904 AQUILA (Italian). 1909 LUIGINO (Italian). 1914-5 scrapped in Italy.

1. 1872 STEINMANN

1,263. 68,02 x 9,02. (223.2 x 29.6).I—S—C2—10. Wigham Richardson & Co, Walker-on-Tyne (engines Thompson, Boyd & Co, Newcastle). 1872 (/) launched. 1872 (12/10) MV Antwerp—New York. 1877 (8/2) LV ditto. 1877 ALEXANDRE SMYERS (Belg). 1881 (18/10) foundered off Hanstholm, Skagerrak.

2. (1873) C.F. FUNCH

1,501. 85,58 x 9,96. (280.8 x 32.7). 1—3. I—S—C2—10. J. Key & Sons, Kinghorn. 1871 (9/1) launched as ALPS (Br). 1873 C.F. FUNCH (White Cross). 1873 (15/5) FV Antwerp—New York. 1876 (24/8) arrived in Flushing Roads with cargo on fire; beached; burnt out; broke in two. (0).

3. 1874 AUGUST ANDRE
   (1879) HELVETIA

1,472. 81,95 x 9,99. (268.9 x 32.8). S—1—2. I—S—C2—10. Forges & Chantiers de la Méditerranée, La Seyne. 1874 (29/5) MV Marseilles—New York—Antwerp. 1874 (28/7) FV Antwerp—New York. 1879 (Mar) LV ditto. 1879 renamed HELVETIA. 1879 (Jul) FV Antwerp—New York. 1882-5 seasonal voys Antwerp—Quebec—Montreal. 1885 (9/5) foundered off Scatterie, CBI on voyage Antwerp—Montreal.

4. (1877) DANIEL STEINMANN

1,790. 84,57 x 10,51. (277.5 x 34.5). S—1—2. I—S—C2—10. Cockerill, Antwerp. 1875 (Jul) launched as KHEDIVE (Belg). 1877 DANIEL STEINMANN (White Cross). 1877 (9/3) FV Antwerp—New York. 1884 (20/3) sailed Antwerp—Halifax—New York. 1884 (3/4) foundered near Sambro Island, Nova Scotia (123).

5. (1877) HERMANN LUDWIG

1,505. 82,84 x 9,81. (271.8 x 32.2). 1—3. I—S—C2—10. J. Key & Sons, Kinghorn. 1870 (11/8) launched as ANDES (Br). 1877 HERMANN LUDWIG (White Cross). 1877 (Feb) FV Antwerp—S America—New York (arr 9/6)—Antwerp. 1877 (16/7) FV Antwerp—New York. 1878 (28/9) sailed New York—Antwerp; went missing (50).

6. 1879 HENRY EDYE

2,417. 94,82 x 10,67. (311.1 x 35.0). S—1—2. I—S—C2—11. W. Doxford

& Sons, Sunderland. 1879 (25/3) launched. 1879 (2/6) MV Sunderland—
New York—Antwerp. 1879 (15/7) FV Antwerp—New York. 1881 (19/11)
sailed Antwerp—New York; went missing.

7. 1881 HERMANN
2,879. 98,20 x 12,19. (322.2 x 40.0). C—1—3. I—S—C2—11. Sunderland
Shipbuilding Co (engines G. Clark, Sunderland). Bought on stocks from
D.G. Pinkney & Sons. 1881 (28/4) launched. 1881 (30/6) MV Antwerp—
New York. 1894 (3/12) LV Antwerp—Boston—New York. 1894 HERO
(Nor). 1907 SUCCESS (US). 1908 JACOB LUCKENBACH (US). 1916
(5/7) sunk in collision with ss EDDYSTONE near Downs Light Vessel,
English Channel.

8. (1883) LUDWIG
3,087. 99,97 x 12,89. (328.0 x 42.3). C—1—3. I—S—C2—11. Caird & Co,
Greenock. 1861 (23/8) launched as HANSA (NDL). 1883 LUDWIG
(White Cross). 1883 (2/7) sailed Antwerp—Montreal; went missing
(70-80). (See NDL - 60).

Note: The following Engels Line steamers ran in a joint White Cross - Engels service
(See Chapter 108):-

1879-94   DE RUYTER
1879-80   MERCATOR
1879-83   PLANTYN
1880-88   JAN BREYDEL
1881-89   PIETER DE CONINCK

FUNNEL: (a) 1872. Black
    (b) 1888. Black with reproduction of houseflag.

FLAG: Red; white cross.

SOUTH WALES ATLANTIC STEAMSHIP COMPANY

(British)

The SOUTH WALES ATLANTIC STEAMSHIP COMPANY owed its existence to the Marquess of Bute, who was one of the principal shareholders and had also played a prominent part in the construction of Cardiff Docks. Thanks to him, the Company was excused payment of dock dues at Cardiff and the ships were bunkered there free of charge.

The first unit of the fleet, the 2,411 ton iron screw GLAMORGAN, was launched by W. Simons & Co of Renfrew on 4 September 1872, and sailed from Cardiff on 12 October of the same year for New York with 38 passengers. On her second voyage, starting on 2 December, she encountered strong westerly winds and high seas and was compelled to put in at St John's Newfoundland, to replenish her supply of coal.

A sister ship, the 2,410 ton PEMBROKE, started her maiden voyage on 24 March 1873 and, like the GLAMORGAN, was lighted by gas on the principle adopted for the White Star ADRIATIC and CELTIC. The arrangement was not a success. The two ships offered saloon, second cabin and steerage accommodation and the Company advertised that they 'provided every improvement for the comfort and convenience of passengers' - including pneumatic bells, libraries and pianos. [1] Steerage passengers were provided with mattresses; a stewardess was carried for female emigrants. [2]

During 1873 the Company arranged 12 sailings to New York, of which the GLAMORGAN and PEMBROKE were responsible for 11 and averaged 103 passengers a voyage, westbound. The final voyage of the year was undertaken by a chartered steamer, the 1,974 ton DELTA, which did not carry passengers on that occasion nor on a second voyage in 1874, when also the 1,638 ton ANDES made two round voyages carrying cargo only. With the assistance of these ships, 1874 voyages rose to 17 but that did not mean that the Company was doing well. Westbound passengers dropped to an average of about 30 a voyage and freight revenue fell equally sharply. The departure of the GLAMORGAN from Cardiff on 13 January 1875 was the Company's last - a sure sign that free coal and the absence of dock dues do not by themselves make for success.

A third steamer, the 3,000 ton CARMARTHEN, was never commissioned by the Company. It remains to add that a 400 ton steamer, the ESKDALE, was launched by G.W.Dodgin & Co of North Shields on 14 December 1871 for F.Ireland & Co of Middlesbrough. She was intended to run between Wales and France as a feeder steamer for the South Wales Atlantic Line, [3] and it can be assumed that her activities did not prove at all profitable.

[1]   *The Times* 9/4/1873 (advt)
[2]   *The Times* 5/7/1873 (advt)
[3]   *Mitchell's Maritime Register* 22/12/1871

1. 1872 GLAMORGAN
2,411. 97,56 x 11,15. (320.1 x 36.6). S—1—2. I—S—C2—11. W. Simons & Co, Renfrew. 1872 (4/9) launched. 1872 (12/10) MV Cardiff—New York. 1875 (13/1) LV ditto (arr 30/1) (16 RV). 1879 (8/4) FV for Warren (c), Liverpool—Boston. 1880 (17/2) FV for Adamson & Ronaldson (c), London—Boston (4 RV). 1882 reverted to Warren (c). 1883 (16/2) foundered on voyage Liverpool—Boston.

2. 1873 PEMBROKE
2,410. 97,95 x 11,15. (321.4 x 36.6). S—1—2. I—S—C2—11. W. Simons & Co,Renfrew. 1873 (15/2) launched. 1873 (24/3) MV Cardiff—New York. 1874 (7/10) LV ditto (arr 23/10) (12 RV). 1878 (19/1) FV for Warren (c), Liverpool—Boston. 1881 (20/5) sank off Boston after collision with ss GANOS; salved. 1883 MURCIANO (Spanish). 1893 (24/9) stranded at Chincoteague, Virginia; refloated; towed to Newport News; converted to barge.

CARMARTHEN
3,000 (Never ran for Company).

Total 32 RV (including two each by chartered steamers DELTA and ANDES).

FUNNEL: Black with two narrow white bands near top.

FLAG: White burgee with Prince of Wales' feathers in red.

(Note: Funnel and flag details should be accepted with caution).

PLATE, REUCHLIN & CO

(Dutch)

An unsuccessful attempt was made during the early 1850s to establish a steamship service between Holland and the United States, one of the promoters being F.J.Plate, head of a Rotterdam firm of shipping agents. Almost exactly 20 years later his son, Antoine, aged 24, decided that the time was ripe to make a further attempt and with the co-operation of O. Reuchlin, head of another Rotterdam shipping agency, founded a limited liability company, PLATE, REUCHLIN & CO, whose articles of association were signed on 8 February 1871. Capital of the company was 900,000 guilders (£75,000).

Orders were placed for the 1,700 ton iron screw ROTTERDAM and MAAS, contract prices being about £30,000 each, leaving the Company a working capital of less than £15,000. Dimensions of the ships were restricted by the size of the locks of the Voorne Canal, through which ships proceeding between Rotterdam and the North Sea had to pass as the New Waterway had not yet been completed. Much consternation was caused, therefore, when one of the heads of Henderson, Coulborn & Co, the builders, announced with pride at an after-dinner speech during the inaugural run of the ROTTERDAM from Glasgow to Rotterdam that as his firm always endeavoured to give good value for money the length of the ship was slightly greater than specified. Fortunately, when she entered the canal locks it was found that there were a few inches, but no more, to spare.

The ROTTERDAM, which had accommodation for eight first class and 288 steerage passengers, sailed from Rotterdam on 15 October 1872, called at Plymouth on the 20th and reached New York on 5 November with cargo and 67 passengers. She was consigned to Funch, Edye & Co. The MAAS followed on 20 November, experiencing strong westerly gales and was obliged to put in at Halifax on 16 December for coal. On her second voyage, the ROTTERDAM also had to call at Halifax for the same reason. In fact, she met with such appalling conditions that the second officer was washed off the bridge by a giant wave and drowned.

Before many months passed, it became abundantly clear that Plate, Reuchlin & Co had insufficient capital to continue the service. It was decided, therefore, to form a joint stock company, NEDERLANDSCH-AMERIKAANSCHE STOOMVAART MAATSCHAPPIJ, to take over their assets and liabilities. Details are in Chapter 100.

RED STAR LINE

1871. International Navigation Company (of Philadelphia)
1893. International Navigation Company (of New Jersey)
1902. International Mercantile Marine Company
(United States)

1872. Société Anonyme de Navigation Belge-Américaine
(Belgian)

1893. International Navigation Co Ltd (of Liverpool)
1927. Frederick Leyland & Company Limited
(British)

The INTERNATIONAL NAVIGATION COMPANY was founded in Philadelphia in 1871, receiving its charter from the State of Pennsylvania on 5 May that year, [1] less than a month after its neighbour, the American Line. Better-known as the RED STAR LINE from its houseflag of a red star on a white 'swallow-tail', the International Navigation Company was essentially an American concern even though its Red Star fleet flew the Belgian flag during the first 20 years or more of its existence. Some steamers continued to do so for much longer.

Principal instigators of the line were Peter Wright & Sons of Philadelphia, aided and abetted by the Pennsylvania Railroad. A partner of the firm, Clement Acton Griscom, born in 1841, was responsible for most of the preliminary negotiations. He proceeded to Europe in 1872 to attend the launching on 21 August of the first of the Company's steamers, the VADERLAND, [2] and to complete arrangements with John Bernard von der Becke, a well-known Antwerp shipowner, and William Edouard Marsily, a prominent Antwerp shipbroker, and others, for the formation of a Belgian subsidiary, SOCIÉTÉ ANONYME DE NAVIGATION BELGE-AMÉRICAINE, which was founded in Antwerp on 5 September 1872. Clement A. Griscom, Thomas A. Scott and another were nominated by the International Navigation Company and Peter Wright & Sons to seats on the board of the 'Société Anonyme', [3] the first-named choice being an obvious one and that of Scott very astute as he was senior vice-president of the Pennsylvania Railroad. There is nothing to show, however, that this giant corporation had any financial interest in the International Navigation Company or its subsidiary, but there was clearly close co-operation between the parties, and the same could be said of the International Navigation Company *vis-à-vis* the American Line, in whose foundation the railroad had played a leading part.

The Pennsylvania Railroad built a new ocean terminal at Philadelphia in preparation for the arrival of the first Red Star ship, together with warehouses and grain elevators and at a convenient site in the vicinity installed gear for handling petroleum from shore to ship. The fact that they also undertook to provide free docking facilities does not by any means indicate that they had a financial interest in the line. The main objective of the railroad was the rail haul of passengers and freight; provision of these port facilities was an indication that they were determined to get a full share of both.

1873 VADERLAND 2,748 tons
Designed for passengers and petroleum in bulk but
never carried the latter.

A product of Palmers Shipbuilding & Iron Company Limited, of Jarrow-on-Tyne, the 2,748 ton iron screw VADERLAND was the first steamer designed to carry petroleum in bulk and for this reason bore some slight resemblance to the tanker of the 1920s and 1930s, her funnel and engines being placed aft, between the mainmast and the mizzen. Petroleum exports from Philadelphia in 1871 had reached a total value of nearly £3,000,000 and Peter Wright & Sons were the leading firm in the trade, shipments to Antwerp having hitherto been made, in barrels, by sailing ship. [4] The VADERLAND had berths for 30 first class and 800 steerage passengers, the intention being to carry passengers and merchandise westbound and passengers and petroleum eastbound.

Sailing from Antwerp on 20 January 1873 and from Falmouth on the 30th, the VADERLAND encountered a severe gale in the Atlantic, was compelled to put in at Halifax for coal, left on 14 February and reached Philadelphia on the 17th with 105 passengers and a fair cargo from Newcastle and Antwerp. [5] She sailed again on 26 February, being advertised to carry cabin and third class passengers to Antwerp at fares of $100 and $30, respectively. At an invitation dinner on board two days previously, James A. Wright of Peter Wright & Sons 'explained the construction of the vessel and its arrangements for carrying liquid freight'.

[6] However, it is certain that she carried neither petroleum nor petroleum products, and her cargo consisted of bark, hides, lard, tallow, tobacco and large consignments of bacon. [7] Nor did the dangerous combination of passengers and petroleum take place on subsequent eastbound voyages. It is evident that the American authorities had banned the arrangement.

It was stated in Philadelphia on 27 May 1873 that the 2,554 ton ABBOTSFORD, 'pioneer steamer of the Red Star Line's Liverpool service, arrived yesterday from Liverpool and Queenstown on her first voyage, bringing 294 passengers.' [8] She had been launched in March 1873 for Williamson, Milligan & Co of Liverpool for the South American trade. Although no pains had been spared to prevent sailings of this new service clashing with those of the American Line on the same route, there was justification for the general public getting the impression that the two services were competitive. However, this was not the case as the 25th annual report of the Pennsylvania Railroad, issued on 20 February 1872, stated that arrangements had been reached between the American Line and the International Navigation Company for certain interchanges, of which this was undoubtedly one. The reason for Red Star being called in was that the American Line was endeavouring to obtain an American mail subsidy. Considerable emphasis had been laid on the fact that the company came into being with American capital and that the ships, having been built in America, flew the 'Stars and Stripes'. With negotiations still in progress, it would have been the height of folly to introduce into the American Line service chartered ships wearing the British flag, so it was a logical move for the line to arrange, temporarily, with Red Star to operate the chartered steamers.

A sister ship, the 2,595 ton KENILWORTH, which had been completed a year previously, was scheduled to leave Liverpool on 11 July. Soon afterwards advertisements stated that the International Navigation Company (Red Star Line) fleet consisted of the ABBOTSFORD, KENILWORTH and two other steamers (no names mentioned) of 3,250 and 3,340 tons, respectively, which were under construction. Fares quoted were £18 saloon, 9 guineas intermediate and 6 guineas steerage. [9]

After further sailings by the VADERLAND, the 2,114 ton RYDAL HALL was chartered in August 1873 for two round voyages between Antwerp and Philadelphia pending the commissioning, in November 1873, of the 2,839 ton NEDERLAND. Shortly afterwards advertisements stated that the Red Star fleet consisted of the VADERLAND, NEDERLAND, SWITZERLAND and RHYNLAND. The SWITZERLAND was nearing completion, but it was not until 1879 that a ship bearing the name RHYNLAND was commissioned. The NEDERLAND and SWITZERLAND, unlike the VADERLAND, had engines amidships and two masts instead of three. A description of the

831

1874 SWITZERLAND 2,816 tons
Unlike the pioneer VADERLAND, had her
engines amidships. Sister ship NEDERLAND.

launching of the SWITZERLAND in January 1874 stated that she was intended for carrying oil. [10] In all probability both ships were laid down with this in mind, but it is certain that neither actually did so.

The ABBOTSFORD and KENILWORTH continued to sail at approximately four-weekly intervals until March 1874 when, without warning, the Red Star service was withdrawn and both joined the PENNSYLVANIA and her three sisters in the American Line's service between the same ports, that is to say, Philadelphia and Liverpool. Some little time previously the American Line had closed their offices in Philadelphia and had appointed the Red Star agents, Peter Wright & Sons, to represent them. There was a further justification for the transfer of the two ships, the final one being that all efforts on the part of the American Line to obtain an American subsidy had failed. They did, however, secure a mail contract, the terms of which did not debar them from chartering foreign ships.

A development of far-reaching importance, came on 11 March 1874 in the form of a subsidy of $100,000 (£20,000) a year for ten years being awarded Red Star by the Belgian Government, with certain other privileges worth an additional $30,000, in return for a new line of steamers between Antwerp and New York. This was opened on the date mentioned by the 1,980 ton CYBELE, chartered from the Donaldson Line, for whose Glasgow - South America service she had been launched in the previous January. The second New York sailing, and her maiden voyage, was undertaken on 24 April by the SWITZERLAND, which was to have been followed a month later by the NEDERLAND. Instead, however, the COLINA was substituted. This 2,001 ton sister ship of the CYBELE had been completed for the Donaldson Line a year previously. She made five round voyages for Red Star and acted as the SWITZERLAND's consort on the New York route until the end of 1874. The CYBELE had only undertaken one round voyage between Antwerp and New York, but subsequently made two to Philadelphia before returning to her owners. The VADERLAND and NEDERLAND were then jointly responsible for the Antwerp - Philadelphia service until the early months of 1877.

After completing her Red Star service, the COLINA was replaced by the 2,488 ton STATE OF NEVADA, which was temporarily superfluous on the State Line's Glasgow - New York route. She had accommodation for 75 first class, 35 intermediate and 550 steerage passengers.

The ABBOTSFORD was wrecked on Anglesey in July 1875, but the KENILWORTH remained in American Line service until the following December. Three months later she sailed at short notice for Red Star in place of the STATE OF NEVADA and for a year acted as consort of the SWITZERLAND on the Antwerp - New York service. Just before the start of her eighth voyage, having been bought by the Company, her name was

1877 RUSLAND 2,595 tons
Built 1872 as KENILWORTH. Wrecked during
first Red Star voyage as RUSLAND.

changed to RUSLAND (the Flemish name for Russia) and 12 days later, on 17 March 1877, she went ashore at Long Branch, New Jersey. Despite high hopes that she would be refloated, she became a total loss.

From the spring of 1877 onwards, the SWITZERLAND, NEDERLAND and VADERLAND shared responsibility for the New York service, and in May 1878 were joined by the 2,866 ton JAVA, built for Cunard in 1865. After her third voyage she was renamed ZEELAND. The Antwerp - Philadelphia service was discontinued from March 1877 for about a year.

1879 RHYNLAND 3,689 tons
Typical of the Red Star fleet of the 1880s

Despite the many difficulties experienced by the North Atlantic lines during the 1870s and the fact that two other Belgian lines - White Cross and Engels - started services between Antwerp and the USA at about the same time as Red Star, the latter not only weathered the storm but went ahead much more successfully that either of them and in 1879 was able to commission the 3,700 ton BELGENLAND and RHYNLAND, which were more than 15 metres (50 feet) longer than any previous units of the fleet. Each had a straight stem, single funnel and four masts, passenger capacity being 150 first class and 1,000 steerage.

It will now be appropriate to refer to what many have hitherto regarded as the Red Star Line's mystery ship - the 3,446 ton PERUSIA, which had been commissioned in 1857 as the P&O NEMESIS and had been employed on the North Atlantic by Cunard, Inman and Norddeutscher Lloyd. In 1878 she was acquired by the Société Anonyme de Navigation à Vapeur Belge and renamed PERUSIA. It transpires that this concern had no connection with the Société Anonyme de Navigation Belge - Américaine, [11] although through some mistake Lloyd's Register included her in their fleet list, and this was largely responsible for the confusion.

Red Star advertisements in January 1881 mentioned the 'new' steamer WAESLAND which, in fact, was none other that the ex-Cunarder RUSSIA, dating from 1867. Before re-entering service she was lengthened from 109,11 to 132,61 metres (358.0 to 435.1 feet) and thereby lost her well-nigh perfect proportions, although the addition of a fourth mast preserved some sense of symmetry. Opportunity was also taken to fit her with

835

compound engines which, nine years later, were converted to triple-expansion. In her altered condition she had a tonnage of 4,752 and accommodation for 120 first class and 1,500 steerage passengers.

A third Cunarder joined the fleet in 1882 in the form of the PENNLAND (ex-ALGERIA). This time there was no lengthening, but her engines were compounded and six years later a new spar deck was added, increasing her tonnage from 3,428 to 3,760.

In 1882, for the first time, the Company had sufficient tonnage to run a weekly service between Antwerp and New York plus an occasional one between Antwerp and Philadelphia. Their intention was to increase the latter to fortnightly at the first opportunity.

The 5,736 ton WESTERNLAND, built in a dry dock, was floated by Laird of Birkenhead on 4 August 1883 and was notable as the first steel unit of the fleet. She was also the first with two funnels. On the following 1 November the same builders launched the 5,212 ton NOORDLAND, which had a length of 121,91 metres (400 feet) compared with the WESTERNLAND's 134,10 metres (440 feet) and had a single funnel.

1883 WESTERNLAND 5,736 tons
Red Star Antwerp—New York service. Funnel
markings are those from 1893 onwards.

1884 NOORDLAND 5,212 tons
Consort of the WESTERNLAND but slightly
smaller.

Until 1878 the usual arrangement had been for the VADERLAND and NEDERLAND to run to Philadelphia and the others to New York. From then until 1882 there was a degree of interchangeability between the two services, and from time to time both steamers ran to New York whereas various other units, including the SWITZERLAND, ZEELAND,

WAESLAND and, on one occasion, the BELGENLAND proceeded to Philadelphia. From early days, the New York service was clearly regarded as the more important and was not only the more frequent but usually had the newest and best ships. From 1884 onwards the WESTERNLAND, NOORDLAND, RHYNLAND, BELGENLAND, PENNLAND and WAESLAND were the steamers normally responsible for maintaining the weekly service to and from New York.

In the space of ten years the Company had increased its fleet from three to ten ships, the latest of which had a tonnage appreciably greater than the combined tonnage of the first two. The next move, in 1884, was of an entirely different character and resulted in the purchase by the International Navigation Company (Red Star Line) of the four American-flag steamers of the American Line's Philadelphia - Liverpool service. This was continued under its existing name without any important change. Two years later the Company's position was strengthened still further by buying the British-owned Inman Line, which had gone into liquidation, together with its fleet of five steamers. All continued to run under the red ensign. The Inman Steamship Company Limited was renamed Inman & International Steamship Company Limited.

An interesting result of the acquisition of the American Line by International Navigation Company was that the former's 3,300 ton ILLINOIS and PENNSYLVANIA were detailed in 1887 to the Antwerp - New York service as extra steamers, and the INDIANA made one similar voyage in 1889. At first they carried a limited number of second class as well as steerage passengers, but from the latter part of 1889 onwards merchandise only was carried, at any rate westbound. In 1890 the 2,328 ton cargo steamer SACROBOSSO was bought by the International Navigation Company after being damaged by fire at Baltimore, scuttled and refloated. She was renamed CONEMAUGH and, sailing under the American flag, took part spasmodically in the Antwerp - New York service until 1897. The ILLINOIS and PENNSYLVANIA were fitted with triple-expansion engines in 1891. From the spring of 1892 onwards their Red Star activities were confined to the Red Star Antwerp - Philadelphia trade.

Red Star landed an average of well over 25,000 passengers at New York each year between 1881 and 1889. The steerage figures were remarkably consistent during this period, but the combined first and second class figures rose steadily from 1,500 to over 4,000 a year. This satisfactory state of affairs enabled the Company to place an order for the 7,100 ton single-screw FRIESLAND, which started her maiden voyage from Antwerp to New York on 7 December 1889. Her passenger complement was 226 first class, 102 second and 600 steerage, she was the only ship laid down by the Company to have a clipper stem and was the first with triple-expansion engines. The pioneer VADERLAND and the ZEELAND, first of the ex-

1884 NOORDLAND 5,212 tons (left)
1889 FRIESLAND 7,116 tons (right)
Two successful ships that eventually ran for
American Line.

Cunard ships, were sold. Red Star were obviously justified in building the FRIESLAND as they carried no fewer than 5,504 first and second class and 35,870 steerage passengers from Antwerp to New York in 1891, the combined total of 41,374 being exceeded only by two British and two German lines.

The four surviving Inman & International ships began to trade under the style American Line in 1893. Two were transferred to the American flag under the ownership of the reconstructed INTERNATIONAL NAVIGATION COMPANY, of New Jersey, and the others retained their British registry, shortly afterwards coming under the ownership of the INTERNATIONAL NAVIGATION COMPANY LIMITED, of Liverpool, formed on 13 July 1893. An interesting result of these moves was that both the Red Star and American lines adopted the Inman black funnel with white band.

Major changes in the Company's fleet came in 1895. First and foremost, the 8,600 ton twin-screw SOUTHWARK and KENSINGTON, which flew the British flag and had been completed rather more than a year previously for the American Line's Philadelphia - Liverpool service, were transferred to the Antwerp - New York trade. It is important to note that they carried second and third class passengers and cargo only, and were at the time the largest and finest ships to dispense with first class. In exchange, the PENNLAND, BELGENLAND, RHYNLAND and WAESLAND joined the American Line's Liverpool fleet.

In October 1895 a weekly Red Star service began to operate from New York to Antwerp on a mail subsidy basis of $4 a mile eastbound. Ships employed were the SOUTHWARK, KENSINGTON, FRIESLAND, WESTERNLAND and NOORDLAND, with occasional assistance from the BERLIN, which had become superfluous to the American Line's Southampton - New York service following completion of the ST. LOUIS and ST. PAUL, but returned to it for a short time during the Spanish-American War of 1898. A few weeks later she was bought by the US Government. The BERLIN's consort, the CHESTER, never ran for Red Star, although a tanker of that name made some voyages - not for Red Star - between Antwerp and the USA during the 1890s.

The average tonnage of the Company's regular New York fleet at this time was 7,800 - a very commendable figure, and one that was exceeded only by the steamers running on the premier services of the American, CGT, Cunard, Hamburg American and White Star lines.

The ILLINOIS, PENNSYLVANIA, NEDERLAND and SWITZERLAND were available for the Antwerp - Philadelphia service until 1897, when the first two were sent to the Pacific.

During the autumn and winter of 1898-9 greatly increased cargo requirements resulted in the chartering of the Hamburg American ITALIA,

SCOTIA, ARAGONIA and ADRIA for a total of 11 round voyages between Antwerp and New York; the ITALIA and ARAGONIA were subsequently responsible for a similar number between Antwerp and Philadelphia. All carried cargo and third class passengers only for Red Star. On the ADRIA's second westbound voyage from Antwerp starting on 19 January 1899 her captain was knocked down by a giant wave when descending from the bridge to the cabin and was picked up dead. Further misfortune followed as on 9 March, at the start of her third voyage, the ADRIA collided with the British steamer AMARYLLIS in the River Scheldt. She returned to Antwerp for repairs and resumed her voyage on 21 March.

It was announced in July 1889 that four large steamers were under construction for Red Star, two in Britain and two in the United States. First to be completed was the 11,899 ton twin-screw VADERLAND (II), launched by John Brown of Clydebank on 12 July 1900. She had the then-popular combination of two funnels and four masts and was propelled by two sets of quadruple-expansion engines, which gave her a service speed of about 15 knots. Accommodation was provided for 342 first, 194 second and 626 third class passengers. Her maiden voyage started on 8 December 1900 from Antwerp to New York, with a call at Southampton to augment the American Line service, the regularity of which had been affected by the stranding of the PARIS on the Manacles, Cornwall, in May 1899. A similar voyage followed, and then she made three purely American Line voyages from Southampton to New York via Cherbourg.

1901 ZEELAND 11,905 tons
Built in Britain, as was sister ship VADERLAND.
Consorts built in USA: KROONLAND,
FINLAND.

The second of the British-built ships, the ZEELAND (II), took her place in the Company's service in April 1901. Both newcomers were registered in the name of the International Navigation Company Limited, of Liverpool, and therefore flew the British flag, but from 1903 until the outbreak of World War I the VADERLAND was transferred to the Société Anonyme de Navigation Belge-Américaine under Belgian registry, probably owing to the disposal of many of their older Belgian-flag steamers and a desire to keep the Belgian flag prominently before the public.

Similar in most essentials to their immediate predecessors except that they flew the American flag and had triple instead of quadruple-expansion engines, the second pair, the KROONLAND and FINLAND, were completed by Cramp of Philadelphia in 1902. Owing to their higher speed, the quartette were capable of maintaining a weekly service between Antwerp and New York whereas previously a minimum of five ships had been required. Although there were a number of larger steamers in other services by this time, all four exceeded in tonnage the largest unit of the American Line fleet.

In 1902 the International Navigation Company, of New Jersey, under the guidance of J.Pierpont Morgan, and aided and abetted by W. J. Pirrie, head of Harland & Wolff, changed its name to INTERNATIONAL MERCANTILE MARINE COMPANY and increased its capital from $15,000,000 to $120,000,000, following or in preparation for the purchase of the entire share capital of the White Star, Dominion, Atlantic Transport and Leyland lines and the acquisition of an interest in Holland America. The activities of the Red Star and American lines were not affected and they continued to work together in close harmony. Moreover, the International Navigation Company Limited, of Liverpool, continued in operation without change of name and became the registered owners of two British-flag additions to the American Line fleet - the 11,635 ton HAVERFORD and the 11,621 ton MERION. The former made four Red Star voyages to New York in 1901-2, and the latter one in 1907.

From time to time, there were many interchanges of tonnage between the various wholly-owned subsidiaries of IMM and for a variety of reasons. The transfer of the WESTERNLAND and NOORDLAND to the American Line's Philadelphia - Liverpool service in 1901 and of the FRIESLAND in 1903 was due entirely to the commissioning of the new Red Star quartette, and would undoubtedly have taken place irrespective of the formation of IMM. The transfer in April 1903 of the KENSINGTON and SOUTHWARK to the Dominion Line's Liverpool - Quebec - Montreal service came about for the same reason. They remained the property of the International Navigation Company Limited of Liverpool.

Starting in December 1900, certain Red Star steamers began to call at Southampton outwards and homewards, but the arrangement cannot have been an unqualified success - perhaps because it was trespassing on American Line preserves - as it was discontinued in 1902. Instead, Red Star ships put in at Dover outwards and homewards from August 1904, and this arrangement continued until the outbreak of World War I.

During 1904 the Antwerp - Philadelphia service was operated by the SWITZERLAND, BELGENLAND and RHYNLAND, the two last-named having returned to Antwerp after several years in the American Line's Philadelphia - Liverpool service. Both were long past their prime

NAS–24 **   841

and, along with the NEDERLAND, were sold in 1905-6. They were replaced by the 7,000 ton MANITOU, MENOMINEE and MARQUETTE, which were no longer required by Atlantic Transport on the London - New York route following the completion of the MINNEAPOLIS, MINNEHAHA and MINNETONKA.

1908 GOTHLAND 7,755 tons
Built in 1893 as White Star GOTHIC.

Red Star's American-flag fleet was augmented in July 1906 by the 7,913 ton Atlantic Transport MISSISSIPPI, which sailed as such from Antwerp and upon arrival at New York was renamed SAMLAND. The 7,755 ton White Star GOTHIC, well-known for many years in the New Zealand trade, became the Belgian-flag GOTHLAND in 1907. She was sent to Harland & Wolff for conversion into an emigrant carrier, with accommodation for over 1,800 third class passengers, all in four-berth rooms. Three years later the SAMLAND was transferred from United States to Belgian registry. Between 1911 and 1913 both ships were temporarily transferred to White Star as the British-flag BELGIC and GOTHIC, after which they resumed their Red Star names and Belgian registry. In addition, the Dominion CAMBROMAN made four round voyages between Antwerp and New York in 1907, a year when steerage business was booming, and carried well over 1,000 passengers on each westbound voyage.

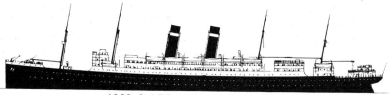

1909 LAPLAND 17,540 tons
Commissioned under the Belgian flag but later flew
the British.

The 17,540 ton twin-screw LAPLAND was launched on 27 June 1908 and started her maiden voyage from Antwerp to New York on 10 April

1909. Her instant success and the increasing Holland America competition, led to an order for the 27,000 ton BELGENLAND (II), which was launched on 31 December 1914.

The White Star REPUBLIC had been sunk in collision a few weeks before the LAPLAND entered service, and as Red Star had a surplus steamer they were glad of the opportunity to transfer the ZEELAND to the White Star Liverpool - Boston service during much of 1910-1. -She already sailed under the British flag, but when she completed her White Star duties she joined the LAPLAND and VADERLAND as a Belgian-flag unit of the Société Anonyme de Navigation Belge-Américaine. Between 1908 and 1912 the American-flag FINLAND and KROONLAND were also transferred to Belgian registry. A likely reason for these moves was the friendly relationship that existed between King Leopold (II) of Belgium and Pierpont Morgan, who still had an active interest in IMM.

The Hamburg American Line and Norddeutscher Lloyd, in association with Holland America and Red Star, started a joint passenger service in the spring of 1909 between Hamburg, Bremen, Rotterdam, Quebec and Montreal. From 1911 onwards Red Star contributed occasional sailings - at first by the SAMLAND and GOTHLAND, but the ZEELAND made a call at Halifax in 1912 *en route* to New York and the VADERLAND did the same in 1913.

The rapid advance of the German army through Belgium in August 1914 and the threat to Antwerp quickly resulted in the transfer of the Red Star headquarters and European terminal to Liverpool, and the decision to place all the Belgian-flag ships except the GOTHLAND and SAMLAND under the British flag. This meant that they were re-registered in the name of the International Navigation Company Limited, of Liverpool - a decision largely influenced by the fact that shippers thereby had the benefit of the British war insurance scheme for cargo.

The KROONLAND sailed from New York on 15 August 1914, the original intention being for her to proceed to Antwerp. Instead, she was diverted to Liverpool and left there for New York on 28 August, followed at weekly intervals by the FINLAND, ZEELAND and VADERLAND. Upon arrival at New York the ZEELAND was despatched to Canada to join the 31 other ships of the convoy in which the First Canadian Expeditionary Force sailed for England on 3 October. Another member of this convoy was the LAPLAND which, at the conclusion of these duties, was detailed to White Star's Liverpool - New York service. The ZEELAND then made one voyage for White Star - Dominion from Liverpool to Quebec and Montreal. Subsequently, the VADERLAND and she proceeded to Halifax and Portland owing to the winter closure of the St Lawrence.

In the spring of 1915 the ZEELAND was renamed NORTHLAND and

the VADERLAND became the SOUTHLAND in order to overcome the unpopularity of the latter's German-sounding name which, however, was really Flemish. Shortly afterwards, both were taken up by the British Government as troopships. The SOUTHLAND was torpedoed in the Aegean Sea in September 1915, managed to reach port, was repaired and in August 1916 detailed again to White Star - Dominion, for whom she was joined at once by the NORTHLAND. The SOUTHLAND's reprieve was, unfortunately, only temporary as she was torpedoed and sunk off the Irish coast on 4 June 1917.

After completing two or three round voyages between New York and Liverpool, the KROONLAND and FINLAND, still under Red Star auspices, undertook one and three voyages, respectively, between New York and the Mediterranean. Next, they each made some voyages during 1915 for the allied Panama Pacific Line between New York, the Panama Canal and San Francisco. Then came one or two voyages between New York and London for the American Line before they were detailed, early in 1916, to the same company's service between New York and Liverpool, an arrangement that continued until the United States entered the war in 1917, when they were taken up as American transports.

The SAMLAND ran as an Atlantic Transport cargo steamer between London and New York from 2 October 1914 until 29 February 1916, after which she and the GOTHLAND made at least three voyages each between New York, Falmouth and Rotterdam for the Belgian Relief Commission.

The MESABA had joined her sister ships MANITOU, MARQUETTE and MENOMINEE in the Antwerp - Philadelphia trade in May 1914 and had undertaken two earlier voyages between these ports. Sooner or later all four resumed ATL service between London and New York. The MESABA was torpedoed and sunk in September 1918.

An event that passed almost unnoticed owing to the war was the appointment, in April 1915, of a receiver to handle the affairs of the International Mercantile Marine Company. At that time the market value of the stock was approximately $26,500,000, whereas the paper value was almost $172,000,000. Thanks to the efforts of the receiver, P.A.S.Franklin, and the shipping boom brought about by the war, the market value had risen barely a year later to $165,000,000. In recognition of his great work, Franklin was appointed president of the company.

In August 1919 Franklin proceeded to Belgium to make arrangements for the early resumption of Red Star's Antwerp - New York mail service. The SAMLAND and GOTHLAND were already running as cargo and emigrant carriers and, in addition, the Leyland Line cargo steamer LANCASTRIAN had been detailed to the route. In due course the Company operated a wide variety of American-flag cargo steamers on behalf of the United States Shipping Board.

It was not until 3 January 1920 that the LAPLAND, still flying the red ensign and having undergone a drastic reconditioning which increased her gross tonnage to 18,565, sailed from Antwerp for Southampton and New York. The 13,639 ton MANCHURIA and MONGOLIA, of the American Line, each made one call at Antwerp *en route* from Hamburg to Southampton and New York and then, in April 1920, the American-flag KROONLAND and FINLAND re-entered the service, as did the British-flag ZEELAND four months later. The Southampton call became a permanent feature westbound, and from 1921 the steamers also put in at Cherbourg. From time to time they proceeded via Halifax to cater for passengers to Canada. The eastbound itinerary was New York - Plymouth - Cherbourg - Antwerp.

Resumption of sailings by the ZEELAND brought the service up to strength, and enabled the GOTHLAND and SAMLAND to be transferred to a new cargo and emigrant service between Libau (Liepaja), Danzig (Gdansk), Hamburg and New York, in which they were joined in 1921 by the 6,849 ton POLAND, formerly the MANITOU of the pre-war Antwerp - Philadelphia service. Libau sailings continued until September 1923, but in April 1922 the POLAND and the White Star VEDIC started a new White Star emigrant service between Bremen, Southampton, Cherbourg, Quebec and Montreal.

The BELGENLAND (II) had been completed without her upper and lower promenade decks and commissioned in June 1917 as the troopship BELGIC under White Star management. After the Armistice her funnels were, despite her White Star-sounding name, painted black with a white band - presumably to show her Red Star origins or intentions - and she ran in the White Star cargo service between Liverpool and New York until early 1921. She then returned to Harland & Wolff for an extensive overhaul and the addition of her passenger accommodation. Upon arrival at Antwerp for the first time in March 1923 few people would have recognised her as the same ship since, quite apart from her now lofty superstructure, she had three funnels and two masts instead of two funnels and three masts, as formerly.. These alterations had increased her gross tonnage from 24,547 to 27,132. She had reverted to the name BELGENLAND but continued to fly the British flag, her registered owners still being the International Navigation Company Limited, of Liverpool. She had dimensions of 204,32 x 23,89 metres (670.4 x 78.4 feet), and at that time was the ninth largest steamship in service in the world. Her triple screws were driven by a combination of triple-expansion engines and a low-pressure turbine on the well-known Harland & Wolff principle, giving her a service speed of 17 knots. To begin with, she catered for 500 first, 500 second and 1,500 third class passengers, but in April 1927 part of the second class and the best of the third class accommodation was devoted to a new class known officially

1917 BELGIC 24,547 tons
Reverted to BELGENLAND when passenger
accommodation was added in 1923.

as tourist third cabin to which, two years later, her entire second class accommodation was transferred. During the course of her career, the BELGENLAND undertook several round the world cruises.

1923 BELGENLAND 27,132 tons
Completed in 1917 as White Star cargo steamer
BELGIC with two funnels and three masts.

The KROONLAND and FINLAND completed their Red Star service shortly before the BELGENLAND's first sailing from Antwerp for New York on 4 April 1923. For the next few months they ran for the American Line between Hamburg and New York and then, in the autumn of 1923, were transferred - not for the first time - to the allied Panama Pacific Line for service between New York, the Panama Canal and San Francisco. Both were scrapped in 1928. The BELGENLAND, LAPLAND and ZEELAND, occasionally helped by the GOTHLAND and SAMLAND, took care of the mail service during the next year or two, but for several weeks during the summer of 1924 the poor state of the River Scheldt made it inadvisable for the BELGENLAND and LAPLAND, on account of their size, to negotiate the awkward reaches below Antwerp and each was diverted to London for two or three voyages. At that time the BELGENLAND was the largest steamer ever to have visited the Thames.

Early in 1925 the White Star PITTSBURGH and ARABIC joined the Red Star service and a year later the former was renamed PENNLAND (II). She was a triple-screw steamer of 16,322 tons, had been laid down before the war for the American Line but since 1922 had been running for White Star. The ZEELAND made her last Red Star voyage in November 1926 and in the following year became the ATL MINNESOTA. The emigrant-carrier GOTHLAND was scrapped in 1926, but the SAMLAND survived for another five years, although she was laid up during some of this time. She was the last unit of the once-extensive fleet of the Société Anonyme de Navigation Belge-Américaine.

The Leyland Line's 10,405 ton WINIFREDIAN and the 12,153 ton DEVONIAN each made two or three voyages between Antwerp and New

York starting in November 1927, and carrying tourist third cabin passengers and cargo. The reason behind this move, which but for poor trading conditions would probably have continued indefinitely, was that the International Navigation Company Limited had been taken over by Frederick Leyland & Company Limited, together with the BELGENLAND, LAPLAND and PENNLAND. The Leyland Line had already acquired the Dominion Line's REGINA, a sister ship of the PENNLAND. In 1930 she was renamed WESTERNLAND (II) and detailed to the Antwerp - New York service in place of the ARABIC.

The worldwide trade depression during the early 1930s brought new problems to all North Atlantic lines. One of the most seriously affected was the Atlantic Transport, whose 22,000 ton MINNEWASKA and MINNETONKA catered for 369 first class passengers and no less than 1,000,000 cubic feet of cargo - that is to say, 25,000 tons measurement. It was found impossible to keep the ships profitably employed in the London - New York trade during the slump and the ATL service closed down. The MINNEWASKA and MINNETONKA were, therefore, transferred to Antwerp to act as consorts to the Red Star PENNLAND and WESTERNLAND, which had recently been catering exclusively for tourist and third class passengers. From now on they carried tourist only and the two 'MINNE' ships followed suit by the simple expedient of calling their first class accommodation tourist.

The BELGENLAND was laid up at Antwerp during the greater part of 1932, but in the summer of that year employment was found for the LAPLAND by despatching her on a series of Mediterranean cruises from London. These were repeated in 1933, but owing to disappointing financial results she was sold to Japan in October 1933 for scrapping. The BELGENLAND was brought out of retirement in July 1933 to undertake three Mediterranean cruises, but was then laid up again. She was subsequently transferred to the Atlantic Transport Company of West Virginia, renamed COLUMBIA and scrapped in 1936.

Unfortunately, the transfer of the MINNEWASKA and MINNETONKA to Antwerp brought no improvement in results, and the latter started her last voyage from Antwerp on 29 September 1933. The MINNEWASKA was to have followed a fortnight later, but the voyage was cancelled and both were laid up until the autumn of 1934 when, only 10 - 11 years old, they were sold for scrap. The PENNLAND and WESTERNLAND, with assistance between April and October 1934 from the Leyland cargo steamers DAKOTIAN and NUBIAN, made a few more voyages until 12 December 1934, when the sailing of the WESTERNLAND from New York for Havre, London and Antwerp marked the close of the Company's active career. The total number of passengers carried during 1934 was under 4,000. In comparison the 1913 total had been over 117,000,

848

but, of course, at that time three classes were carried and emigration from Europe to America was booming.

For some months previously negotiations had been proceeding for the purchase of the BELGENLAND, PENNLAND and WESTERNLAND by a British group headed by Major (later Lieut-Colonel) Frank Bustard, who planned to carry passengers across the North Atlantic at exceptionally low fares, with meals on a cafeteria basis. The British Treasury had, however, just advanced a vast sum for the completion of the QUEEN MARY and the building of a sister ship, and fearing the effect the proposed venture might have on the fortunes of Cunard-White Star, refused to give their sanction. The result was that the PENNLAND and WESTERNLAND were sold early in 1935 to Arnold Bernstein of Hamburg, who continued to employ them in the Antwerp - Southampton - New York trade under the description Bernstein (Red Star) Line.

During the greater part of the 61 years between 1873 and 1934 when the Red Star Line was in operation it could be regarded as one of the major North Atlantic lines, and throughout its life had a safety record second to none. However, its principal claim to fame was undoubtedly that it was the *raison d'être* of the International Mercantile Marine Company - the greatest international shipping organisation the world has ever known - and, almost equally important, it was the ancestor of the present-day United States Lines.

[1] Dr.William H. Flayhart (III) : *The American Line* 1873-95
[2] Dr.William H. Flayhard (III) : *The American Line* 1873-95
[3] Letter to N.R.P.Bonsor from the late F.J.HERMANS of Borgerhout, Belgium.
[4] Dr.William H. Flayhart (III) : *The American Line* 1873-95
[5] *Philadelphia North American & United States Gazette* 18/2/1873
[6] *Philadelphia North American & United States Gazette* 25/2/1873
[7] *Philadelphia Commercial List & Price Current* 1/3/1873
[8] *Philadelphia North American & United States Gazette* 27/5/1873
[9] *Liverpool Journal of Commerce* 8/8/1873
[10] *Mitchell's Maritime Register* 23/1/1874
[11] Letter to N.R.P.Bonsor from the late F.J.HERMANS of Borgerhout, Belgium.

1. 1873 VADERLAND (I) (B)
     2,748. 97,68 x 11,73. (320.5 x 38.5). S—1—3. (engines aft). I—S—C2—13. (I—30 (later 70); III—800). Palmers Shipbuilding & Iron Co, Jarrow-on-Tyne. 1872 (21/8) launched. 1873 (20/1) MV Antwerp—Falmouth—Halifax—Philadelphia. 1873 (25/3) FV Antwerp—Philadelphia. 1876

(29/11) FV Antwerp—New York. 1877-87 Antwerp—New York or Philadelphia. 1887(26/10) LV Antwerp—New York; subsequently Antwerp—Philadelphia. 1889 (Mar) GÉOGRAPHIQUE (French). 1889 (Oct) sunk in collision.

1a. 1873 ABBOTSFORD (c) (Br)
    2,554. 105,15 x 11,37. (345.0 x 37.3). S—1—2. I—S—C2—10. (I—20; III—500). Gourlay & Co, Dundee. 1873 (29/3) launched. 1873 (10/5) MV for Red Star (c), Liverpool—Queenstown—Philadelphia (7 RV). 1874 (11/3) FV ditto for American Line (c). 1875 (19/7) wrecked off Anglesey, Wales (0).

2. (1873) KENILWORTH (c) (Br)
    (1877) RUSLAND (B)
    2,595. 105,15 x 11,34. (345.0 x 37.2). S—1—2. I—S—C2—10. (I—20; III—500). Gourlay & Co, Dundee. 1872 (Aug) launched. 1873 (11/7) FV for Red Star (c), Liverpool—Philadelphia (6 RV). 1874 (25/3) FV for American Line (c) ditto. 1875 (Dec) LV ditto. 1876 (16/3) FV for Red Star (c), Antwerp—Philadelphia. 1877 (17/1) FV Antwerp—New York. 1877 RUSLAND (Red Star). 1877 (5/3) sailed Antwerp—New York. 1877 (17/3) wrecked at Long Beach, New Jersey (0).

2a. (1873) RYDAL HALL (c) (Br)
    2,114. 100,73 x 10,36. (330.5 x 34.0). 1—3. I—S—C2—10. London & Glasgow Co, Glasgow. 1871 (Jul) launched for R. Alexander, Liverpool. 1872 (Aug) FV for Beaver (c), Liverpool—Quebec—Montreal (1 RV). 1873 (Aug) FV for Red Star (c), Antwerp—Philadelphia (2 RV). 1873 CHILIAN (West India & Pacific). 1894 (29/1) abandoned in N Atlantic on voyage Norfolk—Liverpool.

3. 1873 NEDERLAND (B)
    2,839. 100,33 x 11,76. (329.2 x 38.6). S—1—2. I—S—C2—13. (I—70; III—800). Palmers Shipbuilding & Iron Co, Jarrow-on-Tyne.1873 (23/6) launched. 1873 (Nov) MV Antwerp—Philadelphia. 1877 (31/5) FV Antwerp—New York. 1877-96 Antwerp—New York or Philadelphia. 1895 (approx) III only. 1896 (26/11) LV Antwerp—New York; subsequently Antwerp—Philadelphia except 1905 (11/4) LV Antwerp—New York. 1906 (May) scrapped in Italy.

3a. 1874 CYBELE (c) (Br)
    1,980. 97,40 x 10,54. (319.6 x 34.6). S—1—2. I—S—C2—10. (I—16; III—284). A.Stephen & Sons, Glasgow. 1874 (21/4) launched for Donaldson. 1874 (12/3) MV for Red Star (c), Antwerp—New York (1 RV). 1874

(Apr) FV Antwerp—Philadelphia. 1874 (Jun) LV ditto (2 RV). 1874 (Sep) FV for Donaldson, Glasgow—S America. (See Donaldson - 109).

4. 1874 SWITZERLAND (B)

2,816. 100,39 x 11,76. (329.4 x 38.6). S—1—2. I—S—C2—13. (I—70; III—800). Palmers Shipbuilding & Iron Co, Jarrow-on-Tyne. 1874 (17/1) launched. 1874 (24/4) MV Antwerp—New York. 1878 (Oct) FV Antwerp —Philadelphia. 1878-84 Antwerp—New York or Philadelphia. 1884-1904 Antwerp—Philadelphia except 1 RV to New York in 1884, 1886, 1888 and 1901. 1897 (approx) III only. 1904 (26/10) LV Philadelphia—Antwerp. 1905 SANSONE (Italian). 1909 scrapped in Italy.

4a. (1874) COLINA (c) (Br)

2,001. 97,31 x 10,60. (319.3 x 34.8). S—1—2. I—S—C2—10. (I—14; III—250). Barclay, Curle & Co, Glasgow. 1872 (31/10) launched for Donaldson; ran Glasgow—S America. 1874 (13/5) FV for Red Star (c), Antwerp—New York. 1874 (5/10) LV ditto (4 RV). 1874 (Dec) resumed Glasgow—S America for Donaldson - 109. (qv).

4b. (1875) STATE OF NEVADA (c) (Br)

2,488. 101,22 x 11,06. (332.1 x 36.3). S—1—3. I—S—C2—12. (I—75; intermediate 35; III—700). London & Glasgow Co, Glasgow. 1874 (2/6) launched for State. 1875 (26/2) FV for Red Star (c), Antwerp—New York. 1875 (11/12) LV ditto (7 RV). (See State - 99).

5. (1878) JAVA (B)
   (1878 ZEELAND (I) (B)

2,866. 102,74 x 13,07. (337.1 x 42.9). C—1—3. I—S—C2—12. (I—160; III—800). J. & G. Thomson, Glasgow. 1865 (24/6) launched for Cunard. 1878 (30/4) FV for Red Star, Antwerp—New York (2 RV). 1878 (Aug) FV Antwerp—Philadelphia (1 RV). 1878 ZEELAND (Red Star). 1878)2/11) FV Antwerp—New York. 1878-89 Antwerp—New York or Philadelphia. 1889 (23/2) LV Antwerp—New York. 1889 (Mar) ÉLECTRIQUE (French). 1892 LORD SPENCER (British sailing ship). 1895 (9/4) sailed San Francisco—Queenstown; went missing. (See Cunard - 13).

6. 1879 BELGENLAND (I) (B)

3,692. 122,79 x 12,25. (402.9 x 40.2). S—1—4. I—S—C2—14. (I—150; III—1,000). Barrow Shipbuilding Co. 1878 (24/12) launched. 1879 (30/3) MV Antwerp—Philadelphia (1 RV). 1879 (20/5) FV Antwerp—New York. 1895 (6/7) LV ditto. 1895 (31/7) FV for American Line (c), Phil-adelphia—Liverpool; (II—150; III—1,000). 1903 (17/10) LV ditto. 1903 (Nov) resumed for Red Star, Antwerp—Philadelphia; (III only). 1904 (7/12) LV Philadelphia—Antwerp. 1905 VENERE (Italian). 1906 scrapped.

851

7. 1879 RHYNLAND (B)

   3,689. 122,76 x 12,25. (402.8 x 40.2). S—1—4. I—S—C2—14. (I—150; III—1,000). Barrow Shipbuilding Co. 1879 (10/3) launched. 1879 (10/6) MV Antwerp—New York. 1895 (27/7) LV ditto. 1895 (Aug) FV for American Line (c), Philadelphia—Liverpool; (II—150; III—1,000). 1903 (4/3) LV ditto. 1903 (29/4) resumed for Red Star, Philadelphia— Antwerp; (III only). 1904 (28/12) LV ditto. 1905 (28/3) resumed Antwerp —New York. 1906 (22/5) LV ditto (3 RV). 1906 RHYNA (sic) (Italian); scrapped in Italy.

8. (1880)WAESLAND (B)

   4,752. 132,61 x 12,77. (435.1 x 41.9). C—1—4. I—S—C2—14. (I—120; III—1,500). J. & G. Thomson, Glasgow. 1867 (20/3) launched as RUSSIA (Cunard). 1880 WAESLAND (Red Star); lengthened from 109,11 metres (358.0 feet); compound engines by builders. 1880 (6/12) FV Antwerp— New York. 1889 triple-expansion engines by builders. 1895 (17/8) LV Antwerp—New York. 1895 (11/9) FV for American Line (c), Philadelphia —Liverpool; (II—120; III—1,500). 1902 (5/3) sunk in collision off Anglesey with ss HARMONIDES (Br) (2). (See Cunard - 13).

9. (1882) PENNLAND (I) (B)

   3,428. 110,08 x 12,53. (361.2 x 41.1) . S—1—3. I—S—C2—12. (I—200; III—1,000). J. & G. Thomson, Glasgow. 1870 (12/7) launched as ALGERIA (Cunard). 1882 PENNLAND (Red Star); compound engines by J.Jack & Co, Liverpool. 1882 (13/5) FV Antwerp—New York. 1888 new spar deck fitted; tonnage 3,760. 1894 (15/12) LV Antwerp—New York. 1895 (11/4) sailed Antwerp—Philadelphia. 1895 (18/5) FV for American Line (c), Philadelphia—Liverpool; (II—200; III—1.000). 1901 (6/4) LV ditto. 1901 (4/5) resumed Antwerp-New York. 1901 (Aug) resumed Antwerp—Philadelphia. 1902 III only. 1902 (27/3) LV Antwerp —New York (3 RV). 1903 (23/9) LV Philadelphia—Antwerp (15 RV). 1903 scrapped in Italy. (See Cunard - 13).

10. 1883 WESTERNLAND (I) (B)

    5,736. 134,10 x 14,38. (440.0 x 47.2). S—2—4. S—S—C2—14. (I—80; II—60; III—1,200). Laird Bros, Birkenhead. 1883 (4/8) floated from dry dock. 1883 (3/11) MV Antwerp—New York. 1901 (30/3) LV ditto. 1901 (May) FV for American Line (c), Liverpool—Philadelphia; (II—170; III—1,200). 1906 (14/3) resumed Antwerp—New York for Red Star. 1907 (27/1) LV ditto (3 RV). 1908 (Sep) LV for American Line (c), Liverpool— Philadelphia. 1912 scrapped.

11. 1884 NOORDLAND (B)

    5,212. 121,91 x 14,32. (400.0 x 47.0). S—1—4. S—S—C2—13. (I—63; II—

56; III—500). Laird Bros, Birkenhead. 1883 (1/11) launched. 1884 (29/3)
MV Antwerp—New York. 1901 (9/3) LV ditto. 1901 (Apr) FV for
American Line (c), Liverpool—Philadelphia; (II—160; III—500). 1906
(28/3) resumed Antwerp—New York (2 RV). 1908 LV for American Line
(c), Liverpool—Philadelphia. 1908 scrapped.

11a. (1887) ILLINOIS (c) (A)

3,341. 104,54 x 13,10. (343.0 x 43.0). S—1—2. I—S—C2—12. W. Cramp
& Sons, Philadelphia. 1873 (Jun) launched for American Line. 1874 (23/1)
MV Philadelphia—Liverpool. 1886 (7/7) LV Liverpool—Philadelphia.
1886 (17/12) FV for Red Star (c), Philadelphia—Antwerp. 1887 (16/3) FV
Antwerp—New York. 1891 triple-expansion engines by builders; (inter-
mediate and III only). 1892 (27/2) LV Antwerp—New York (20 RV).
1892-7 Antwerp—Philadelphia. 1898 (Mar) sailed Philadelphia—San
Francisco. (See American - 101).

11b (1887) PENNSYLVANIA (c) (A)

3,343. 104,54 x 13,10. (343.0 x 43.0). S—1—2. I—S—C2—12. W.Cramp &
Sons, Philadelphia. 1872 (15/8) launched for American Line. 1887 (25/5)
Fv for Red Star (c), Antwerp—New York. 1891 triple-expansion engines
by builders; (intermediate and III only). 1892 (9/3) LV Antwerp—New
York (16 RV). 1892-7 Antwerp—Philadelphia. 1898 (11/4) sailed
Philadelphia—San Francisco. (See American - 101).

11c. (1889) INDIANA (c) (A)

3,335. 104,54 x 13,10. (343.0 x 43.0). S—1—2..I—S—C2—12. W.Cramp &
Sons, Philadelphia. 1873 (25/3) launched for American Line. 1889 (6/3)
FVfor Red Star (c), Antwerp—New York (1 RV). (See American - 101).

12. 1889 FRIESLAND (B)

7,116. 133,19 x 15,60. (437.0 x 51.2). C—1—4. S—S—T3—15. (I—226;
II—102; III—600). J. & G.Thomson, Glasgow. 1889 (15/8) launched. 1889
(7/12) MV Antwerp—New York. 1903 (10/1) LV ditto. 1903 (25/3) FV for
American Line (c), Liverpool—Philadelphia; (II—300; III—600). 1911
(May) LV ditto. 1911 LA PLATA (Italian); two masts. 1912 scrapped.

13. (1890) CONEMAUGH § (A)

2,328. 91,43 x 11,31. (300.0 x 37.1). S—1—3. I—S—C2—12. Bartram,
Haswell & Co, Sunderland (engines J. Dickinson, Sunderland). 1882
(11/2) launched as SACROBOSSO (Br). 1890 (13/1) fire damage from
burning grain elevators at Baltimore; scuttled; salvaged; sold to International Navigation Co; renamed CONEMAUGH. 1890 (6/12) FV
Antwerp—New York. 1897 (31/8) LV ditto (15 RV); transferred to New
York—Seattle trade. 1904 (28/3) sailed from Coronel; went missing.

13a. (1895) SOUTHWARK (c) (Br)

8,607. 146,30 x 17,43. (480.0 x 57.2). S—1—4. S—2S—Q8—14. (II—100; III—929). Wm Denny & Bros, Dumbarton. 1893 (4/7) launched for American Line. 1895 (8/8) FV for Red Star (c), Philadelphia—New York —Antwerp. 1895 (31/8) FV Antwerp—New York. 1899 (or earlier) II increased to 250. 1903 (21/3) LV Antwerp—New York. (See American - 101).

13b. (1895) KENSINGTON (c) (Br)

8,669. 146,30 x 17,43. (480.0 x 57.2). S—1—4. S—2S—Q8—14. (II—100; III—929). J. & G. Thomson, Glasgow. 1893 (26/10) launched for American Line. 1895 (28/8) FV for Red Star (c), Philadelphia—New York —Antwerp. 1895 (21/9) FV Antwerp—New York. 1899 (or earlier) II increased to 250. 1903 (14/3) LV ditto. (See American - 101).

13c. (1895) BERLIN (c) (Br)

5,525. 148,91 x 13,47. (488.6 x 44.2). C—1—3. I—S—T3—14. Caird & Co, Greenock. 1874 (27/10) launched as CITY OF BERLIN (Inman). 1893 BERLIN (American Line). 1895 (31/8) FV for Red Star (c), Antwerp— New York. 1896 (1 RV); 1897 (2 RV); 1898 (3 RV)). 1898 (16/4) LV ditto (total 7 RV). (See Inman - 28).

13d. (1898) ITALIA (c) (G)

3,564. 104.99 x 13,25. (344.5 x 43.5). S—1—2. S—S—T3—11. (III— 1,400). Armstrong, Mitchell & Co, Walker-on-Tyne (engines Wallsend Slipway Co). 1889 (2/4) launched for Hapag. 1898 (6/11) FV for Red Star (c), Antwerp—New York (1 RV). 1899 (Jan) FV ditto, Antwerp—Phil- adelphia (1 RV). (See Hapag - 53).

13e. (1898) SCOTIA (c) (G)

2,558. 97,53 x 12,22. (320.0 x 40.1). S—1—2. S—S—T3—12. (III— 550). C.Connell & Co, Glasgow (engines J. & J. Thomson, Glasgow). 1890 (20/5) launched as GRIMM (Hansa). 1894 SCOTIA (Hapag). 1898 (10/11) FV for Red Star (c), Antwerp—New York (2 RV). (See Hapag - 53).

13f. (1898) ARAGONIA (c) (G)

5,446. 123,13 x 15,24. (404.0 x 50.0). S—1—2. S—2S—T6—13. (III—235). Flensburger Schiffsbau, Flensburg. 1897 (28/1) launched as BURMAH (Hamburg—Kalkutta). 1897 ARAGONIA (Hapag). 1898 (26/11) FV for Red Star (c), Antwerp—New York. 1899 (Mar) FV ditto, Antwerp—Phil- adelphia. 1900 (Jun) LV ditto (10 RV). 1900 (28/7) LV Antwerp—New York (5 RV). (See Hapag - 53).

13g. (1898) ADRIA (c) (G)

5,458. 121,70 x 15,27. (399.3 x 50.1). S—1—2. S—S—Q4—13. (III—1,100). Palmers Co Ltd, Jarow-on-Tyne. 1896 (27/5) launched for Hapag. 1898 (8/12) FV for Red Star (c), Antwerp—New York. 1899 (21/3) LV ditto (3 RV). (See Hapag - 53).

14. 1900 VADERLAND (II) (Br-B-Br)

11,899. 170,92 x 18,35. (560.8 x 60.2). 2—4. 2S—Q8—15. (I—342; II—194; III—626). John Brown & Co Ltd, Glasgow. 1900 (12/7) launched. 1900 (8/12) MV Antwerp—Southampton—New York (British flag). 1901 (11/12) FV for American Line (c), Southampton—Cherbourg—New York. 1901 (8/4) LV ditto (3 RV). 1903 (16/5) FV Antwerp—New York (Belgian flag). 1914 (25/7) LV ditto. 1914 (22/9) FV Liverpool—New York (British flag). 1914 (Dec) FV for White Star-Dominion (c), Liverpool—Halifax—Portland. 1915 (Feb) LV ditto (3 RV). 1915 SOUTHLAND (International Navigation Co); taken up as troopship. 1915 (2/9) torpedoed in Aegean Sea; reached port; repaired. 1916 (Aug) FV for White Star-Dominion (c), Liverpool—Quebec—Montreal. 1917 (4/6) torpedoed and sunk by German submarine U.70 off Irish coast (4).

15. 1901 ZEELAND (II) (Br-B-Br)

11,905. 171,16 x 18,35. (561.6 x 60.2). 2—4. 2S—Q8—15. (I—342; II—194; III—626). John Brown & Co Ltd, Glasgow. 1900 (24/11) launched. 1901 (13/4) MV Antwerp—New York (British flag). 1910 (5/3) LV Antwerp—Dover—New York. 1910 (19/4) FV for White Star (c), Liverpool—Boston. 1911 (Sep) LV ditto (14 RV). 1911 (21/10) resumed Antwerp—Dover—New York. 1912 (13/7) FV ditto (Belgian flag). 1914 (18/7) LV ditto. 1914 (11/9) FV Liverpool—New York (British flag). 1914 (Nov) FV for White Star-Dominion (c), Liverpool—Quebec—Montreal. 1914 (Dec) FV ditto, Liverpool—Halifax—Portland. 1915 (Jan) LV ditto. 1915 NORTHLAND (INCo). 1915 (Mar) FV for White Star-Dominion (c), Liverpool—Halifax—Portland. 1915 (Jun) LV ditto, Liverpool—Quebec—Montreal. 1915 troopship. 1916 (Aug) resumed for White Star-Dominion (c), Liverpool—Quebec—Montreal. 1917 (Apr) LV Liverpool—Halifax (7 RV). 1919 (Feb) FV for American Line (c), Liverpool—Philadelphia. 1919 (Jun) LV ditto (4 RV). 1920 (18/8) resumed Antwerp—Southampton—New York as ZEELAND (British flag). 1923 (Apr) cabin; III. 1926 (8/10) LV ditto. 1927 MINNESOTA (ATL); tourist only. 1927 (30/4) FV London—New York. 1929 (21/9) LV ditto. 1930 scrapped at Inverkeithing.

15a. (1901) HAVERFORD (c) (Br)

11,635. 161,84 x 18,04. (531.0 x 59.2). 1—4. 2S—T6—14. (II—150;

III—1,700). John Brown & Co Ltd, Glasgow. 1901 (4/5) launched for American Line. 1901 (9/11) FV for Red Star (c), Antwerp—New York. 1902 (8/3) LV ditto (4 RV). (See American - 101).

16. 1902 KROONLAND (A-B-A)

12,760. 170,68 x 18,35. (560.0 x 60.2). 2—4. 2S—T6—15. (I—342; II—194; III—626). W.Cramp & Sons, Philadelphia. 1902 (20/2) launched. 1902 (28/6) MV New York—Antwerp (US flag). 1908 (7/11) FV Antwerp—New York (Belgian flag). 1912 (13/1) FV ditto (US flag). 1914 (1/8) LV Antwerp—Dover—New York. 1914 (15/8) FV New York—Liverpool (2 RV). 1914 (15/10) FV New York—Gibraltar—Naples—Piraeus (1 RV). 1915 (21/5) FV for Panama Pacific (c), New York—Panama Canal—San Francisco. 1916 (30/1) FV for American Line (c), London—New York (1 RV). 1916 (20/2) FV for ditto, New York—Liverpool. 1917 (31/1) LV Liverpool—New York (9 RV). 1917 US troopship. 1919 I.—242; II—310; III—876; tonnage 12,241. 1920 (14/4) resumed Antwerp—Southampton—New York. 1923 (16/1) LV ditto. 1923 (21/6) FV for American Line, New York—Plymouth—Cherbourg—Hamburg; (Cabin; III). 1923 (15/9) LV Hamburg—Cherbourg—New York (3 RV). 1923 (18/10) FV New York—San Francisco for Panama Pacific. 1928 scrapped at Genoa.

17. 1902 FINLAND (A-B-A)

12,760. 170,68 x 18,35. (560.0 x 60.2). 2—4. 2S—T6—15. (I—342; II—194; III—626). W.Cramp & Sons, Philadelphia. 1902 (21/6) launched. 1902 (4/10) MV New York—Antwerp (US flag). 1909 (Jan or earlier) FV Antwerp—New York (Belgian flag). 1909 (6/3) FV Naples—New York for White Star (c). 1909 (5/6) LV New York—Naples (3 RV). 1912 (21/1) FV Antwerp—New York (US flag). 1914 (8/8) LV ditto. 1914 (22/8) FV New York—Liverpool (2 RV). 1914 (21/11) FV New York—Naples—Piraeus. 1915 (24/3) LV Genoa—Naples—New York (3 RV). 1915 (30/4) FV for Panama Pacific (c), New York—Panama Canal—San Francisco. 1915 (Oct) LV San Francisco—Panama Canal—New York. 1915 (26/10) FV for American Line (c), New York—Falmouth—London (2 RV). 1916 (19/1) FV for ditto, New York—Liverpool. 1917 (18/2) LV Liverpool—New York (11 RV). 1917 US troopship. 1917 (28/10) torpedoed 150 miles from French coast; reached St Nazaire; repaired. 1919 I—242; II—310; III—876. 1920 (28/4) resumed Antwerp—Southampton—New York. 1923 (22/3) LV ditto. 1923 (1/6) FV for American Line (c), New York—Plymouth—Cherbourg—Hamburg; (cabin; III). 1923 (29/9) LV Hamburg—Cherbourg—New York (4 RV). 1923 (1/11) FV New York—San Francisco for Panama Pacific. 1928 scrapped at Blyth.

18. (1905) MANITOU (c) (Br)
   (1920) POLAND (Br)
   6,849. 144,92 x 15,91..(475.5 x 52.2). 1—4. S—T3—14. (II—120). Furness,
   Withy & Co Ltd, West Hartlepool (engines T.Richardson & Sons Ltd,
   West Hartlepool). 1897 (31/7) launched as VICTORIA (Wilson's &
   Furness-Leyland). 1898 MANITOU (ATL). 1905 (Aug) FV for Red Star
   (c), Antwerp—Philadelphia. 1914 (Jul) LV Antwerp—Boston—Philadelphia. 1914 (31/10) resumed London—New York for ATL. 1914
   (22/12) LV ditto (2 RV). 1921 POLAND (Red Star); (III—1,100). 1921
   (20/1) FV Antwerp—New York. 1921 (17/2) FV New York— Hamburg
   —Danzig—Libau. 1921 (25/5) LV Philadelphia—New York—Danzig.
   (1½ RV). 1922 (26/4) FV for White Star (c), Bremen—Southampton—
   Quebec—Montreal. 1922 (Jul) LV ditto (3 RV). 1925 NATALE: scrapped.
   (See ATL - 123).

18a. (1905) MENOMINEE (c) (Br)
   6.919. 144,77 x 15,94. (475.0 x 52.3). 1—4. S—T3—14. (II—120).
   A. Stephen & Sons, Glasgow. 1897 (2/8) launched as ALEXANDRA
   (Wilson's & Furness-Leyland). 1898 MENOMINEE (ATL). 1905 (Sep)
   FV for Red Star (c), Antwerp—Philadelphia. 1914 (Jul) LV ditto. 1914
   (18/8) FV Antwerp—London (dep 5/9)—New York. 1914 (28/10)
   resumed London—New York for ATL - 123 (qv).

18b. (1905) MARQUETTE (c) (Br)
   7,057. 148,27 x 15,94. (486.5 x 52.3). 1—4. S—T3—14. (II—120).
   A. Stephen & Sons, Glasgow. 1897 (25/11) launched as BOADICEA
   (Wilson's & Furness-Leyland). 1898 MARQUETTE (ATL). 1905 (Sep)
   FV for Red Star (c), Antwerp—Philadelphia. 1914 (Aug) LV Antwerp—
   Boston—Philadelphia. 1914 (3/10) resumed London—New York for
   ATL. 1914 (30/12) LV ditto (3 RV). (See ATL - 123).

19. (1906) MISSISSIPPI (A)
   (1906) SAMLAND (A-B)
   7,913. 149,46 x 17,74. (490.4 x 58.2). 1—4. 2S—T6—14. (III—1,900). New
   York Shipbuilding Corporation, Camden, NJ. 1902 (15/12) launched as
   MISSISSIPPI (ATL). 1903 (16/4) MV Baltimore—London. 1903 (30/9)
   LV London—Baltimore (3 RV). 1906 (7/7) FV for Red Star, Antwerp—
   New York. 1906 (24/7) FV as SAMLAND (US flag), New York—
   Antwerp. 1910 (1/1) FV Antwerp—New York (Belgian flag). 1911 (7/1)
   LV Antwerp—Dover—New York. 1911 (7/4) FV Hamburg—Antwerp—
   Quebec—Montreal (2 RV). 1911 (30/8) BELGIC (White Star - Australian
   service; 10,151 tons. 1913 reverted to SAMLAND (Red Star; Belgian flag;
   9,748 tons). 1913 (27/12) resumed Antwerp—New York. 1914 (2/10) FV
   London—New York for ATL (c), (cargo only). 1916 (13/2) LV ditto. 1916

(12/3) FV New York—Falmouth—Rotterdam for Belgian Relief Commission (3 or more RV). 1919 (28/2) resumed Antwerp—New York. 1931 (6/2) LV Antwerp—New York (arr 19/2; dep 28/2)—Halifax—London—Antwerp. 1931 scrapped.

19a. (1907) CAMBROMAN (c) (Br)
6,059. 131,02 x 14,11. (429.9 x 46.3). 1—4. S—T3—12. (III—1,275). Laird Bros, Birkenhead. 1892 (6/10) launched. 1907 (8/3) FV for Red Star (c), Antwerp—New York. 1907 (9/11) LV ditto (4 RV). (See Dominion - 93).

19b. (1907) MERION (c) (Br)
11,621. 161,68 x 17,04. (530.5 x 59.2). 1—4. 2S—T6—14. (II—150; III—2,000). John Brown & Co Ltd, Glasgow. 1901 (26/11) launched for American Line. 1907 (16/11) FV for Red Star (c), Antwerp—New York (1 RV). (See American - 101).

20. (1908) GOTHLAND (B)
7,755. 149,55 x 16,21. (490.7 x 53.2). 1—4. 2S—T6—14. (III—1,800). Harland & Wolff, Belfast. 1893 (28/6) launched as GOTHIC (White Star; New Zealand service). 1906 wool cargo caught fire; beached and flooded upon arrival at Plymouth. 1908 GOTHLAND (Red Star) after conversion by Harland & Wolff as emigrant carrier. 1908 (11/7) FV Antwerp—New York. 1911 (6/5) FV Hamburg—Antwerp—Quebec—Montreal (1 RV). 1911 (24/6) LV Antwerp—New York. 1911-3 GOTHIC (White Star; Australia/New Zealand service). 1913 (23/4) resumed Antwerp—New York as GOTHLAND. 1914 (23/6) struck on Gunner Rocks, Scilly Isles; towed off after three days; repaired at Southampton. 1916 (20/4) FV New York—Falmouth—Rotterdam for Belgian Relief Commission (3 or more RV). 1919 (6/5) resumed Antwerp—New York (cargo only). 1920 (7/8) resumed as passenger ship. 1925 (Mar) LV Antwerp—Philadelphia. 1925 (Nov) sold. 1926 scrapped at Bo'ness.

21. 1909 LAPLAND (B-Br)
17,540. 184,64 x 21,45. (605.8 x 70.4). 2—4. 2S—Q8—17. (I—450; II—400; III—1,500). Harland & Wolff, Belfast. 1908 (27/6) launched. 1909 (10/4) MV Antwerp—Dover—New York (Belgian flag). 1914 (4/7) LV ditto. 1914 (1/9) FV Liverpool—New York. 1914 (29/10) FV ditto for White Star (c) (British flag). 1917 (Apr) mined off Mersey Bar lightship; reached Liverpool. 1917 (Jun) troopship under Liner Requisition Scheme. 1918 (23/11) FV after Armistice, Liverpool—New York for White Star. 1919 (2/8) LV ditto (6 RV). 1919 (16/9) FV Southampton—New York for White Star (c). 1919 (27/11) LV ditto (3 RV). 1920 (3/1) resumed Antwerp—Southampton—New York for Red Star (British flag); 18,565 tons; (I—389; II—448; III—1,200). 1927 (Apr) cabin; tourist; III. 1932

(29/4) LV Antwerp—Southampton—Havre—New York (arr 8/5; dep 11/6)—Cobh—Antwerp. 1932-3 Mediterranean cruises from London. 1933 (Oct) sold to Japan. 1934 scrapped at Osaka.

21a. (1912) MESABA (c) (Br)
6,833. 146,93 x 15,91. (482.1 x 52.2). 1—4. S—T3—14. Harland & Wolff, Belfast. 1897 (11/9) launched as WINIFREDA (Wilson's & Furness-Leyland). 1898 MESABA (ATL). 1912 (Jun) FV for Red Star (c), Antwerp —Boston—Philadelphia. 1913 (Jun) 2nd RV ditto. 1914 (May) LV ditto (3 RV). (See ATL - 123).

22. (1923) BELGENLAND (II) (Br)
27.132. 204,32 x 23,89. (670.4 x 78.4). 3—2—C. 3S—T8 & ST—17. (I—500; II—500; III—1,500). Harland & Wolff, Belfast. 1914 (31/12) launched as BELGENLÁND. 1917 completed as White Star troopship and cargo steamer BELGIC (two funnels; three masts; 24,547 tons). 1918 (Nov) FV after Armistice, Liverpool—New York. 1921 (8/3) LV ditto; returned to Belfast for completion as passenger liner; renamed BELGEN-LAND. 1923 (4/4) FV for Red Star, Antwerp—Southampton—New York. 1927 (Apr) I; II; tourist; III. 1929 (May) I; tourist; III. 1932 (17/6) LV Antwerp—New York; many cruises New York—West Indies. 1933 (18/3) LV New York—Southampton—Havre—Antwerp; laid up. 1933 (Jul-Sep) three Mediterranean cruises from UK; laid up at London. 1935 (10/1) sailed London—New York in ballast. 1935 (26/1) renamed COLUMBIA (Panama Pacific) (US); cruises to West Indies. 1936 (22/4) sailed New York—Bo'ness; scrapped.

23. (1925) PITTSBURGH (c) (Br)
   (1926) PENNLAND (II) (Br)
16,322. 175,06 x 20,66. (574.4 x 67.8) 2—2—C. 3S—T8 & ST—15. (Cabin 600; III—1,500). Harland & Wolff, Belfast. 1913 (Nov) laid down for American Line. 1920 (11/11) launched for ditto; completed in White Star colours. 1925 (20/1) FV for Red Star (c), Antwerp—Southampton—Cherbourg—Halifax—New York. 1926 (2/4) FV as PENNLAND ditto. 1930 (Jan) tourist; III. 1934 (16/11) LV Antwerp—Havre—Southampton —Havre—Southampton—New York (arr 25/11; dep 30/11)—Havre—London—Antwerp. (See White Star - 88).

23a. (1926) ARABIC (c) (Br)
16,786. 179,88 x 21,24. (590.2 x 69.7). 2—2. 2S—Q8—17. (I—266; II—246; III—2,700). AG Weser, Bremen. 1908 (7/11) launched as BERLIN (NDL). 1920 (Nov) sold to White Star; renamed ARABIC. 1926 (30/10) Fv for Red Star (c), New York—Plymouth—Cherbourg—Antwerp. 1927 (Apr)

859

repainted in Red Star colours. 1929 (27/12) LV Antwerp—Southampton —Cherbourg—New York. (See NDL - 60).

23b. (1927) WINIFREDIAN (c) (Br)
10,405. 168,39 x 18,07. (552.5 x 59.3). 1—4. S—T2—13. (Cabin 135). Harland & Wolff, Belfast. 1899 (11/3) launched for Leyland. 1927 (19/11) FV for Red Star (c), New York—Southampton—Antwerp. 1928 (30/1) LV ditto (2½ RV). (See Leyland - 106).

23c. (1927) DEVONIAN (c) (Br)
12,153. 177,38 x 18,38. (582.0 x 60.3). 1—4. 2S—T6—14. (Tourist 250). R. & W. Hawthorn, Leslie & Co Ltd, Hebburn-on-Tyne. 1902 (25/2) launched as HANOVERIAN (Leyland). 1903 MAYFLOWER (Dominion). 1903 CRETIC (White Star). 1923 DEVONIAN (Leyland); tonnage reduced from 13,518 to 12,153. 1927 (10/12) FV for Red Star (c), New York—Plymouth—Antwerp. 1928 (9/3) LV Antwerp—Southampton— New York (3 RV). (See White Star - 88).

24. (1930) WESTERNLAND (II) (Br)
16,314. 175,06 x 20,66. (574.4 x 67.8). 2—2—C. 3S—T8 & ST—15. (Tourist; III). Harland & Wolff, Glasgow. 1913 laid down as REGINA (Dominion). 1917 (19/4) launched. 1925 transferred to White Star. 1926 (Jun) cabin; tourist; III. 1930 (10/1) FV for Red Star as WESTERN-LAND, Antwerp—Southampton—Cherbourg—New York; (tourist; III). 1934 (30/11) LV Antwerp—Havre—Southampton—New York (arr 10/ 12; dep 12/12)—Havre—London—Antwerp. LV of line. (See Dominion - 93).

24a. (1932) MINNEWASKA (c) (Br)
21,716. 183,11 x 24,50. (600.8 x 80.4). 1—2—C. 2S—ST(SR)—16. (Tourist 417). Harland & Wolff, Belfast. 1923 (22/3) launched for ATL. 1932 (13/5) FV for Red Star (c), Antwerp—Southampton—Havre—New York. 1933 (15/9) LV ditto (10 RV). 1934 (Nov) scrapped at Port Glasgow. (See ATL - 123).

24b. (1932) MINNETONKA (c) (Br)
21,998. 183,11 x 24.50. (600.8 x 80.4). 1—2—C. 2S—ST(SR)—16. (Tourist 413). Harland & Wolff, Belfast. 1924 (10/1) launched for ATL. 1932 (27/5) FV for Red Star (c), Antwerp—Southampton—Havre—New York. 1933 (29/9) LV ditto (12 RV). 1934 (Nov) scrapped at Bo'ness. (See ATL - 123).

NOTES: (A) - US-flag steamer.
          (B) - Belgian-flag steamer.
          (Br) - British-flag steamer.
          (G) - German-flag steamer.
          §   - cargo steamer.

FUNNEL: (a) 1873. Black; broad white band with red star.
           (b) 1884 (or earlier). Buff with red star; black top.
           (c) 1893. Black; white band.

FLAG: White swallow-tailed pennant with red star.

STATE LINE

(State Steamship Company Limited)

(British)

The STATE STEAMSHIP COMPANY LIMITED was advertised to start services from Glasgow and Liverpool to New Orleans and from Glasgow to New York during the spring of 1872. [1] In fact, the New York service was delayed a whole year, but the first sailing to New Orleans took place in August 1872, when the 1,869 ton iron screw LOUISIANA left Glasgow via Liverpool. She and a sister ship, the MINNESOTA, subsequently made the Mersey their home terminal. From time to time, calls were made at Bordeaux and Havana.

Pioneer unit of the New York fleet was the 2,472 ton PENNSYLVANIA, which sailed from Glasgow on 18 April 1873, calling at Larne the following day to await arrival of the cross-channel steamer from Stranraer with the London mails. The 2,473 ton VIRGINIA sailed on 6 June, a few days after the start of the PENNSYLVANIA's second voyage, and the 2,313 ton ALABAMA followed on 24 June. The last-named had been built for the New Orleans trade, to which she was transferred after her second voyage. By that time the 2,490 ton GEORGIA was ready to take her place alongside the PENNSYLVANIA and VIRGINIA, each of which had accommodation for 65-70 first class passengers, 35-40 intermediate and 400 steerage.

Although the State Line was registered in Britain a considerable portion of its capital had been subscribed in the United States, hence the choice of names for the ships. Unfortunately, these were, or had been until recently, duplicated by steamers of the American, Guion and National lines and there was a good deal of confusion. In December 1873 the words 'STATE OF' were wisely added to each name.

The 2,488 ton STATE OF NEVADA, the 2,528 ton STATE OF INDIANA and the 3,155 ton STATE OF FLORIDA were commissioned in 1874, the intention being to run a weekly service to New York, six steamers being required for the purpose. By the time they were ready to sail however, a serious slump had set in and after completing five round voyages between Glasgow, Larne and New York the STATE OF NEVADA was chartered to the Red Star Line, whose service between Antwerp and New York had started in March 1874. She did not sail again from Glasgow until June 1876.

1873 STATE OF PENNSYLVANIA 2,472 tons
Completed as PENNSYLVANIA; renamed to
avoid confusion with other ships.

The STATE OF FLORIDA was scheduled to start her maiden voyage to New York on 16 October 1874, but this sailing was cancelled and, instead, she was transferred to the Queen Line's Indian service and renamed QUEEN MARGARET. The New Orleans service was affected even more seriously by the slump and was withdrawn in 1875, the STATE OF MINNESOTA being sold to the Royal Mail Steam Packet Company. The STATE OF LOUISIANA and the STATE OF ALABAMA were retained, but neither was employed on the North Atlantic during the two succeeding years.

There had been only 26 sailings to New York in 1875, but trading conditions improved sufficiently by the end of 1877 for a weekly service to be started, following the return of the STATE OF LOUISIANA from a Far Eastern voyage. She was wrecked in Lough Larne in December 1878, and in the following July the STATE OF VIRGINIA was wrecked on Sable Island. The STATE OF ALABAMA had already been recalled to the North Atlantic, but even so the Company had only five steamers at their disposal and the 3,034 ton MIKADO was chartered for three round voyages.

Soon afterwards, in April 1880, the QUEEN MARGARET made one voyage to New York under that name, attracting no fewer than 517 passengers, a complement not far short of being the Company's record. Before starting a second voyage she reverted to her original name, STATE OF FLORIDA.

The 3,986 ton STATE OF NEBRASKA sailed from Glasgow for New York for the first time on 5 November 1880 and was a considerable improvement on all previous units. Accommodation was provided for 100 saloon, 75 intermediate and 825 steerage passengers. The STATE OF ALABAMA again became a spare steamer, but in April 1884 the STATE OF FLORIDA was sunk in collision with the Canadian bark PONEMA with the loss of over 100 lives, and from then until the end of 1886 the STATE OF ALABAMA found regular employment. Her last voyage as a passenger steamer started on 17 February 1888, but she made a few subsequent voyages carrying cargo only.

One of the aftermaths of the depression of the 1870s was the continued decline in the cost of passages. In 1873, for instance, the Company's saloon fare was 13 or 15 guineas, according to accommodation, whereas in 1885 it ranged between 6, 8, 10 and 12 guineas. Corresponding reductions also took place in intermediate and steerage fares. Advertisements in 1888 stated: 'Lowest cabin fares on the Atlantic.'

On the other hand, the years 1886-8 were the best the Company ever experienced from the point of view of passengers carried. In 1886 they landed 14,889 at New York (including 2,530 saloon and intermediate) during the course of 47 voyages, compared with the Anchor Line's total for the same route of 19,065. In 1888 they did even better with a total of 16,691 spread over 50 voyages, an average of 334 a voyage. Clearly, serious inroads were made into the Anchor Line's business, but this old-established company had many other interests and was able to bear the strain. The State Line, unfortunately, had been struggling from the first to keep its head above water.

One of the travel bargains of all time was offered by the Company in 1889: 'Summer Voyage. The cheapest ocean holiday tour is to New York and back to Glasgow, occupying about a month, allowing a few hours in the north of Ireland and about one week in New York. Fares for Round, 13 guineas to 16 guineas, according to berths selected.' [2]

The satisfactory passenger figures for 1886-8 were destined not to be repeated, the total falling to 10,773 in 1889 and to 9,143 in 1890. It is not surprising, therefore, that with freight takings also at a low level the Company went into liquidation in 1890. Many expected that the Anchor Line would make a takeover bid but, instead, the fleet and goodwill were sold to the Allan Line in March 1891 for £72,000. They had had a certain amount of previous experience of the New York trade and, of course, had extensive connections with Glasgow.

Of the six ships sold to the Allan Line, the STATE OF ALABAMA and STATE OF PENNSYLVANIA were re-sold without undertaking any further North Atlantic voyages, while the STATE OF INDIANA and STATE OF GEORGIA made only one and two, respectively. The STATE OF NEVADA made a few more before being re-sold in 1893, and it was left to the STATE OF NEBRASKA to justify her existence. She continued until 1901 to sail from Glasgow to New York via Moville, the Irish port of call having been changed from Larne to Moville in February 1890. A seventh ship, the 4,244 ton STATE OF CALIFORNIA, was in an advanced stage of construction at the time of the takeover. After her completion later in 1891, she saw useful service for Allan, who continued a Glasgow - New York service until 1905 under the description ALLAN-STATE LINE. (Chapter 44).

[1]   *Glasgow Herald* 20/10/1871 (advt)
[2]   *Glasgow Herald* 20/5/1889 (advt)

1. 1873 PENNSYLVANIA
   (1873) STATE OF PENNSYLVANIA
   2,472. 101,03 x 11,06. (331.5 x 36.3). S—1—3. I—S—C2—12. (I—65; intermediate 35; III—400). London & Glasgow Co, Glasgow. 1873 (12/2) launched. 1873 (18/4) MV Glasgow—Larne—New York. 1873 (Dec) re-named STATE OF PENNSYLVANIA. 1873 (19/12) FV ditto as ditto.

1891 (27/3) LV Glasgow—Moville—New York. 1891 STATE OF PENN-SYLVANIA (Allan) but did not run for them. 1893 MEDINA (Turkish). 1900 MARMARA (Turkish). 1915 (5/9) reported sunk by Russian destroyers off Kefken.

2. 1873 VIRGINIA
   (1874) STATE OF VIRGINIA
   2,473. 100,94 x 11,09. (331.2 x 36.4). S—1—3. I—S—C2—12. (I—70; intermediate 40; III—400). London & Glasgow Co, Glasgow. 1873 (29/3) launched. 1873 (6/6) MV Glasgow—Larne—New York. 1873 (Dec) renamed STATE OF VIRGINIA. 1874 (3/1) FV ditto as ditto. 1879 (20/6) LV ditto. 1879 (15/7) wrecked on Sable Island (9).

3. 1873 ALABAMA
   (1874) STATE OF ALABAMA
   2,313. 97,92 x 11,03. (321.2 x 36.2). S—1—3. I—S—C2—12. (I—30; intermediate 50; III—200). T. Wingate & Co, Glasgow. 1873 (11/3) launched. 1873 (24/6) MV Glasgow—Larne—New York. 1873 (Dec) renamed STATE OF ALABAMA. 1873 (Dec) FV Liverpool—New Orleans as ditto. 1874 (27/2) FV Glasgow—New York. 1888 (17/2) LV ditto; subsequently carried cargo only. 1891 STATE OF ALABAMA (Allan) but did not run for them; resold. 1896 scrapped.

4. 1873 GEORGIA
   (1873) STATE OF GEORGIA
   2,490. 100,67 x 11,06. (330.3 x 36.3). S—1—3. I—S—C2—12. (I—70; intermediate 40; III—400). London & Glasgow Co, Glasgow. 1873 (13/6) launched. 1873 (12/9) MV Glasgow—Larne—New York. 1873 (Dec) renamed STATE OF GEORGIA. 1873 (5/12) FV ditto as ditto. 1891 (7/3) LV Glasgow—Moville—New York. 1891 STATE OF GEORGIA (Allan). 1891 (22/5) FV Glasgow—Moville—New York. 1891 LV ditto (2 RV). 1893 STATE OF GEORGIA (Aberdeen Atlantic). 1896 (23/12) sailed Danzig—Halifax; went missing (32).

5. 1874 STATE OF NEVADA
   2,488. 101,22 x 11,06. (332.1 x 36.3). S—1—3. I—S—C2—12. (I—75; intermediate 30; III—550). London & Glasgow Co, Glasgow. 1874 (2/6) launched. 1874 (19/7) MV Glasgow—Larne—New York. 1874 (19/12) LV ditto (5 RV). 1875 (27/2) FV for Red Star (c), Antwerp—New York. 1875 (11/12) LV ditto (7 RV). 1876 (2/6) resumed Glasgow—Larne—New York. 1891 (20/3) LV Glasgow—Moville—NewYork. 1891 STATE OF NEVADA (Allan). 1891 (25/4) FV Glasgow—Moville—New York. 1892 (2/9) LV ditto (9 RV). 1893 MEKKE (Turkish). 1914-8 reported as war loss.

6. 1874 STATE OF INDIANA

  2,528. 100,54 x 11,03. (329.9 x 36.2). S—1—3. I—S—C2—12. (I—75;
intermediate 30; III—550). T. Wingate & Co, Glasgow. 1874 (27/8)
launched. 1874 (6/9) MV Glasgow—Larne—New York. 1891 (23/1) LV
Glasgow—Moville—New York. 1891 STATE OF INDIANA (Allan).
1891 (17/4) FV Glasgow—Moville—New York (1 RV). 1893 ISMIR
(Turkish). 1912 sunk by Turks as blockship at Smyrna (Izmir).

7. (1875) STATE OF LOUISIANA

  1,869. 91,52 x 10,73. (300.3 x 35.2). S—1—3. I—S—C2—12. (I—30;
intermediate 50; III—200). T. Wingate & Co, Glasgow. 1872 (19/8)
launched as LOUISIANA (State). 1872 (Aug) MV Glasgow—Liverpool—
New Orleans. 1874 renamed STATE OF LOUISIANA. 1875 (19/3) FV
Glasgow—Larne—New York. 1878 (12/11) LV ditto. 1878 (24/12)
wrecked in Lough Larne (0).

7a. (1879) MIKADO (c)

  3,034. 113,28 x 10,97. (371.7 x 36.0). S—1—4. I—S—C2—14. Aitken &
Mansel, Glasgow (engines J. & J. Thomson, Glasgow). 1873 (15/4)
launched for D. R. Mcgregor & Co (Br). 1879 (12/9) FV for State (c),
Glasgow—Larne—New York. 1880 (16/1) LV ditto (3 RV). 1881 KOST-
ROMA (Russian Volunteer Fleet). 1887 (17/5) wrecked at Kreslopp,
Sakhalin Island.

8. (1880) QUEEN MARGARET
 (1880) STATE OF FLORIDA

  3,138. 113,28 x 11,73. (371.7 x 38.5). S—1—3. I—S—C2—13. (I—90;
intermediate 30; III—500). London & Glasgow Co, Glasgow. 1874 (28/8)
launched as STATE OF FLORIDA (State). 1874 (16/10) scheduled to sail
Glasgow—New York; voyage cancelled. 1874 QUEEN MARGARET
(Queen). 1880 (23/4) FV Glasgow—Larne—New York as QUEEN
MARGARET (1 RV). 1880 (4/6) FV ditto as STATE OF FLORIDA.
1884 (22/3) LV ditto. 1884 (18/4) sunk in collision with Canadian bark
PONEMA (123).

9. 1880 STATE OF NEBRASKA

  3,986. 117,40 x 13,19. (385.2 x 43.3). S—1—3- I—S—C2—13. (I—100;
intermediate 75; III—825). London & Glasgow Co, Glasgow. 1880 (6/9)
launched. 1880 (5/11) MV Glasgow—Larne—New York. 1890 (24/10) LV
Glasgow—Moville—New York. 1891 STATE OF NEBRASKA (Allan).
1891 (8/5) FV Glasgow—Moville—New York. 1901 (28/9) LV ditto.
1902 scrapped.

STATE OF CALIFORNIA
4,244. (Did not run for Company; see Allan Line - 44).

NOTE: The 1,858 ton MINNESOTA, commissioned in 1872 for the New Orleans service and in 1873 renamed STATE OF MINNESOTA, did not run for the Company on the North Atlantic.

FUNNEL: Buff with red band; narrow black top.

FLAG   :Blue swallow-tailed pennant; red and narrow white stripe at top and bottom; white star and white 'S'.